Consumer Culture and
TV Programming

Critical Studies in Communication
and in the Cultural Industries
Herbert I. Schiller, *Series Editor*

CONSUMER CULTURE
AND
TV PROGRAMMING

―――――――

ROBIN ANDERSEN

WestviewPress

A Division of HarperCollins*Publishers*

Critical Studies in Communication and in the Cultural Industries

Copyright © 1995 by Westview Press, Inc., a Division of HarperCollins Publishers, Inc.

Published in 1995 in the United States of America by Westview Press, Inc., 5500 Central Avenue, Boulder, Colorado 80301-2877, and in the United Kingdom by Westview Press, 12 Hid's Copse Road, Cumnor Hill, Oxford OX2 9JJ

A CIP catalog record for this book is available from the Library of Congress.

ISBN 0-8133-1541-7
ISBN 0-8133-1542-5 (pbk.)

Printed and bound in the United States of America

The paper used in this publication meets the requirements
of the American National Standard for Permanence of Paper
for Printed Library Materials Z39.48-1984.

10   9   8   7   6   5   4   3   2

For Guy

Contents

Acknowledgments

I would like to thank Herb Schiller, Doug Kellner, Elayne Rapping, and George Gerbner for offering their encouragement and support when this book was first proposed. For research and involvement at all stages of the manuscript I am indebted to Roger Logan. He was the most intelligent and sympathetic reader I could ever hope to find. Michael Yellin also gave unselfishly of his time, offering wise comments as each chapter was completed. Pamela Smorkaloff read portions of the manuscript, offered encouragement, and showed a keen eye for clipping relevant newspaper articles and sending them off to me. Jim Naureckas and Kathy Leary offered helpful hints on television and press reports, as did many other of my friends and colleagues. For computer expertise, especially wizardry at retrieving files lost in cyberspace, there is no one like Stephen Yorke. I also wish to thank my friends Nancy Bermon and Chuck Singleton for their creative consultations.

For his guidance and support I am indebted to Everett Parker. His advice and counsel are always given with careful and affectionate consideration. I have benefited immeasurably from his vast experience and understanding of broadcasting. The writings of Joel Kovel have profoundly influenced my thinking, and his review of portions of the manuscript was greatly appreciated. My thanks also go to the kindred spirit of Gerry O'Sullivan, whose humor and critical intelligence are always inspiring.

Even though the writing is mine, Ellen Braune co-authored the chapter on talk shows. My ideas developed through the course of our discussions to the point where I can no longer separate her understandings from my own. I benefited enormously from the camaraderie, and from the curiosity about everything related to television and culture, of my colleagues in the media group of CUNY Cultural Studies, whose members included Paolo Carpignano, Bill DiFazio, Stanley Aronowitz, Jeff Schmidt, and Elayne Rapping. Many thanks to Paolo, whose good-humored encouragement and stimulating arguments contributed to the ongoing development of this book.

Michael Letwin shared his writings and sources on criminal justice issues, and Warren Harry carefully read the docu-cop chapter and offered the benefit of his experiences. Guy Robinson Sr. and Bee Ring took time from their own writing to read mine. Their comments and encouragement are always helpful.

I owe a special debt of gratitude to my students at Fordham University, whose comments and enthusiasm inform much of this work. The book was nurtured with them in mind. For her research on the economics of broadcasting, I would like to thank Kalin McNichol. For bringing programs, advertisements, and newspaper clippings to my attention, I owe thanks to Aaron Kaplan, Joseph Conte, Ariel Diaz, Elizabeth Jenkins, Steve Rocco, Steven Sakadales, and many more who always had their eyes open. I hope I do not offend those whose names are omitted here. For her support in every way, I thank Rose Muccioli. I am grateful to Fordham University for providing financial support for this work through faculty research grants. No question was too silly for my colleagues in the Office of Research, Nancy McCarthy and Laura Ebert, who answered my numerous queries with grace and attention.

Gordon Massman at Westview Press watched with a careful eye over this book from beginning to end. I remember fondly Meredith Sund's encouraging remarks after reading the first draft of the manuscript. It was always refreshing and informative to talk to Scott Perrizo. And Dave Jenemann and Jane Raese are careful, thorough, and intelligent editors. I could not have hoped for a better copy editor than Christine Arden.

I am, of course, indebted to my parents, Bernadette and Harold Bennetto. They taught me to be critical. Finally, for his immeasurable support—emotional, intellectual, and every other kind—I thank Guy Robinson. His collaboration, enthusiasm, and encouragement when the going got tough can never be overstated or repaid. I am passionately grateful. Any wrongheadedness found in these pages is, of course, my own.

Robin Andersen

Introduction

IN A WILDERNESS SETTING, two good friends, a man and a woman both in late middle age, sit in camping chairs in front of a tent. Night has fallen and the scene is tranquil. He begins to blow up a small air mattress.

> HE: I never thought I'd be using one of these damn things, but since my sciatica started acting up. . . .
> SHE: You want some Advil?
> HE: You got any?
> SHE: Uh-huh, I always carry it around for my bursitis.
> HE: I've got some Ben-gay, if you get achy.
> SHE: You do?
> HE: In the side pocket there. (*Points to his backpack*)
> SHE: I'll use it before I go to bed.

He lights up a cigar and offers one to her. She accepts. They pour and drink some brandy and sit happily outside, comfortable. The camera pans back, framing the moment, holding it emotionally.

This scene is similar in structure to many advertisements. It is fictional, played by charming characters in a pleasing setting with references to the products incorporated into a naturalistic dialogue. But the scene is not an advertisement. It is part of a program. Or we might better say, it is an advertisement within a television program. The characters are Ruth-Anne and Holling, and the program is an episode of the popular CBS series *Northern Exposure*.

The only difference between this scene and a television commercial is that these characters use the word "damn" and smoke cigars, details that would not appear in spot advertising. But these foibles reflect the personalities of the characters who are, by most standards, eccentric anyway. And that is just the point: These are characters with established identities who already appeal to a loyal audience. It is acceptable for familiar characters—whom viewers know and love—to smoke cigars and say "damn" (especially on *Northern Exposure*). In fact, it is essential that the characters act naturally. What is gained is authenticity, and in this age of commercial clutter and a highly competitive commercial market, advertisers strive to incorporate their products within the broader media environment. In this way, persuasive messages appear to be authentic sectors of the landscape of popular culture, rather than deliberate advertisements urging consumers to buy products.

For Holling and Ruth-Anne the mention of Advil and Bengay is as natural as any other part of the dialogue. Or is it?

The president of ABC network, Robert Iger, talked about "product placement" and *Northern Exposure.* He explained that the encapsulated advertisement within the program was the result of the program's popularity and its high production costs. According to Iger, the producers of *Northern Exposure* were the "hottest television creators" in Hollywood. For this reason, half a dozen television entities began vying for their services, and that "drove the price sky-high." As the program became more expensive, the producers sought to "make better sense of that business economically" and an arrangement was made "between the creator and the studio to . . . put product placement in the show." This helps pay for the cost of production.

Over the past decade, the economic dynamics of network television underwent a dramatic transformation. Throughout the 1980s programming production costs rose steadily. At the same time, network television lost a considerable portion of its audience to other programming services. Iger, referring to that loss as "network erosion," explained that "as our ratings decrease . . . the value of the commercial on network television" has also decreased. National advertisers, concerned with the weakening of their advertising messages, "are looking for ways to increase the value of their commercials." Iger went on to say, "We foresee that national advertisers will become more involved in programming product in order to protect the value of their advertising."

Indeed, direct involvement at the level of television production would afford advertisers more control over creative design and guarantee programming as the appropriate environment for the display of their products. What Iger sees in the future of network television is a return to the past, when advertisers not only sponsored programs but created them. In other words, "advertisers may go . . . into producing" in much the same way they did during the 1950s. They will begin to "use the program to sell the products," eventually resulting in what Iger calls "commercialtainment."

The prospect of commercialtainment raises troubling issues for broadcasters. As Iger cautions, "If the commercial entity ultimately gets more involved in the creation of that product, and in some form or another with storyline . . . I think there is a concern." Even though Iger does not believe this situation to be imminent, he acknowledges the increasing pressures from advertisers and describes as "frightening" the prospect of commercialtainment. A look back to the days when sponsors controlled programming will shed some light on his concerns.

In 1951 Ralph Bellamy starred in the popular series *Man Against Crime,* sponsored by Camel cigarettes. Camel exerted near total control over both the writing and the directing of the episodes. Erik Barnouw (1975) has documented the numerous mimeographed instructions telling writers what to include in the plot.

Camel found that viewers were fascinated with murder and therefore wanted it included early and often; "somebody must be murdered, preferably early, with the threat of more violence to come" (Barnouw 1975, 132). Romance also had to be included. The presence of at least "one attractive woman" was essential, but the instructions warned, "Don't let it stop the forward motion of the story." Action had to "rise to a cliff hanger" before the middle commercial to ensure that the audience stayed tuned (Barnouw 1975, 133).

Numerous directions were also included about the presentation of cigarettes. Cigarettes had to be "smoked gracefully, never puffed nervously." They could not be associated with "undesirable scenes or situations." Arson could not be a plot element because it might "remind a viewer of fires caused by cigarettes." And doctors could not be antagonized. Indeed, they were to be shown only in "the most commendable light" because of tobacco companies' fears of the coming reports on the health effects of smoking (Barnouw 1975, 132).

Direct control over content and creative design by the sponsors in the early days of television ended after the quiz-show scandal of the late 1950s. The discovery that sponsors had rigged questions and selected certain contestants to win over others was considered a national disgrace. Broadcasters used this opportunity to regain control of airtime they had previously handed over to sponsors.

For broadcasters, the prospect of returning to the days of sponsor-controlled storylines may be a frightening one, but hands-on production of content is only the most conspicuous form of advertisers' influence. In fact, the 1980s witnessed the increasing encroachment of commercial influences on television programming. Advertising is now inserted directly into programming through product placement, and advertisers demand that programs be the vehicle for their product image. In many ways, the future—"commercialtainment"—has already arrived.

Consider, for example, the concept of "programming environment," which advertisers take into account before they buy commercial time on television. When *Broadcasting* reported that the Fox network was having trouble lining up sponsors for its provocative late-night show *Studs*, not much notice was taken. Advertising executives complained that the show would not provide the right programming environment for their products. Full of contrived sexual innuendo and ribald humor, *Studs* was not particularly endearing to those concerned with the public interest. But sponsors' demands for appropriate programming environments have led to so-called hit lists of shows, ranging from *Alf* to *Sally Jessy Raphael*, that advertisers view as inappropriate surroundings for their advertisements. The *Washington Post* reported "a growing number of companies that are concerned about the content" of TV shows (Lawrence 1989, E1). For instance, Domino's Pizza, which spends more than $25 million on TV advertising, will not buy time on the often irreverent, and sometimes mildly politically critical, *Saturday Night Live*. The candymaker Mars Company, which spends an estimated $91 million a year on network advertising, will not advertise M&Ms on a total of fifty programs, from the *Golden Girls* to *20/20*. And Exxon Corporation reportedly has a thirty-show list that it would not reveal to the *Washington Post*.

A spokesman for Foote Cone & Belding Communications Inc., which represents enormous corporate advertising accounts for companies such as Colgate, Nabisco, RJR, Kraft, Mazda, Levi Strauss, Coors, and Campbell's Soup, notes that the concern over "unacceptable" programming "has certainly increased" (Lawrence 1989, E6). Indeed, a study commissioned by a TV industry newsletter, *Market Shares*, found that the "hit lists, while they have long existed, are said to be longer and covering a broader array of programming than before" (Lawrence 1989, E1).

The highly competitive advertising environment has only increased the demand that programming conform to advertiser's wishes. Shows that do not provide suitable vehicles for advertising become a source of friction between sponsors and broadcasters. Over the years advertisers have come to expect that an appropriate "programming environment" will be part of the deal when they purchase airtime from broadcasters. And broadcasters have long understood that the development of programming must be achieved with two audiences in mind: the mass viewing audience, and the sponsors who view their pilots before deciding to buy time. As Todd Gitlin (1983, 253) has observed, network executives would be happy with the ratings if they showed *The Texas Chainsaw Massacre* every night, but it would not sell Hamburger Helper.

Clearly, program design is torn between two conflicting demands; yet both of these demands stem from the needs of national advertising. On the one hand, if a program is to reach a wide audience with commercial messages (thus keeping advertising revenues high), good ratings are essential. On the other, creation of the right programming environment, though increasingly important, is often at odds with the desire for ratings. These contradictory demands have become more glaring as advertisers actively seek more powerful advertising strategies. And because networks are less dominant now than before, programming environments that produce quality audiences are used to compensate for "network erosion."

Manufacturers and their agency representatives are no longer satisfied simply with quantity—the number of people watching TV shows. Now they are concerned with audience "quality" as well. And there is a fundamental connection between programming environment and audience quality. A "quality" audience is one that has been primed, with the appropriate programming, to be more receptive to advertising messages.

To truly understand the implications of this development, we must look more closely at the definition of *audience*, a term that has undergone a notable transformation over the years. Now more frequently referred to as "viewers," even as "readers" of television (Fiske 1987) who participate in the production of television meanings, the audience is nevertheless conceptualized by the makers of television primarily in terms of its market value.

It is a Hollywood joke that broadcasters are selling eyeballs to advertisers. It is fair to say, then, that in selling commercial time to advertisers to sell products, broadcasters are also selling a product—their audiences. It also stands to reason, as in any market relationship, that all steps will be taken to increase the profitability of that transaction. And just as any product needs to be developed and packaged to increase its salability and market share, so too must the viewers be packaged into more desirable commodities. Extensive research is thus conducted to ensure that the product—viewers—will be appealing to the buyers. Broadcasters are enlisting increasingly sophisticated audience research methods from the A. C. Nielsen Company and others, in an effort to determine which demographic groups are watching specific programs and in which proportions. In effect, the broadcaster's product—the audience—is transformed into a segmented market. The various divisions of that market can then be sold to advertisers either separately or cumulatively as target markets. Working together in this way, ad agencies and broadcasters can reach each segment with just the right commodity and sell a product with a precise advertising message that appeals to the specific tastes of those people watching the targeted programming. In short, packaging the audience to increase its salability involves creating programs that prime the product (viewers) to be receptive to advertising messages. Commercial value is thus increased, and the audience becomes a more desirable commodity.

Viewers watching *Northern Exposure,* for example, have already been conceived of as a market—as both a set of demographics and, not coincidentally, an important target market for the products advertised during the program. The program, in turn, has delivered the various segments of its audience to the advertisers. Indeed, during the "creative process" the program was conceived in terms of its demographic appeals. These practices helped determine what kinds of characters would be included, defined by their appeal to particular audience segments.

In the fall of 1993, NBC and Kellogg formalized the unity between product and audience marketing. It is neither a coincidence nor simply a case of "realistic" stage setting that Kellogg cereals are displayed on the kitchen shelves of Jerry Seinfeld's apartment. The kitchen serves as a key location for much of the action and dialogue on the program, tying Kellogg cereals to Jerry's home and character. This is only one aspect of what *Advertising Age* referred to as a "huge integrated" arrangement made by NBC with Kellogg to feature the cereal maker as a "co-star" (Mandese 1993). The NBC/Kellogg arrangement connected the stars of *Seinfeld,* and five other NBC shows, with Kellogg in a "marketing program that matches consumers of specific cereal brands with shows they are most likely to watch" (Mandese 1993, 1). For instance, Seinfeld viewers were deemed more likely to eat

Low Fat Granola than other cereals, so the four leading cast members appeared on Granola cereal boxes (see Figure I.1). In addition, a special "Seinfeld" bowl was offered as a premium.

The deal has also included a "watch and win contest" promoted by Kellogg with "in-store" displays tied to the premieres of ten new NBC prime-time shows. And, indeed, NBC's prime-time lineup makes for a perfect demographic fit with Kellogg consumers. Raisin Bran has been tied to *Fresh Prince,* with a sweepstakes tie-in. Both the NBC show *Wings* and Kellogg's Frosted Bran are popular with eighteen- to thirty-four-year-olds. And the show *Blossom* has "family appeal," making it an appropriate vehicle for Corn Flakes. Of course, it is not coincidental that the program's demographics match the desired cereal markets. TV programs are designed to appeal to demographic segments that can be sold to advertisers, and cereal is a TV advertising staple. The NBC/Kellogg deal is the logical outcome of media marketing practices. It merely formalizes the relationship, making it more explicit.

The reciprocal arrangement embeds the cereals within NBC programming, and NBC is "tagged" at the end of Kellogg TV commercials that run not only on NBC but on independent stations and cable as well. This is the first time a network logo has appeared on cereal boxes. The Kellogg/NBC deal is believed to be the largest ever between a marketer and a network, and it represents the definitive unity of media and product marketing. Conservatively valued at $100 million, it has become "the focus of both companies' entire fourth-quarter strategy" (Mandese 1993, 1).

Of course, the contents of the programs will not contradict the product images; nor will they question the benefits of consuming overpriced cereals,[1] or of consumption in general. Jerry Seinfeld "already had a reputation" as a cereal afficionado, but in case there was any doubt, NBC arranged a special taste test for Seinfeld to sample Low Fat Granola. "Asked whether the comedian actually uses the product, Mr. Cohen said, 'He does now.'" (Mandese 1993, 32). The merger of cereal marketing with television shows illustrates the final result of "appropriate programming environment." The program ultimately becomes a program-length commercial.

As the link between advertising and programming tightens, advertising agencies have beefed up their TV divisions. During the 1980s, competing agencies hired their own TV experts, such as Jon Mandel at Grey Advertising and Steve Sternberg at Bozell, whose job it is to "keep the people in Hollywood in tune with the people who are paying for the shows" (Berger 1994, 2-25). Agency TV advisers have begun to exert enormous clout. One of the most quoted sources in the ad business is Saatchi & Saatchi TV expert Betsy Frank, who was featured on page 1 of the *New York Times* Arts & Leisure section (July 10, 1994). Entitled "The Amazing Secrets of a Television Guru," complete with a full-color photo of Frank, the article quoted president of NBC Entertainment Warren Littlefield, who admitted to being "more and more receptive every year to what the advertisers have

FIGURE I.1 Kellogg's Cereal Box

TV programs are designed to appeal to demographic segments that can be sold to advertisers. In the fall of 1993, this unity between product and audience marketing was formalized with a contract signed by NBC and Kellogg. For the first time, a network logo appeared on cereal boxes. Cereal consumers were matched with shows they were most likely to watch. In this case, Kellogg's Low Fat Granola was designed to appeal to the demographics for *Seinfeld*.

to say" (Berger 1994, 2-25). And agency reps are talking. Frank publishes an annual booklet listing her favorite shows on a scale from one to ten. She also receives "scripts and videotapes from producers and stars seeking her opinion and perhaps her endorsement as they vie for places on the network schedules" (Berger 1994, 2-25). Acknowledging the increased influence that advertising "prognosticators" have on programming, president of CBS Entertainment Peter Tortorici concurred: "Our direct consumer is the advertising community, and we must maintain an open dialogue with them" (Berger 1994, 2-25). Now a "power player," Saatchi & Saatchi's Frank sometimes "meets with and advises top network executives" (Berger, 1994, 2-25).

To better understand the extent to which product marketing has influenced programming content, consider the films made during the 1980s. Product placement—the insertion of products directly within film narratives—was widely adopted in that decade. The practice offset spiraling production costs, but as Mark Miller (1990) argues, it had a dramatic effect on the creative design of the films themselves. Miller notes that film pacing and narrative structure are changed when products are inserted into the dialogue. Narrative progression itself is sometimes interrupted to feature stars talking about and asking for particular products.

When film stars begin to serve dual roles as characters and product promoters, character depictions are also invariably altered. Celebrity association with products demands a singularly positive "image." Thus, when selling products becomes the primary motive, there is no place for dark anti-heroes, or even complex personalities. Such characters do not make appropriate bonds with products. Recall that Burt Reynolds's contract as promoter of beef and orange juice was canceled when he and Loni Anderson divorced, and initial charges (not conviction) of child molestation prompted Pepsi-Cola to immediately distance itself from Michael Jackson.

The sodas, snack foods, and cereal so often inserted in films demand happy, upbeat environments. Then, as the film accommodates those products, becoming an appropriate product environment, it too must display the superficial mindless happiness characteristic of promotional culture. This trend, argues Miller (1990), accounts for the proliferation of so many happy endings and unidimensional heroes in American films of the 1980s, when product placement became the norm.

And as we have seen, product placement is now an integral part of what is considered the highest-quality fiction programming on television. Throughout the history of television, until now, direct product placement within fiction has not been a significant marketing strategy. This new broadcasting/marketing configuration marks a another definitive step in the history of the commercialization of television.

∾   ∾   ∾

This book is an exploration of the interconnections between media economics and communication discourse. The recessionary, highly competitive economic environment of the 1980s, which affected networks, independent broadcasting, and the media industry in general, has been widely noted in the business pages of the national press. But the dramatic effects on programming wrought by the financial strategies of this period are yet to be understood. Marketing factors account for the heightened emphasis on programming environment during the 1980s. But what are the full implications of the practice of audience marketing and the creation of appropriate programming environments?

When audiences are no longer principally conceptualized as people wanting to be entertained but, rather, are seen as products needing to be sold, programming itself is profoundly influenced. Designed to prime viewers and viewed primarily as a landscape for product promotion, TV shows have taken on the specific characteristics of "commercialtainment."

The accelerated movement toward "commercialtainment" is the focus of this book. It seeks to understand the impact of business practices, especially the spiraling commercial imperative, on program content. As marketing and advertising strategies become primary forces in the creative design of programming, the embedded commercial messages begin to merge with fictional formats.

Advertising is understood to be one aspect of the larger culture of consumption. Consumer marketing in general, with its assumptions about and imperatives for product promotion, is now integral to TV programming. We must explore the parameters of consumer culture and the nature of commercial discourse in order to understand their broad influence on media culture. Modes of advertising communication, long defined as openly persuasive, were previously considered to be distinct from entertainment and information communication. But as advertising begins to penetrate the entire media spectrum, these modes become incorporated into other programming strategies.

The dominant aesthetic of contemporary advertising is to routinely draw on a variety of intertextual media references. Many ads are constructed as combined fragments or mini-copies of entertainment genres and formats. Just as products are embedded within entertainment, entertainment is incorporated into commercial messages. These "creative" practices have forged yet another set of unities between advertising and media content.

Chapter 1 details the economic transformations that took place throughout the media industry during the 1980s. The loss of revenues caused by the availability of cable and VCR technologies, combined with the demand for maximum profits in the short term, placed severe economic constraints on the industry as a whole. Deregulation of broadcasting set in motion yet another set of economic pressures, resulting in a demand for greater profitability among broadcast groups, including news departments. The print media, similarly affected by economic concerns, became more susceptible to advertising pressures.

Over the past decade, advertisers have sought to increase the value of advertising. One strategy has been to insert product promotion directly into programming. Other strategies include product placement in films, advertiser-friendly copy or "advertorials" in newspapers and complementary copy in magazines, and video news releases and "infomercials" on television. All such techniques have been successful in promoting products and brand names within media content itself.

The culture of commodity promotion has now been fully incorporated within the fictional media environment. As motifs, advertising themes and marketing practices are now in the foreground of numerous TV shows, predominantly depicted from a sympathetic point of view.

To understand the effects of advertising on media content, we must trace the development of promotional strategies and contemporary persuasive communication. Chapters 2, 3, and 4 explore the nature of advertising messages and consumer culture in general from a variety of perspectives. In Chapter 2 the interconnections among production processes, economic forces, and consumption are redrawn. The corporate "globalization" practices of Nike, entailing the movement of factories to low-wage labor pools, are compared to its advertising messages, which celebrate human liberation and fulfillment. The Nike example is used to illustrate the economic linkages among American job loss, a falling standard of living, and consumer culture. The positioning of the public as consumer, in both advertising messages and television programming, has resulted in the mystification of these economic relationships. As consumers are positioned outside economic and political perspectives, the promise of their personal well-being and social satisfaction cannot be fulfilled.

Chapter 3 provides a behind-the-scenes look at a contemporary marketing research method—the focus group. Product promotion is now achieved primarily through emotional persuasion. The psychological techniques used in focus groups uncover a range of emotional needs and psychic longings. Based on the feelings and anxieties evoked in these groups, the advertising industry establishes pathways of desire for products.

To successfully tie human emotions to products, advertisers must use associative modes of communication capable of forging arbitrary connections between product consumption and human well-being. In the present age of advertising dominance, this mode of communication is no longer unique to commercial messages; indeed, it has been adapted to a variety of media strategies.

Thematically speaking, contemporary advertising has embraced a pseudotherapeutic discourse that promises the satisfaction of emotional needs and psychic well-being. The search for solutions to a range of human needs, social problems, and even economic hardships takes place within the realm of consumption through the discourse of therapy. With the merger of advertising discourse within television programming, then, therapy has become a primary theme woven into the fabric of television itself.

In Chapter 4 the current postmodern theoretical approach to much of popular culture is discussed in terms of its effectiveness as a tool for the analysis of advertising and consumer culture. Much of contemporary postmodern criticism tends to separate consumption from material and economic forces, preferring to evaluate consumer behavior within the realm of culture and to appreciate advertising messages as aesthetic forms. From this standpoint, advertising is social communication or simply postmodern symbolic expression. Although this analytic separation is crucial to an understanding of advertising messages and cultural representations, it is necessary to reconnect commodities to the social and political worlds that give them meaning, and to the material and economic forces that produce them. Only then can we assess the impact of the incorporation of consumer culture within the broader media environment.

Chapters 5 and 6 delineate the ways in which advertising themes and the general preoccupations of consumer marketing are assimilated into television programming. TV representations are heavily influenced by the economic practices and marketing techniques of the television industry. For this reason, the same themes of personal well-being and therapeutic promises found in advertising also characterize entertainment programming.

Chapter 5 traces advertising's discourse of therapy through *thirtysomething,* a program that arguably appealed to the baby-boom generation's desire for community. In this case, however, underlying media marketing strategies transformed the representation of community into "lifestyle" categories, defined by marketing practices. Marketing strategies also affected the portrayal of the family and gender relationships. Marketing's "new traditionalism" sold products to female consumers and became a dominant force in the fictional representation of family on *thirtysomething.* As a vehicle for consumption, the program assumed an individualized psychological discourse void of the social, political, and economic contextualizations needed for the representation of community and gender equality.

In Chapter 6 a therapeutic discourse is also found to be the guiding principle of talk shows. As the chapter points out, these shows developed in response to the ossification of traditional news formats. At first innovative, talk television provided an alternative to the fragmented, delinked constructions of sound-bite news representations and official statecraft. The new talk format offered the potential for a democratic, participatory discussion of issues of common concern. However, because of economic competition, the demand for ratings, and the influence of marketing themes, talk shows have devolved into spectacles of pseudotherapy.

Like contemporary advertising, talk shows appeal to viewer's needs for social belonging. But the commodification of programming has telescoped talk-show content into purely personal categories. This individualized language of consumption obscures the causes and solutions to social, economic, and even personal problems.

As with advertising strategies, the attempt to apply therapeutic practice to television talk shows is profoundly lacking. Pain, regret, and private exposure, commodified as entertainment, transform discourse into spectacle, often provoking scorn, ridicule, and disdain for the participants. And when suffering is commodified in this way, media content is significantly altered. Ultimately, the commodified talk show becomes a ritual of exclusion, not a healing narrative of inclusion or redemption.

"Reality"-based police shows are the topic of Chapter 7. These programs employ modes of communication once reserved for persuasive messages. Advertising's associative language permeates the representations of news and nonfiction programming. An in-depth look at the program *Cops,* for example, demonstrates a use of associative language that results in the lack of explanatory narratives. In short, this mode of communication is incapable of providing information necessary to understand the complex social, political, and economic forces that have caused the social problems so explicitly portrayed on these programs.

Also delineated in this chapter are the interconnections between "reality"-based police shows and the "war on drugs" being carried out in America's cities. The docu-cop crime formula proliferated at the same time the government instituted a drug policy focusing on criminalization and street-level narcotics enforcement in urban communities. Cheap to produce but deceptive, these TV representations of police activities misrepresent the nature of drug use and its relationship to crime and violence. Indeed, such programs have led to a lack of public understanding of drug use and the connections between urban poverty and the policies of drug prohibition. Criminal justice issues have been further skewed by the dramatic imagery of the street-level drug trade. In some instances, the policies of the war on drugs and their media representations have led to the curtailment of civil liberties and to unequal criminal justice practices applied to black and white Americans.

As with advertising and TV talk shows' therapeutic discourse, "reality"-based police programming appeals to authentic needs but offers false formulations and resolutions. The new crime programming invokes the public's need for safety and security, but it is only when the public participates from an informed perspective on criminal justice issues that the problem of crime will be solved. In the absence of a solution to this problem, the new crime programming offers spectacles of fear, punishment, and retribution commodified as entertainment.

Chapter 8 examines the media coverage of the Gulf War, which was presented through a discourse whose substance, language, and visual rhetoric closely resembled the persuasive logic of advertising. Distorted forms of communication that incorporate goods into the lives of American consumers (and into other forms of popular media culture) were consistent with the distorted modes of representation that incorporated the war into the symbolic rhetoric of American life.

The media misrepresented the war as something acceptable to the public because of its recognizable depictions. Accordingly, the chapter delineates the shared language between the presentation of war and the promotion of product. Advertising language that presented conformity as choice, the denial of problem complexity and responsibility, a positive attitude, solutions achieved through products and technology, the acceptance of contradiction, and the total disassociation of image from the material world also characterized media representations of the Gulf War.

Chapter 9 examines the ways in which the 1992 presidential campaigns were incorporated into a variety of fictional, nonfictional, and advertising genres and formats. The argument here is that both the Republican and Democratic campaigns were formulated to resonate with existing television themes, informed by the now-dominant media marketing strategies. Clinton became the first presidential candidate to fashion his campaign around the talk-show format and its therapeutic themes. And advertisements designed by the Bush camp tapped into the discourse of fear and anxiety, prominent themes of the "reality"-based police and crime programs. The connections among entertainment, advertising, and political discourse led to what some have referred to as "politainment."

The *Murphy Brown* episode to which Dan Quayle referred, as well as the use of "new news" and "direct-access" formats for political discussion, can be seen as responses to the crisis of official news detailed in Chapter 6. For a brief moment during the second presidential debate, policy issues were connected with public concerns, and the talk-show format facilitated a participatory and democratic discussion. For the most part, however, when put to the use of political marketing and persuasive practices, talk-show therapeutic themes merely provide another way for politicians to engender a false sense of sincerity and public trust, and thereby to avoid authentic political discussion. Within this media environment, the 1992 presidential campaign offered clear choices—but these were primarily of a discursive nature, rather than choices that resulted in real political and economic change.

In essence, contemporary marketing research and media business strategies have blurred the boundaries among fiction, nonfiction, and commercial programming. The new programming environment has led to changes in narrative structure, modes of address, and visual and linguistic devices. These changes, in turn, have led to a near-total lack of distinction in contemporary programming between modes of communication intended to persuade and those intended to entertain and/or inform.

To fully understand these dynamics, particularly the increased influence of media marketing and advertising on a wide range of television programming, we must examine the variety of communications media that have experienced very direct pressures from advertisers. This is the subject of Chapter 1, to which we now turn.

1

Advertising, Economics, and the Media

The "Golden Age" of Television

The most enduring historical example of the influence of advertising on program design comes from early television drama. Sponsor-controlled programming established patterns of advertising influence that have endured to the present. As television was posed to become a mass medium, sponsors learned which type of programs supported and reinforced advertising messages. By the early 1950s they had discovered that some programs, no matter how good, were not conducive to advertising messages. If story lines could not be changed according to the wishes of sponsors, they did not remain on the air. Sponsors succeeded in discontinuing the programs now considered to represent the "golden age" of television.

The New York theater community became involved in the presentation of Live Drama Anthologies in 1953–1955. The flagship production of *Marty* by Paddy Chayefsky told the story of a romance between a young butcher from the Bronx and a young woman outside of established social circles. These anthology dramas were touching and well executed. They drew consistently high ratings, but "one group hated them: the advertising profession" (Barnouw 1975, 163). In an effort to mold the programs more to their liking, sponsors continually requested script changes because, as Erik Barnouw (1975, 163) argues,

> most advertisers were selling magic. Their commercials posed the same problems that Chayefsky drama dealt with: people who feared failure in love and in business. But in the commercials there was always a solution as clear-cut as the snap of a finger: the problem could be solved by a new pill, deodorant, toothpaste, shampoo, shaving lotion, hair tonic, car.

In short, writers of drama depicted human problems in a way that revealed their complexity, emotional motivations, and human character. "They were forever suggesting that a problem might stem from childhood and be involved with feelings toward a mother or father. All this was often convincing—that was the trouble. It made the commercials seem fraudulent" (Barnouw 1975, 163).

Clearly the anthologies were not appropriate vehicles for the sale of products. As a result of sponsor pressure, they left the airwaves of American television. The subsequent history of programming is marked by the exertion of influence from broadcast executives and advertisers on producers to create programs that do not contradict the world of commodity consumption—a world that offers product solutions to complex social and psychological issues. This dynamic has always been part of the structure of commercial television, but the economic factors brought to bear on the media during the 1980s accelerated commercial pressures.

Promotional influences are not unique to television.[1] A look at the increased advertising leverage across the media spectrum will shed some light on the commercial imperatives that now define television programming.

Complementary Copy and Women's Magazines

In *Sex, Lies, and Advertising,* Gloria Steinem (1990) chronicles her ten-year experience working as the advertising representative for the women's magazine *Ms.* Steinem details her struggle with advertisers over who would determine the content of the magazine—the editorial board of *Ms.* or the advertisers. Securing ad schedules from major manufacturers requires an overall environment compatible with ad campaigns. And, indeed, women's magazines, offering the combination of a target market and quality color visuals, provide the multibillion-dollar cosmetic and fashion industries with effective advertising. At the same time, the magical make-over world of glamour constitutes the primary content of articles, features, and editorial pages of women's magazines. The numerous fashion, beauty, and health articles, often placed adjacent to corresponding advertisements, reinforce the products, their image, and their use. Referred to as "complementary copy" in the industry, this practice refers to the creation of editorial content that enhances the promotion of products and their advertising themes. *Ms.* found it impossible to compete for advertising revenue without following suit.

The marketing wisdom that advertising must be placed within a broader media environment that supports product promotion directs content in a number of ways. "Adjacencies" must express an appropriate emotional tone and thematic content, and topics antithetical to the product or its image are eliminated. Steinem notes that during the 1980s, advertisers' control over the editorial content of women's magazines had become "so institutionalized that it is written into 'insertion orders' or dictated to ad salespeople as official policy" (Steinem 1990, 26). Advertisers' demands include the following:

- Dow stipulates that ads for its Vivid and Spray 'n' Wash products should be adjacent to "children or fashion editorial. . . . If a magazine fails for 1/2 the

brands or more," the Dow order warns, "it will be omitted from further consideration."

- Bristol-Myers, the parent of Clairol, Windex, Drano, Bufferin, and much more, stipulates that ads be placed next to "a full page of compatible editorial."
- S. C. Johnson & Son, makers of Johnson Wax, lawn and laundry products, insect sprays, hair sprays, and so on, orders that its ads *"should not be opposite extremely controversial features or material antithetical to the nature/copy of the advertised product"* [italics in original].
- Maidenform, manufacturer of bras and other apparel, leaves a blank for the particular product and states: "The creative concept of the — campaign, and the very nature of the product itself appeal to the positive emotions of the reader/consumer. Therefore, it is imperative that all editorial adjacencies reflect that same positive tone. The editorial must not be negative in content or lend itself contrary to the — product imagery/message (*e.g., editorial relating to illness, disillusionment, large size fashion, etc.*)" [italics added].
- The De Beers diamond company, a big seller of engagement rings, prohibits magazines from placing its ads with "adjacencies to hard news or anti/love-romance themed editorial."
- Procter & Gamble, one of this country's most powerful and diversified advertisers . . . : its products were not to be placed in *any* issue that included *any* material on gun control, abortion, the occult, cults, or the disparagement of religion. Caution was also demanded in any issue covering sex or drugs, even for educational purposes. (Steinem 1990, 26)

If editors do not comply, they lose advertising revenue. Take, for example, the exclusive story that *Ms.* published in 1980 about four women from the Soviet Union who produced underground books there. This timely article, which won a Front Page award, included the first news about the peace movement and the struggle to end the war in Afghanistan, predicted the coming era of *glasnost,* and presented an intimate view of Soviet women's lives. The cover featured a picture of the four women. What the editors considered a "journalistic coup," however, spoiled "years of effort to get an ad schedule from Revlon" (Steinem 1990, 23). Why? Because according to Steinem the Soviet women on the cover were not wearing makeup. The magazine had failed to reinforce the image of women defined primarily by their appearance. Women's magazines are required to present an overall look compatible with the image conscious fashion and cosmetics industry. Even "real" women featured for their success or achievements wear makeup and are dressed in credited clothes, notably accessorized.

Women use these magazines, in part, to glean fashion and beauty tips, hoping that the writers' experience and talent will help them make informed selections. A good portion of such copy includes direct mention of specific merchandise and brand names, a standard feature of magazines competing for increasingly fewer ad dollars. Complementary copy and advertorials mislead readers into believing that products featured in columns are chosen on the basis of quality and design, when in fact fashion and beauty content is determined by which manufacturers have paid for advertising.

The industry habit of regarding women's magazines primarily as advertising vehicles precludes an extraordinary range of information and debate. Steinem's reflections illustrate that, for advertisers, complementary adjacencies and overall look are not adequate assurances that the magazine will provide the appropriate programming environment. In addition to positive editorial support, censorship is openly requested. The directives of Procter & Gamble represent the most sweeping demands on content. Certain topics are to be excluded from the entire issue in which any of this manufacturer's ads appear. This rule encompasses controversial topics as well as material simply offensive to corporate managers; but by no means is it restricted to Procter & Gamble. Keep in mind, too, that many of the same advertisers buying space in magazines also buy advertising time on television. In the end, *Ms.* realized that in order to represent (and protect) the interests of its readers as the magazine defined them—intelligent, independent women, eager for credible information relevant to their needs—it was simply forced to stop carrying advertising.

"The Slimmest Slim in Town"

The case of the tobacco industry best illustrates the connection between advertising and censorship. When cigarette advertising was banned from television, magazines took over the promoting of tobacco. This decision has had an enormous impact on the content of women's magazines. One women's magazine, *True Experience,* instructs writers and editors to omit all negative references to cigarettes.[2] The third item of a four-page style sheet reads, "Take out all mention of cigarette smoking. For example, no one in our stories dies of lung cancer caused by smoking." The author of one story entitled "How I Murdered My Husband" (all stories are promoted as true testimonials based on real experiences) is a disgruntled wife who researches the major causes of death for men. She finds that the culprits are smoking, fatty foods, alcohol, and motorcycle riding, all of which she encourages her husband to do. But by the time her story was published, all references to cigarettes had been taken out by the editor. Smoking no longer had a role in the story. Among the bowdlerized lines was this one: "Al did smoke, but not much. I'd find a way to make him smoke more." And on another page: "When a smoking table appeared beside his chair he didn't even bother to ask where it came from. Or to notice that new packs of cigarettes appeared nightly." One line reads "The money I saved . . . went into booze and cigarettes for him." The word *cigarettes* is penciled out, and "fatty, unhealthy snacks" is penciled in the margin.

A study of women's magazines done by Lauren Kessier at the University of Oregon, published in *Journalism Quarterly,* found a direct correlation between cigarette advertising and editorial content. The study examined the copy of six large-circulation women's magazines. All but one carried cigarette advertising. During the five-year period between 1983 to 1987, not one of the magazines "published any full-length feature, column, review or editorial on any aspect of the dangers of smoking" (quoted in Kilbourne 1991, 7).[3] During the same period, lung cancer was determined to be the number-one killer of women, surpassing even breast cancer. Not one of the magazines surveyed mentioned this fact.

Cigarette advertising has targeted women, especially young women, to replace older, higher-income, better-educated segments of the population who have quit smoking. Another study, published in *Health Education Quarterly*, found that "proportionately more cigarette ads were placed in women's and youth-oriented magazines than in magazines targeting other population segments" (Kilbourne 1991, 7). The atmosphere of the fashion industry provides an ideal environment for tobacco ads. Moreover, advertising associates smoking with slimness, offering a way for women to conform to the rigid weight standard of the glamour industry. The marketing of Capri, a new women's cigarette, targets young women and features tall, slim models announcing "The Slimmest Slim in Town."

In two disturbing instances of complementary copy, "*Cosmopolitan* and *McCall's* published short items associating smoking positively with weight control" (Kilbourne 1991, 7). Another example is the December 1993 issue of *Glamour*, which included a long piece on "smokers' rights." The content paralleled the tobacco industry's promotion of a smokers' rights point of view.

The Pressure Spreads

The direct and forceful ways in which advertisers demand complementary copy, along with the exclusion of antithetical material in women's magazines, is considered one of the most conspicuous cases of advertiser influence. It has not generated great concern, however, because women's magazines are not deemed to be journalistically legitimate. They have a long history of functioning as consumer vehicles. The transformation of *Ms.* from a commercial magazine to a journal that no longer carries advertisements illustrates the difficulty of carrying authentic journalism and advertisements under the same cover. At the same time, it has become clear that Steinem's experience with advertising pressure is not unique.

Because of increased economic pressures felt across the media industry, commercial interests have been more successful in shaping media content through demands similar to those brought to bear on women's magazines. In the face of economic recession and shrinking ad dollars, together with bottom-line management, the media have dropped even the pretense (once so adamantly asserted) that editorial and sales departments were separated to protect the integrity of media content. Indeed, it is now standard practice for newsmagazines as well as newspapers to design special consumer "Home" and "Style" sections that carry complementary copy. These publications also routinely attempt to disguise persuasive promotional material as legitimate news and feature stories through the use of "advertorials." In addition, both print and broadcast outlets have engaged in self-censorship on subjects known to be a problem with sponsors and advertisers. A report entitled *Dictating Content* by Ronald Collins (1992), co-founder of the Center for the Study of Commercialism, documents the escalation of advertising pressure and the numerous cases of economic censorship that characterize the present media environment.

Paul Farhi, a business reporter for the *Washington Post,* identified the problem in this way:

> Thanks to deregulation of the broadcasting industry, hard times and cut-throat competition for shrinking ad dollars, even the most reputable broadcasters and publishers are knocking new holes in the wall that traditionally has separated news and entertainment from their advertising departments. (Farhi, quoted in Collins 1992, 44)

The deregulatory atmosphere that characterized the 1980s is responsible for much of the economic pressure bearing down on the media industry.

Deregulation

Mark Fowler, head of the Federal Communications Commission under Reagan, rolled back the principle components of broadcast regulation during the 1980s. For example, under the long-standing "three-year rule," which Fowler rescinded, broadcast entities could not be sold for three years after the date of purchase. This anti-trafficking rule ensured that a station remained viable and intact. In the words of Everett Parker, former head of the Office of Communication for the United Church of Christ and long-time media public-interest advocate, "Regulatory structures set in place throughout the history of broadcasting served to stabilize the industry and worked well for broadcasting and the American public."[4] When the three-year rule was rescinded, any corporate investor could buy a broadcast entity and, as Parker explains, "fire the staff and reporters, lower the general overhead and sell the station at a profit in less than a year."

Before deregulation, corporate speculators did not purchase stations solely for the purpose of commodity trading. After deregulation, however, speculators who had no interest or experience in the media bought and sold stations simply to make a profit. This practice set a trend for broadcasting that resulted in the devastation of news departments, increasing demands for low-cost programming, and the escalating competition for short-term profits. As Eugene Secunda (1989, 3) has observed, it was during the 1980s that all three networks and many independent stations were acquired "by bottom-line-minded entrepreneurs, intent on getting a fast return on their investments." The establishment of bottom-line concerns prioritized profits at the expense of both news values and the public interest.

Historically, network news was designed to fulfill the regulatory public-interest mandate. It served to justify the private use of spectrum space. News divisions were subsidized by entertainment departments as representing the portion of the broadcast day designed in the public "interest, convenience and necessity." Long-time producer of CBS's *60 Minutes,* Don Hewitt, speaking at a seminar at Fordham University, revealed that for years the show was unique among news programming because it actually made a profit. Other network news shows were allowed to operate at a deficit because they brought prestige to the networks. Before bottom-line management, network economics traditionally protected news producers from the budgetary and ratings pressures that now characterize all broadcast news divisions.

The Waning Power of Advertising

Another step taken during the deregulatory fashion of the 1980s created a "commercial clutter" on television that overwhelmed viewers and diminished advertising's effectiveness. Until about fifteen years ago, advertising's persuasive appeal was impressive. Viewers watched advertisements attentively, and research revealed that they remembered a great deal of what they saw. But deregulation allowed more commercials on every broadcast hour. In addition, the standard 30-second commercial gave way to a proliferation of shorter 10- and 15-second spots. These changes created a TV environment in which "the number of spots appearing on network TV during an average week has nearly tripled to more than 5,000" (Secunda 1989, 4).

Just as the commercial storm hit 1980s television, remote-control technology provided viewers with a way to escape. Commercial-avoidance patterns reconfigured viewing habits as audiences began to zap, mute, and fast-forward ads within programs that had been videotaped. When viewers physically, or subconsciously, turned them off, advertisements lost a great deal of their persuasive power. The world of marketing began to notice that "heavy television advertising was no longer producing commensurate sales at the supermarket" (Secunda 1989, 4). With this realization, marketers have stepped up their search for ways to bring back advertising's persuasive power. One result has been increased demands that programming content support and reinforce advertising messages. Another has been the need to devise strategies that hide the promotional character of segments and programs so that viewers will be more accepting of persuasive messages.

Network Decline in the 1980s

The increased pressure for profits brought to bear on broadcasting during the 1980s, especially on the three networks, resulted in unprecedented influence by advertisers in broadcaster-controlled programming. In this decade, a variety of factors resulted in shrinking audience shares for the Big Three. The growth of independent stations, stronger competition from cable and videocassette recorders (VCRs), the fourth network (Fox), barter syndication,[5] and the preempting of network programming by affiliated stations—all contributed to viewing-level declines for the networks.

By the end of the decade, network executives realized that cable, and other media, posed a serious challenge to their once-axiomatic domination of the indus-try.[6] As noted in *Broadcasting* (1988, 72), "The continuing influx of cable into homes is further destabilizing the networks' position in the marketplace. . . . Even if they're [cable stations] only viewed in just tiny bits—you're going to have an erosion impact." Indeed, *Broadcasting* (1983, 44) had earlier warned that "net-work erosion isn't a geographic or temporary fluke; it's a nationwide, permanent, snowballing effect." By the fall of 1992, the network's prime-time schedule had "dropped to a collective 60% of the nightly audience, a record low" (Jensen 1993a, B1).

In the face of network decline, sponsors changed their approach to media buy-ing. Not only did advertising reps have more options in terms of media vehicles, but their clients were spending less on advertising due to the lagging economy. Advertisers often waited until the last possible moment to commit time, forcing the networks to reduce their rates. In turn, the networks had to compete with a variety of cheaper cable and broadcast outlets that were financially attractive to contemporary media buyers. Other media could produce effects at a fraction of the cost. Network CEOs realized that "the lush life once enjoyed at all three net-works is a thing of the past" (*Broadcasting* 1987, 70). By 1987 diminished advertis-ing sales had caused network executives to assert that "the pool of advertising rev-enues can no longer feed even a subsistence level" (*Broadcasting* 1987, 70).

Effects on Broadcast News

In 1986, within nine months' time, all three networks changed hands and the "new owners all had the same mantra: cut costs or die" (Auletta 1991b). Hardest hit by the new bottom-line management were the network news divisions. When, for example, General Electric bought RCA (NBC's parent company), GE chair-man and CEO Jack Welsh immediately demanded that the news budget be cut by 5 percent. Then, because NBC's ratings were high, NBC News president Lawrence Grossman concluded that there was no need to make the cut, in the belief that it would only hurt NBC's ability to produce a quality newscast. Welsh replaced Grossman with Michael Gartner, and the cut was made.

Economic pressure on local newscasts, treated as cash cows since the early 1970s,[7] also escalated. Already tight budgets in the news departments of indepen-dent TV and network affiliate stations became even tighter. As Eugene Secunda (1989, 3) has noted, "Network affiliates in the top 25 markets cut back their news staffs an average of 7%; the next ranking 25 markets saw cuts of 5%." Even as staff members were being fired, demands for ratings increased because early-evening news shows are viewed by managers as crucial lead-ins to their prime-time pro-grams.

Although production costs for hard news were cut, "soft" news provided the salve for network erosion. As *Broadcasting* (1990a, 34) observed, the networks are indeed striving for "viewer friendly, profit-making news." In 1990 Steve Friedman, executive producer of NBC Nightly News, said that "major TV news networks have to realize that in the modern TV age being good journalists is not enough. To win the hearts and minds, and, more importantly, the viewership of the audiences, we have to exist in the landscape of television" (*Broadcasting* 1990a, 34). Existing in that landscape has meant the consolidation of "infotainment."

Make It Cheap . . . and Keep the Ratings High

During the 1980s the costs of prime-time programming escalated, whereas revenues plateaued. Television began to rely more on in-house productions. Many high-cost entertainment shows were replaced with cheaper nonfiction programming and specials. "Reality" programs, many of which were produced by independents for national syndication, became the inexpensive new popular format across the video spectrum. The cost of producing a one-hour entertainment program is now more than twice the cost of producing a news magazine show.

The emergence of "trash" television, "genre" news, and TV tabloid "magazines" responded to the need for viewer-friendly infotainment and reduced overhead, but it has led to what David Altheide and Robert Snow (1991) call the "post-journalism era." One station stands out as emblematic of changes made in news formatting and content in order to accommodate the new economic atmosphere of the 1990s. This station is the Fox affiliate WSVN in Miami, which has begun programming 7 hours a day of MTV-style news in order to compete with network rivals. Using jazzy, fast-paced tabloid techniques to reach Miami's younger, minority audiences, WSVN turns raw video into grainy *verité*, then slows it down or speeds it up. Such techniques, along with various graphic sensationalized images and headlines, characterize the hybrid format.

If it bleeds it leads on WSVN, a station that marshals an assortment of the tragic, bloody, and bizarre. One program that aired during the summer of 1993 included the following curiosities before the first commercial break: two plane crashes, three rapes, three hit-and-run accidents (two fatal), a wild monkey attack, an anti-gay protest in Washington, a white plot to blow up blacks, the theft of fake breasts (possibly by a band of transvestites), children who murdered a grandmother, and a train accident. Producers search far and wide for such reports; most do not originate in Miami. Viewers are drawn in by the tabloid techniques and wise-cracking colloquial style typified by the following line: "Cops nailed one of the suspects at a stoplight." As one reporter admitted on the air, "Hey, we do what it takes to get ratings."

Local community leaders have complained that the content and tone of the WSVN news is racist. Paul Steinle, director of journalism at the University of Miami, refers to WSVN as the "worst example of local news I have ever seen in the United States" (Steinle, quoted in Rohter 1993, C34). Yet the *Wall Street Journal* has reported that WSVN is one of the most successful independent stations in the nation and "a trendsetter for the entire television industry" (Jensen 1993b, 1). With the success of WSVN and such programs as *A Current Affair, Hard Copy,* and *Inside Edition,* Rupert Murdoch is reported to be considering WSVN as the model for Fox network's national news.

Although format changes in "serious" news are undoubtedly needed (see Chapter 6), the movement toward altered video and sensationalized rapid-fire stories, along with the pursuit of ever more graphic views of mayhem, does not move the genre any closer to relevancy or thoughtfulness. Instead, such developments mark the total descent of information representation into entertainment for profit. The grabby, stimulating formats using direct address, subjective camera techniques, dramatization, "visualization," and "live reality" video are not meant to explain. On the contrary, tabloid news is designed to jolt the viewer into awed fascination. These strategies were devised to keep audiences tuned, so as to see more of the "real" curiosities on video display.

Economic Censorship

Deregulation, falling profits, and advertising's newfound clout have created an overall atmosphere that influences editorial judgments and the evaluation of newsworthiness. As a result, the boundaries that (at least attempted to) separate reporting and advertising have become the quaint remnants of a past journalistic era. Nowhere is this more apparent than in consumer news.

Even as the media/marketing industry positions the viewing public as consumers, an enormous amount of consumer information is restricted by advertisers' direct influence on the media. In particular, advertisers have been successful in censoring stories critical of their industry or business practices. Numerous cases of direct censorship have become a concern to public-interest advocates. From stories on real estate and housing issues, to automobile pricing and safety, to unfair pricing at supermarkets and department stores, reports have been spiked to appease advertisers' demands.

Debra Zeyen, vice-president and general manager of WBZ(TV) Boston, has expressed great concern over what she called a serious type of broadcast censorship. Because 25 percent of local TV advertising comes from car dealers, "you will never see an investigative report on [local] car dealers. It's an unspoken rule."[8] She also noted that economic censorship on the part of advertisers has become generalized. If a station does a report critical of one product, a station may lose revenue because other advertisers "shy away from anything controversial."

In 1984 WLWT-TV in Cincinnati hired consumer reporter Noel Morgan for its *Five on Your Side* news segment. During the five years he worked for the station he came into conflict with local car dealers on several occasions. Among his stories that were either "killed or toned down were investigations into reported schemes that misled consumers" (Collins 1992, 22). These stories included information about unfair credit rating practices, inflated pricing, bait-and-switch tactics, false advertising, and odometer rollbacks. Morgan's contract was not renewed even though he won two Emmy awards. "They didn't want the kind of thing I did anymore" (Collins 1992, 23). According to a former manager of WCCO-TV in Minneapolis, "As the financial situation in broadcasting has deteriorated and the fight for advertising dollars becomes more fierce, the dealers have come to sense their increasing power, and they know their money can make a significant differ-ence in the profitability of a station" (Collins 1992, 19).

News and public-affairs directors are made keenly aware that advertisers are paying close attention to their programming, and that to contradict corporate sponsors or their advertising messages would have a negative financial impact on the station and, by extension, their jobs. Cable programming is not exempt from these pressures. When CNN's *Capitol Gang* was summoned to carry out a mock program in front of a group of advertisers,[9] the producers and commentators were sent a clear message—namely, that the program's content will be monitored with great interest. Under these circumstances it is unlikely that information un-acceptable to CNN advertisers will be included.

One bright spot in consumer reporting came with the development of Consumer Reports Television, a division of the research organization known as Consumer Union, which in turn publishes *Consumer Reports* magazine. News re-ports featuring consumer information, running about 90 seconds in length, are distributed nationally to fifty-eight subscribing stations. Because they accept no advertising, corporate donations, or corporate foundation funds, the syndicated news service is able to provide independent information. As producer Joyce Newman explained in an interview with the present author (1994), "We're not in the same position as broadcast journalism . . . where advertising has a direct im-pact on what they're producing." However, major markets such as Los Angeles, Chicago, Boston, and Miami have not subscribed, even though the televised Consumer Reports are a fraction of the cost of segments produced by individual stations. The most likely reason is the no-advertising clause carried by the Consumer Reports' syndication contract. Because the Consumer Reports allow no commercial use or advertising tie-ins in any of their material, they are pre-vented from "selling advertising on the basis of programming content." Stations cannot use the segments as adjacencies to draw advertising sales, as is the case with most TV "inserts" produced by outside sources.[10]

Although such consumer reporting is beneficial, the need for an outside news service for critical information is itself a measure of the loss of both journalistic independence and the general ability of the press to function outside the con-straints of promotional requirements. At any rate, a greater trend in TV news fea-tures provided by outside sources has been for stations to air *video news releases* produced by public-relations firms promoting products through "news" seg-ments, as discussed in the next section.

Print Journalism

Throughout the 1980s a close relationship between advertising and editorial de-partments developed in newsrooms across the country. Jim Collins, working as a staff reporter for the *Scranton Times* in 1985, wrote a story on the auto industry using quotes from a car dealer who advertised exclusively with the paper's compe-tition, the *Scranton Tribune*. For doing so, he was pilloried by the city editor for not checking with the advertising department first.[11] Now, stories on consumer issues from store openings to features about flowers before Valentine's day must be approved by the advertising department first. No photograph of a grand opening appears in the paper if the store has not purchased advertising. This close relationship between editorial desk and ad reps at the paper is best illustrated by the *Progress Edition,* a supplement printed once a year. For this special advertising vehicle, which is not identified as such, the editors let advertisers write their own copy. Collins believes that "the people reading them are being misled; they think the paper writes the copy." The *Scranton Times* now publishes such special sections on a regular basis.

Advertorials, like complementary copy, are designed to camouflage their commercial identity and capitalize on the public's trust in journalistic integrity. Many papers now seek to please advertisers with tailored special sections containing copy written either by advertisers or by staff writers who create friendly features that serve as vehicles for advertisements. For instance, the *News* in Birmingham, Alabama, featured an "Auto World" section designed to attract local car dealers. A twenty-three-year veteran reporter for the paper, Dennis Washburn, was fired when he admitted that editors would be "extra careful about doing an exposé" critical of business practices in that section (Collins 1992, 24).

The real estate industry, representing more than 18 percent of the classified ads in daily newspapers also makes its demand for a positive media environment clear to newspaper editors. Still reeling from the economic recession that hit the industry after the inflationary 1980s, real estate advertisers demand friendly coverage. As Elizabeth Lesly (1991, 21) has noted, "Now the mildest critical reporting provokes the industry's wrath." The findings of a confidential survey of forty-two real estate editors, conducted by *Washington Journalism Review,* reveal the extent of advertisers' influence. More than 80 percent of the editors said that advertisers had threatened to pull advertising because of critical reporting, and "more than a third knew of advertisers that had done so" (Williams 1991, 24).

Advertisers have also been successful in acquiring advertorial sections in newspapers. Many of these sections simply embellish the real estate industry's own press releases, which amounts to little more than "industry-generated hype." This national trend has occurred in spite of the need for critical consumer information on housing, pricing, the reliability of real estate brokers and builders, and the stumbling blocks involved in acquiring a mortgage. The result has been to deprive consumers of information they need for one of the most important financial transactions they will ever make. In response to this trend, the *Washington Journalism Review* has observed that "some revenue-hungry newspapers are siding with advertisers against their readers" (Lesly 1991, 21).

With their jobs and the profitability of their papers in mind, editors are asked to consider advertising interests over those of the public. Ronald Collins (1992) has documented disputes between editors and management over the "business-boosting" style of many newspapers. One such editor was Bill Kovach, who left the *Atlanta Journal-Constitution* in 1988. Kovach stated in an interview: "The trend for the past decade has been to promote editors who, if they are not business people, then they are business-conscious" (Collins 1992, 35).

A newspaper in Utah, the St. George *Daily Specter,* published an article advising consumers that the recession had created a buyers' market. In a section providing tips on how to buy a new car, it revealed that car dealers try to make a 7.5 percent markup on a new car, but that "hard bargaining can cut that margin in half." After complaining bitterly, local dealers organized an advertising boycott. In response, "the *Specter* retracted the article, apologized and blamed an editor for exercising poor judgment" (Collins 1992, 20–21).

Cost Cutting and Investigative Journalism

In this age of bottom-line management, tight budgets in news departments make it difficult for editors to assign staff writers to lengthy investigative assignments. Accepting press releases is cheaper than the legwork and digging needed for hard-hitting inquiries. *Albuquerque Tribune* reporter Eileen Welsome won the 1994 Pulitzer Prize for breaking the story on secret government plutonium experiments performed on American citizens. Acknowledging that the "dollar figures" for investigations are "dutifully taken into consideration," she added, "I'm concerned about that. . . . "Economic issues really do play a role in small to mid-sized newspapers."

Increased Corporate Control

The economic recession and the national deregulatory atmosphere, together with financial speculation and corporate conglomeration, ended diversity of media ownership. A succession of media mergers took place during the 1980s. From Capitol Cities Communications' union with ABC to the Time/Warner merger, each was progressively larger, setting one historical precedent after another. At present, less than twenty-four corporations control a vast industry—a true case of corporate monopoly control.

Emblematic of mega-corporate media ownership was the acquisition of the NBC network by General Electric, the largest weapons contractor in the world. A growing body of evidence now illustrates the dangers of such unchecked corporate control of media outlets. Particularly well documented is GE's willingness to control program content. Consider, for instance, the removal of negative information about GE from a segment that aired on NBC's *Today* show. The following lines were cut from a story about defective bolts in nuclear plants: "Recently, General Electric engineers discovered that they had a big problem. One out of every three bolts from one of their major suppliers was bad. Even more alarming, GE accepted the bad bolts without any certification of compliance for 8 years" (Putnam 1991, 4).

GE also successfully blocked NBC's coverage of a boycott of its products being carried out by Infact, a grassroots organization promoting corporate responsibility.[12] In another example, the bureau chief of *Marketplace,* the financial program that airs on public radio, is reputed to have said (or screamed), in response to the possibility of reporting on the GE boycott, "Media censorship, media smensorship, I have a family to support. You're nuts if you think we can do anything on it. . . . I know for a fact they'd run me out of here" (Collins 1992, 29). The former president of NBC News, Lawrence Grossman, recalled a phone call from GE's president, Jack Welsh, complaining about coverage of the 1987 stock-market crash. Negative terms like *Black Monday* had caused GE's stock to fall (Collins 1992, 30).

GE welcomes advertorials, however. NBC stirred controversy when it aired a feature documentary favorable to nuclear power shortly after GE purchased the network. Viewers were not informed that NBC was owned by GE, a leader in the nuclear industry. Nor were they informed that GE was the manufacturer of a new machine used to detect breast cancer, which was featured three nights in a row (June 20–22, 1990) on *NBC Nightly News.* A total of 14 minutes, the equivalent of half of one newscast, was devoted to the "story," which, for obvious reasons, neither CBS nor ABC picked up (Putnam 1991).

It should come as no surprise that during the same time corporate ownership and control of the media took place, information critical of corporate America became harder to find on the news agenda. This relationship is demonstrated by Carl Jensen's (1993) ongoing Project Censored. The majority of the top twenty-five censored news stories for 1992 dealt with corporate malfeasance. Whereas during the late 1980s the top underreported stories involved political scandal, in the 1990s stories critical of corporate practices constitute the majority of censored stories. From reports on toxic dumping to the blackout of news about electric cars, journalists and editors have pulled away from their historical role of keeping "big business" accountable to the public.

The $10 Billion Threat

In addition to media ownership, corporations have the wealth and legal know-how to block information critical to their interests. The threat of libel suits and the financial drain they cause hangs over newsrooms as an ominous specter. Upon receiving the George Polk award for radio commentary, Daniel Schorr noted the "great fear of libel" that inhibits many editors from taking the risks necessary to keep the public informed. For instance, Philip Morris brought a $10 billion libel suit against ABC news on March 24, 1994, even though the information—that tobacco companies have increased the amount of nicotine in cigarettes—had been advanced by the U.S. Food and Drug Administration. The clear intent was to send a warning message to the media.

In another example, General Motors successfully negotiated with NBC to retract statements made about dangerous gas tanks in Chevy trucks. Even though the tanks were ruled dangerous in the courts, and GM was finally forced to make compensation, NBC's rigging of a crash test left the network in no position but to publicly retract its disclosures. But this blunder, ultimately a consequence of the need for visuals and, by extension, ratings as well, did not make the information any less legitimate. Libel, even the threat of libel, is undoubtedly effective in the intended goal of casting a chill over the hard-hitting reporting needed to bring secretive corporate operations to the light of public scrutiny.

The Tabloidization of News

The post-journalism press is largely a consequence of economic pressures brought to bear in the newsroom. Demands for profits in broadcasting and competition to sell papers accelerated as the bottom-line mentality came to dominate the corporate media industry, closing out other mandates historically associated with journalism and the free press. As corporate malfeasance became increasingly blocked from public view, sensationalized stories in the media reached a crescendo. The lurid reporting styles used in these stories, especially those dealing with crime and violence (see Chapter 7), have raised questions involving rights to privacy and a fair trial. Indeed, issues raised by such tabloid practices now dominate professional seminars and public-interest discussions.[13]

In many such instances the victims and their families are further victimized by the press. Speaking at a forum sponsored by the Society for Professional Journalists,[14] Ellen Levine, mother of Jennifer Levine, victim in the "Preppy Murder Case," reported being astounded by the false, sensationalized "facts" published about her daughter. "Dealing with the press," she said, "was the worst thing that happened in my life after the murder of my daughter." In a related vein, New York *Daily News* crime reporter Jerry Capeci, responding to charges that journalists have become more aggressive and less willing to respect the rights of those they cover, acknowledged, "There is no question that economics has something to do with the way stories are told and the types of stories being reported. Journalists are under tremendous pressures." Capeci, formerly with the *New York Post*, explained that journalists are no longer protected by the Newspaper Guild, now that Rupert Murdoch has dismantled the Guild. Allan Wolper of *Editor & Publisher* confirmed that, over and above wages and benefits, the Guild had previously provided protection for journalists from economic and editorial pressures. But it no longer has the power to do so, and journalists are left vulnerable to those influences.

The prioritization of profits over the public interest has led to trash journalism, which in turn has created a public backlash against the press. It is not surprising that, as Schorr acknowledged at the George Polk award ceremony, "the public won't forgive us our press passes. They don't love us much anymore." In short, public animosity has led to calls for censorship and the restriction of private information from journalists. Even though the media themselves have evoked these public sentiments, the fact remains that they endanger the First Amendment mandate and the democratic need for an uninhibited information environment.

"Fake News"

Video News Releases

The influence of advertising on media content has led to hybrid media forms that fuse advertising with journalism, blurring the distinction between them. Consider, for instance, the *video news release* (VNR), an advertisement that adopts the form of a television news feature. *TV Guide* referred to VNRs as "fake news" (Lieberman 1992). These "news" stories are produced at public-relations (PR) firms and sent, free of charge, to stations around the country over satellite or by videocassette. VNRs provide high-quality segments that are made to look as if they had been produced by local reporters. Their target destinations are the 700 local news divisions around the country, but network news programs have also used them. At a cost of about $30,000 for each complete segment, VNRs represent only a fraction of the cost of prime-time advertising.

As news departments cut personnel and overhead expenses, their ability to compete for ratings is diminished. Of the many news professionals who lost their jobs in broadcasting during the 1980s, a sizable number are now employed by PR firms to create the latest state-of-the-art VNR segments. News departments pick them up because competing for ratings is easier with high-quality product.

As one independent video producer who has worked on VNRs explained, "The strategy is to develop a news 'angle' around a product."[15] For example, if the VNR is for Clairol, the news angle might be something like this: "Women are getting promoted to higher management positions and are thus more concerned about the way they look, so they're coloring their hair more often. We spoke to somebody from Clairol about this phenomenon." Or the producer could take a health angle on skin cream: "Yes, doctors say that all women should use face protection every time they go outside. Even if they're only walking around New York, they can apply a Neutrogena cream containing number 15 sunblock protection." Clearly, then, the VNR is the video equivalent of complementary copy and advertorials.

Major advertisers have embraced this new media device to compensate for the waning power of advertising. The VNR is powerful because its commercial content is hidden. Hiding the persuasion is part of the VNR formula. According to one video producer, "You have to be careful about the way it's scripted. You can't be too blatant about mentioning the client or the product too many times. You have to meander around it."[16]

The techniques used to construct VNRs reveal other aspects of their deceptive nature. For instance, they are carefully designed to mimic news reporting. Fully produced ready-to-air VNRs are available, but stations usually prefer to interject their own correspondents and anchorpersons for the sake of "authenticity." For this purpose, PR firms provide a track with natural sound and footage, called a "B-roll," that can be reassembled at individual stations and voiced by their own correspondents. In many cases, visual and audio spaces are also left in interviews so that local reporters can fill in the blanks with questions. In turn, the interviewee is stage-managed to look toward an invisible reporter and nod just as he or she would in an actual interview. In this way viewers are led to believe that their hard-working reporter has done the legwork and asked the questions. But in fact the question-and-answer session has been designed by the PR firm.

Creation of the VNR entails the transformation of information into persuasive discourse. The controlled message of the VNR is designed to benefit from the public's trust in journalism while excluding the very news judgments that legitimate the profession. Proponents of the VNR argue that it is simply an electronic version of the printed press release. But as a representative from one of the largest pharmaceutical firms told a 1990 Food and Drug Law Institute conference in Washington, D.C., VNRs "allow us to make sure we can control the message as much as possible and not depend on a journalist to interpret data that would be in a news release kit" (Taylor and Mintz 1991, 482). Responding to this situation, David Jones, a former vice-president for public affairs at Abbot Laboratories who left Abbot over disputes about objectionable marketing and promotional practices, said, "The media aren't doing what the public expects them to do—which is screen, evaluate and judge the information they get" (Taylor and Mintz 1991, 482).

After a VNR has been distributed, the PR firm follows up with air-check calls to see if it is being picked up. One pharmaceutical representative estimated that about 300 TV stations regularly carry the segments. And Nielsen Media Research group estimated that marketers produced about 4,000 VNRs in 1991. Nielsen, together with Medialink, the largest VNR distributor, also surveyed television news directors. Among those polled, 15.2 percent reported using one unedited VNR each week, and 78 percent said they used one they had edited. Another Nielsen questionnaire commissioned by Medialink found that more than 46 percent of the nation's news directors predicted that national newscasters will increase their use of VNRs over the next five years (Lieberman 1992, 26).

A sad irony is that the VNR, as a "news segment," does not fall under the same truth-in-advertising restrictions that regulate advertising. Pharmaceutical companies are required by the FDA to include in their advertisements a warning about potential misuses and hazardous side effects. VNRs effectively circumvent these regulations.

The pharmaceutical industry is estimated to be the single largest user of VNRs. Drug advertisements disguised as news segments frequently air on the popular health segments of local news programming, stimulating public demand for the products featured. And of course public demand is exactly the point of such advertisements. But because negative information is excluded, VNRs help drive up the cost of drugs "by creating inappropriately high expectations of what a drug can do" (Taylor and Mintz 1991, 484). It is not surprising that, from 1981 to 1989, overall inflation rose 46 percent while prescription drug prices rose 128 percent.

In short, VNRs are advertisements dressed as news to hide their intent and increase their effectiveness. The ultimate example of the unity of programming and advertisements, this media device has gone a long way toward transforming the presentation of news into advertising discourse.

Infomercials

Infomercials represent another set of formatting strategies designed to hide the persuasive strategies of advertising. They mimic various types of programs, from cooking shows to investigative news reports. Often resembling talk shows, they feature "real people" who attest to the value and effectiveness of the products they plug. A deliberately deceptive aspect of these program-length commercials is the insertion of shorter pieces that promote the product directly. Woven into the longer format, these discrete segments appear to be conventional spot advertisements, making the program itself appear more authentic.

The intent is to stimulate a type of compulsive on-the-spot purchase. Infomercials are therefore designed as forceful persuasive formats, making exaggerated claims seemingly authenticated by the personal testimonies they feature. Public-interest organizations, including the Center for the Study of Commercialism (1992), have submitted a petition to the FCC requesting continuous on-screen labeling to notify viewers that they are watching a commercial message. (A similar request has been made regarding VNRs.) According to the petition, the infomercial "preys upon the unsuspecting viewer's assumption that any program one half hour in length could not be an advertisement" (Center for the Study of Commercialism 1992, 3).

Under the guidelines of the Communications Act of 1934, the FCC requires that stations "fully and fairly disclose" the identity of those who pay to air their commercial messages. But the producers of these programs (like those of VNRs) have resisted continuous identification because it would warn viewers that the programs' intent is not to inform but, rather, to persuade.[17] Viewers' knowledge of the fact that people are being paid to make their claims, and that their words are scripted, not the authentic discourse of human experience, would clearly diminish the effectiveness of infomercials.

In 1990 the U.S. Congress investigated infomercials, focusing on the ways in which the public received their messages. It concluded that "consumers need more protection against not only fraudulent infomercial claims but also sales pitches disguised as objective reporting" (Center for the Study of Commercialism 1992, 12). In turn, the Center's suit concludes, "The infomercial is a commercial form designed to exploit audience unawareness that they are watching advertising," the same characteristic that defines the VNR. Both formats are a consequence of the advertising industry's quest for more vigorous forms of persuasion in the face of the waning power of their trade. The producers' resistance to identification is significant because it indicates that these strategies work. Viewers are indeed less critical and therefore more susceptible to persuasive messages when they are unaware of the commercial motives behind them.

Historically, television modes of communication have been distinct, with advertising, entertainment, and nonfiction communication separated by clear boundaries. Indeed, broadcast regulation depended on this separation. Recall that, until 1984, commercials were limited to 16 minutes per broadcast hour.[18] The reasoning behind this restriction was that the public interest is not served when viewers are bombarded with commercial programming throughout the entire broadcast day. The public should have the right to be entertained or informed without being constantly goaded to make a purchase. Until 1984, then, the FCC blocked the broadcast of program-length commercials: Since each entire program was a commercial, it violated the 16-minute time restriction.

In 1984, however, commercial restrictions on broadcasting were eliminated in the "spirit" of deregulation, and infomercials proliferated with astounding force. Together with the home-shopping network, infomercials are currently the fastest-growing programming services on cable TV.

Until now, the primary users of infomercials have been small manufacturers and distributors who used the format as the only means of selling their product. Today, however, "major corporations like General Motors and Volvo are entering the infomercial arena" (Center for the Study of Commercialism 1992, 11). In addition, with the continuing economic instability of broadcasting, network executives have suggested that they might reduce their prime-time schedules to cut programming costs. Howard Stringer, president of the CBS broadcast group, predicted that if network prime-time hours were reduced, "those open hours would be filled with junk" (Carter 1991b, D6). Media observers feel that affiliates would turn to more game shows and tabloid "magazines," and that infomercials would "make their way into prime time" (Carter 1991b, D6). Infomercials are indeed on the cutting edge of media marketing. Forecasts for media spending in 1994 specified a 7 percent increase. Fueling that growth is a strong national television market "stimulated by home shopping, infomercials and other forms of electronic marketing."[19]

The willingness of broadcasters to relinquish their airtime to free programming in order to cut costs, combined with the willingness of major manufacturers to again become involved in television product, harks back to the structure of early television when sponsors controlled programming. At the end of this road back to the future is full-blown "commercialtainment," of which Robert Iger spoke.

VNRs and infomercials are on the cutting edge of strategies designed to tear down the barriers between advertising and media content. The merging of fiction and nonfiction programming with persuasive communication is a feature of the 1990s' commercial imperative. But equally important to the promotion of products within this new media environment are advertisements that resonate with the existing media landscape.

Intertextuality and the Embeddedness of Advertising

Infomercials, VNRs, advertorials, complementary copy, product placement, and programming environments—all seek to unite the product and its message with news and entertainment programming, thereby increasing persuasiveness. The advertisements themselves must also fit stylistically with other media forms. According to the dominant aesthetics of contemporary advertising, commercial messages must resemble the news and entertainment within which they are embedded. "Intertextual" advertising is the means by which products are merged aesthetically with the broader terrain of media culture.

Intertextuality, as defined by John Fiske (1987), involves the use of recognizable textual references that allow the viewer to read the text in relationship to other texts. Playful references to media genres, story formulas, and familiar characters ensure that "a range of textual knowledge" will be brought to bear upon the present text. Analysis of television's intertextual aesthetic has focused on its usefulness as a device for audience participation. Intertextual references work by assuming a degree of cultural literacy and knowledge among the "readers" of television. For the variety of subjective positions and viewer experiences that results there is a corresponding multiplicity of textual interpretations. However, the theoretical emphasis on audience participation through intertextual play (Olson 1987) overlooks the importance of intertextuality as a commercial strategy.

With regard to advertising, intertextuality refers to the creation of commercials that incorporate the product within the context of television itself. When Candice Bergen appears as the spokesperson for Sprint, the pleasure of watching Murphy Brown, with all her endearing, wacky, bellicose independence, is transferred to Sprint and incorporated within the promotion. In this way—through advertisements that refer to the characters, formats, and genres of the surrounding media environments—products and their messages are allowed to resonate with existing cultural attitudes (see Figure 1.1).

The most common form of advertising intertextuality is the presentation of TV characters within commercial messages. As students of advertising are told, "Research suggests that celebrities enhance attention value and persuasion" (Roman and Maas 1992, 22). The stars come out from their programs to shine in product promotions now on a regular basis. When James Earl Jones starred in *Gabriel's Fire* he also promoted NYNEX Yellow Pages. Well-known actor Michael J. Fox promotes Diet Pepsi. And Angela Lansbury from *Murder, She Wrote* brings her determination as well as her gift for always having the right answer to her promotion of aspirin.

Then there's the fictional doctor from *All My Children* who appears in a TV ad proclaiming, "I'm not a doctor, but I play one on television." This admission should immediately discount whatever opinions he might have about medicine. But his medical advice is persuasive, not because of his expertise but because of the relationship of trust and recognition that has been established through his fic-

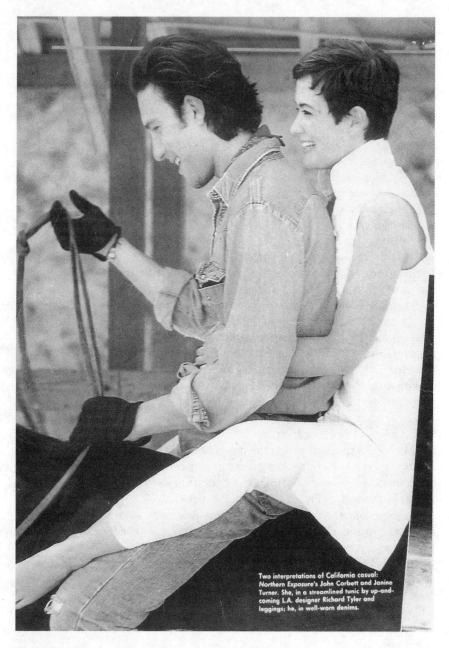

Two interpretations of California casual: Northern Exposure's John Corbett and Janine Turner. She, in a streamlined tunic by up-and-coming L.A. designer Richard Tyler and leggings; he, in well-worn denims.

FIGURE 1.1 Chris and Maggie from *Northern Exposure*
The most common form of advertising intertextuality is the presentation of TV characters within commercial messages. Here, John Corbett and Janine Turner, who play Chris and Maggie on *Northern Exposure,* pose for a fashion layout in a magazine advertisement. The outdoor setting of the advertisement matches the program's emphasis on the natural environment. The commercial imperative is often the motivation for the aesthetics of intertextuality.

tional character. In effect, that relationship is carried into the commercial message.

The best celebrity appeals are not simple endorsements but, rather, those in which the image of the celebrity has merged with that of the product. For example,"Bill Cosby is not just a spokesperson for Jell-O; he is Jell-O. Like Jell-O, he is fun and wholesome—and always a kid at heart" (Roman and Maas 1992, 22). The characters of *Northern Exposure* are also favorites of an industry banking on the ratings success of the program. Each of the commercials done by these actors features the personae of the *Northern Exposure* characters they play.

A commercial for Gold MasterCard tells the story of a young woman who has recently acquired (through the card) the financial means to replace the grandfather clock she broke as a child. The narrative voice is that of Joel Fleischman. The card provides the young woman with the ability to deal with "childhood issues" and finally become an adult. And of course the therapeutic theme fits Joel's character as well as the numerous "self-actualizing" story lines of *Northern Exposure.*

The voice of Holling, owner of the eating establishment called The Brick on *Northern Exposure,* is recognizable in a commercial for Eggo Waffles, which airs during the program. And it is clearly Chris, the philosophical radio host, who reads scripts designed particularly for that character on Isuzu advertisements. For her part, Maggie, the airplane pilot, appropriately plugs another set of mechanical vehicles, Chevrolet automobiles.

It is as natural to see Jerry Seinfeld promoting American Express as it is to see him eating Kellogg's cereal on his program. His sidekick George, the neurotic egomaniac, is also featured in character, selling snack food. Now standard advertising practice, the use of popular actors has not always been such conventional fare for commercials. In the early 1980s, when the entire cast of *M*A*S*H* was reunited in an advertisement for IBM computers, fans and media observers alike expressed concern. When George C. Scott first did a car commercial, he felt compelled to announce that he did not usually do such things. And when the John Lennon song "Revolution" was first appropriated for a Nike commercial, the ad was received poorly and pulled off the air amidst the threat of a lawsuit. Over time, the intertextual use of popular culture by advertising has become an industry habit.[20]

This point is best illustrated by the remarks of two professional actors who create characters for radio and television commercials. They explained that, by the end of the 1980s, there was considerably less work in their field[21]—not because their talent for portraying a variety of audio characters had declined, but because the industry had moved toward using the voices of familiar actors.[22]

Advertising's use of star power, which accelerated with the waning power of commercial messages, must be understood as part of the increased commercialization of media culture that took place during the 1980s.

Advertainments

Some ads create narratives so closely related to actual programs that the viewer can be momentarily fooled. Susan Lucci sits at a desk penning a letter. She sobs as she writes how sorry she is for leaving and says she wants to come back. The letter could be meant for Jackson Montgomery, her romantic interest on the daytime soap opera *All My Children*; it fits so well with the on-going plot. But it turns out to be directed to Wendy's, the hamburger chain. Lucci, now an advertising favorite, also promotes Ford automobiles and has appeared in a coffee commercial that makes reference to her part on daytime TV. In this spot she complains that she has not yet received an Emmy for her acting efforts.

Another example is the touching father/child conflict between Homer and Bart Simpson that is replayed in an ad for Butterfinger. As Homer tries to steal Bart's candy bar, Bart—this time—is allowed to scold Homer. The advertisement incorporates the product into the viewer's familiarity with *The Simpsons*. There's also the unmistakable voice of Robin Leach featured in Midas Muffler commercials. And in a parody of *Lifestyles of the Rich and Famous*, Leach goes to the home of the now-famous Honda salesman, who has trouble selling "the car that sells itself."

Many TV commercials find inspiration for their mini-dramas in television fiction as well as nonfiction formats. Some car advertisements are structured like press conferences. Others are more plot oriented: One ad for Honda is a narrative fragment of a crime drama, with the salesmen yelling through a megaphone outside the would-be consumers' home, trying to convince them to come out—and down to the showroom.

Sports

Probably the most commercialized sector of popular entertainment is the result of the merger between sports and product promotion. The examples of this unity are too numerous to detail. Suffice it to say that, from corporate sponsorship to celebrity endorsements, promotion has penetrated the world of professional sports.

The comprehensive incorporation of Budweiser, Nike, and Reebok (among other products) into the Super Bowl represents the comprehensive assimilation of football into the culture of consumption. The 1993 Super Bowl garnered the largest TV audience in the history of television (133 million viewers), and the 1994 game set ad rates at $900,000 for 30 seconds. Indeed, advertising was a main event for Super Bowl 1994. A replay of the touchdown made by Emmitt Smith of the Cowboys was immediately incorporated into a Reebok commercial and aired before the game ended. Images of the Reebok shoe being pumped up were actually inserted within the play. Then Smith was heard to say, "I can't tell you how good it feels to be in my shoes." Through the double meaning, Reebok became instantly synonymous with the accomplishment of the player himself.

In the "Bud Bowl" commercials, which feature simulated football games between bottles of Bud and Bud Lite, ball players themselves are transformed into products. As in the actual game, each side scores points in the series of commercials (and a cash prize is offered for the correct numbers). The commercials use the film techniques developed for *Who Framed Roger Rabbit?*, allowing the coaches from the real game to interact with the giant bottles. During the game the commentators look skyward and the camera focuses on the Budweiser Blimp, a commercial specter that hovers over the stadium in the night sky.

The list of professional ball players who endorse the array of overpriced gear they are paid to wear is a long one indeed. As potential consumers of products from Gatorade to McDonald's, kids are told to Be Like Mike. "Air" Jordan not only endorses Nike, he has his own shoe. Who will ever forget the disappearing stomach of Tommy Lasorda after his endless advertisements for Slim-Fast. Jimmy Connors boosts Nuprin, whereas Andre Agassi confirms that reality is all an image for Canon. By mimicking and appropriating the games, the players and coaches, the bars and locker rooms, advertisements have become integral to the world of corporate-dominated sports.

Similarly, Olympic content was worked into the themes of the advertisments shown during the 1994 games on CBS. Polar bears drinking Coca-Cola mimicked the various events being aired; Dave, the owner of Wendy's, was shown looking for a figure-skating partner; and another commercial featured bobsledding. Meanwhile, Nancy Kerrigan worked out in Reeboks and gained strength from Campbell's Soup. After winning, of course, she went to Disney World.

Moviemercials

In the early days of broadcasting, film celebrities did not appear on television shows, much less commercials. But times have changed, and the wheels of advertising roll on, picking up whatever talent they can find—even if it's a nicer version of the monster from the *Alien* movies who's looking for a Diet Pepsi.

After the success of Spike Lee's *Do the Right Thing,* Ossie Davis and Ruby Dee, who had parts in the movie, were featured sitting at a table eating Oreo cookies. Following *Mo' Better Blues,* Spike Lee's Nike commercial was entitled "The mo' colors, the mo' better."

Many commercials now copy the themes and recognizable scenes of popular movies. For instance, the voice-over on a television advertisement for Wheaties Honey Gold whispers, "If you make it, they will eat it." Then various players walk out of a field of corn onto a baseball field—carrying bowls of Wheaties. Of course, the commercial recalls the movie *Field of Dreams.* In conjunction with the release of *Lethal Weapon II,* one automobile ad mimicked the antics of two police officers, one black and one crazy-looking—complete with car chase. A "team" of Revlon models played baseball in a TV commercial simulation of *A League of Their Own.* And the same armor that enclosed the Batmobile appeared in TV advertisements. Mark Miller (1990) documents the creative crossover by film directors into commercial production during the 1980s. Ridley Scott, director of *Blade Runner* and *Thelma and Louise,* may be the best known of these multifaceted talents.

Recently the Coca-Cola company shook up the advertising industry when it signed a contract with Creative Artists Agency (CAA) in Beverly Hills. In doing so, it forced its ad agency, McCann-Erickson World Wide in New York (which held the Coke account since 1955), to work with "Hollywood's most powerful talent agency" (Elliott 1993b, D1). What CAA brought to the commercial campaign was its ability to "tap into Hollywood's pool of talent behind the camera, like directors Rob Reiner, Richard Donner and Phil Joanou" (Elliott 1993b, D22). The resulting 1993 series of Coca-Cola commercials was infused "with a contemporary appeal" more in tune "with production techniques borrowed from movies like fast-paced cuts, special effects and elaborate animation" (Elliott 1993b, D22).

This agreement between a conventional Madison Avenue advertising agency and a Hollywood talent agency underscores Coca-Cola's desire to blend more authentically within the landscape of popular entertainment. Indeed, TV and film directors are well suited to the job of creating fictional narratives for entertainment/advertising.[23] In a spot directed by Rob Reiner, which also features his narration, Coke helps a romance blossom over five decades.

This trend will undoubtedly continue; as *Advertising Age* reported, CAA, looking for a bigger role in advertising, has hired an executive with ties to Madison Avenue. Among the business opportunities the agency hopes to develop, along the lines of multimedia product endorsement, is "advertising-supported programming" (Johnson 1993, 1). The new executive is likely to be effective in placing the agency's clients—film and TV stars—in commercial venture of all sorts. As he pointed out, "I have one foot in entertainment, and I have one foot in advertising. These lines are blurring day by day" (Johnson 1993, 32). With its new focus, CAA wants "to take advantage of changing media such as infomercials." Its plans portend the movement toward slicker, star-studded, and more persuasive infomercials.

Nostalgia

Advertising's propensity for intertextuality extends backward in time, evoking memories of past media pleasures. By the 1980s, as the baby-boom generation was entering its prime income-earning years, media nostalgia promoted everything from Coors Beer to paint. The Coors company incorporated the home-movie look into its 1960s-generation ad campaigns,[24] which attempted to appeal to the sphere of life that baby boomers undoubtedly share. This large generation represents a broad cross-section of demographic segments, life trajectories, opinions, and attitudes. But its members also share memories of popular culture still deeply ingrained among their adult sensibilities. Remembering that westerns dominated 1950s television, McDonald's styled a series of ads in which horse-drawn wagons pull up to make their orders and groups of cowboys on horseback thunder across the screen. Clearly the appeal is to memories etched by the long hours many of us spent after school watching Clint Eastwood as Rowdy Yates on *Rawhide*.

In a related example, a pregnant woman sitting in a chair tries to get up as a motown beat pounds. We hear the words of a song, "Hold on, I'm comin'." And in another ad, Nike appropriates John Lennon's song "Instant Karma." Here, music evokes the memories of a generation, forging powerful connections between personal histories and contemporary products while changing the meaning of the song itself. In the original, Lennon enjoins us to recognize our brothers. But the lyrics selected for the ad convey instead a privatized fantasy of the buyer as "super star." By wearing the shoes, we will "all shine on."[25] Then, too, Eagle Snacks' use of the Odd Couple, Tony Randall and Jack Klugman, still playing the roles of Felix and Oscar, certainly reminds older viewers of earlier times. Oscar pours chips all over the table, an action calculated to irritate the character Felix.

Postmodern Aesthetics and Advertising

In a scene from the 1948 RKO comedy *Mr. Blandings Builds His Dream House*, Myrna Loy asks a contractor for a particular color of red paint, describing it as "practically an apple red, somewhere between a healthy winesap and an unripened Jonathan." This footage was inserted into a television spot created by Gianattino & Meredith Advertising for Benjamin Moore paints. As Stuart Elliott (1992a, D5) notes, "The use of footage from vintage movies and television shows for advertising purposes is a growing trend in an industry that already assiduously mines popular culture for inspiration and imagery." In a similar vein, Diet Coke's award-winning commercial entitled "Nightclub" features Louis Armstrong, Humphrey Bogart, and James Cagney. These classic stars appear with contemporary pop singer Elton John. To achieve the composite, the producer mixed footage from four different films, colorizing Bogart and Cagney. Amidst bitter criticism from movie buffs and the creative community for dismantling the original artistic cohesiveness of the films, a similar computer-edited advertising amalgam allows Paula Abdul to dance with Fred Astaire. And ever since Turner Home Entertainment acquired the MGM film library in 1986, it has pursued business from advertising by merchandising thousands of films for commercial use. (Other owners of films and TV shows such as the Universal Television division of MCA—which owns the rights to *Leave It to Beaver*—are also selling rights to advertisers.)

Decontextualized fragments of popular culture, past and present, are mixed and matched, creating an endless environment of (re)contextualized samplings of other forms. This recombination of cultural fragments has been referred to in the context of postmodern culture—an endless pastiche of now groundless images torn from their previous referents. The commercial imperative that currently demands the unity of media content and advertising messages is well served by the new aesthetic. And, indeed, postmodernism has been highly successful in embedding products within the false unity of cultural fragments. A product can now pop up and careen in and out of any number of familiar images, to the great satisfaction of an industry attempting to insert its commodities anywhere and everywhere in the jumbled chaos that constitutes popular culture. The visual/cultural pastiche forges the desired associations, which in turn tie products and product images to the profusion of narrative and visual pleasures, past or present. In short, advertised products now exist as an integral part of the entertainment environment.

As the executive vice-president for Lintas New York, the agency that created the aforementioned Diet Coke spot, reflected: "We're selling a form of entertainment" (Elliott 1992a, D). This new homogeneity of advertising and entertainment has created an interesting paradox: Just as advertisements are becoming rapid-fire forms of mini-image entertainments lifted from the longer narratives of fictional genres, programming formats are being converted into long-form advertisements.

Television and Marketing

Capitalizing on the sense of immediacay and relevance conferred to live television, Prodigy advertisments insert themselves in real time into TV programming. "We're live on Prodigy at 10:47 P.M.," they interrupt. Up-to-the-minute scripts relate directly to program content. Marilyn doesn't do much talking on *Northern Exposure,* but you can ask her all the questions you want on Prodigy. Thus, as advertising and program content merge, TV itself is rendered an effective marketing device.

Other marketing schemes, too, tie programming to product promotions. To entice advertisers, broadcasters now engage in a variety of "value-added" schemes. One such venture was a collaboration among CBS entertainment programming, the New York Times Company magazines (*Family Circle* and *McCall's,* among others), and four of the nation's largest advertisers such as Ogilvie hair-care products, General Motors, and Sears Roebuck and Company. This amalgam created the "Eye on Women National Tour," which visited shopping malls in twenty-five markets over a twenty-five week period, setting up booths "with themes of interest to demographically desirable female consumers" (Elliot 1993c, D22). Among the promotional activities offered was the Ogilvie booth, which provided interactive video technology allowing shoppers to visualize themselves wearing the hairstyles of the stars on CBS programming. As head of CBS marketing and communications operations George F. Schweitzer told the *New York Times,* "Network television has to redefine itself, not just as an advertising vehicle, but as a marketing tool" (Elliott 1992b, D1). Mr Schweitzer is credited with creating the "sophisticated partnerships" between the network and its advertisers.

The marketing possibilities for ABC's *Home Improvement* are vast. The program itself is a deft vehicle for product promotion. Week after week the show displays an array of tools for its large share of male viewers. On page 1 of "The Home Handyman" section of the *San Francisco Chronicle* (June 19, 1993, C1), a father's-day promotion invited Macy's shoppers to "Meet 'Al' from TV's *Home Improvement.*" Richard Karn, who plays Al, Tim's co-host on "Tool Time" (the show-within-the-show), autographed *Home Improvement* T-shirts at 11:00 A.M. It was "tool time at Macy's."

Another marketing strategy utilized by CBS to deal with its economic decline is aggressive self-advertisement. In fact, the network runs about 8,000 of its own promotional spots annually. Collectively, these ads are worth about $500 million in air time—that is, "eight times more than what the biggest Madison avenue shop turns out" (Elliott 1992b, D22). For this they have also staged collaborative events at malls, ski resorts, and college campuses with advertisers such as Pepsi-Cola, Kmart, AT&T, and IBM. These ventures include contests, product give-aways, and visits by stars such as Joe Regalbuto (Frank) of *Murphy Brown*. The aggressive promotion of CBS and its advertisers is credited with moving the network into the number-one rating slot for the 1991–1992 season for the first time in seven years. This was especially impressive considering that CBS came in third during the previous year. No network had ever "leaped from worst to first in a single season" (Elliott 1992b, D1).

In fact, much of television programming is now designed to promote the networks, their other programming, the stars, or the media themselves. Consider, for example, the detailed piece of feature journalism on David Letterman produced by the local news division of channel 2, a New York CBS station. Including comments and impressions about Letterman from "people on the street," as well as interviews in his old neighborhood with childhood acquaintances, it gave David Letterman the type of journalistic attention usually reserved for public figures in trouble[26] or political candidates. The piece was aired during the shaky transition period during which Letterman moved from NBC to CBS and subsequently slipped in the ratings. Seeing CBS's David Letterman, late-night host, on CBS's late-night news feature was not a matter of journalism; it was CBS's promotion of its own programming.

Journalism in the service of promoting products, network programming, and the journalists themselves is now a common feature of the profession. The late news regularly carries stories complete with interviews of the "real" people featured on the made-for-TV movies and docudramas—now that the latter are so popular. This synergistic formula reinforces the ratings for both formats, advertising the movies beforehand and keeping audiences tuned into late news.

The appearance of CBS's *60 Minutes* cast on CBS's *Murphy Brown* in the fall of 1993 was just as much a promotion as an intertextual play. In that episode, Murphy authorizes a biography of herself. In the course of researching Murphy's life, the biographer interviews her friends and colleagues. Meanwhile, an apprehensive Murphy has a dream in which the cast of *60 Minutes* (along with some republican senators involved in the Thomas/Hill hearings) appear and remark on her character and personality. They all make reference to her behavior at the 1980 Republican National Convention. In this quintessential piece of intertextual television, reality is fused with fiction as the boundaries between the two are blurred. Real journalists speak about a fictional journalist, placing her within actual political history as a participant (all this in 1980, before Murphy had been invented!). As meta-television (Olson 1987), this episode infused the real with the fantasy, exposing its nature as constructed fiction for the entertainment of the culturally literate viewer.

Of course, it also served as an advertisement for *60 Minutes,* promoted the journalist themselves as celebrities, and offered a ratings boost for the network and both programs. The year before, Katie Couric, Joan Lunden, Faith Daniels, Paula Zahn, and Mary Alice Williams all appeared in an episode of *Murphy Brown* as guests at their colleague's baby shower. The appearance of journalists on fictional television augmented their roles as reporters, turning them into celebrities. In turn, their increased star power made them better prospects for further promotional activities.

This blurring of distinctions among journalists, celebrities, and product promoters reached its ultimate conclusion in January 1994 when Mary Alice Williams, who spent twenty-five years in broadcast journalism (and attended Murphy's baby shower), became the spokeswoman for NYNEX. Amidst dramatic corporate restructuring, which involved the firing of one-third its work force, the powerful persuasive appeal of an Emmy Award–winning journalist was brought into the company's PR campaign. In one TV spot created by Ogilvy & Mather New York, Williams introduces the company's changes by explaining to viewers that "NYNEX will be the name for a lot of the new things that'll make your life more manageable." Making a clear reference to her previous role as a credible journalist, she continues with "My job is to stay on top of what they're doing and keep you posted." The spot ends as she repeats the new campaign's theme: "At NYNEX right now."

The use of a well-known journalist involved in a massive PR effort, one willing to mouth corporate slogans, gave pause to *New York Times* advertising writer Stuart Elliott (1993a, D21). In his view, this crossover exemplified "the rapid blurring of the distinction between editorial content and advertising" and raised "disturbing issues about the credibility and veracity of communications."

Williams was not the first journalist to turn to advertising. After working for ABC and NBC, Linda Ellerbee appeared in a Maxwell House commercial that mimicked a newscast. Joan Lunden of *Good Morning America* (also in attendance at Murphy's baby shower) appeared in a newscast-like commercial for Vaseline Intensive Care lotions. Subsequently, with the publicized birth of her daughter, she became the consummate model of the successful career woman/mother, an image she utilized to plug Gerber babyfood. The jolly NBC weatherman of the *Today* show, Willard Scott, has also done commercials. And CBS's Charles Osgood now reads advertising copy.

By 1994 the commercialization of television, along with the cost-cutting strategies and bottom-line policies of corporate owners had proved economically successful. Television profits had increased as audiences returned, national advertisers were appeased, and cable ratings reached a plateau. Broadcasting is once again one of the most profitable businesses in the world. But amidst this renewed affluence, there is no willingness to reverse the market priorities of the past decade that decimated the concern for the public interest in broadcasting or the media in general. Journalism itself has been the greatest casualty of an era of cost cutting and the prioritizing of profit. The commercialization of entertainment television continues apace as more products and promotions enter the plot lines of fictional narratives, thereby creating "appropriate" programming environments.

The escalating unity of entertainment, news, and advertising on television has of course been discussed on television itself. As an intertextual self-referential medium, television talks about itself more than anything else. Part of that discourse refers to its own economic structure, its advertising practices and its promotional strategies. These topics have all become the subject of television fiction. The ways in which such issues are treated and resolved in fictional narratives reveal much about the commercialization of television programming and of the media in general.

Product Promotion and Television Fiction

Love and War *and Newspaper Advertising*

An episode of *Love and War,* which aired in the fall of 1993, deals with the issue of advertising's encroachment on newspaper content. The story begins in the restaurant where Jack, the newspaper columnist, is reading his friends an editorial he has written. It is a resounding condemnation of the practice, recently established at his newspaper, of placing advertising on the front page. When the editors read the column, they demonstrate their displeasure by assigning Jack to the "style" beat for two weeks. His first assignment is to cover the closing of a department store in Manhattan.

The telling of the story involves a wealth of comedic situations that revolve around shopping, which all the characters find the opportunity to do. One character continues to get lost, the women complain about their appearance under the fluorescent lamps in the dressing rooms, and they all try on clothes and have encounters with sales clerks and staff. Shopping is rendered in the usual situation-comedy manner, as a hilarious part of life. (In addition, the script is littered with references to The Gap.) The episode ends with Dana and Jack back at the restaurant, sharing the last half of an egg-salad sandwich that Dana brought back from the store. Dana associates the sandwich with the fond memories of childhood shopping sprees accompanied by her mother.

Jack has found the shopping experience not only fun but interesting. An old elevator operator proved to be a valuable source on the history and charm of the store. Finding compelling material for his column, his assignment on the "style" beat was not so bad after all. Jack writes a piece of sentimental journalism about days gone by. Thus did television fiction refer to the uniquely important issue of advertising influence on the media; but it offered a rendering that trivialized the issue and portrayed it as a development easily accommodated by writers who make the best of the situation. Above all, the point seems to be that shopping is fun.

Frasier *and Product Promotion*

A November 1993 episode of the situation comedy *Frasier* consisted of 30 minutes of prime time devoted to advertising strategies.[27] Playing a talk-radio psychologist, Frasier must decide whether or not to become a radio spokesperson for the advertisers who buy time on his program. At first he is reluctant, not wanting to degrade his program by plugging "Chow's Chinese Food." But when he understands the amount of money involved in telling people where to get their takeout, his resistance evaporates. He happily plugs a list of products until it comes to nuts. He draws the line there, feeling that the use of "nuts" as derogatory slang for mental patients would offend his listeners and demean his professional status.

With this depiction, fictional television has essentially endorsed its own commercialization while maintaining an aura of integrity. Frasier accepts the general concept of incorporating product promotion within his program, yet refuses to follow through in one specific instance. In short, the program maintains a sense of legitimacy by appearing critical but endorses the practice in its broad outline.

Infomercials and L.A. Law

In 1992 infomercials featured in one of the knitted narratives of *L.A. Law.* Roxanne, the secretary who has decided to have a child, successfully helps her ex-husband sell a product called First Phone. The device, a ridiculous instrument that appears to have been designed by a cartoonist, is promoted as a telephone used by mothers to speak to their unborn children. With Roxanne's help, her ex-husband produces an infomercial featuring the actor Buddy Hackett. Just when it seems the infomercial will (justifiably) be a complete flop, Buddy Hackett breaks out of his crass-comedian character and delivers a heart-rending monologue on the joys of having children. Roxanne is also inspired to attest passionately to the delights of carrying her baby. *L.A. Law* ends happily inasmuch as the emotional persuasion of the infomercial, which had nothing to do with the actual quality of the obviously ridiculous product, becomes a huge success. So many orders are made on the 800 number that the warehouse sells out of First Phones. Not coincidentally, Roxanne is reunited with her now financially successful husband, and he shares half the profits with her. This type of media marketing is represented as a positive force in people's lives, even though the product was a blatant fraud and the infomercial an obvious emotional manipulation.

Another narrative woven into *L.A. Law* (this time, during the 1993 season premiere) dealt with a compulsive consumer and a cable home-shopping network. A woman and her husband bring suit against a cable service for prompting the woman—who is addicted to home shopping—to spend as much as $1,500 a week on products. Her desire to acquire something new every day is articulated as a quest for well-being and happiness that other aspects of her life are incapable of providing. Even though the program recognizes the problem of compulsive consumption, the jury rules against her suit in favor of the defendant. The latter, owner of the cable service, is portrayed as a savvy small businessman who sees the profit potential in the woman's compulsive behavior. The narrative resolves with the hiring of the compulsive shopper as an on-air host for the shopping network. Everybody benefits. Thus did television fiction endorse and promote the commercial exploitation of TV consumers.

Consuming Television Programming

Indeed, explicit portrayals of consumption itself, rarely featured on television in years past, has become a main theme in TV programming. For instance, when the character Hayden Fox on ABC's *Coach* fails to recruit a star player for his team, he eases his disappointment by buying a very large new bed from the player's grandfather, who just happens to be in retail sales—selling mattresses.

An entire episode of *Roc,* a show about a black working-class family, revolves around the decision to purchase a car. Roc resists buying the car, arguing that the family's priority must be to save money for a home. At first his wife pleads; then she demands that they make the purchase. The show ends with Roc getting up in the middle of the night to look out the living room window and admire the car. He speaks of "her" smooth, beautiful lines. Entirely satisfied with his purchase, Roc has learned his lesson of consumption well.

Product Placement

Television production companies employ buyers who purchase the clothes, makeup, furniture, and other accoutrements for television studios. They often work with retailers and manufacturers, selecting trendy items available for consumption that can be displayed on the programs. Special arrangements are made between either set designers or production companies to place commodities where they can be seen or even used by actors. To mention just one example, a buyer for *Beverly Hills 90210* purchased a complete set of eye shadows in a handy carrying box made by Revlon. Then the item was carefully placed within the scene to appeal to young fashion-conscious consumers.

Until recently, direct product plugging voiced by television characters was resisted because it conflicted with spot advertising. As product-placement film executive Marvin Cohen explained, "How would you feel if you bought advertising time on a program and the competitor's product was featured in the program itself?"[28] But conventional advertising practices have begun to change, and product plugging is now being systematized as standard advertising procedure. By 1994 the characters on *Northern Exposure* had managed to mention, among other products, Dove ice-cream bars, Cheerios, Good and Plenty candy, Advil, Bengay, Tourister Luggage, Franco-American Spaghetti, Chef Boy-ar-dee, Prozac, the Sundance catalog, Armani suits, and an expensive brand-named shirt that Joel had in his car (see Figure 1.2).

Programming has long been a commercial showcase for fashion, but the promotion of clothes, style, and lifestyle is becoming more overt every day. This trend is well illustrated by the cover story of *TV Guide* (for April 3–9, 1993). A photograph

FIGURE 1.2 Ed with Dove Box

Product placement, an advertising strategy applied to the film industry during the 1980s, is now a common occurrence on prime-time television as well. Here, throughout an extended sequence, *Northern Exposure's* Ed holds up a box of Dove ice-cream bars.

of Heather Locklear of *Melrose Place* modeling a full-length red evening dress, along with the headline "Your Guide to What Those *Hot* Stars Are Wearing This Season," appears on the cover. The article inside is a full fashion layout for both *Beverly Hills 90210* and *Melrose Place,* showing the stars adorned in brand-name clothes. Also supplied were the names of the clothes makers and retail outlets, where available.

Synergy, Jurassic Park, *and Children's Media*

Termed *synergy* in the industry, this new totalizing commercial environment is multimedia in nature. In other words, promotion can be attached to and combined with a number of different media, all of which serve to reinforce the products being sold. TV characters appear in magazine advertising layouts. Sports contests are combined with product giveaways, celebrities, and TV advertising. Music videos are made from popular movies, which promote tie-in products as well as the soundtracks. And TV advertising campaigns regularly attach products and fast food to releases of "blockbuster" films. *Jurassic Park* offers the most striking recent example of synergy (see Figure 1.3).

As the film began to set box-office records, making $50.2 million in its first week of release, a wave of dinosaur products hit the retail market. The TV advertising campaign for McDonald's offered Jurassic mugs with meals. Ranging from Double Flavored Raptor Eggs to Jurassic Jaw Breakers that took "eons to eat," T-shirts, and tooth brushes, this marketing scheme of truly monstrous proportions

FIGURE 1.3 *Jurassic Park* Products
As Jurassic Park set box-office records, making $50.2 million in its first week of release, a wave of dinosaur products hit the retail market. Although very young children were not allowed to see the film because of its violent content, they were specifically targeted by advertisements for thirty different toys, a host of coloring books, postcards, and "admission tickets" to Jurassic Park.

encompassed 1,000 official products worldwide.[29] The marketing of Rex-appeal included thirty different toys, from 3-D puzzles to backpacks, an assortment of mugs, a host of coloring books, postcards, and admission tickets that furthered the pretense that a Jurassic Park actually exists. There was a journalistic tie-in as well. The same week the movie was released, a front-page article in the *New York Times* announced "DNA from the Age of Dinosaurs Is Found" (Brown 1993, A1).

Emblematic of the effects of marketing on media content was the insertion of products for sale within the film itself. Recall the scene in which the camera pans the inside of the park's souvenir store, revealing the Jurassic products lined up on the shelves waiting to be purchased.

When Michael Crichton's (1991) novel (of the same name) is compared to the movie, a number of ironies and insights become apparent. The first pages of the novel contain a scathing criticism of the commercialization of scientific practice—specifically, genetic engineering done for profit without considering social benefit.[30] Crichton writes, "The commercialization of molecular biology is the most stunning ethical event in the history of science." With scientists and companies flocking to make a profit on biotechnology, suddenly "everyone wanted to become rich." Certainly everyone wanted to become rich with *Jurassic Park*. Unfortunately the marketing affected the film's content.

In particular, plot changes downplayed Crichton's commercial criticisms. In the book the park's greedy inventor comes to a well-deserved demise, devoured by a pack of the unpleasant creatures he had unwisely created for profit. In the movie this character is a loving grandfather first, profiteer second. Unlike the book's character, he agrees to allow underprivileged children to enter the park free, and at the end of the movie he is left alive.

As Janet Wasko (1993) points out, international marketing demands action-packed visuals needing few subtitles. And, indeed, the Jurassic characters of few words seemed to be cardboard cutouts of real people. But the most glaring commercial contradiction was the massive product marketing directed to small children, who were not allowed to see the film because of its frightening violence. The marvelous illusions of thundering dinosaurs, created by state-of-the-art computer graphics, were kept from the eyes of children for whom they would have been the most magical. The same inappropriate marketing to children occurred in the case of *Batman II*, creating an outrage on the part of parents that was rekindled by *Jurassic Park*'s commercial exploitation of the young. Crichton's book contains the violence depicted in the movie, but it is presented to adult readers and thus appropriately contextualized.

Probably the most disturbing and ethically reprehensible commercial development in media and marketing during the past fifteen years has been the selling of American children as consumers. Deregulation led to the proliferation of program-length commercials in children's television, and to the total domination of children's broadcasting by the toy industry (Engelhardt 1986). With the prioritizing of profit, Saturday-morning television abandoned any attempt to produce educational programming, and children's TV became dramatically more violent, gender based, and commercialized (Liebert and Sprafkin 1988).

The Paper of Record

As we have seen, commercial pressures on the media are not restricted to women's magazines. They now constitute the dominant influence across the media spectrum. No commercial medium (not even public broadcasting) escapes advertising's pull, from the tabloid magazines to the papers of record. Consider the headline on the first page of the *New York Times* home section of June 13, 1994, which tells us, "Softly, Armani pushes men ahead: page C10." It includes a picture of a model with the caption "Giorgio Armani's new six-button suit." In the fall of 1993, the *New York Times Magazine* had featured an entire second issue it called Part 2 of the magazine. Entitled "Fashions of the Times," the advertising supplement was filled with designer clothes, cosmetics, and shoe advertising.

One month later, the entire magazine was again devoted to fashion. The cover article, "How Fashion Broke Free," contained a "special report on a half-century of fashion of the times." It constituted a good portion of the magazine's copy and

FIGURE 1.4 All the Fashion News That's Fit to Print
This merger of news and advertising discourse appeared in the *New York Times Magazine*. The paper of record lent its famous slogan "All the news that's fit to print," which has always signified journalistic integrity, to the department store that purchased advertising in its magazine. The *New York Times*'s own fall 1993 advertising supplement, entitled "Rethinking the Rules," was also incorporated into the A&S advertisement.

featured many photographs. Here we are reminded of the words of Gloria Steinem (1990, 19), who pointed out that advertisers "expect to be surrounded by fashion spreads." Most interesting, however, is an A&S department store advertisement that takes up two full pages. It depicts a group of young people in a loft-like setting, all sitting on a couch looking at the same magazine—the *Times*'s own Fall 1993 advertising supplement, "Rethinking the Rules." Printed on the left page is "All the fashion news that's fit to print," with the A&S logo just below it (see Figure 1.4). So the merger of news and advertising discourse is now complete: A paper of record lends its famous slogan, which has always signified journalistic integrity, to the department store that purchases advertising in its magazine.

The emphasis on fashion reporting is certainly not a function of its newsworthiness. Rather, it is better explained by the balance sheet of, say the *New York Times Magazine,* which has had to struggle to keep its advertisers in this faltering economy. The magazine "saw a 26.3 percent decline in advertising pages for the first six months of 1991" (Carmody 1991, D6). In short, the fashion "news" that's fit to print now indicates that serious journalism is influenced by the same pressure once thought to be unique to women's magazines.

This fact became evident when the *Times* created its Style section, an obvious advertising vehicle designed to carry advertorials. One front-page story reads, "At

Nike Town Chicago, shoppers can test sneakers on a basketball court featuring a 35-foot photograph of Michael Jordan and a quotation from William Blake" (Sella 1992, 3). It goes on to describe the "life-size plaster statues of mountain bikers suspended from wires in the three-story atrium" and tells readers that New Age music is playing. Scattered around the store are "inspiration boards." And buyers walk on a video–sea floor of "sharks, drifting sea weed and sand washing over conch shells." The $34 million installation is referred to as a "mythology." Its vast inventory is detailed in the article—a staggering amount of merchandise from every kind of shoe imaginable to athletic clothes and an astounding variety of socks.

It was left to a reader, in a letter to the editor (given only a couple inches of copy compared to the entire page consumed by the article), to point out that the piece was "rhapsodic" promotional fluff that lacked journalistic balance. The reader then asked, "How innovative is it to gain enormous wealth by exploiting the poor and the helpless?" (De Vinck 1992). Her letter included information on the exploitative wages that Nike pays its Indonesian workers. Certainly such a topic would have been more appropriate to the *New York Times* than the advertorial it carried.

The web of interconnections among media and product marketing, advertising design, and programming content justifies the term *commercialtainment* as an accurate description of the media environment. But what are the consequences of this harmony between advertising and media content? What are the implications of the demand that information and entertainment programming conform to the persuasive parameters of advertising communication? To begin to answer these questions, we now take a look at one of the most effective and influential advertising campaigns ever—that of the Nike corporation. A comparison of Nike's advertising to its corporate policies will shed some light on the commercial media and their willingness to bend content to the needs of product promotion.

2

The Producers and Consumers of
Nikes and Other Products ...

OVER A CLOSE-UP, sharp-focus image of a woman aggressively twisting her head back and forth, thrusting it out of the water that engulfs her, a voice narrates, "You were born, and oh how you wail." Emerging from the water, she climbs the steps out of a small pool. Her leg bends up close to her body, a display of awesome strength and agility. The setting is futuristic, mellowed black and white. Now she's running with long beautiful strides across a bridge. Stark contrasts define heavy shadows on the steel landscape. Its feeling is modern and urban, yet clean and safe. She dominates the steel power with her own human power. "Your first breath is a scream, not timid or low, but selfish and shattering." The image is only a little slowed, adding to the feeling of a world transformed, where human power and spirit are allowed to find the ultimate fulfillment. "With all the force of waiting 9 months, under water." Indeed, the miracle of life and the celebration of human liberation define the very nature of this world, as the woman runs through another spacious loft-like area decorated with small fountains and arches, classic, yet fully advanced. "The rest of your life should be like that. An announcement." Her gleaming body, long and perfectly formed, is centered within the frame. Again it dominates the space with its resplendence and power. Her muscles move with the momentum of her running, but in slow motion, accentuating the physical vigor that defines her. On the screen, after the image goes blank, reads the Nike slogan: "Just do it."

In another, very different world is a young woman working in a factory in Indonesia. Sadisah toils long hours to make less than $2.00 a day. The image of the woman of power was created to sell Nike shoes. The disempowered Sadisah makes them. Writing for *Harper's* magazine, Jeff Ballinger (1992) analyzed Sadisah's pay stub and determined what her wages can buy. Working at Sadisah's rate of pay leads to acute levels of economic and social depravation. She can afford to rent only a "shanty" without electricity or running water. The UN's International Labor Office (ILO) found that 80 percent of Indonesian female workers are malnourished. The vast majority of those working in the textile industry are women. Sadisah's body is undoubtedly not the finely tuned essence of vitality that is the promise of Nike.

The Makers of Running Shoes and Designer Clothes

At an average of $1.80 a day, Indonesia has the second lowest minimum wage in Asia, after Bangladesh. Yet fewer than 40 percent of employers actually pay minimum wage. Nike, for example, pays its workers less than that. In order to be paid, Sadisah had to work for 7.5 hours. In one month she worked six days a week at an average of 10.5 hours per day. For the 63 hours of overtime Sadisah received an extra 2 cents per hour. Sadisah has neither the time nor the energy after work to exercise, and she could not possibly afford to buy the running shoes she makes. In one month she earns less than half the retail price for a pair of Nikes, even though, working on an assembly line, she will make hundreds of pairs. As Ballinger points out, "The labor costs to manufacture a pair of Nikes that sells for $70 in the United States is approximately $1.66."[1]

Jabotabek is the industrial complex in Indonesia that supplies European and North American markets with such products as Nike, Reebok, and Adidas running shoes, Levi-Strauss jeans, and Calvin Klein underwear. South Korean and Taiwanese companies, under license to Western label owners, manufacture a variety of commodities using cheap Indonesian labor. The products are bought by Nike, Reebok, Levi, and Calvin Klein, whose labels—because of sophisticated marketing and lavish advertising campaigns—allow them to mark up the price for Western markets. Writing on the subject of human rights for the *New Internationalist & Amnesty,* Peter Hitchings (1993) documented the conditions under which popular training shoes, famous-maker jeans, and other fashionable products are made. Indonesia's Jabotabek complex "may seem a happy image of incipient Third World capitalism," but, he warns, "a closer look shows the underbelly of one of the world's nastiest regimes whose industrial-relations policy makes England's during the Tolpuddle massacre seem almost benign" (1993, 24).

Working conditions in these factories, and the political repression needed to maintain them, have come to the attention of Amnesty International. Workers who dare to complain about factories in which "the minimum international standards for health and safety are ignored" find themselves "rounded up by the military, interrogated and permanently unemployed" (Hitchings, 1993, 25). Interrogations may last six hours; and as one Amnesty researcher explained, "A lot can be done to a human being in six hours" (Hitchings, 1993, 25). Beatings and electric shock torture are common, and in some cases "interrogators simply lay a revolver on the desk, or put it against the victim's head," shouting at them to talk (Hitchings 1993, 25). The screams of workers who try to assert their right to human dignity—the essence of Nike advertising—are probably shattering; they are screams not of selfishness but of pain.

Employers routinely abuse their workers to the fullest degree by, for example, cutting off wages if employees make an unauthorized trip to the toilet. The military is essential in keeping the work force in line. As Hitchings notes, "The key precondition for business success in Indonesia is having a chum in the military," since it is authorized to intervene in industrial disputes (1993, 25). The clean, safe, humanistic environment inhabited by the consumer of Nike in the advertisement is far from the factories that constrain the life force of those who produce the shoes. The tight security in these factories (and in those of other countries as well) producing Western goods makes them equivalent to military compounds. Maternity and sick leave are denied to all but a handful of those with the temerity to fight for statutory rights.

In 1991, 8,500 women making Calvin Klein and Triumph jackets and underwear in Indonesian factories went on strike against "pitiful wages, 13-hour days, and the practice of docking one-fifth of wages for going to the toilet without authorization" (Hitchings 1993, 25). As one woman asked, "Why can't we have decent wages when each jacket we produce costs $425?" The organizers of this strike were rounded up, "interrogated," and permanently blacklisted. Another strike—this time by 30,000 workers in Medan, Northern Sumatra, in 1994—also resulted in a military crackdown. The number of arrests made caused a major setback for the labor movement and its effort to improve working conditions in the country. Hitchings (1993, 26) notes that Indonesia, which is "cozily patronized by Western multinationals," has preferential trade agreements with the United States. In June 1992 the U.S.-based human rights organization Asia Watch asked the Clinton administration to review labor rights and practices in Indonesia. Through the Generalized System of Preferences (GSP), U.S. law links workers' rights to tariffs and international trade agreements.[2] If a country does not take steps to "afford internationally recognized workers' rights," the president can end preferential trade agreements. But according to Asia Watch, no progress was made in securing workers' rights during the president's trip to Indonesia in late 1994, and trade pressures on the Indonesian government were removed.[3] In fact, the leader of one independent union was jailed for three years only days before Clinton's visit to Jakarta.[4]

Globalization and the American Economy

To some, the comparison between Nike's advertising and the conditions of its work force may seem unfair, "unbalanced," or simply irrelevant. Others may insist that these are the facts of life. American consumer lifestyles should not, after all, be compared to conditions in the Third World. Corporate America is not responsible for those conditions; it simply does what it must to make a profit. This is the way the free market works, and the free market brings prosperity, to everyone, ultimately. It does not render as fraudulent the message of human dignity and spiritual fulfillment received by the viewer/buyer in the United States. For some, it will remain a positive communication after all, a force for good, promoting the values of human dignity and fulfillment—even if only within the realm of media discourse, which, many would argue, in the postmodern age, is more real than the material world. To answer these assertions we must dig a little deeper into the world of commodities and the world of economic production by taking a closer look at the relationship between consumer culture and the economic, social, and political forces at work in the United States.

The Run-Away Shop

There is an important connection among Sadisah, her working conditions, and the general well-being of most Americans. During the 1980s, U.S. corporations moved an enormous number of lucrative manufacturing jobs, regarded as the economic basis for a strong middle class, to the Third World. And they continue to do so. Nike offers a clear example of what is now referred to as globalization. Nike's corporate headquarters in Oregon closed its last U.S.-based factory in Saco, Maine, in the mid-1980s. At that time the average wage paid by the U.S. rubber-shoe industry was a whopping $6.94 an hour. Not wanting to pay U.S. labor costs, Nike moved its footwear manufacturing to South Korea and hired cheaper non-unionized workers. Nike's actions are standard procedure for the shoe industry as a whole, resulting in the loss of 65,300 footwear jobs in the United States between 1982 and 1989.

By the late 1980s South Korean laborers won the right to form unions and to strike. In response, Nike moved again—this time to Indonesia, where "labor rights are generally ignored and wages are but one seventh of South Korea's" (Ballinger 1992, 46). Winning a huge share of the footwear market, Nike now makes 80 million pairs of shoes annually, contracting globally with several dozen factories in countries including Indonesia, China, Malaysia, Thailand, and Taiwan. As Ballinger (1992, 46) notes, "By shifting factories to cheaper labor pools, Nike has posted year after year of growth." The company made a 700 percent increase in profits between 1987 and 1992.

Demand created by a massive advertising effort allows Nike to charge exorbitant prices for its shoes. With the low rates it pays workers, the profit margin is enormous. As Ballinger pointed out to CBS, 1 percent of Nike's advertising budget "could put 15,000 workers above the poverty line."[5] Instead, Nike's advertising budget has continued to rise—from $230 million in 1993 to $281 million in 1994—showing a net increase of 21.9 percent. But it is the advertising that sells Nike shoes. When the May 1993 *Consumer Reports* gave its top rating for quality and value to an American-made brand, the Saucony Jazz 3000, sales doubled. Subsequently, the *New York Times* reported that the "$68 dollar running shoe has been flying off retailers shelves . . . depleting inventories and causing some shortages for retailers" (Shapiro 1992, D1). But as the marketing consultants who spoke to Shapiro (1992, D1) pointed out, Saucony "lacked the advertising budget to make a lasting impression." The company did plan to raise its advertising budget from $2 million to $5 million a year—but the latter was still no match for Nike. So, the better product cannot compete with the manufactured image.

The Job Crisis

In the summer of 1993, the *New York Times* announced on its front page that "Strong Companies Are Joining Trend to Eliminate Jobs." Even as President Clinton voiced public concern that too many jobs were being eliminated and that employers should view workers as an asset, Procter & Gamble announced its "decision to eliminate 13,000 jobs during a year of record earnings" (Uchitelle 1993, A1). Explaining that in the current economic climate it was impossible to raise prices to keep profits high, and not wanting to offer discounts to boost sales, the company would have to eliminate workers. This action "called attention to a surprising aspect of America's job crisis: profitable companies with booming sales are shedding jobs." Thus Procter & Gamble "embraced a practice that has quietly become daily regimen at such profitable companies as General Electric, AT&T, Johnson & Johnson, the Chubb Group of Insurance companies, Raytheon and many others" (Uchitelle 1993, A1). The practice of "shedding" jobs was indeed a part of corporate strategy throughout the 1980s. Consider General Electric, a company that since 1981 has laid off 25 percent of its work force—a total of more than 100,000 employees. As Martin Lee and Norman Solomon (1992, 77) have observed, "These cutbacks occurred at a time when the company was earning record profits."

Management strategies that consistently cut labor costs to maintain profit margins have led to a declining standard of living. Louis Uchitelle (1993, D3) notes that "the growing impact of job-cutting is increasingly evident in national statistics. Wages are falling as a percentage of national income, while profits are rising." And in her bestselling book *The Overworked American,* Juliet Schor (1992, 109) confirms that the decline in wages has been "a phenomenon of the last 10 years." Inequality in income distribution increased dramatically during the 1980s, and "many people . . . have experienced substantial declines in their standard of living. Others have maintained their incomes only by working longer hours" (Schor 1992, 109). Another study, this one performed by the Washington-based research group called the Economic Policy Institute, found that wages continue to shrink while the quality of new and existing jobs deteriorates. Lawrence Mishel, co-author of the study, confirms that "wages of just about every education group over the last 20 years among men . . . are down" (Mishel, quoted in Herbert 1993, A23). Even though figures indicate an economic "recovery" since 1991, "there have been broad-based wage reductions during the recovery, including severe wage reductions for both blue- and white-collar men" (Herbert 1993, A23).

The consequences of corporate "job-shedding" strategies reverberate throughout the economy. Further disparities in income levels, a shrinking middle class, and a falling standard of living concentrate wealth in fewer hands and impoverish increasing numbers of Americans. Schor estimates that as a consequence of the "recent surge in [economic] inequality," the portion of the population at the bottom end of the economic scale has risen to a full one-quarter of the population. In the mid-1970s many working-class families, "often by dint of considerable overtime hours," were able to finance their home, buy nice cars, and otherwise manage a middle-class lifestyle. But in the 1980s, "as lucrative manufacturing jobs for men have disappeared," many more now live on the margins struggling to get by" (Schor 192, 114).

Throughout the 1980s higher-paying manufacturing jobs were replaced with low-wage and part-time positions. The Labor Department admits that 40 percent of job loss is now considered permanent, not temporary (as in the case of layoffs). A study of want ads done by a Harvard labor economist "found that the number of job openings available to an unemployed worker has declined by 37 percent since 1984" (Uchitelle 1993, D3). Following the low-wage, no-benefit trend of job creation during the Reagan/Bush era, 60 percent of the 800,000 jobs created between January and July of 1993 were part time. These processes have increased the numbers of the working poor, an employed population that can no longer be considered middle class. As Schor (1992, 114) describes them, "among those who do have jobs, hourly pay is very low; long hours or multiple jobs are necessary just to make a subsistence income. They are clearly not working in order to sustain a middle-class life style." As the job market becomes more competitive, companies are successful in demanding more work for less pay and lower benefits. When these working people, whose lower wages and part-time work translate into corporate profits, cannot afford health care, public money—taxes from all Americans—must pay for various entitlement programs. Therefore, the general public has subsidized, in many ways, increasing corporate profits that benefit the few. In addition, the wealthiest Americans—those making the profits—received significant tax breaks during the Reagan era. By the end of 1994 these economic trends caused Clinton administration Labor Secretary Robert Reich to comment on the troubling bifurcation of the U.S. economy. After evaluating 1993 economic figures he warned, "We are hurtling toward a two-tiered society composed of a minority who are profiting from economic growth and a majority who are not. Concerned by what some have called the "jobless recovery," after two years of economic expansion since 1991, he notes that corporate profits are up, but real wages are down. The bottom 60 percent of American families have experienced a fall in real income. The poorest Americans have been hit by a 17 percent drop, while the well-off have scored an 18 percent hike.[6]

As a result of these economic forces, poverty increased dramatically in the United States. A 1989 Gallup poll found that 13 percent of those surveyed "reported that there were times during the last year when they did not have money to buy food" (Schor 1992, 114). And a higher proportion, 17 to 21 percent, reported that with their incomes they could not afford clothes and medical care.[7] Recent research has also revealed that during the seven-year period between 1985 and 1992, hunger in America increased by an enormous 50 percent.

A 1984 survey taken by pollster Louis Harris found that 21 million Americans were experiencing hunger. Similar finding were reported in 1985 by the Harvard School of Public Health, which estimated the number of hungry Americans to be 20 million. Using three separate methodologies, researchers continue to report consistent findings: As of 1992 approximately 30 million Americans were hungry.[8]

Wal-Mart

With the loss of white-collar and mid-level management jobs in the late 1980s and 1990s, on top of the drastic cut in manufacturing during the 1970s and 1980s, "white-collar workers without jobs constitute a much bigger percentage of total unemployment than they did in the mid-1970s" (Uchitelle 1993, D3). These jobs are also being lost due to corporate policies that increase or maintain profits at the expense of jobs. The hugely successful and rapidly expanding discount chain of Wal-Mart stores offers an example of management practices that embrace job cutbacks as a basic strategy. For example, numerous duties are now compressed into one position. Previously, most stores had an employee checking the electronic scanners at the checkout counters making sure they were up to date with price changes. But that chore has now been added to the existing duties of store clerks.

Insecurity that one might lose one's job at any time has led to an environment of anxiety and overwork. As Bob Herbert (1993, A23) reports, there is "fear in the workplace, tremendous fear. . . . Everyone worries that he or she will be the next to go." And in *The Overworked American,* Schor (1992) confirms that people are working longer and harder. People with jobs are forced to make continuing concessions on a broad range of issues, from health care to wage cuts to increased responsibility.

"Paying to Lose Our Jobs"

The issue of jobs became a main campaign theme during the 1992 presidential election. While on the campaign trail, then-candidate Bill Clinton accused the Bush administration of funding government programs that were responsible for taking jobs away from American workers and exporting them to cheaper labor pools. During the nationally televised vice-presidential debate between Senator Al Gore and Vice-President Dan Quayle, Gore raised the criticism again, accusing the incumbent administration of using tax dollars to shift American jobs to other countries. Quayle dismissed Gore's accusation with a chuckle, saying, "That's just totally ridiculous." The accusation was unfortunately true.[9]

Candidate Gore was referring to a report entitled *Paying to Lose Our Jobs,*[10] which had been the subject of a *Nightline* investigation. The issue was also explored on a *60 Minutes* exposé entitled "Hire Rosa Martinez," which aired the week before the debate on September 27, 1992. Rosa Martinez was a young Salvadoran woman featured in an advertisement that was placed in a prominent

U.S. trade journal. The ad pictured a young woman working at an industrial sewing machine, and the text, in bold print, read as follows: "Rosa Martinez produces apparel for U.S. markets on her sewing machine in El Salvador. *You* can hire her for 57 cents an hour." In slightly smaller print, the text continues: "Rosa is more than just colorful. She and her co-workers are known for their industriousness, reliability and quick learning. They make El Salvador one of the best buys." Businesspeople reading this ad were told to find out more about "sourcing" in El Salvador by contacting "FUSADES, the private, non-profit and non-partisan organization promoting social and economic development in El Salvador."

In *Paying to Lose Our Jobs* (1992), the authors state, "It is difficult to imagine, but U.S. tax dollars actually paid for this ad" (italics in original). They go on to document the variety of ways in which government funding helped export American jobs in the apparel and electronics industries to Central America and the Caribbean.

Since 1984 a little-known organization, the Salvadoran Foundation for Economic and Social Development (FUSADES), received $102,397,000 from the U.S. government. That sum constituted 94 percent of the organization's total budget. With this funding, FUSADES paid for the Rosa Martinez ad; it also operated "investment promotion offices" in New York and Miami that targeted U.S. firms. FUSADES approached businesses, attempting to convince them to move their manufacturing operations to El Salvador.[11] The industry focus was apparel, but it also included electrical assembly manufacturing. The U.S. Agency for International Development (USAID) even advised the Salvadoran organization where to concentrate its efforts; "within the U.S. the regions with the greatest concentration for relevant firms are likely to be in the Northeast and Southwest" (Kernaghan 1992, 12).

The U.S. Department of Commerce has also actively promoted El Salvador as a low-wage offshore production site. As Charles Kernaghan (1992, 12) quotes from an *Investment Climate Report*, "Business with significant labor requirements should consider the positive factors of the Salvadoran labor market and make technological decisions reflecting the availability of an eager supply of inexpensive labor."

Realizing that the lack of available factory space was a "critical disincentive" to potential investors in 1988, "the U.S. Government allocated more than $32 million to help fund the start-up cost for the eventual construction of 129 factory buildings" (Kernaghan 1992, 15). This factory space facilitated the flight of U.S. firms. Another $5 million allocated to U.S. Food for Peace Aid to El Salvador "was used to build a 72,000 square foot free zone factory which is now occupied by a U.S. manufacturer" (Kernaghan (1992, 15). USAID lauded FUSADES for accomplishing the task of creating 16,400 jobs in El Salvador over a two-year period. Three thousand jobs alone were secured in one free-trade zone—as USAID noted, "thanks to FUSADES' help in bringing in U.S. investors interested in obtaining the benefits of the Caribbean Basin Initiative" (Kernaghan 1992, 16–17).

The implication is that the U.S. taxpayer "paid approximately $6,244 for each of the 16,400 jobs 'created', many if not most diverted from the U.S." (Kernaghan 1992, 17).

FUSADES is only one of more than ten Central American and Caribbean investment promotion organizations in the United States operating "with U.S. government funding obligations totaling more than $289 million since 1983" (Sheinkman 1992, 8). A variety of other organizations funded by the U.S. government provide incentives for American businesses to move their manufacturing operations to cheaper labor pools. And more than a billion dollars has been committed since 1980 to other investment and trade promotion projects such as worker training, zone development, and lines of credit. Not only is the cheap labor of Rosa Martinez and her co-workers available, but businesses have also secured low-interest loans, tax breaks, and subsidized job training programs for their Central American workers. As one businessman told *60 Minutes*, "It's much easier to set up down there than it is here."

In Guatemala, too, the textile and apparel industry is expanding enormously. A 1991 International Trade Commission study found that "manufacturers in Guatemala producing for the U.S. market identified during 1990 included Levi Strauss, Van Heusen, Calvin Klein, Liz Claibourne, and Arrow. One U.S. manufacturer of women's sportswear closed its U.S. facility and relocated to Guatemala in 1990 to take advantage of lower cost labor" (Kernaghan 1992, 33). By one industry estimate, the clothing manufacturing industry in Guatemala grew by 800 percent between 1986 and 1990.

One Honduran woman, Maria del Carmen Portillo, came to New York under the auspices of the Amalgamated Clothing and Textile Workers' Union. Working in a garment factory in the Chip Choloma Free Trade Zone, Portillo sewed zippers into nylon running suits for a Korean company under license to Wilson's Sporting Goods. She made an average of $21 per week for working 11-hour shifts, sewing as many as 1,000 zippers a day. In her testimony of the working conditions in a plant making clothes that were shipped to Kansas City, Missouri, she described the followng experiences. One day she was caught "chewing gum at her machine." A foreman yanked the wad from her mouth, stuck it to her forehead, and made her leave it there all day. Supervisors "periodically slapped co-workers in the face or banged their heads with screwdriver handles for not producing fast enough. For punishment they'd make a woman stand for hours facing a wall, balancing a big spool of thread on her head." Foremen also beat and sexually abused the women workers, threatening "to cut their faces if they complained" (Gonzalez 1992).

These trade initiatives, collectively termed "Trade, Not Aid" by the Reagan administration (initiated as part of the Caribbean Basin Initiative), have had a dramatic impact on the U.S. economy. For more than a decade, approximately 2,000 apparel jobs have been lost each month, totaling one-half million jobs. Since 1980 apparel employment in the United States has fallen 18.9 percent. Real wages for the jobs that remain have fallen 17 percent. And another 194,800 American electronics workers have lost their jobs (Kernaghan 1992, 34). Since 1990 alone, at least fifty-eight apparel factories have closed, leaving more than 12,000 employees without jobs. Job loss has also affected the trade deficit. In 1980, 70 percent of all apparel bought in the United States was made domestically. Now imports account for only half the total apparel market. In 1991 "the apparel trade deficit accounted for 37 percent of the total U.S. merchandise trade deficit" (Kernaghan 1992, 37). Once again we find that routine business employment practices that maximize corporate profits are carried out at the expense of workers' wages and contribute to the overall decline in the living standard.

Sending jobs offshore has been a major factor in the decline of real wages in the United States. As Ray Marshall, former secretary of labor under the Carter administration, told CBS, "I think American wages are being ratcheted down, and I have no doubt at all that these kinds of subsidized job activities tend to drive wages down in the U.S." In addition, current business practices hold wages at artificially low rates in the host countries. As the *Paying to Lose Our Jobs* (1992, 7–8) report documents, Central American and Caribbean workers "have seen their wages slashed by their governments' programs to make their country more attractive to foreign investors." They have been "denied their most fundamental human and workers rights." And per capita income and living standards have fallen "to levels not seen since the 1950s."

Haiti provides a vivid example of the devastating effects of the demand for cheap labor pools. Sears, Wal-Mart, and J. C. Penney are among the more than fifty U.S. companies that continue to do business with Haiti in spite of an embargo imposed by the Organization of American States after the military coup of 1991. The United States bought $154.3 million in goods from Haiti in 1993, an increase of almost 50 percent over the previous year. Real wages dropped to less than 14 cents per hour on average.

U.S. baseballs and softballs are assembled in Haiti by workers paid 2 cents a ball—a wage totaling as little as 70 cents a day. The U.S. government purchased many of the 2.54 million softballs imported to the United States duty free during 1993. Home of Champions, one of the major manufacturers, has responded to attempts to organize a union at its plants with illegal firings.

As early as 1980 USAID began funding studies that showed it was "far cheaper for U.S. companies to produce goods in Haiti than in the United States" (Briggs and Kernaghan 1993, 38). USAID also spent more than $100 million enlisting the support of the country's small business elite. When Jesuit priest Jean-Bertrand Aristide won an unexpected victory in the 1990 election, gaining the presidency with 67 percent of the vote, USAID invested $26.7 million—this time, to oppose his subsequent efforts to raise the minimum wage in Haiti to 50 cents an hour.

Cajuste Lexiuste, the secretary general of the General Confederation of Labor in Haiti, living in exile in Brooklyn, New York, explained that the malnourishment and health problems stemming from low wages and long hours are devastating: "The Haitian people want to work, but we want to make a living, not be destroyed by our very work." Since the military intervention on October 15, 1995, analysts fear that calls to bring about the "structural readjustment" of the Haitian economy will do nothing to improve working conditions. Allan Nairn, writing in the *Multinational Monitor,* summarized the plan, entitled "Strategy of Social and Economic Reconstruction" (cited in Ives 1995). In it, Haiti commits to making drastic cuts in tariffs and import restrictions, enforcing an "open foreign investment policy," and "[limiting] the scope of state activity." Another analyst notes that, under the current political configuration, as Aristide's power is diminished, so is his ability to work for improved working conditions and wage increases (Ives 1995).

Whose Economy Is It?

After reading reports on USAID policy, one is compelled to ask, How could this have happened? How could USAID have done this to our economy? Columnist Juan Gonzalez (1992) described it as "a policy so traitorous to American workers it defies belief." One reels at the overall effects of such actions on developing countries. But the United States is affected as well—by unemployment and the resulting devastation of communities, the continuing economic decline of urban areas (where much textile industry had been concentrated), the overall loss of real wages, and the generally lower standard of living for most Americans. The simple fact (and the only answer to the above questions) is that USAID represents only one sector of the American economy, and that this sector measures economic well-being solely in terms of corporate profits. But corporate interests (evaluated by short-term profits) are far more narrowly defined than are the economic interests of the vast majority of the American people. Exploiting the cheap labor pool abroad is a practice shown to have devastating consequences for working Americans. In short, economic well-being, narrowly defined by corporate indicators, obscures an understanding of the economic health of the rest of the country. Raising corporate profits by exporting jobs increases the wealth of the few, even as it destroys national economic well-being.

But there are some important repercussions recognized as problems by the corporate managers who "shed" jobs. Unfortunately these have nothing to do with concerns about communities or with the damage to the human spirit brought about by unemployment, underemployment, a lower standard of living, and even poverty. Instead, corporate-funded research is directed quite specifically at other questions. For example, "no issue is more troublesome to managers and workers than the impact of job-cutting on the employees who survive" (Uchitelle 1993, D3). The Conference Board, a research organization funded by corporations, has found that firing people creates anxiety among those who continue to work.[12] But it is not the psychic distress to the human spirit that troubles them (as corporate advertising would have us believe); rather, it is the impact that low morale may have on productivity. Says Helen Alex of the Conference Board, "If you keep on downsizing, as many companies are doing, then you keep people on tenterhooks and perhaps in the long run reduce their efficiency" (Alex, quoted in Uchitelle 1993, D3).

Here's another question regarding massive firings that has come to the attention of corporate researchers: "Does the conspicuous loss of jobs at many companies create the sort of anxieties among workers that may deter them from spending as much as they otherwise would?" (Uchitelle 1993, D3). Increases in corporate profits depend on our continued spending. As Raymond Williams (1980, 187) puts it, "We are the market, which the system of industrial production has organized. We are the channels along which the product flows and disappears. In every aspect of social communication, and in every version of what we are as a community, the pressure of a system of industrial production is towards these impersonal forms."

The "impersonal forms" of consumption are nevertheless very personalized when they become advertising messages. Americans, constantly compelled to consume, are after all the primary market for American corporations, even as they lose their capacity as producers. Corporations must therefore question just how much of a living-standard decline the country can take without affecting the sales of their products. As Albert Sommers, another economist at the Conference Board, recently warned, if corporate job "shedding" continues, affecting an increasing number of jobs and companies "there might eventually not be enough wages for people to buy things; then the economy gets hurt" (Uchitelle 1993, D3).

Evident from the language used in this quote is the assumption that "the economy" affects only corporate profits. Clearly, corporate America's view of the economy is not the same as that of most Americans. We take responsibility for the economy as a whole; it does not.

As consumers we are led to believe that the economy belongs to all of us. When the holiday shopper tells the local news cameras, "Yes, I've spent a lot of money, I'm doing my bit for the economy," the attitude is "when I spend, we all prosper." The very fact that the obligatory Christmas news story seeks to answer the question "Will this be a good season for retail sales?" assumes that the issue is of interest to everyone. When the stock market crashed in 1987, the dominant media theme was also about spending, referred to as "consumer confidence." The headline of the *New York Post* on October 23, 1987, read, "Prez reassures nation, 'THE SYSTEM IS WORKING. Don't panic, keep spending!'" The entire country worried that people would stop buying and that the economy would be sent into a downward spiral. The assumption is that the economy is something we all share, and that when it is good we all reap the benefits. If we do our part and spend, like good consumers, our efforts will be rewarded. But in fact we do not all benefit when the economy is good. As discussed, when corporate profits are high, managing executives still "shed" jobs, a practice that continues to shrink the middle class and impoverish increasing numbers of Americans.

Under these conditions, consumers actually view the profits of corporate America as equivalent to their own economic interests, when in actuality they are not. Spending impoverishes the consumer personally. And as real wages fall, consumption must increasingly be carried out on credit. Many people find themselves overwhelmed, servicing only the debt on their credit cards. Banks charge up to 22 percent in consumer interest rates, all the while paying less than 3 percent on savings. We the consumers become individually impoverished. Spending goes against our own private economic interests, yet we are assured that it will make the economy "get better." However, as the corporate policies of the 1980s made abundantly clear, even when the economy is better, corporate profits are not shared: Jobs are not created. In fact, the corporate economic strategies of the 1990s, which focus on profits, have become more relentless—jobs are now *cut* even when profits are high.

NAFTA

The economic practices detailed above, with their devastating consequences to the quality of life for most Americans, will be accentuated under the North American Free Trade Agreement. When President Clinton embraced NAFTA, he chose an economic and trade policy that would sacrifice inestimable numbers of American jobs to benefit the profit margins of large corporations. "Lowering of trade barriers" translates into the abandonment of regulations designed to prevent exploitative employment practices and to ensure safe working conditions, workers' rights to unions and collective bargaining, and environmental protection. The flight of American jobs, abuse of workers in Central America, maintenance of low wages in the United States, and environmental devastation have all been exacerbated by the "free-trade zones" detailed in *Paying to Lose Our Jobs*. Free trade only allows these practices to continue as standard business strategy.

When Clinton carried out NAFTA, a policy designed during the Bush years, he ensured the continued decline of the standard of living for most Americans, the very people who voted for him. The justification for NAFTA—that increased markets will cause corporations to grow, thereby providing jobs—is erroneous, as we have seen. Those who work for less than survival wages in assembly plants, especially the *maquiladoras* in Mexico and Central America, do not have the money to buy consumer goods. And even as corporate profits grow from cheaper labor and favorable trade, they do not expand employment opportunities in the United States because of corporate job "shedding."[13]

Employment Themes in Advertising

These corporate management policies go hand in hand with corporate advertising strategies. The incredible celebration of individualism and self-worth, the hope for fulfillment and the good life, and the general philosophical humanistic attitudes that pervade the magic of advertising are completely at odds with the policies that have such devastating effects on the world in which we live. Granted, the hope of prosperity for all is an authentic aspiration. But the policies and their negative repercussions for a majority of Americans define the actual quality of life.

During the 1980s advertising began to make reference to the problematic conditions of employment in America. The persuasive strategies used to sell products
in this difficult economic climate have been numerous. The mythic power fantasy
associated with Nike shoes is only one of many "soft sell" tactics designed to elicit
a variety of emotional responses. The celebratory ecstasy and jubilation created as
"environments" for some products exist at one and the same time with other less
euphoric messages. Also popular in advertising circles is the exploitation of more
troubling sensitivities and misgivings. Various approaches play on feelings of anxiety, many of which stem from unemployment and the declining economic situation in general. Even as AT&T was "shedding" jobs, it ran a series of advertisements that played on employees' fears that they might lose their jobs. In one such
ad, a youngish midlevel manager is shown throwing water on her face in the company bathroom, rehearsing in the mirror what she will tell her boss when he discovers the phone system she ordered is not as good as AT&T's. And both
Chevrolet and Ford currently air TV advertisements that depict white-collar
workers being demoted after displeasing their bosses. One is shown answering the
phone at the end of the ad; the other is sweeping the showroom floor.

Stouffer's Lunch Express

Another television commercial, this one for Stouffer's Lunch Express, offers a
product solution to increases in white-collar overtime and harder work. It opens
with a frenetic strained voice singing, "Work, work, work, work, work. . . . " A hy-
per-modern office is depicted, almost cartoon-style, in black and white; only the
woman's dress is a mauve color. Fellow workers rush by and the hands of the clock
race around the dial. The woman types at a computer, responds to questions, and
answers the phone—all at the same time. People make demands on her as she
struggles to keep up. Suddenly a Stouffer's lunch cart is pushed through the office
by an attractive young man on rollerblades, and a placating voice announces, "If
you can't get away for lunch, now you can feel like you did. Stouffer's Lunch
Express—14 microwavable choices." The arrival of the product transforms the office into a park-like setting. The woman's desk turns into an outdoor table, a big
shade tree pops up from the ground, and shrubs appear as the office furniture
falls away. The woman relaxes. The young man with the Stouffer's lunch cart is
there to serve her. A close shot shows her eating with a look of pleased satisfaction
on her face. After lunch the outdoor garden spot turns back into an office, but one
that is much less hectic, and, this time, in color—mauve, blues, and buff instead
of black and white.

The use of a hectic work scenario to sell convenience food implies recognition
of the increasingly long hours experienced by those with full-time jobs. Their
anxiety is soothed by Stouffer's Lunch Express, offered as a solution to highly un-
satisfactory working conditions and increased responsibilities. The practice of
substituting a sense of control and fulfillment through a product (in the realm of
consumption) for situations that actually arise from the experience of work (in

the realm of production) has been noted by Raymond Williams (1980) and Sut Jhally (1989). As the latter author (1989, 228) states, "At work we are not in control." But advertising's habitual practice of posing work-related problems, then inviting the sufferer into the pleasing world of product solutions, "naturalizes the loss of control [at work] and instead offers us control in another realm—consumption." Jhally (1989, 228) goes on to argue that consumer culture offers a false sense of democracy "in as much as people have 'choices' about the products they can buy, but not the productive arrangements under which they live."

Proud to Be Your Bud

Another advertising strategy in the age of job loss has been to present mythic images of work settings that celebrate such attributes as physical strength, camaraderie, and power and control. As the slogan "Proud to be your Bud" is sung with great revelry on the television beer commercial, images of people working together illustrate the sense of skill and accomplishment achieved under ideal working conditions. In one shot a team of people work on a huge outdoor lighting system. The woman's position is highlighted, and the workers all go for a Bud following a job well done. In another setting a clean, safe, high-tech airplane factory is pictured, and again people gather after work to relax with a refreshing Budweiser. This ad campaign speaks to the desire for challenging hard work, rewarding and high-paying work, exactly at a time when that work is in short supply. It offers the sensation of a gratifying working experience realized within the fantasy world of advertising, which in turn resides within the realm of consumption.

In yet another advertisement, this one for the soft drink Dr. Pepper, a man operates a massive crane with the words *LINK BOLT* printed on the side. In the heat of the outdoor setting, sweat pours down his face and he wipes his brow. Over shouts of "I want more of that taste I've been looking for," the well-built heavy-equipment operator swings the magnetic boom above a Dr. Pepper truck he sees and succeeds in getting more of the Dr. Pepper taste. A scenario portrayed with a comic tone, with references to erector sets, this ad is a ritualized demonstration of power over the production process. The man's physical potency dominates the equipment he runs and allows him total control of the situation. He moves huge objects through space to satisfy his own deep-felt needs—for consumer products.

In short, the incorporation of images of production within advertising is a recent phenomenon that can be understood as a response to the ambient national anxiety about the American job crisis. The loss of 10 million manufacturing jobs since the 1980s has led to advertising images of idealized employment scenarios that speak to the longing evoked by that loss. These images manufacture a shiny gloss over which to cover the country's jobless rates. Unfortunately, the desire—even the demand—for jobs will not be satisfied by either beer or soda. But it will maintain corporate profits. Meanwhile, the state of denial (along with advertising's counterfeit celebration of work) effectively distracts consumers from identifying the source of longing as well as the solution, which can be found only within the realm of production.

What the Magic Hides

As Stuart Ewen (1988) observes, the culture of consumption has been associated historically with the concept of democracy. The variety of choice, the satisfaction of human needs through products—indeed, the very multiplicity of advertising images—have come to define democracy—the attainment of human well-being, a high standard of living, "our way of life." Yet participating in the "democracy of consumption" will not create what Williams (1980, 187) refers to as genuine democracy, "in which the human needs of all the people in the society are taken as the central purpose of all social activity." Only then would politics truly be a system of self-government, such that the systems of production and consumption would be "rooted in the satisfaction of human needs and the development of human capacities" (Williams 1980, 187).

Today, the desire for satisfaction and the development of human capacities are for the most part addressed by the fantasy world of advertising. And one of the most proficient ad campaigns of all has been carried out by Nike. Even as it takes jobs out of this country, an action that destroys self-worth and the ability of people to control their own lives, Nike presents magical images of empowerment, personal control, and human liberation. The enormous amounts of money needed to produce such advertising campaigns celebrating the human spirit are acquired at the expense of the humanity of Nike's underpaid workers in the Third World. Again, even as it takes jobs out of the United States to save money, it spends millions to persuade American consumers that our lives will be enriched if we buy a pair of extravagantly priced "trainers," which many of us cannot afford and will never use for running.

Consumers' confusion as to the actual economic dynamics that impoverish them is one of the consequences of a media environment highly influenced by marketing and promotion. Advertising's habitual equation, which promises that products can solve problems and that emotional happiness and well-being in general can be found within the sphere of consumption, distracts our attention and prevents us from understanding how the economic world works. The most pernicious effect of advertising is to keep us striving for the good life within the realm of consumption, when the attainment of a truly better life can be accomplished only within political and economic realms where decisions are made that direct wealth and resources in one direction or another. As Williams (1980, 186) puts it, "The system of organized magic which is modern advertising is primarily important as a functional obscuring of this choice." Commodities cannot relieve the loss, disruption, and anxiety brought about by unemployment and underemployment, the falling standard of living, and the general decline in what has been called "social capital." The only way that prosperity for the majority can be accomplished is through changes in the economic and political practices that determine the allocation of wealth and power.

The public's participation in the economy is now primarily defined through consumption—by seeking the good life in the shopping mall and ensuring a good season for retailers. But economic democracy can be achieved only if the public participates in, understands, and influences the creation of public policies that address economic issues. As Jhally (1989, 228) points out, "The important decisions made about the structure of society are made at the realm of production." Seeking solutions for social needs through consumption, then, only amplifies the problem. The paradox is this: By accepting Nike's offer of empowerment and liberation when we buy a pair of Nike shoes, we endorse and promote the very production practices and corporate policies that preclude our own economic well-being.

Fictional Representations of Consumption

As advertising discourse becomes increasingly embedded within television programming, and as programming strategies strive to accommodate the needs of advertising by creating an appropriate vehicle for the display of products, the images and narratives of consumption proliferate. These practices are particularly noticeable in the programming developed during the 1980s to target working-class viewers; yet they define those audiences within the realm of consumption, not within the world of work. A closer look at one program that failed is revealing.

Using elements similar to those now found in the successful ABC series *Roseanne,* CBS developed a situation comedy called *Lenny,* about a working-class family man. (The show featured a stand-up comedian as the star.) Billboards along Webster Avenue in the Bronx promoted the series to its target market, working-class and low-income households. Lenny worked for the Boston Gas and Electric company, but he also held a night job as a hotel doorman to make ends meet. Given its subject matter, about a baby-boomer white working-class guy with an attitude, *Lenny* might have made it through the season, and even on to another one, had it not been so stilted, badly written, stereotypical, and just plain bad. *Lenny* was bad, but not because talented people are hard to find among the elite of television production professionals in Hollywood. It was bad because of programming strategies that convert creative motivations into the business of audience media and consumer marketing.

With the expansion of cable and the home VCR market during the 1980s, the once-dominant Big Three television networks lost a portion of their audiences. Up to 20 percent of viewers departed from prime-time TV on any given night, choosing cable or a home movie instead. In short, the demographics of the prime-time audience changed. Working-class and low-income viewers who could not afford VCRs or cable, or who did not live in the affluent communities wired for cable, were left in front of prime-time programming in greater numbers than ever before. It was for this reason network television finally discovered the working class and began to represent it on national programming. As Stanley

Aronowitz (1989) points out, before that time the working class was largely absent from the world of television. George Gerbner and Larry Gross (1976) have also documented the historical overrepresentation of professional/technical employees, whose numbers on television far exceed their proportion in the actual population. But with the economic motivations and market segmentation of the 1980s, working-class characters began to proliferate on prime-time television.

The opening sequence for *Lenny* consists of visual flashes that introduce the main character to the audience. First we see him coming up out of a manhole in a hard hat. Next he is shown sitting in a bright yellow truck with *Boston* printed on the side. Lenny and his fellow workers sit on a low wall during lunch break and survey a passing woman. Then, dressed in his hotel doorman's uniform (for his night job), he lifts a heavy suitcase out of the trunk of a taxi. Over these images the theme song tells us, "I'm just a man who holds his family sheltered from the rain" and, in a repeating refrain, "no one backs me down."

When *Lenny* debuted, it did so with matching national advertising. Immediately following the opening sequence was a commercial so visually similar to the program introduction that it was difficult to distinguish. As in *Lenny's* opening segment, the first image of the advertisement featured a man in a hard hat emerging from a manhole. But this time two men, both in hard hats, survey not a woman but a Chevrolet Lumina (see Figures 2.1 and 2.2). The ad flashed back and forth between the two guys on the job; rather than working, they were looking at and talking about the car. This scene was intercut with images of a woman demonstrating the "zero-gravity modular seats" and other features. The ad was edited in such a way that its pacing closely resembled that of *Lenny's* opening. The hard hats were the same color as the truck Lenny occupies—bright yellow. While talking about "bio-rhythms," the workman about Lenny's size made a disparaging comment (mirroring Lenny's attitude about anything "new age"), and the commercial ended. In short, this advertising dove-tailed with the visual style, mood, and content of the show, thereby incorporating the product fully within the programming format.

Just one of the programs in the working-class lineup, *Lenny* represented an attempt to appeal to the tastes and sensitivities of blue-collar, service, and low-income audiences. In the first episode, Lenny distinguishes himself from the affluent yuppies living in the upscale world of *thirtysomething*. When his wife asks him how long it's been since they spent any quality time together, he sneers, "Oh what, have you been watching *thirtysomething* again? Do you know how much I hate that word *nurturing?*" Ultimately, however, *Lenny* had neither the production values nor the attention to detail characteristic of programs aimed at more affluent audiences.

Turning again to the first episode of *Lenny*, we find a plot so contrived it could have been a parody. Lenny discovers that his father is in a great deal of pain and needs a hip replacement. Apparently never having heard of Medicaid or a doctor's second opinion, Lenny quickly finds a way to borrow the $5,000 necessary to pay the deductible for his father's operation. Giving new significance to the classic

FIGURE 2.1 Opening of *Lenny*

criticism of situation comedies—as vehicles featuring happy people with happy problems that are always solved—is a scene in which Lenny's father gets up from the couch (while watching television) and goes through the motions of a hula dance to demonstrate the complete success of the procedure to his proud son.

But the show does not end there. Lenny has had a difficult time borrowing money. Not wanting to go to his credit union (because "everybody's gonna know"), he tries to secure a bank loan. But because he has prided himself on never borrowing money, he has no credit and the banks turn him down. By the end of the episode, having learned his lesson (how to borrow money and feel good about it), he decides to go further into debt and buy his wife the engagement ring he always-promised-her-but-could-never-afford. As he and his wife slip into bed, before the lights go out, he says, "I'm goin' in debt, I'm goin' in big time. Happy engagement." Struggling to survive, forced to hold two jobs, Lenny has nevertheless learned to borrow and, even more important, to spend more money.

The first line of *Lenny*'s theme song is "When I come down the boulevard/cut me slack 'cuz I work hard." But as we have seen, network television portrays its newfound working class audience not through the world of work but through that of consumption. Lenny was never depicted as negotiating his conditions of employment, as having to deal with physical labor or the demands of supervisors, the threat of losing his job(s), or any other conditions that would constitute the definition of production. Rather, Lenny's world was about borrowing money to satisfy the consumer demands of his dependent family. Again, in the first episode, one of Lenny's daughters begs him to buy her a $150 pair of (what else?) sneakers.

FIGURE 2.2 Chevy Lumina Ad
Advertisements now often mimic the programming that carries them. Immediately following the opening of the situation comedy *Lenny* is a commercial for Chevy Lumina, which
coincides thematically with the program and visually parallels the opening sequence. The
program's opening, shown on the previous page, shows *Lenny* emerging from a manhole
wearing a hard hat. Above, the first image of the advertisement is a man in a hard hat
emerging from a manhole. Themes of consumption also characterize the program, positioning the working-class Lenny as a *consumer* rather than as a producer.

Along the way, the writers work into the plot other ways to represent spending
money on consumer goods. During the course of the program, the characters
manage to mention a Toyota Land Cruiser, a Winnebago, and a Lincoln Town
Car. And Lenny's mother is shown purchasing utterly useless items from the
home-shopping channel when the family is wired for cable TV.

Lenny was made ludicrous by the logic of consumption embedded within the
structure of the program. In essence, teaching *Lenny* to spend money was the
"creative motivation" that propelled the design of the program. Though consistent with the needs of advertising, this objective was at odds with the needs of its
audience; thus the show can be considered an example of "commercialtainment."

Lenny and his wife do not communicate in any significant way through the superficial one-liners they throw back and forth. Their love for each other is not expressed through a dramatic incident that might demonstrate his affection or de-
votion. Instead, it must be expressed through a product, as in so many of the
commercials we have seen over the years. (We no longer notice, much less object

to, the utterly specious assertion that a product can buy love.) Lenny has a similarly noncommunicative relationship with his father, made more explicit than that with his wife. His children, too, seem to be props that move in and out of the frame. Their purpose is to augment Lenny's stand-up comedian routine—and to ask for commodities of course.

Working people, when they have been represented on TV at all, have historically not been depicted at the level of production. Archie Bunker most often appeared sitting in his favorite chair in his living room, not working on the job. As Aronowitz (1989) points out, the working-class job most often depicted on television is police work. Another work-place image, notable for its rarity, occurred in the program *Laverne and Shirley,* which occasionally depicted the bottling factory where the two characters worked. This image achieved even more notoriety when it was the subject of parody in the movie *Wayne's World.*

The depiction of ABC's *Roseanne* as a factory worker in the early episodes was yet another rare exception to the rule. Recall, however, that she was quickly removed from that setting (specifically, when she led a strike and everyone was fired.) After that she worked her way up to private enterprise. One of her more significant jobs, working in a beauty parlor, can be viewed as an intertextual reference to the movie *Steel Magnolias,* an overt celebration of the traditional role of women. Over the years the absence of fictional representations of the world of work—with the emphasis on consumption instead—has helped define working-class Americans as consumers, not producers. With the growing influence of advertising on commercial television, in addition to advances in audience measurement techniques that more accurately define the audience as market, the ongoing incorporation of the logic of consumption within programming has increased.

The tendency of commercial television, which accelerated during the 1980s, is to set up dramatic scenarios about products and to present people as consumers. This tendency became more apparent with the introduction of "working-class" shows, which, as noted, make very few references to conditions of production but, rather, focus on issues of consumption. Lenny's activities as a working-class consumer are emblematic of an entertainment environment tied to the promotion of an ethic of consumption. The positioning of the audience as consumer pervades program design and excludes representations of production, in the broad definition of the term—that is, representations of people taking part in directing the social and economic forces that determines their lives.

In the next chapter we will look at the marketing research methods used to shape advertising campaigns. With the help of increasingly sophisticated focus group research, advertising succeeds in presenting the world of consumption as the only place capable of satisfying human needs and providing feelings of well-being. In this sense, advertising has taken on a therapeutic role, presenting consumption as the panacea to an increasingly problematic economic reality.

3

Emotional Ties That Bind:
Focus Groups, Psychoanalysis, and
Consumer Culture

AN AD FOR ROGAINE opens with the words "I'll never forget." A tight close-up on the face of a boy pitching a baseball (see Figure 3.1) cuts to the scoreboard, which reads *Strike 2*. The voice continues, "It was the big game, and it was all up to me." This time the tight shot is on the batter's face. As the pitch glides over the plate in slow motion the boy holding the bat never swings. The umpire shouts, "Strike. You're out." The sound track carries a dull, ominous background noise. The slow motion and reverberating noise together create an eerie tone. As the ball passes home plate, the low register of a deep voice echoes three times: "Go for it." As if in a prolonged dream sequence the camera holds the look of anguish on the boy's face, which slowly fades into the face of a grown man who, we find, is the one speaking. His remembrance is now over and we are in the present. He is sitting on the benches behind a baseball diamond. He speaks to us as if we have all been sharing his dream memory, "For years I've been wishing I'd swung at that pitch. Hit or miss, at least I'd have given it a shot. So if you're a guy who wants to find out more about Rogaine with minoxidil, whether it's for you, don't just stand there with a bat on your shoulder, find out about it."

At this point the image cuts to a brochure as an anonymous authoritative voice intones, "To find out about Rogaine topical solution. . . . " An 800 number is featured, and the voice promises that Johnson & Johnson will send you an "informative brochure and a list of local doctors who can help you decide about it." The man, who has a full head of hair, returns to the screen and, as he follows through batting at an imaginary ball, repeats, "Don't stand there with a bat on your shoulders. Make the call now." The phone number is printed below his face.

Nowhere does this commercial state that the product will actually cause hair to grow on the buyer's head. In fact, baldness is not even defined as the problem. Rather, anxiety is the key to this appeal. And it's not simply the anxiety of going bald. The narrative depicts a painful incident from childhood and evokes a sense

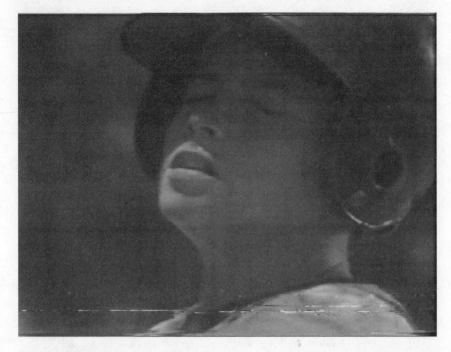

FIGURE 3.1 Rogaine Dream Sequence
The television commercial for Rogaine evokes feelings of regret, anxiety, and frustration by depicting the unpleasant childhood memory of striking out. It then promises relief from such long-held disappointments. This pseudotherapeutic discourse, common to many advertisements, promises emotional comfort through the use of products that are inherently incapable of providing such comfort.

of regret and frustration. It establishes a mood of disappointment, which in turn, sets up an emotional response. The story is from one man's life, but the narrative is not unique. It is designed to work on the dissatisfaction that pervades the general psychic atmosphere. The use of commonly shared elements, at some point experienced by virtually everyone—a missed opportunity, feelings of inadequacy and regret, failure at sports or at competition in general—allows any number of people a moment of emotional convergence with the emotions expressed. This ambient anxiety is tied to the threat of not trying a product and going bald as a consequence. The product Rogaine, even if it does not prevent baldness (the commercial makes no promises) will heal the wound of a past torment. It will finally relieve the sense of self-blame and remorse felt all those years for not swinging at a pitch—or whatever. "Hit or miss, at least I'd have given it a shot." What the ad offers is psychic healing. The product and its functional qualities are irrelevant.

This ad is only one of a plethora of psychological maneuvers that have become popular in the therapeutic discourse of advertising. Keying into psychic desires, needs, frustrations, and anxieties, and then tying those feelings to products, has become the strategy of choice for an industry always searching for the most effective mode of persuasion.

Emotional persuasion has been greatly enhanced in recent years through the use of new research methodologies, most notably the focus group. The success of focus group techniques has greatly facilitated the current passion for the emotional persuasions used in much of contemporary advertising.

The Rise of Focus Groups

In a feature article for *New York* magazine, Bernice Kanner (1989, 35–36) entered the world of marketing research and discovered a vast array of techniques employed to discover the psychocultural motivations that compel consumers to buy products:

> Researchers have respondents finish sentences ("Tide washes————," "M&M's candies went to a party last night and————"). They ask them to sketch drawings, tell tales, match up companies with various animals, colors, places, and types of music, and paste up photocollages of the people they associate with different brands. Recruits are also asked to act out their expectations for a product, fill in the balloon captions of cartoon characters, make clay models, keep diaries about their relationship with certain products, and even write obituaries for brands and companies.

Although focus groups are disparaged by some on the creative side of advertising, they now dominate the field of market research. Focus group findings are taken very seriously by the clients who commission them. More intimate than the quantitative survey approach, this new strategy is designed to discover the emotional and psychological desires that drive buying behavior. Usually eight to ten individuals are invited to sessions that turn out to be in-depth probes of their hidden landscapes of feelings and aspirations. Afficionados of the new approach believe traditional survey questions "elicit only superficialities or lies, not the subconscious desires that drive behavior" (Kanner 1989, 36). It is widely believed that people do not reveal the truth about their lives when asked, simply because they do not know it themselves. Focus group researchers are determined to tap that collective source, one way or another.

To discover the psychic bonds that can be used to tie consumers to products, focus groups go beyond straightforward questions about commodity benefits such as "What do you think about product X? And when do you use it?" Instead, researchers employ innovative procedures capable of retrieving a multiplicity of personal data that, until now, were unobtainable.

Psychological Probing

Scouting the new frontiers of private sensibilities requires room to maneuver. And, indeed, the architects of contemporary marketing understand that focus sessions cannot be rigidly structured. The guide sheets prepared for the moderators, those who will lead the focus groups, cannot be burdened with "multi-page detailed lists." If they are, one consultant warns, the client or advertising firm conducting the focus groups has a "basic misunderstanding of the nature of qualitative research."[1] Questionnaires that direct the moderators are to be "short and very general." Strategically worded open-ended questions allow for creativity and brainstorming. The approach is to create fragments of meaning and have respondents fill in the numerous blank spaces. The moderators are told to follow the open-ended discussion of the group and remain responsive to change, "casting a wide net" and leaving "the way open for surprises."

Evocative sketches are used as props to encourage imaginative fantasies. The recruits' own visual renderings are also encouraged. During sessions that make use of the "photo and tale technique," for example, subjects are given a picture and asked to fill in a face, or invent a story about the product or company itself. As a participant in one interview, Kanner (1989, 34–35) was asked to tell "a tale about what happens before someone needs shampoo and conditioner and after she's applied them." In other variations of these methods, the moderators ask subjects to draw their own pictures, sketching their feelings about a product.

Moderators encourage flights of fancy using an array of procedures devised to evoke a broad range of psychic and emotional sensations. In some workshops, volunteers are encouraged to act out their feelings about a product, or to express what it feels like to be in need of one. One researcher reported that in these animated groups, people often "raise their arms, stand up, smile, hit themselves on the heart or act bored" (Kanner 1989, 38). These "psychodramas" are then interpreted to ascertain the emotional needs they express. For example, volunteers who conducted an orchestra and steered an imaginary ship "demonstrated that they want control."

As a participant, Kanner was also asked to describe what parts the products would play if they appeared in her dreams. Indeed, focus group fantasies often evoke the associational imagery of dreams. For instance, the ad agency Ogilvy & Mather has asked business travelers to dream about an airline's voice and attitude. They found that businesspeople "must grudgingly give up control when they fly." Consequently, they wanted to be "taken care of and pampered, treated like an only child" while in the air, "not like pledges rushing to a fraternity house" (Kanner 1989). This probe of two hundred people prompted Ogilvy & Mather to replace its "festive, high-flying" ad campaign with one more appropriate to the travelers' emotional needs.

In another exploration of the psychic makeup of businesspeople, anthropologists at the Saatchi & Saatchi ad agency have identified some of the emotional motivations for choosing a hotel. A "psychological probe" uncovered their "unconscious underlying separation anxieties and need to feel dependent but ultimately in control." Therefore, according to Saatchi & Saatchi, the hotel should offer emotional support so as to "restore . . . self-esteem" while the "road warriors" relax and refuel. These emotional findings, derived from focus groups, determined the theme for Saatchi & Saatchi's campaign pitch, even though the data contradicted what businesspeople told them directly. When simply asked, businesspeople "claim they pick a hotel because of its location, reputation, or service" (Kanner 1989, 40).

Emphasizing the product's function, benefits, or use-value is no longer the strategy of choice for ad agencies. Contemporary advertising has moved away from campaigns designed to "inform" the consumer about the "conscious, rational product benefits" and toward campaigns aimed at "psychoanalytically interpreted emotional and cultural values that drive behavior" (Kanner 1989, 40). These psychocultural appeals[2] offer the advertiser many advantages over simple details concerning physical characteristics, performance, or price. As one professional has put it, "Rational benefits are vulnerable, because with today's technology it's easy to knock off a competitor's innovation quickly or play on his marketing turf. Emotional bonds, on the other hand, are hard to break" (Kanner 1989, 37). Such bonds explain consumer's preference for Classic Coke as well as their rejection of the newer recipe that failed.

Even contemporary "benefit probes" translate product benefits into emotional values. Respondents may note that mouthwash has breath-cleaning properties. "This," says Kanner (1989, 39), "might to lead to citing the fact that it eliminates worry and fosters confidence, which might snake into making one feel fresh, relaxed and happy."

In many cases today, the product takes a back seat to the soft-sell approach of marketing strategies. This trend is particularly important in the context of new products introduced into the market. Finding the emotional niches for these products is as important as designing the products themselves. As one professional puts it,

> You don't come up with a product and then try to sell it to consumers through advertising messages. Rather, the successful marketer begins with the minds of consumers and tries to identify potentially unmet needs there. If one or more is discovered, then a product is either designed to fill the need or an existing product is "redefined" to fill the need. (Larson 1989, 381)

Finding unmet needs allows advertisers to create pathways of desire that connect the product to those needs. But these often arbitrary associations must be presented as genuine. To successfully forge emotion/product associations, the ad campaign must ring with authenticity, speaking the perceived language of real people's lives.

The Quest for Authenticity

It is essential that advertising language sound authentic, not like the tired jingles of obvious persuasion. After nearly a century of advertising's promotion of mass consumption, the industry now confronts a cynical public, culturally literate and on guard against persuasive appeals. As one advertising executive told a group of students learning copywriting techniques, "If it sounds like any advertisement you've ever heard before, throw it out." Always looking for words that evoke real people, focus groups provide marketers with genuine speech, not counterfeit slogans. The use of slang and colloquial phrases connects advertising to popular discourse, which in turn mirrors everyday life.

The proceedings of focus groups are usually recorded, whereupon "creative" researchers scan the tapes looking for recurring words, phrases, and images. This, the stuff of real lives, is what ads are made of. The most effective ads are those in which consumers recognize some part of themselves. Commodities must be wrapped with symbolic packaging that elicits the consumers' actual feelings, attitudes, and words. So the consumers are given back what they put in. Tony Schwartz (1973) uses the term *resonance* to describe this strategy.

The most successful campaigns bounce creative energies and direct language back to the consumer, but only after they have been transformed into promotional appeals. Consider, for instance, the slogan that enthusiastic people shout in a television spot done by J. Walter Thompson for Prodigy personal computer service: "You gotta get this thing!" As Frank Nicolo, executive vice president and senior creative director at Thompson, explains, This phrase was "really an expression we heard consumers use in focus groups" (Nicolo, quoted in Elliot 1992b). Similarly, Michael Evans, a spokesperson for Burger King, notes, "Your way right away" sounds like an ad slogan, whereas "What d'ya say? What d'ya say?" makes the ad "more realistic." With vernacular like "gotta," "yo," "gonna," "uh-huh," and "hey," advertisements mimic the language of everyday. Pepsi-Cola's carefully formulated "The choice of a new generation" was dropped in favor of "You got the right one baby, uh-huh," and "Gotta have it." And the New York State Lottery's formulaic "All you need is a dollar and a dream" gave way to "Hey, you never know."

Nonverbal Techniques

A number of focus group techniques are designed to bypass verbalization altogether. One popular strategy is to ask recruits to sort photographs. This technique goes directly to the connotative visual imagery of advertising, whereby the message no longer has to be mediated by language. The results of such probes yield invaluable information, as Kanner (1989, 37) reports: "General Electric decided to 'bring good things to life'—and to its image—after photosorters associated GE with older, conservative business-suit types." GE's now-familiar ad campaign, featuring soft-focus shots of smiling employees, epitomizes diversity and humanism rather than the corporate priorities that actually steer the organization.

Nor is the psychic makeup of children considered off limits to marketing researchers. One of the largest markets in the 1980s, children represent the fastest-growing investment made in broadcast advertising. In the field of marketing it is widely acknowledged that kids are difficult to draw out through conversation. "The main thing is to get involved in interaction," through techniques such as "role playing and simulated shopping," says Cindy Clark, owner of a children's research company (Clark, quoted in Spethmann 1992, 51).

Focus groups designed to elicit emotions, imagery, and dramatic fantasies use innovative techniques, many of which were originally designed as psychological probes. The thematic apperception test, or TAT, was designed in 1938 by Harvard psychologist Henry Murray. Now agencies such as D'Arcy Massius Benton & Bowles apply a version of the test to focus groups, whose members are asked to "read" their feelings into a picture. This method was used effectively to market Entenmann's baked goods. In one session participants were shown a picture of a woman holding a knife, standing at a checkout counter with a package of Entenmann's cake. Drawn without eyes or nose, the figure was given a degree of anonymity. The participants were asked to tell a story about what it would feel like if they were placed in her position. According to Kanner, "The story that often got told was how the woman cut one little piece until the whole thing was gone" (Kanner 1989, 38). With these findings, the "Splendid Obsession" campaign was launched, featuring the theme of uncontrollable cravings. In one spot a couple ventures into the pouring rain late at night in order to satisfy their yearning for Entenmann's.

Studies of poor southern women done by McCann Erickson for the makers of the pesticide Combat uncovered a level of psychic distress some would consider disturbing. The probe was intended to find out why Combat was not selling well in the South, whereas its competitor, Raid, was in high demand. Why would pesticide users prefer a spray can of Raid to a product in plastic trays that kills insects quickly and with no mess? Focus groups provided the answer: "When asked to draw and tell a story about a roach, dozens of poor southern women depicted the insect as a man who comes around when he wants something (like a free meal) and leaves once he's gotten it." Analyzing these findings, researchers at McCann Erickson understood that "Raid gave them some feeling of control and an outlet for their hostility that Combat could not."

The soft sell is now the persuasive method of choice in an industry hocking many products with little difference between them. Anthropologists and psychologists employed by ad agencies spend hundreds of hours probing their subjects to determine the hidden desires that motivate behavior. For example, the large advertising firm Saatchi & Saatchi has six clinical psychologists on staff. As noted earlier, the research they do involves finding ways to quantify consumers' emotional bonds with products. Meanwhile, "at McCann, recruits rate 24 feelings, such as happiness, sexiness, and safety, that they'd most like to derive from a toothpaste, beer, or nail polish" (Kanner 1989, 39). Researchers at this agency strive to find ways to connect cigarettes with relaxation and to associate fast food with a feeling of safety. Other scales list as many as 58 emotions, which are rated to determine an "ideal emotional expectation for a particular product category."

Focus Groups as Therapy

Focus groups have been called "the modern-day equivalent of the consciousness-raising groups of the seventies" (Kanner 1989, 36). In such groups, sociologists and anthropologists as well as clinical psychologists discover anxieties and unhappiness as well as needs for power and control, safety and security. They use dream sequences and a variety of emotional and psychological probes to assess psychic passions. Volunteers often feel secure enough to engage in various emotive behaviors such as taking off their pants to demonstrate the comfort of their underwear. In one focus group on dentures, participants even removed their false teeth. Indeed, the groups provide recruits with an outlet for the expression of an array of emotional needs and psychic desires. The similarity to therapy sessions is not coincidental: Some of the same dynamics of therapeutic practice come into play during focus groups. Both contexts allow participants to verbalize their desires and to express sometimes extremely intimate longings as well as pain.

Many of the psychological probes employed by focus group moderators are clearly derived from the practice of psychology and psychoanalysis. Joel Kovel's (1989, 136) description of the expressive language of psychoanalysis developed by Freud reveals the similarities between psychoanalysis and much of what goes on in focus group sessions. Freud discovered that the unstructured, open-ended discourse of dreams and associations revealed hidden subjective desires:

> He gave the patient the initiative, and realized that the peculiar, seemingly disjointed speech which spilled forth obeyed the same, alternate logic as the dream thoughts he was also investigating. We might call this kind of speech "desiring speech," since its words express the inchoate longings of the inner self. Freud learned to follow the thread of this language of the self, to decipher it, and [to] give its strange contours the forms he was to call psychoanalysis.

The "creative brainstorming" in focus groups evokes fantasy thought and emotionally charged creative associations. This technique is similar to the "free association" and dream analysis used in psychoanalysis.

Ernst Dichter, who pioneered motivational research and later applied his methods to contemporary marketing practices, also referred to focus groups as group therapy sessions. He asked the members of focus groups to speak personally and "in-depth from a general point of view." After asking an initial question, "he let people talk very freely. Usually they did not even know what the product was."[3] Focus groups certainly provide a context for emotional expression; but they also bring into play the flattering proposition that at least someone cares about what the average person thinks, needs, and feels. The context is a singular one in which the consumer is given voice, allowed to talk back to the monolith that has become marketed media culture. And in such verbal and emotional flights of fancy there exists the liberating elements of a therapeutic process. The "desiring speech," as Kovel has come to call the discourse of therapy that pours forth when someone takes the "talking cure," offers emotional release:

> Its original impulse contained an emancipated moment—and . . . this moment is reproduced every time a person unburdens her/himself to a therapist. It is only a moment, that is, a bit of dialectical human power, unfrozen for an instant and entering historical time. The moment can be refrozen, distorted, even obliterated—but it is real.

Marketing research takes these "emancipated moments" of unburdening, when the "desiring speech" of the self is given voice, and indeed does distort them. As with the psychoanalytic practice of free association, the emotional revelations evoked by focus group techniques are released—but not to a healing professional. Rather, they are appropriated by the architects of persuasion. And instead of offering the keys to self-fulfillment, these revelations become part of the wisdom of persuasion, used by marketers to construct the vast array of promises made to appeal to the innermost needs of the buying public. The problems, pain, and disappointments, the hopes, dreams, and fantasies of the self, are translated into powerful advertising images that offer the world of consumption as the vehicle for fulfillment of emotional need and psychological want.

But the vast majority of promises made by the emotional appeals of the soft sell can never be kept. Anonymous hotels designed to accommodate large numbers of "guests" by means of characteristically overburdened staffs cannot provide emotional support for the travelers experiencing feelings of separation anxiety. Nor can a small number of flight attendants treat every fearful passenger like an only child. And most assuredly, spraying roaches with Raid cannot put an end to the poverty and patriarchy that engender such rage in poor southern women.

To understand the power of advertising and its ability to make such assertions, however inauthentic its discourse and improbable its emotional promises, we need to look further into the psychic and emotional appeal of its persuasive techniques. As we have seen, the success of that appeal owes a great deal to focus group revelations.

Advertising and Psychoanalysis

A Montage of Images

The themes raised in advertising—friendship, romance, nostalgia, success, pain, rediscovered happiness, and so on—are explored in the fleeting glimpses of fragmented yet highly evocative images. Within at most one minute, a story must be told, a scenario set up, emotions evoked, and needs gratified. Advertising therefore speaks an abbreviated language in which meaning is produced through a rapid-fire sequence of powerful juxtapositions. Advertisements tell their stories not with complete or coherent narratives but with a series of image associations.

Take, for example, the Shady Brook Farms ad that opens with a succession of beautiful pastoral scenes. Following these evocative fragments are images of turkey parts. The golden hues of sunshine on fields of grain cut to the bronze color of roasted thighs and drumsticks. The trusted voice of Burgess Meridith croons, "Ah, you can just taste it, the warmth of the sun, the pure country air, the golden green of the land." The images continue, alternating between tranquil landscapes and turkey parts. Finally, as the entire extended family sits around an outdoor table, the proud mother presents a platter of turkey parts; then a boy bites greedily, with great satisfaction, into a piece of turkey. The voice again assures, "You can just taste the farm freshness in every part of a Shady Brook Farms turkey. In this whole world there's no better turkey." The last image, just before the product package, features a horse-drawn cart full of yellow hay making its way off a covered bridge—the perfect image of rural bliss.

This Shady Brook Farms advertisement relies on a specific mode of communication to transfer positive value and good feelings to its turkey parts. Specifically, it juxtaposes a series of images united by the color yellow: Recall the sunlit landscape and the bronze hue of the turkey. It is through the use of color that the images are incorporated. They become a set, a category of things with shared characteristics. The positive pleasure of sun and land is thus merged with the turkey. In short, the series of representations produces signification at the connotative level. The goodness depicted reflects onto the turkey and becomes the essence of that turkey. The meaning derived is good taste.

As discussed earlier, advertising strategies rarely inform viewers about a product's use-value or physical attributes. Instead, they tie values and meaning to the product through montage, transferring the connotative quality of one image to the next. This associative technique creates a series of fast-moving images in which meaning is derived through the logic of association, not through channels of reasoning applied by the analytic mind.

Associative Drift

In *Unconscious for Sale,* two psychoanalysts, Doris-Louise Haineault and Jean-Yves Roy (1993), explore the language of advertising. They argue that its mode of discourse is analogous to what they call the "associative drift" of the unconscious mind. The logic of associative drift is "a mode of understanding specific to the human mind . . . and its consequences for psychic life to this day remain barely measurable" (Haineault and Roy 1993, 90). Fundamentally, the unconscious mind works through associations, which in turn follow the "law of series." That is, "representations regroup among themselves, form series, sequences, cohorts from analogous elements" (Haineault and Roy 1993, 90). Meaning emerges from these representations in series—in short, from images ordered in sequence.

Associative drift is used in psychoanalysis to tap into the patient's psychic makeup, information that is not available at a conscious level. The purpose of the therapeutic process is to find meaning in the patient's free association. As noted, Kovel (1989, 136) referred to this practice as "desiring speech." As the analyst "strives to extract meaning from the associative sequence," he or she must attempt to understand associative logic, the progression in which meaning is developed (Haineault and Roy 1993, 90). In psychoanalysis, one image or thought leads to another, evoking chains of representation that begin to reveal the self. Signification is produced by this psychic process of drift as the analyst works with the "analysand" to grasp its message.

Haineault and Roy (1993) argue that advertising uses the associative mode of discourse, which speaks directly to the unconscious mind. Earlier, Scott Lash (1988) had noted that postmodern discourse (especially that of advertising) does not follow the systematic rules of language but, rather, uses a "figural" visual mode based upon perceptual "memories" unique to the unconscious mind.

Dreaming Advertisements

Responding to the findings of numerous surveys in which people report that they do not remember advertisements, Haineault and Roy (1993) reason that the ads are not recalled because "they are dreamed." In other words, advertisements engage the human psyche at the level of dream associations. And, as we have seen, focus group techniques in which people are asked to dream about products help marketers create associative sequences that appear authentic. Visualizations and other psychoanalytic strategies tap into authentic human desires and fears so that those affective states can be affiliated with products. This is the use to which advertisers' lists of emotions and corresponding products are put.

Desire and the Unconscious

Powerful visual juxtapositions, the *lingua franca* of advertising, encourage the viewer to engage in associative drift, producing a range of meanings derived from that engagement. The beautiful images of fields of grain, blue skies, sunshine, and babbling brooks of Shady Brook Farms evoke any number of possible associations. The viewer might drift from love of country to the serenity of nature, all the while experiencing nostalgia for a past never actually experienced—sensations that mingle with feelings of warmth, tranquillity, leisure, and freedom.

Because the logic of association is polysemic, in that the series of representations evokes a range of possible meanings, it engages the viewer at the level of "play," investing the associative sequence with psychic desire. The initial sequences in advertisements are necessarily ambiguous, leading to a multiplicity of possible interpretations. With this presentation of ambiguity, advertisements take a certain risk, but a necessary one. For without polysemy, the associative chain of desire is not sparked. The ambiguity is what excites and engages the viewer. As Haineault and Roy (1993 98–99) point out, "Some representations that, absurdly, are neutral do not hold our interest: without a gap in significance, desire has no place in which to invest itself. Advertising did not invent this rule; all one can say is that it exploits it to the maximum." Lash, too, has noted that the figural language of advertising speaks directly to the "primary processes" of desire. Differentiation and distance are lost as the viewer becomes immersed in the immediate emotional desire evoked by the message.

After the initial associative play, the advertisement must work to direct awareness back to the product. Television advertisements are structured "to make possible meanings converge toward a desired meaning. From the initial polysemics of original representations, one will attempt to conclude with a final monosemy"

(Haineault and Roy 1993, 91–92). Psychoanalysis employs associative drift to understand the human psyche; advertising utilizes the associative discourse of desiring speech in another way. It attempts to control and direct the spectator's associative drift toward a *product*.

As discussed earlier, advertisements invite desire through fantasies of wish fulfillment; but they also rely on powerful negative emotions. In such cases, it is the desire to avoid pain and anxiety that directs psychic affect. The strategy used to sell Rogaine, now a popular formula, introduces a painful or anxiety-inducing scene followed by a product remedy. In other ads, frenetic black-and-white images shot at unpleasant angles, often depicting ugly urban environments, noisy and crowded, are juxtaposed with serene color images of quiet beauty featuring the product being sold. One TV commercial for Dannon yogurt features a sequence of black-and-white anxiety-provoking scenes, then jumps to a soft-focus color image of a woman and her child eating yogurt as a voice reassures the viewer that the goodness of Dannon yogurt is one part of your life you can control. Another example is a Nike advertisement in which an entire page of print lists a series of psychological fears and offers Nike as the tangible alleviation of those fears.

Haineault and Roy (1993, 105) characterize this formulaic structure as a kind of tryptic: "a conflict, a product, a conflict resolved." This approach is effective precisely because the dread aroused requires consoling. Closing images of products in commercials are successful "to the degree that they are capable of reducing the tension the first association provokes" (Haineault and Roy 1993, 98). The final monosemous meaning points to the product as a way of easing the tension raised by the ad.

As we found earlier in the example of Stouffer's Lunch Express ad, anxieties brought up in one sphere, the realm of production in that case, were "solved" in the realm of consumption. So, too, we find that when advertising provokes affective states, it offers material acquisition to resolve and/or direct those feelings. As Haineault and Roy (1993, 96) put it, "The advertisement works to the extent to which we willfully confuse *having* and *being*." Advertisements such as these work by conflating the desire for emotional well-being with obtaining a product.

A viewer confuses *having* with *being* when advertisements successfully strike such an emotional chord. And, indeed, the objective of the advertisement is to spark a psychic conflict, or wish, and then to offer an "easy way out." The affective state is immediately replaced with a false reassurance. The viewer welcomes the solution because "it is easier to endorse the false self" than to contemplate the effort involved overcoming fears or apprehensions, or in finding a realistic way of understanding and approaching what is desired. "The affective steady forward progress we forget, in these advertising situations, in order to let ourselves be duped by the provisional euphoria" (Haineault and Roy 1993, 97). In short, it is easier to accept the product solution than to contemplate the affective difficulty of resolving psychological conflict, unpleasant working environments, urban problems, or lack of fulfillment.

Advertising and Repression

Looking again at the turkey commercial, we find that it can be understood as a set of dream associations disconnected from what Stuart Ewen (1988) calls "material reality." Also embedded within such messages is a profound psychic repression. Bucolic images of fields of grain have little to do with turkey farming; they constitute a false set of associations. Yet the images are beautifully crafted and have a pleasing effect. Such images depend on the viewer's willingness to participate, with good feelings, in its dynamic aesthetic form. The ad, then, is appreciated at the level of aesthetics. In that respect, it is well done.

Who wants to venture behind those images to "drift" to the actual conditions under which turkeys are raised for the consumer market? Even though we see that the *turkey has been cut into parts,* we are not compelled to contemplate the fact that it was once alive and has been slaughtered and then butchered. We allow that distressing reality to remain repressed. What viewer is willing to contemplate images of turkeys crowded together in dirty pens that bear no resemblance to the clean open fields presented to us? Who is willing to endure the psychic distress of pondering the machinery of slaughter instead of the grain harvester shown in the commercial? The industrial management by which turkeys are raised and butchered has nothing to do with the mythic icons and warm feelings of amber waves of grain, even if Burgess Meridith's reassuring voice insists it that does. And yet as viewers we are not disturbed by this contradiction because we have been offered emotional fantasies and aesthetic forms. We do not look behind the images. The repressive power of advertising is its ability to obliterate the clear illogic of this contradiction. It succeeds in doing so by evoking the viewer's desire to avoid psychic disturbance.

Emotional Poverty

The associative discourse of advertising is effective precisely because it engages the unconscious mind, which accepts emotional propositions that the analytic mind would reject. Buying a pair of shoes cannot alleviate psychological fears, and eating yogurt or turkey parts will not provide a shield from increasingly unsafe and unpleasant urban environments. William Leiss and his colleagues (1989) have referred to these strategies in terms of the inherently false communication implicit in advertising discourse. Indeed, the emotional promises made by advertisements cannot be fulfilled. As Haineault and Roy (1993, 96) point out, "The advertiser has oriented the connotative chain toward material representations of affective content, banalizing, by the same stroke, actual anguish just as much as potential happiness, reducing them both to a factual tangibility." In doing do, the advertiser cynically mocks authentic desire. The consequence of this process is essentially a sense of emotional poverty:

[Desire] is evoked in a properly accessible real situation and then, right on the spot, a needlessly sparked flame is extinguished. Well beyond the consumption such maneuvers incite is the corrosive and constantly banalizing usury of an authentic desire that, from one message to another, repeats itself insidiously. (Haineault and Roy 1993, 106)

In these strategies of emotional manipulation, desire or anxiety is aroused and then avoided or repressed. Advertising counts on the fact that "we ourselves are going to collaborate in the repression of what is problematic—and in this sense we are ourselves authors of our own perversions" (Haineault and Roy 1993, 108). We actively participate in the process in order to avoid psychic pain, and along the way, awareness of the counterfeit nature of advertising's therapeutic discourse is lost.

Consumer Culture and Therapy

Through the vast glittering array of advertising, the world of consumption is presented as the key to profound human satisfaction—the end of longing and the fulfillment of desire. Products promise to affirm and to heal broken relationships, to transform a needy and unwanted self into the object of desire. They promise power, as well as freedom from the obligations and strains of a troubled world. The symbolic icons of advertising images even offer spiritual liberation, as when the Nike ad orders us all, for our own benefit, to "Just do it."

The cumulative effects of these emotional appeals is to constrain yearning for well-being within the realm of consumption. Advertising's therapeutic discourse, which promises that life will be good (for the price of the product), coexists with a political and economic context increasingly incapable of offering "the good life" (itself an ad slogan). Advertising's promise that emotional well-being can be selected from the multiplicity of products for sale is effective because so few opportunities for emotional healing actually exist. Tracing the historical trajectory of professional therapeutic services will shed some light on how advertising came to assume its ersatz therapeutic role in contemporary society.

No Money for the Talking Cure

In post–World War II America, mental health services had begun to develop into a full-blown social-service industry, nurtured by public funding and federal policy. It was the Kennedy administration that viewed psychotherapy as a necessary aspect of an improved quality of life. Community clinics providing therapeutic services to low- and middle-income residents around the country were publicly funded. In those halcyon days at the beginning of the 1960s, federal policy attempted to extend mental health services even, for example, to people in the South Bronx. Kennedy allocated funds for over 2,000 comprehensive community mental health centers (CMHCs), which were to be completed by the end of the 1980s.

During this time, resources were allocated and prevailing attitudes supported a therapeutic model that allowed doctors to spend time with patients. The emphasis was on the "talking cure," which, in its most helpful form, entails "sitting down with someone, trying to make sense of his/her life, communicating this in a way that makes a difference" (Kovel 1988, 92). But by the 1970s, as the economy was starting to contract, "resident psychiatrists were getting the back of Washington's hand, the line workers who pulled the real load in the mental health industry were being laid off, and the once proud community health centers were being shut down" (Kovel 1988, 93).

Since the mid-1970s, the "fiscal crisis of the state has led to a more or less inexorable cutting back of resources" for public-funded health care facilities. These cutbacks have brought working conditions in most mental health facilities to a "truly hellish level" (Kovel 1989, 136). Today only about 700 CMHCs serve the entire country, and Joel Kovel characterizes them not as viable institutions able to have an impact on public well-being, but as "typically dreary and understaffed pill-pushing bureaucracies." These demoralized institutions now characterize public mental health facilities where doctor/patient therapy is "no longer based on talk, but pills. . . . Pills are substantially cheaper than nurses and therapists for the state and insurance companies, who have to pick up the tab for the care of madness" (Kovel 1988, 93–94).

The Political Consequences of Speaking Freely

Funding cuts are not the only reason that public mental health clinics have failed to fulfill their mandate to provide services to the poor. Deeper social and political dynamics have also prevented the continued funding of public therapy. One such dynamic, the process of giving voice to the innermost needs of the self, is especially problematic. "Desiring speech," now encouraged in marketing research's focus groups, and contained within much of advertising's persuasive appeals, has been discovered to be a politically disruptive process. According to Kovel (1989, 140), "When Freud developed the method of free association, dialogue became invested with the radical demands of desire. . . . This form of speech is inherently political and potentially subversive."

The talking cure allows not detached observations (such as those made on the other side of the mirror by strategists watching focus groups) but "dialogue, and dialogue [has] allowed those on the bottom—women, people of color, the poor in general—to speak up and even back" (Kovel 1988, 94). The discourse that engages the patient, and the therapist in the life of that patient, is a dialogue that touches on the collective moments—the personal history and social context—of someone's life. This dialogue has been considered the real menace of psychoanalysis, especially when used to treat those on the bottom end of the socioeconomic scale: It gives powerless people a voice. As Kovel (1989, 137) argues,

Since an individual's life history is a narrative drawn from the history of society, in which all the actors have roles defined by class, gender, and context, Freud's psychoanalysis became the forum for a new politics of desire. Freud opened a door, and through it poured all the pent-up forces which have made the body and personal life zones of conflict in our time.

While working with people in the South Bronx, psychologists discovered that "the gun was loaded." According to Kovel (1989, 40), "Though the CMHC could not begin to provide the economic basis for full empowerment, it gave a vision of power within its own therapeutic system. It offered desiring speech." The contradiction between desire and the reality of the South Bronx led the voices of desiring speech to become unruly demands that challenged power structures by calling economic inequality into question. In 1969 the Lincoln CMHC at Lincoln Hospital in the South Bronx, one of the most impoverished communites in the country, was taken over and occupied by its patients, members of the community, and the nonmedical staff. As Kovel (1989, 140) observed, these were people "who had the effrontery to take seriously the radical promptings of the desiring speech set into motion" by the therapeutic practices encouraged there.

In effect, these collective "emancipated moments" of unburdening raised to consciousness the inequities in relations of power. As Freud discovered at the end of the century, "desiring speech" is liberating speech—and the consequence is a demand for empowerment. Connecting personal well-being and expectations of a better life to actual economic and political structures creates social instability when there is no way to affect those entrenched structures. After the aforementioned disruption at Lincoln Hospital in the South Bronx, Kovel (1989, 140) concluded that genuine therapeutic practice is "deemed a threat to the orderly keeping of everyone in their place. We should learn the lesson well: the demands of desiring speech can only be realized in a better world." Since that time there has been a "steady drift of the mental health industry downward and Rightward, to its present pathetic state" (Kovel 1988, 94).

Social and economic circumstances have gotten not better but worse. As the need for therapeutic services has increased, the mental health industry's ability to deliver such services has decreased. Within this context, advertising has effectively presented the culture of consumption as the key to emotional well-being. By assuming an ersatz therapeutic role, its dream images offer commodities as the end of psychological dissatisfaction. A look at the nature of the commodity form itself will help explain the success of advertising's strategies.

The Commodity Form

"Desiring speech" is continually being reconnected, with the help of focus groups and advertising's emotional appeals, to commodity needs. The commodity form itself, which is appropriately vague and mystified, lends itself to this practice. It was in *Capital* that Karl Marx (1887) first noted the peculiar properties of the commodity, which he referred to as fetishism. He argued that the product hides, even from its producers, the social and economic relations of its own production. It does this in two ways. Under industrial production the labor process is fragmented and segmented and workers no longer oversee, or are even apprised of, every aspect of the creation of the product. The "miraculous" industrial revolution, which produced (and still does produce) the commodities we consume daily, was based on assembly-line labor entailing repetitive, dispiriting work over which workers had very little control. Nor could they provide input into the design of the products. In short, they had no view of the process from inception to completion. The terms Marx used to describe these industrial practices were *specialization* and the *division between mental and manual labor*. He also called them alienating.

Embodied (but hidden) within the commodity is the step-by-step process of production, but no one sees and experiences all those steps. So the commodity is viewed as appearing rather than as being produced and thus becomes a fetish when it is offered for sale on the market. The labor practices—the social relationships of production—incorporated within the product are essentially invisible, then. When we buy a pair of Nike trainers, as consumers we have no way of understanding the conditions under which that pair of shoes was made. The negative aspects of the exploitative manufacturing process (detailed in Chapter 2) are taken to a further remove as advertising becomes added to the formula. The meanings inherent in the original context—the conditions of exploitation—are omitted from the discourse, and new meanings are created through advertising. Spiritual liberation is now defined as the essence of the same commodity that destroys that spirit.

Given the properties of commodity as fetish, a vast array of arbitrary meanings can be assigned to products at the convenience of marketers, after the meaning of their relationship to production has been suppressed. And contemporary advertising has perfected that practice to a fine science. Focus groups, by scouting the most intimate terrains of desire, allow advertising practitioners to create an array of mythic associations, all tied to products. Moreover, they accomplish this end in such a way that the associations do not appear, at least at first glance, to be fraudulent. Advertising speaks to real people's fears, anxieties, joys, and longings, offering a glittering assortment of ways, through spending, to fulfill them. Within the therapeutic mode, the product itself becomes increasingly irrelevant. The role of the commodity is primarily a mediating one, between the psychic desires posed and the quest for emotional satisfaction promised through the magic of advertising.

In the short term, on a superficial level, consumption appears to be a satisfying activity, thereby causing a further rupture between the conditions of production and the fantasy meanings associated with products. "Thus," notes Raymond Williams (1980, 189), "the fantasy seems to be validated, at a personal level, but only at the cost of preserving the general unreality which it obscures: the real fail-ures of the society which however are not easily traced to this pattern."

Observing the nature of the commodity and its cultural meanings, Raymond Williams has noted the contradiction of modern industrial society. Many criticize consumer culture for its materialistic values, but as he argues:

> If we were sensibly materialist . . . we should find most advertising to be of an insane irrelevance. Beer would be enough for us, without the additional promise that in drinking it we show ourselves to be manly, young at heart or neighborly. A washing machine would be a useful machine to wash clothes, rather than an indication that we are forward-looking or an object of envy to our neighbors. (Williams 1980, 185)

The contradiction inherent in the material nature of consumer cultures is that "objects are not enough but must be validated, if only in fantasy, by association with social and personal meanings" (Williams 1980, 185). We do not really buy products anymore. We buy advertising messages, which promise happiness, fun, popularity, and love. Take, for example, the following clothing advertisement for *theo*miles.[4] A dreamy image of romance showing a close-up kiss shared between a man and a woman stands alone on one page. On the opposite page the text reads "It's like love. No maybe it's like marriage. Face it, love is all about this immediate rush. Which is how you feel when you buy some gorgeous little blouse." The ad goes on to assure the spectator/buyer that her blouse is more like marriage be-cause it will "work with your new blazer." And "Yeah, if he's marriage material, he'll really love you at nine months [pregnant]."

But the fulfilling interpersonal relationships so often promised for the price of a product remain elusive. This fact becomes clear when we realize that, ultimately, the act of purchasing does not satisfy the needs that the products have been asso-ciated with. Buying a blouse will not produce the same emotional "rush" that comes with love, marriage, and children. Parent-child relationships will not be-come more loving when families eat at McDonald's. And a child will not love his mother more because her laundry detergent makes clothes whiter and brighter.

In some ads, the product itself is absent—yet another indication that con-sumers' desire is not for the product but for the promise. Research also confirms that having material objects is not really the point. Most telling is the fact that when survey respondents were asked to choose what they cherished most in life from a list of values such as health, family, and betterment of society, "the materi-alist option—'having a nice home, car and other belongings'—ranked *last*" (Schor 1992, 126). In another survey, "having nice things" ranked twenty-sixth in a list of twenty-eight. Clearly we strive for the associative values tied to objects, not for the objects themselves.

The accumulation of objects does not make us happy. The consumer lifestyle has not provided the public with an increased sense of satisfaction. Consider Juliet Schor's (1992) study, in which she correlates levels of consumption with perceptions of happiness. The percentage of people who reported being "very happy" peaked in 1957. By 1978, the last year in which a "happiness" poll was taken, the level of "very happy" had not recovered, "in spite of the rapid growth in consumption during the 1960s and 1970s. Similar polls taken since then indicate no revival of happiness" (Schor 1992, 115).

Incapable of producing true satisfaction, advertising reinforces compulsive behavior both directly (in ads like Entenmann's "Splendid Obsession") and indirectly (by continually making promises that an act of buying cannot fulfill). For an increasing number of compulsive shoppers this paradox sets off a cyclical quest. When the product does not satisfy, the consumer is compelled to continue shopping, still trying to fulfill those needs. As Schor (1992, 108) notes, "For some people, shopping has become an addiction, like alcohol or drugs." Consumer credit has "enabled" this behavior; "compulsive shoppers spend money they don't have on items they absolutely 'can't' do without and never use." This behavior is actually referred to and reinforced in advertising. In the style of "true confessions," an ad for NICOLE shoes[5] features an "average" woman, Lisa Geisenheimer. The text promises to divulge the "Confessions of a Shoe Addict." Printed underneath Geisenheimer's name is the information that she owns "82 pairs." Wedged between the brand name and a picture of a NICOLE shoe is the text "The pair you wear." This ad openly acknowledges that addictive behavior leads to the purchase of products never used. It is not surprising that self-help groups such as Debtors Anonymous and Shopaholics Limited were formed, providing one of very few sources of support for dealing with this peculiarly contemporary behavior.

Advertising makes promises that can never be realized for the simple reason that most emotional commitments cannot be fulfilled within the realm of consumption. The link between emotional satisfaction and commodities is for the most part utterly specious, as Williams (1980, 189) notes: "The attempt is made, by magic, to associate this consumption with human desires to which it has no real reference." How, for example, can women's desire for independence and equality be fulfilled through dependency on cigarettes, even if, as Virginia Slims tells us, we've "come a long way, baby"? And what does *trying* Rogaine have to do with assuaging feelings of regret and inadequacy? There are far too many examples of the false promises made by advertising messages to list here.

We seek social status, respect, health, success, power, and control in the realm of consumption because these things are in such short supply in the social, political, and economic spheres. In doing so, we continue to look for happiness "in all the wrong places" (or so the country-western song goes). As Williams (1980, 190–191) points out:

> If the meanings and values generally operative in the society give no answers to, no means of negotiating, problems of death, loneliness, frustration, the need for identity and respect, the magical system must come, mixing its charms and expedients with reality in easily available forms, and binding the weakness to the condition which has created it. Advertising is then no longer merely a way of selling goods, it is a true part of the culture of a confused society.

Confused by the priorities of consumer culture, we seek satisfaction through commodities because of a failure of social meanings, economic values, and political bearings. As Williams (1980, 188) further notes, "To satisfy this range of needs would involve questioning the autonomy of the economic system, in its actual setting of priorities." Focus group insights have encouraged the creation of pathways of desire disconnected from any context other than consumption. And the transcendent properties of the commodity form, together with the magical preparations of advertising, have created an ambiguity that "obscures the real sources of general satisfaction because their discovery would involve radical change in the whole way of life" (Williams 1980, 189). In essence, the wizardry of advertising "ratifies the subjection of society to the operations of the existing economic system" (Williams 1980, 188). Consumers are thus distracted from participating in the very realm that would have an impact on their lives.

The historical trajectory of consumer culture has obscured social relations of power, and its mystification has prevented the public from even looking for well-being within the spheres that truly matter. The unhappiness, the misguided values, and the lack of psychic well-being and social worth so evident in contemporary consumer society find no remedy outside a cosmetic therapeutic discourse of consumption. The connections between personal life and political and economic processes only become more obscured. And as the external conditions of life become increasingly problematic, negotiating an economic environment characterized by high unemployment, continual recession, and social decline is ever more difficult. As the twentieth century nears its end, the quest for emotional well-being itself remains an elusive object of desire.

The lack of resources and of meaningful mental health care has left a void in American life. And many people have no means of learning the discursive and emotional strategies necessary to achieve emotional and personal fulfillment. It is no wonder that, given the great need for psychological assistance but with so few providers of those services to the general public, the media in the 1980s became the main forum for expressing such needs. The discourse of therapy is now particularly pervasive on television, where talk shows, dramatic series, and advertising language have capitalized on human dissatisfaction and picked up the mantle dropped by the therapeutic profession.

It should also come as no surprise that we would find the same therapeutic discourse of advertising incorporated within dramatic television series. In Chapter 4, accordingly, we will take a look at the baby-boom program *thirtysomething* in an effort to understand the extent to which the pseudotherapeutic language of contemporary advertising has become incorporated within entertainment programming design. We will then turn to the nonfiction format of the talk show and trace its development as a national forum for artificial therapeutic expressions.

4

Postmodern Theory and Consumer Culture

In the preface to his book *Consumer Culture and Postmodernism,* Mike Featherstone (1991, ix) explains that his interest in the study of postmodernism was an outgrowth "of the problems encountered in attempting to understand consumer culture, and the need to explore the direct links made between consumer culture and postmodernism by Bell, Jameson, Baudrillard, Bauman and others." He goes on to point out that postmodern theorists see "postmodern culture as the culture of the consumer society," and that they share the assumption that "the immanent logic of the consumer capitalist society leads towards postmodernism" (Featherstone 1991, 15).

Consumer and media culture have been centrally located in the discussion of postmodern theory—specifically, because advertising is really the essence of postmodern culture. Postmodernism is the age of the lost referent, an age in which the signs and symbols of culture have been torn from the material world. It refers to a world in which turkey parts spring from fields of grain and places of work are transformed into parks by microwavable food. Advertising largely accounts for the tangled visual terrain that describes the phenomenon of postmodernism. The multiplicity of images tied together with every new ad campaign forge yet another set of arbitrary associations, creating an endless play of depthless surface imagery.

Although it is still difficult to propose a unified definition of postmodernism, there is common ground shared by many authors, even those who do not use the term itself.[1] Frederick Jameson (1984) characterizes postmodernism, the "cultural logic of late capitalism," as a superficial juxtaposition of images pulled from a variety of past styles and recombined into a timeless pastiche of the present. This chaotic landscape has lost its temporal grounding and, hence, any connection with history. Without past or future, systematic connective meaning cannot be read from the signs and symbols of culture; chains of signifying codes no longer produce meaning. The resultant cultural disorientation parallels the historical shift in late capitalism from a society based on productive forces to one dominated by reproductive technologies (i.e., the media, electronic communications, etc.).

Jameson's portrayal of postmodern culture as a series of superficial and meaningless representations is very similar to Jean Baudrillard's (1983) analysis of contemporary culture. Central to Baudrillard's definition is the assertion that the real has been replaced by the "hyper-real." In this formulation, the cultural production of symbolic forms is all-encompassing and overwhelming. Culture is little more than a "hallucination of the real," a "simulational" world characterized by an endless series of copies of previous forms. Of course, meaning is lost, even to the extent that no perceivable distinction can be made between the real and the hyperreal, between image and reality—in Hegelian terms, between surface and essence. In Baudrillard's assessment, "TV is the world."

Many of the visual and cultural phenomena that theorists describe as postmodern are manifestations of promotional modes of discourse in contemporary culture. The ongoing incorporation of commodities at the core of contemporary life has accelerated the associative modes of communication so necessary in assigning value to products for sale. As we discovered in the last two chapters, promotional discourse rarely amplifies the actual manufacturing of a product or promotes its physical attributes to verify quality or benefits. Instead, emotional needs and connotative associations of all kinds are arbitrarily linked to products as the dominant mode of advertising discourse. Fleeting glimpses of a mythic bucolic past merge with images of turkey packaging in order to transfer warmth and tenderness, through association, to the product. History is lost in this endless pastiche of depthless representation. Again, as noted, no mention is made of the history of the turkey itself, or of those who "produced" it, how it was raised, what it ate. The multiple image fragments, the jumbled mergings of disconnected signs emptied of what Stuart Ewen (1988) calls the "material world," and what for Baudrillard is "the social," are primarily a consequence of this promotional discourse.

According to Baudrillard, the postmodern experience makes no sense because signification has been eclipsed by the sheer volume of disordered symbols, which, however meaningless, are nevertheless enchanting. As David Tetzlaff (1992, 49) points out, from the postmodern view "audiences are no longer seen to engage mass-produced culture on the level of ideology, myth or even pragmatic information." Thus consumers of postmodernity derive no meaning whatsoever; instead, they become fascinated "with the spectacular surfaces of media forms, the play of ever proliferating and intermingling signs and images disconnected from their meanings" (Tetzlaff 1992, 50).

In Baudrillard's formulation, meaning gives way to an aesthetic fascination with the endless simulations encountered on a daily basis, and the "everyday and banal reality falls by this token under the sign of art and becomes aesthetic" (1983, 151). Postmodern theorists offer aesthetic categories with which to evaluate and understand this new scene, because, they assert, sociological, political, and economic analyses no longer render understanding. Under this purview, the novel (dis)order that is postmodernism cannot be known through the old classificatory schemes of modernism. According to Jean-François Lyotard (1984), for example, there are no more "meta-narratives" in a world where the order that was once modernity no longer exists. And as Featherstone (1991, 9) has observed,

> For those who take seriously the implications of postmodernism as a mode of critical theorizing or cultural analysis, the attempt to produce a sociological understanding must necessarily fail as it cannot avoid totalization, systematization and legitimation via the flawed grand narratives of modernity: science, humanism, Marxism, feminism, etc.

Supplanting "the social" and other forms of explanation is the notion of the "aestheticization of everyday life." For Baudrillard (1983, 151) "art is everywhere, since artifice is at the very heart of reality." Aesthetic categories, then, become central to the evaluation of postmodernity. According to Featherstone (1991), "It can be argued that postmodernism—especially postmodern theory—has brought aesthetic questions to the fore." Interestingly, it has become fashionable among advertisers themselves to think of their work as forms of art.

Theater of the Mind

TOTEM is a term now popular in advertising, used by practitioners to express the mystique of fun, play, and creativity that they believe characterizes the product of their labors. It is an acronym for Theater of the Mind. Creation of the fantasy associations that tie anything and everything to products and their images is now described as an artistic labor of love that brings pleasure to the senses and enriches the imaginary landscape of the everyday. In the past, arbitrary associations that connected emotional well-being and intimate desires to products were referred to simply as the *soft sell,* a strategy distinct from the rational, informational techniques that appeal to reason. The new term, *TOTEM,* communicates a new attitude. Whereas *soft sell* once had the unwanted connotation of emotional manipulation, *TOTEM* celebrates the imaginary pleasures brought to you by the advertising industry. This thinking parallels postmodern analysis; as Featherstone argues, when advertising becomes art it is no longer a manipulation. Viewing advertising from an aesthetic context, "we get not just skepticism towards advertising's effectiveness, in that its capacity to persuade people to purchase new products—or indoctrinate—is questioned (Schudson, 1986), but a celebration of its aesthetic pedigree" (Featherstone 1991, 25).

Indeed, at one level, there is no doubt that TV and print advertising (and radio at its "best"), with their wild, fanciful imagery, mimic a liberated state of mind. The viewer cannot help but respond, upon gazing at a TV commercial for Swatch in which an animated man dives into a sparkling pool of water that turns into clouds. As he glides through the air, the viewer's lifelong desire to fly, expressed in perfect wish fulfillment, is brought to an ideal closure when the man reaches an island oasis. The worries of life are shed like the dying skin of an animated snake, who is reborn in brilliant hues in another Swatch spot. The animation itself, with its splendid colors, presents a world in which anything is possible and satisfaction is guaranteed—all beautifully crafted and tied to a watch.

The playful imagery in this ad is realized as immediate, if fleeting, pleasure. It gains autonomy from the necessities of life. The viewer's gaze is totally diverted from unpleasant social and political forces. It is fantasy, after all, that is part of life. And who is to say that it's a less important part of life than the rational? There is no doubt that watching the ad is more fun than going to work. How can this liberating, imaginary play be insidious?

Postmodern theory has proposed that the fanciful associations evoked by brilliantly colored snakes and flying humans now construct for us a world indistinguishable from the material one. But is it truly indistinguishable? After all, the advertisement exists to sell something, which, furthermore, is arguably overpriced. In fact, as with Nike ads, the imagery of the Swatch commercial is at odds with its material context. Such beauty makes it easy to forget that the purchase of an overpriced "stylish" watch, soon to be outdated and replaced, requires increased drudgery in the working world. After the point of purchase, when the watch has not fulfilled the promise of well-being, fun, and liberation, its disposal will contribute (as its production did) to the further destruction of beauty in the natural world so enticingly represented in the colorful animation of the compelling commercial. Again, we find the promise that well-being can be realized within the realm of consumption is a false one. The fantasy of the ad and the false promise itself have consequences. The watch has a material existence that lies hidden behind the "postmodern" surface.

However, the process of examining the false communication—the ad's inability to live up to its promise, along with the material reality (such as environmental destruction) connected to the fantasy image—is not nearly so seductive as gazing at the image.

Postmodernism and Production

Theorists of postmodernism define it as a profound historical shift, manifested primarily at the cultural level; but they also include (somewhat vague) assertions that the basic economic structure has undergone a transformation. Jameson (1984) speaks of a qualitative shift into "late" capitalism and stresses the influence of reproductive technologies. For Baudrillard (1983) the new informational and symbolic technologies have supplanted productive forces in what he says has become essentially a postindustrial age. Lyotard (1984) also emphasizes reproductive technology over productive forces and the "computerization of society." And Featherstone (1991, 13) focuses on the centrality of culture, which he now sees as overshadowing productivity: "It is important to focus on the question of the growing prominence of the culture of consumption and not merely regard consumption as derived unproblematically from production." This claim of a reordering of productive and cultural priorities by postmodernists occurs in a society where "a good deal of production is targeted at consumption, leisure and services and where there is the increasing salience of the production of symbolic goods, images and information" (Featherstone 1991, 21).

The proposal of an epochal shift to a world characterized as the "hyper-real," a world broken from the productive forces of modernism, to a global system based on informational technologies is a highly Eurocentric construct. This construct, in turn, is a consequence of the fact that much production is no longer carried out in the developed world, and that the remainder is given little thought. Much of the writing on postmodernism has high regard for the other and for the validity of the multiplicity of subjective views and formulations of the world. Postmodern theory rejects universalized concepts and canonical constructs of the real, determined by one set of social positioning. Therefore, postmodern theory's seeming disregard for the subjective experience of those who continue to labor in almost inconceivable conditions in Third World factories is highly contradictory.

The Eurocentric perspective on postmodernism is evident in the position that production and the commodity form are no longer central to consumer culture. Rather, the contention is that the symbolic culture of media images themselves, and advertising, has come to define the very world in which we live; it has become as real as the material one. But the fact that commodity production—the material world—has largely been removed from the purview of the developed world, and almost totally removed from cultural representation, leaving apparent only the powerful symbolic technologies used to sell products, does not mean that products are no longer manufactured. Clearly goods *are* still produced, and it ought to be obvious that production is central—even if it is no longer the object of cultural representation.

The fascinating, albeit arbitrary, associations of carefully wrought promotions that define this new postmodern era still sell commodities, which in turn have to be made. Indeed, all the wild juxtapositions of the symbolic consumer environment exist for the purpose of selling products. That the product is absent from many of those fascinating images does not mean it is no longer the point. And in order to continue selling the product, advertising continues to promote the mystification of the forces that produce it. That material activity is to a considerable extent what drives the world.

As noted in Chapter 2, the economy depends on consumer spending, and if the conditions of commodity production were associated with the product, spending would very likely slow down. While browsing through the glittering malls of the First World, the consumer *must not* think of actual working conditions when he or she comes across a clothing label that reads "Made in Indonesia." That would definitely take some of the fascination out of shopping.

The celebration of advertising and symbolic culture as that which constitutes the real is a point of view incapable of looking behind the symbols to an existing material world. Because the magical system of advertising has hidden the social relations of commodity production, they have been theorized and aesthetisized out of the picture. In this sense, consumer society has succeeded in hiding the very economic structure and social relations that account for its existence.

A separation has indeed occurred between the signs and images of postmodern culture, on the one hand, and the material world, on the other; but postmodern theorists universalize that loss of meaning. By positing a breakdown of signification as the primary characteristic of the contemporary mileu, they reject the attempt to understand cultural symbols as being imbued with social, cultural, or psychological meanings. A closer look at the way in which meaning is produced in advertising illustrates this disjuncture.

Images and Meaning:
Social Discontent and Consumption

In bold letters that consume the entire inside-cover page of *Rolling Stone* magazine (April 30, 1992), an advertisement screams, YOUR JOB STINKS. YOUR LOVE LIFE STINKS. THE GUY IN THE CAR NEXT TO YOU STINKS. IT DOESN'T GET ANY BETTER THAN THIS. On the facing page, in direct response to this lament, is an image of an empty desert road heading toward a horizon filled with that iconic referent—Monument Valley. This image is inserted into its companion text, which begins, "This is escapism."

The huge bold letters on the left side add up to a shrill pronouncement of distress that speaks directly to the subjective emotional and social frustrations of contemporary life. Facing that message on the right side, answering that grievance, is the open road. Stretched horizontally, slightly higher than midpage, the image positions the viewer behind the wheel of a car. This configuration engages the subject, by virtue of a very personal invitation, to become the driver and thus to participate in the fantasy escape. The promotional text, printed on a thin vertical strip of yellow that runs down the entire page, is visually aligned with the dividing line in the picture of the open road. The layout unifies and reinforces the meanings of both text and image.

Within the yellow strip, the promotional copy proposes the solution to the wail of discontent on the opposite page. Offered as an escape from the emotional stresses of difficult relationships, work-place frustrations, and antisocial feelings is a car stereo.

This is accelerating as the road clears and the CD drops into the slot and "U2's "Streets With No Name" begins. This is cranking it. This is leaving work early on Friday afternoon. This is the Clarion Car Audio 5770 CD AM/FM Stereo CD Player.

The message recognizes workaday malaise and encourages flight from the constraints of duty and responsibility into a world where uninhibited pleasure through consumption is the primary goal. It also incorporates the wild, even subversive, cultural expressions of rock 'n' roll and the drug culture of the 1960s. The ad continues: "This is sex. This is purple haze. This is rock 'n' roll." The social criticism and rebellious attitudes advocated in this (and many other examples of) advertising copy undeniably contain elements subversive to political and economic systems. Certainly these elements are not the symbols that hold existing social structures in place. Or are they?

The inclusion of Monument Valley offers a view of a particularly spectacular geologic formation. But this image does not serve merely as a scene of natural beauty at the denotative level. Rather, it is read as a cultural referent, meant to be recognized for its connotative meaning, as the primary signifying element for the West.

The mythic West stretches out in front of the windshield, the site of a long and continuing American preoccupation, whose meaning is now laden with successive layers of significance. The Old West, set in the vaguely pre-industrial past, became the symbol of the post–World War II American dream. Traversed by horses and the men bold enough to stay on them, it embodied the struggle and hope for what was once called the American Century. Movies and television westerns spoke to a society of endless opportunity and freedom, where bare desert landscapes waited to be mastered. They came to life with the sound of thudding hooves and the sight of dust (we could almost taste it through those early TV screens) kicked up by reckless cowboys come to conquer that terrain. Freedom was that last frontier where the brave and the strong lived by their own rules, with the help of their horses. The tenacious settlers battled the Indians, who, we now remember with a blush, were usually referred to as "redskins," and negative stereotypic portrayals "justified" their slaughter. Even then, middle-class Americans were under attack by people of color, who constituted the greatest obstacle to the fulfillment of happiness ever after in a little house on the prairie.

Monument Valley, and the West in general, as the cultural icon of the last frontier of personal strength and resistance, was most recently reinforced and transmuted in the outlaw road movie *Thelma and Louise.* Here, the codes of the Old West have become fragments intermixed with layers of newer signifying elements. Cars have long since replaced horses, and the symbolic freedom has a distinct contemporary twist: The road tracking inexorably toward Monument Valley symbolizes outlaw liberation. After the cops trail in the dust of Thelma's 1969 green convertible Thunderbird, outlaws, not law enforcement, are (at least for now) the celebrated proprietors of that terrain. As Thelma and Louise speed down the empty desert, hot and dry, the wind and sun remove the last signs of social constraints—the women's hair is no longer styled and their makeup has long since worn off. In the months following the movie, pictures of Monument Valley proliferated in ads framing everything from fashion layouts to automobiles.

But the speeding car on the open road of the New West depicted in the adver-tisement for a car stereo carries neither rugged cowboys nor women on the run from the forces of gender and state repression; rather, its occupants are urban malcontents (with jobs) escaping from social and psychological fantasies never fulfilled. Indeed, the society once portrayed as a dream come true, the embodi-ment of mythic strength, is now predominantly depicted as a nightmare. What lies ahead is no longer hope for an ever-improving way of life (with a little hard work and "elbow grease") but an admittedly temporary escape from a life that "doesn't get any better than this."

Yet these criticisms of the world in which we live are part of the same message that celebrates the achievements of that world by presenting advanced electronic technology as the elimination of discontent; within itself the problematic world contains its own solutions. The ad copy speaks directly to the spectator/buyer pre-senting the latest in audio technology as individual human empowerment:

> This is a removable chassis, single DIN unit that fits almost every car that's been around since you've been around. This is no skipping CDs, regardless of how hot or cold it gets. This is 100 watts of power served up the most efficient way known to mankind: 4 channels each delivering 27 watts respectively.

Through the world of things the insufferable world of work is obliterated, like the desert itself, as the car speeds down the empty highway. Ultimately, though, the message is one of acquiescence and submission to a world that must be accepted as unbearable. All hope for action that could or should be taken to change or improve it has been precluded. The only possibility for action is escape, and then only tem-porarily, from the unpleasant "real" world of work and traffic into the realm of con-sumption. But it is precisely the promise of weekend consumerist escape that keeps the young malcontents going back to work and putting up with all manner of abuse to obtain the income necessary to play the roles of stylistic urban weekend outlaws.

Thus dream-fantasies of noncompliance, mythic American icons of independence and rebellion, and the personalized identification with rock and roll form a package that appears highly subversive. But all this defiance is marshaled and subdued within the realm of consumption, providing false solutions to a disheartening environment while preventing the formulation of real ones. And all this complicated symbolic dis-course has been constructed to sell a car stereo, an item that has actual use-value. Why not just propose that the buyer use it to listen to music? Because the social meaning that sells the product is in the advertising message, not in the product itself.

The Loss of Meaning?

To say that the symbolic world has proliferated, that sequences of images have be-come more complicated and polysemic, and connotative meanings have sifted from one manifestation to the next, is not to say that they carry no signification.

Rather, signification has simply gotten more complicated, remote, and arbitrary, and it most certainly has become more difficult to understand or make sense of. But ultimately there are pathways that can be traced to social and especially psychocultural meanings. A rupture undoubtedly exists between the world of commodities and the material world. Analysis itself must work to recontextualize the two. To find disconnected meanings and connotative significations, analysis must at some point intersect with social and political history and then be reconnected to given material circumstances.

A terrible irony of postmodernism is that the most dramatic rupture of connections of significance has occurred between media theory and media practice. As media/market research steps up its quest to understand the psychocultural world so as to better tap into the powers of that world for its own persuasive purposes, postmodern theorists claim that this objective is not being achieved—and, for that matter, *cannot* be.

Baudrillard's (1983) analysis of postmodernity attempts nothing less than the restructuring of analytic thought. As he and others have theorized, because there is no difference between reality and the hallucination of the real, social and political categories are no longer relevant. So another set of categories, aesthetic ones, has been introduced, and with these categories we are to understand the cultural configuration. But this perspective is hindered by numerous analytical obstacles.

Consumer Culture as Art

Raymond Williams (1980, 184) points out that advertising is "in a sense the official art of modern capitalist society." Michael Schudsen (1989) has also noted that advertising is a particular type of art form that he calls "capitalist realism," the celebration of all that is positive about the current economic system to the exclusion of all that is negative. Postmodern theory has taken these points literally and seeks to understand consumer culture within an artistic mileu. One of the defining characteristics of the postmodern era is what Featherstone (1991), following Baudrillard (1983), has referred to as the "aestheticization of everyday life."

Accounting for at least part of the focus on advertising's artistic qualities would have to be the recognition that advertising has simply gotten much better. Williams made his observations about what he called the "magic system" in an essay written around 1960 (but published in 1980). When he referred to "the jejuned bravado of deeply confused men," he had in mind the advertising of the late 1950s: "It is in the end the language of frustration rather than power. Most advertising is not the cool creation of skilled professionals, but the confused creation of bad thinkers and artists" (1980, 190). At this point, Williams did not yet have to contend with, and had not predicted, the creations of the highly skilled professional marketers and artists working for companies like Nike, Reebok, Levi Strauss, and Coca-Cola.

Featherstone (1991, 25) argues that postmodern culture is characterized by "the migration of art into industrial design, advertising, and associated symbolic image production industries." This "migration" has led to the collapse of the boundaries between art and everyday life and to "the erosion of the special protected status of art as an enclaved commodity." Given the effacing of the boundaries between high art and mass consumer culture, as well as the "aestheticization of everyday life," postmodern theory posits that consumer culture should be evaluated and appreciated for its aesthetic qualities, over and above its function to persuade. As Featherstone (1991, 25) puts it, advertising has become a significant art form, at least in part, because of the creative work of artists themselves: "Many artists have relinquished their commitment to high culture and *avant-gardisme* and have adopted an increasingly open attitude toward consumer culture and now show a willingness to truck with other cultural intermediaries, image-makers, audiences and publics."

One might reply, from a slightly different perspective, that artists have had few alternatives but to truck with other cultural image-makers who have been incorporated within the media industry. Independent sources of income not tied to corporate funding (Schiller 1989) have been greatly diminished, as have other sources of income that allowed artists to subsidize themselves. Indeed, the final stages of gentrification of urban "artistic" enclaves priced artists out of the "loft scene." In the face of such economic circumstances, artists have been incorporated within the industry, in much the same way that, as Russell Jacoby (1989) has argued, public intellectuals were incorporated within academic institutions.

Advertising is, after all, a lucrative profession—a simple fact jokingly acknowledged by those who have chosen a certain lifestyle over struggling to remain independent. Consider, for example, the biographic sketch of Bert Berdis (of Bert and Barz & Company), which explains, among other things, his entry into advertising. Doing a standup comedy routine in Greenwich Village, Bert was approached by an advertising executive [AE] to write a comedy commercial. "What! And prostitute my craft?" he cried. "Too bad," replied the AE. "It pays a thousand bucks." The next hour found Bordello Bert firmly ensconced in McCann-Erickson's New York office.

Those who elevate advertising to an art form seem willfully naive about the creative restrictions that artists must confront daily once they enter that realm. Among other things, "creatives" are accustomed to designing a variety of alternative campaigns because it is the client who always makes the final decision. Speaking to a group of students, a top executive at Bert and Barz & Company recounted an incident in which three possible ad endings were offered to a client. In the executive's opinion, the client chose the least creative/artistic option because the other two did not emphasize the product effectively enough.

Another "creative" at Sloaman/Nussbaum, Inc., in New York, bitterly complained that advertising is losing its creativity because it has become so "research driven." As one analyst put it, "The bottom line to a market researcher is not how clever or creative an advertisment is. It must sell the product."[2] Especially given the advances being made in focus group and other techniques, creative inspirations are not permitted to override research results.

According to Featherstone (1991, 25), the expansion of artistic expression within consumer culture "entails a pluralistic stance toward the variability of taste, a process of cultural de-classification which has undermined the basis of high culture—mass culture distinctions." One can do little but applaud the tendency toward the deconstruction of symbolic hierarchies. In postmodern culture, art is no longer relegated to elite "highbrow" forms. Performance art and body art, which cannot be "mummified" within the enclaves of museums, have forced the boundaries and definitions of artistic expression. True, the emphasis on artistic expression and its incorporation into everyday life are admirable goals. It does not follow, however, that commodity culture and advertising should be declared art. An observation made by Raymond Williams (1980, 190) is pertinent here;

> The structural similarities between much advertising and much modern art is not simply copying by the advertisers. [They are] the result of comparable responses to the contemporary human condition, *and the only distinction that matters is between the clarification achieved by some art and the displacement [that is] normal to bad art and most advertising.* (italics added)

Today, more than ever, it is true that advertisers "must be seen as ultimately involved in the general weakness which they not only exploit but are exploited by" (Williams 1980, 190). The creators of Theater of the Mind did not invent commodity fetishism; nor, for the most part, do they make the corporate decisions that call for short-term profits at the expense of all other considerations. However, they do contribute to a symbolic environment that obscure the workings of the economic forces that drive postmodern culture. In this regard, Williams's distinction between art as clarification and advertising as "magic" contributes much to the debate about postmodernism.

From another perspective we must ask, Is there something that can be identified as an *artistic intention,* as contrasted to a *promotional intention,* and will it affect the work produced? In this connection, Doris-Louise Haineault and Jean-Yves Roy (1993) have offered one of the most compelling distinctions between art and advertising. Comparing the works of filmmakers such as Fellini and Bergman to the artifice of advertising's associative visual chains, they point out that art, unlike advertising, does not direct desire toward a universal settlement of affect; rather, it leaves unanswered the questions that have been raised, thus allowing individual contemplation to carry out the work of self-discovery. When viewing works of art, "one does not feel, as spectator, shielded from the screen. On the contrary, one is confronted by a real void, by a manifest gap so subversive that it sends us back to ourselves and suggests that we make sense, all of us for ourselves, of this void" (Haineault and Roy 1993, 110).

The difference between the associative work of art and advertising is that the latter never leaves questions open to be resolved by the self but, rather, forces meanings to close around the product because the motivation is, after all, to sell the product. Advertising sparks desire through polysemy, but it closes into monosemy, leaving the self with no way to find other meanings. In the end there exist no gaps in significance, no questions left unanswered.

Some advertisements fail to circumscribe meaning and remain polysemous. They more closely resemble a work of art, "because the multiplicity of meanings they evoke is never entirely recentered on an object. In general these are the advertisements most respected in the advertising business, that win prizes or satisfy the artistic wishes of their authors" (Haineault and Roy 1993, 111). But unfortunately they are also the ones that "least often appear on television." As noted earlier, the client typically prevails in closing expression around the product.

Consumption and Participation

Postmodernism's aesthetic perspective on consumer culture has led to explorations of the ways in which consumers actively participate in the realm of consumption, to "aestheticize" themselves and their surrounding on a daily basis. In a similar vein, Anthony Giddens (1993) argues that we live in a "self-conscious" time during which subjects actively "invent themselves." This line of thinking dates back to early modernism, as exemplified by the writings of Baudelaire. Michel Foucault (1986, 41–42) approvingly describes Baudelaire's profile of the dandy "who makes of his body, his behavior, his feelings and passions, his very existence, a work of art." And Featherstone (1991, 67) ties these aesthetic pursuits to the innovative uses of commodities made by those who consume them:

> The dual focus on a life of aesthetic consumption and the need to form life into an aesthetically pleasing whole . . . should be related to the development of mass consumption in general and the pursuit of new tastes and sensations and the construction of distinctive lifestyles which has become central to consumer culture.

According to postmodern theorists, an individualized artistic play takes place within consumer culture. The new "heroes" of consumer culture express "stylistic self-consciousness," as Giddens (1993) has noted. The consumer is "made conscious that he speaks not only with his clothes, but with his home, furnishings, decorations, car and other activities" (Featherstone 1991, 86). But these activities of consumer self-invention should not be restricted to young and affluent shoppers; rather, "consumer culture publicity suggests that we all have room for self-improvement and self-expression whatever our age or class origins" (Featherstone 1991, 86). In short, the heroes of consumer culture have a "sense of adventure"; they like "to take risks" and, in general, to "explore life's options to the full." They are also conscious that "they have only one life to live and must work hard to en-joy, experience and express it."

When (as in Featherstone 1991) the willingness within consumer culture to ex-periment with a variety of cultural expressions is contrasted to, say, moralistic "Thatcherism," which preaches abstinence and moderation, conservatism and rigid traditionalism, for ultimately nefarious political purposes, this line of rea-soning appears liberating, even defiantly resistant. This "calculating hedonism" seems a dramatic break from the social manacles that keep people from realizing their full potential in repressive political systems.

But on closer examination, the points at which the public participates in con-sumption reveal an interface fundamentally characterized not by pleasure and re-sistance but by acquiescence and conformity. As Hall (1986a) points out, empha-sis on the subjective experience of contemporary culture is a useful focus, but it has tended to underplay the processes that shape and restrict the ways in which people interact with mass-cultural forms. Consumers undoubtedly participate actively, but under what constraints? To what degree are they in control of cul-tural practices? Conversely, how are subjectivities influenced by external cultural images? And finally, is it possible to effectively consider these questions without taking gender, income, the psychocultural context, or even the material world into account?

Mediated Desire

In contrast to the focus on the discriminating and liberating participation of con-sumer culture is the more critical perspective of John Berger (1972), Stuart Ewen (1988), and William Leiss et al. (1989), among others, who emphasize the prob-lematic ways in which subjectivity is, in many cases negatively, influenced by con-sumer culture. Ewen (1988) argues that cultural standards of perfection "invite invidious comparisons" that consumers cannot live up to. Trying to emulate the air-brushed perfection of models who exist only in the world of advertising leads to failure and, ultimately, to "loss of the self."

This line of reasoning also dates back to modern and premodern writers. Notable is the work of René Girard (1965), whose analysis of fiction traces a theme of "triangular" or mediated desire. People suffer from mediated desire when sub-jective yearnings are not their own but, rather, have been instilled externally. The quest to emulate an admired Other leaves the Self empty and broken, out of touch with its own subjectivity and a deeper, *authentic* sensibility. This understanding of mediated desire was applied to the world of advertising in the seminal work of John Berger (1972) in *Ways of Seeing*. Berger argues that mediated desire is central to the artifice of publicity images. In other words, it is the desire to be like the glamorous, confident, and conceited personalities who inhabit the world of adver-tising that compels the consumer to want the products that they have.

By the same token, the spectator/buyer is "meant to imagine herself transformed by the product into an object of envy for others, an envy which will then justify her loving herself" (Berger 1972, 134). Thus within advertising culture, desire is not only mediated but commodified, moving further away from the realm of authenticity and into a truly alienated desire. It is a desire for commodity transformation—a desire to resemble the perfect Other. As Berger observes, this strategy leads to subjective confusion and ultimately, to discontent: "The publicity image steals [the consumer's] love of herself as she is, and offers it back to her for the price of the product" (Berger 1972, 134).

Berger's analysis extends to paintings of the nude in nineteenth-century art, which he compares to publicity images. He argues that, because women are constrained by the need to acquire social status through their ability to attract the "gaze" of men, they must learn to survey themselves through the eyes of the Other (men). This split of female subjectivity into Subject and Other is a consequence of defining the value and status of women by their appearance. Berger places advertising images within this context of European paintings, tying both forms of expression to the social and economic relationships from which they sprang.

Certainly the depiction of women has changed dramatically since the advertisements of the 1970s, which Berger uses as his guideposts. And to a considerable extent, women have succeeded in expanding the definition of their social roles. Today, they more frequently enter the public sphere and gain social status based on their actions. They demand respect for the people they are, not simply admiration for the way they look. Within advertising and consumer culture, however, the traditional view of woman as defined by men's gaze remains largely the same.

The progression of advertising campaigns for Hanes nylon stockings and pantyhose illustrates the transformation of the depiction of women within advertising, but it also reveals a convergence with more traditional portrayals. The ads of the 1970s told women that "Gentlemen Prefer Hanes" and rather insultingly depicted a man with wandering eyes peeking at Hanes-adorned legs. But the man was always paired with a woman whose unadorned legs were not on display. This woman had lost his attention, so he was surveying the legs of another. The message to the spectator/buyer was clear: The lack of Hanes nylons leads to the loss of the gaze. The woman has not lived up to society's standard of appearance dictating that legs should be on display for the pleasure of men.

This advertising campaign lasted for years and sold many pairs of nylons. The (not so) veiled threat was actually an ultimatum: Wear nylons or lose the interest of your man. Many woman chose to wear this brand of nylons, and some undoubtedly derived pleasure from it. But behind the (not so) gentle prodding was the menace of what would happen if one chose not to participate. Behind the dream-images of beauty and glamour that set standards of appearance lay the nightmare of rejection that would ensue when one did not measure up to those standards.

But we've come a long way from those bad old days. The more contemporary campaigns of the 1990s assert that "The Lady Prefers Hanes" and feature a series of well-known professional women wearing the product. Gone are the images of a woman living up to a male standard—that of the Other. She now dresses for herself. In one advertisement, Diane English, the influential creator of the television series *Murphy Brown,* is featured sitting in profile on a television set with her Hanes-adorned legs (see Figure 4.1). She is tilting back, her slim legs in the air, knees slightly bent, one held higher than the other. It is an alluring position but also an actively in-control position. And it characterizes much of the new and improved advertising that contains a double message. One part of the message speaks to women's desire for respect, success, and power based on who they are and what they have done. The other still asserts that appearance and the ability to attract the gaze have cultural salience. In fact, as the two halves of the message merge, power becomes associated with appearance.

This theme also has psychocultural appeal. The cultural construct of the *femme fatale* assigns women the power to control men, even to destroy them, by using their beauty and ability to compel men's attraction. Madonna, who has deliberately molded herself in the image of the "blond sex goddess" and become a copy of the original Marilyn, takes that power to its ultimate conclusion. Flaunting constructed beauty and appeal, she simultaneously denies the desire it provokes by engaging in auto-eroticism and remaining unobtainable. This double image is undoubtedly a form of power, one offered to young women who are invited to "invent" themselves according to the standards of attraction, keeping the power and control for themselves. Much of Madonna's appeal to young women is about such power.

Yet this form of power remains constrained within the bounds of patriarchy. A woman choosing to exercise it is confined to the given categories of attraction and appearance. Nonpatriarchal forms of womanly power would look much different, encompassing equal opportunity in the social and political realms as well as shared standards of personal respect and economic fairness. Ironically, Madonna has come close to achieving nonpatriarchal power through the financial success of her image creations.

Depictions of successful, empowered career women in advertisements can be viewed as valuable in themselves, inasmuch as they serve as cultural symbols that applaud women's independence. But we must take those images a step further and evaluate them on a social and economic level, for consumption must ultimately be understood within that broader framework. The fact remains that, although such advertisements appeal to women's desire for success and power, the commodity cannot satisfy these yearnings. One will not become independent, successful, or powerful by wearing Hanes, or any other pantyhose. Social and economic power cannot be bought within the realm of consumption—it cannot be purchased. It will come about only through structural social and economic change.

FIGURE 4.1 Diane English

In this intertextual advertisement, Diane English, the creator of the television series *Murphy Brown,* is selling Hanes nylons. Although the ad features an image of a professional, independent woman, commodified desire remains the persuasive device. What evoke desire are English's talent, wealth, and status—qualities that can neither be purchased nor acquired through use of the product.

The Hanes advertisement thus remains a model of commodified desire. It is the social position and economic rewards possessed by the model/Other, not necessarily the pantyhose, that appeal to the spectator/buyer.

Power and pantyhose may be connected, but only to the extent that wearing the product may help one conform to corporate dress standards. This "dress for success" code is in no way a liberating proposition based on boundary effacement and enjoyment. It merely facilitates dominant norms of appearance; there is no choice or creative play involved in purposeful conformity to external standards. After all, what pleasure could possibly be derived from being forced to copy a model because our economic livelihood depends upon it?

In addition, even though portrayals of liberated women are increasingly numerous, for every independent woman depicted there exists her counterpart who conforms to standards long ago defined by patriarchy—standards that continue to assert that appearance rules women's lives. Certainly enjoyment exists within these boundaries, and negotiating that terrain is (sometimes) fun. But the position of this counterpart is not an independent one; social and economic limits restrict its range of play.

The portrayal of men in advertising has also changed, at least at the level of social communication. If we look, for example, at the advertisements for Eternity, a cologne by Calvin Klein, we see an important shift in the social representation of maleness. The black-and-white photograph of a young man (father?), lying on his back with a small child on his bare chest, forces the boundaries of traditional portrayals of manhood. Representations such as this lift cultural restraints that define men as tough, stoic, and hard, not gentle or nurturing; they also open to consumers the possibility for experiencing a range of sensations traditionally denied by rigid gender boundaries.

As Irving Goffman (1979) first pointed out, historically male stereotypes within advertising have followed strict conventions. The chiseled, expressionless face of the Marlboro Man that epitomized the definition of maleness has at least been added to. Certain advertisements now openly encourage men to enjoy nurturing and tenderness. But here we must question the origins of such portrayals. Is the world of advertising truly on the artistic cutting edge, effacing gender boundaries and allowing for new experiences so that men might experience life to its fullest? Or have psychographics and survey results uncovered trends and inchoate desires that already exist, only to appeal to those longings to sell a product? One could argue that the images of man and child in the Calvin Klein ad are expressions of the "consciousness raising" of baby boomers, and that members of this generation have carried their new sensitivity into parenting. Advertising has followed that inclination merely in order to profit from it. Ewen (1989), among others, calls this practice "appropriation."

But once again we need to go further, to reach deeper into psychocultural categories. Do the Calvin Klein images actually offer liberating sensations and new experiences? Indeed, they do not: Those viewing the ad must do the hard work of making real experiences out of its dream-images. The images are not ends in themselves. They are pleasing to look at, but in no way can they be considered gratifications of the needs they appeal to. The realization of emotional sensitivity and nurturing entails the work of experimenting and learning how to be sensitive. It will not come from the purchase of a bottle of cologne. Nor does the act of consumption offer any guidelines as to how to achieve those emotional goals. The utopian image of bonding, father to child, cannot help men achieve that state. It can only give them the opportunity to purchase a simulacrum of that state.

Social progress capable of forcing political and economic change is also necessary before men and women will be able to redefine gender roles. And as we will see in the following chapter, on the television program *thirtysomething,* increased male sensitivity that might lead to gender equality is foreclosed when it is constrained within the bounds of patriarchal relationships.

In the pleasing world of consumption, images of male sensitivity are mingled with other images that reinforce positions of patriarchal male dominance. Take, for example, the series of magazine advertisements for B and B Brandy (see Figure 4.2). A young, affluent couple in evening clothes is shown in a hotel room. The man leans over the woman, grinning somewhat lasciviously as he clutches her hand. She sits at a table on which a drink is displayed, and her position of vulnerability is emphasized by the giggly look of intoxication on her face. It is the end of an evening and she holds the "Do Not Disturb" sign in her hand. He is poised to take action; she is perhaps the unwitting target.

The image is a clear invitation. It appeals to the masculine need for power, providing a fantasy of female vulnerability and the implicit approval of domination. We cannot evaluate this image without taking into consideration the cultural association of sex and power—and, ultimately, that of sex and violence—which brings to mind the issue of date rape.[3]

Finally, it is at the intersection of income, opportunity, and consumer culture that some of the most destructive manifestations occur. In many cases, the concentrated promotion of expensive (overpriced) commodities to low-income targeted "markets" has devastating results. Dwindling opportunities for economic prosperity, self-confidence, and personal worth, especially among low-income minority youth (as discussed in Chapter 7), are answered by advertising and consumer culture with promises to fill the void. These promises imply the realization of economic and personal needs within the sphere of consumption and commodity display. And so it happens that powerful role models of success—commodified African-American athletes appropriated to sell "trainers," athletic clothes, and "gear" of every variety—contribute to an environment in which children kill other children for the jackets, sunglasses, and running shoes that promise self-worth and social status. The moral indignation often leveled at those children influenced by such appeals is but rarely directed toward an industry that targets $150 commodities to vulnerable groups who can in no way afford such items, making promises of power and contentment in an environment that provides no other opportunities for such fulfillment.

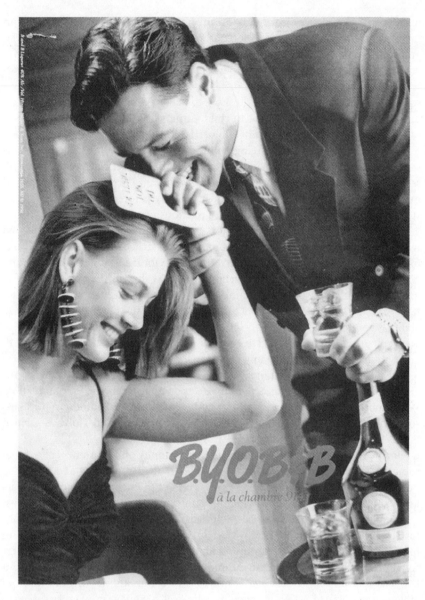

FIGURE 4.2 B and B Brandy Ad
Within the pleasing world of consumption, images of male sensitivity are mingled with other images that reinforce male dominance.

Fragmentation

Antithetical images of sensitivity and of power exist in the same media environment. The chasm separating the different messages is vast, confirming the postmodern assertion of overwhelming chaos in the multiplicity of disconnected signs and symbols. But meaning is not absent; it is simply that much harder to find in an increasingly complex media terrain.

If we look at marketing segmentation, a primary factor behind this increased complexity, the issue will become clearer. Indeed, marketing segmentation is a key to understanding the new media environment. As target markets become more closely defined, mass strategies are replaced by strategies that subdivide the public into smaller marketing units, thus demanding specific, tailored messages. Often, the same product is promoted to different market segments with correspondingly different advertising strategies. Focus group research targeting the psychocultural makeup of increasingly smaller market segments allows each campaign to speak directly to the needs of a specific subgroup.

This strategy is fraught with implications. For instance, it has resulted in a profoundly fragmented media environment. And subgroups of consumers have become accustomed to hearing their particular interests and desires specifically referred to in media messages. Frequently, the message to one market is of little meaning and interest to the next. Images of powerful women that promise equality and success are not targeted to men. Nor are images that promise men power over women placed in women's magazines. In short, images that challenge cultural boundaries generally do not reach a wider audience who might find them threatening. Tailored messages with images of power and control that target men at the expense of women only reinforce patriarchy, which, in turn, is not challenged by images of powerful women targeted only to women. And as long as patriarchy remains unchallenged, both men and women will find it difficult to "experience life to the fullest," making the "liberation" argument for advertising suspect.

Yet such advertisements do contribute to the widespread inability of groups to sympathize, understand, or tolerate the differences of others, with regard either to the opposite sex or to, say, a factory worker on the opposite side of the world. This media environment is clearly not centered on an empathetic view of the Other. Moreover, the lack of empathy facilitates the continuation of a system that subordinates the interests of the majority—consumers—to the interests of a financial minority. As David Tetzlaff (1992, 49) suggests, "Mass-produced culture does contribute mightily to the maintenance of the social order in late capitalism, but . . . it does so more through social and semiotic fragmentation than by forging any sort of ideological unity among the subordinate."

Lifestyle Advertising

Featherstone (1991) ties the notion of creative participation to a particular type of consumption—the expression of taste, personality, and image offered in lifestyle advertising. The "preoccupation with customizing a lifestyle" has become one of the ways in which daily life is aestheticized:

> Rather than unreflexively adapting a lifestyle, through tradition or habit, the new heroes of consumer culture make lifestyle a life project and display their individuality and sense of style in the particularity of the assemblage of goods, clothes, practices, experiences, appearance and bodily dispositions they design together into a lifestyle. (Featherstone 1991, 86)

In throwing off the constraints of "tradition" and "habit," lifestyle consumers are viewed as utterly independent, unaffected by the persuasions of advertising, which have proven to be every bit as powerful as "tradition" and "habit." It is as if the content of lifestyle advertising does not exist, even though the industry's implementation of lifestyle has been adopted by postmodernism as a sociological category.[4] A brief look at lifestyle advertising itself clearly reveals its inherently contradictory messages of freedom and conformity.

Consider, for instance, the television advertisement for Mazda's MX-3 that pictures a red sports coupe screeching to a halt in front of a dry-cleaning establishment (see Figure 4.3). In the window, one wildly colorful jacket stands out from a row of monochromatic garments. The television ad (as well as its print counterpart) asks, "You're not John Doe. Why drive his car?"

Those who drive the Honda Paseo, we learn from another ad, are brave enough to abandon mild and medium salsa and to go all the way to "hot." This nonconformist image of the young, the restless, and the wild promises the members of a youthful target audience that they will be set apart from the boredom of uniformity and the complacency of middle age. Their daring tastes will allow them to recognize themselves not only by what they wear but also by what they eat, which bars they frequent, and, especially, which the cars they drive— very fast.

But the lifestyle sell is a minefield of contradictions that the consumer is invited to negotiate without ever recognizing its dangers. One of the most glaring contradictions revolves around the tension between the desire for group belonging and the promise of individual expression. The intoxicating images of shared group experiences—the life-affirming connections between people who drink milk, Pepsi, Coke, and even Gallo wine—promise the security of belonging. But Mazda sells lifestyle with a new twist, as individualistic nonconformity. An irony exists in the tension between obedience and freedom: "Rebels" must obey the rules of image or risk not being recognized by their fellows as part of the rebellious group. They are a subset chiseled out of the mass by virtue of their adherence to a rigid set of standards. The message is ultimately one of peer-group pressure and lifestyle conformity. Of course, this conformity is heatedly denied

YOU'RE NOT JOHN DOE. WHY DRIVE HIS CAR? A car isn't just something you drive. It's something you wear. The Mazda MX-3 is a new sports coupe for those of us who'd never be seen driving a beige cardigan. Instead of making a car that everyone would like, Mazda engineers made a car that a few people will love. ✴ So what's to love about the MX-3? For a start, it's the only car of its kind with smooth V6 power. And suspension that lets it change direction quicker than a politician in an election year. ✴ Plus a fold-down rear seat that is widely rumored to be more spacious than some Manhattan studio apartments. ✴ These are just a few of the reasons you might love the new Mazda MX-3. But if it's not for you, that's okay. It's not for John Doe, either.

THE MAZDA MX-3 GS

The only 1.8L, 24-valve V6 in its class. Plus 4-wheel independent suspension and disc brakes (ABS optional). And a 36-month/50,000-mile limited warranty with no deductible, "bumper-to-bumper" protection. See your dealer for details. So where do you find one? Call 1-800-639-1000.

mazda
IT JUST FEELS RIGHT.

© 1993 Mazda Motor of America, Inc.

FIGURE 4.3 Mazda Ad

An advertisement for Mazda's MX-3 pictures the red sports coupe at a halt in front of a cleaners. In the window, one wildly colorful jacket stands out from a row of monochromatic garments. The ad asks, "You're not John Doe. Why drive his car?" The ad's TV counterpart features an assemblage of wild symbols that represent distinction from conservative establishment culture—fast-paced edits of tattooed punk youth and apple pie hitting the pavement. These nonconformist images of the young promise a youthful target audience that it will be set apart from the boredom of uniformity. But an irony exists in the tension between obedience and freedom: "Rebels" must obey the rules of image or risk not being recognized as part of the rebellious group. The message says "Conform and be different," at one and the same time.

through an assemblage of wild, uncommon symbols of distinction from conservative establishment culture—fast-paced edits of tattooed punk youth and apple pie hitting the pavement. Thus does contradiction implode in a message that says "Conform and be different," at one and the same time, as any such message must. The object is to sell the commodity, not to challenge behavior.

Being truly nonconformist would, of course, mean jumping off the acquisition treadmill and opting out of the consumer culture image machine. It would mean defining oneself (and establishing a sense of character) in ways less superficial than the purchase and display of commodities that confer social status. The very industrial infrastructure of economies of scale requires that mass-produced products be sold to a mass market, but a mass market consisting of consumers eager to be distinguished as individuals. Lifestyle conformity pushed as individualism is only the latest manifestation of this contradiction. The younger audience is sold an image of wild nonconformity—to which it must conform if it wants to belong.

Note, however, that as a marketing strategy, the grouping of lifestyle in terms of shared buying patterns does not correspond directly to sociological or political categories of lifestyle such as interest groups, subcultures, or communities. Thus, when a particular group or television audience is defined as a target market and lifestyle group, we must ask, How does the marketing process begin to influence the definition and representation of that group? As advertising has come to dominate television programming, the concept of lifestyle permeates the creative design of television fictions. We will consider this issue in the next chapter, which analyzes *thirtysomething*—a program whose creative/fictional representation of the baby-boom generation was greatly influenced by the logic of lifestyle marketing.

Of Authentic Desire and Alternative Pleasures

From the logic of postmodern theory we can formulate the following equation: No meaning can be evidenced from consumer culture, but the merger of art and industry has produced the art of the everyday and created an environment of aesthetic fascination and enjoyment. The assertion that symbolic culture, including advertising, should be evaluated as a form of artistic expression leads to the notion that advertising should be considered independent of its objective to persuade or sell commodities—and, therefore, that its cultural role as artistic expression and pleasurable realization should be defined as the principal evaluative categories.

According to this formula, one reinforces elitist symbolic hierarchies of taste by discounting the enjoyment derived from consumption. So postmodernism abandons critical theory as an "elitist critique" that made "dubious distinctions between real and pseudo individuality, and true and false needs" (Featherstone 1991, vii). Critical theory is viewed by postmodern theorists "as looking down on the debased mass culture and as having little sympathy for the integrity of the popular classes' pleasures. The latter position has been strongly endorsed by the swing to postmodernism" (Featherstone 1991, vi–viii). Though Featherstone warns that this quest should not "merely entail a reverse populist celebration of mass pleasures," postmodernism offers no alternative framework for critical evaluation of the inherently persuasive discourse of advertising. That would be to view culture as manipulation. Instead, postmodern theory is interested in "conceptualizing questions of desire and pleasure, the emotional and aesthetic satisfactions derived from consumer experiences, not merely in terms of some logic of psychological manipulation" (Featherstone 1991, 13).

Just as critical questions are brushed aside by postmodernism's focus on aesthetic categories and assumed liberating participation, so also pleasure as a defining category is advanced unproblematically. The postmodern assertion that pleasurable sensations and iconoclastic tastes are realized through consumer culture fails to examine the persuasive messages tied to the products themselves. Specifically, it fails to assess the ability of the advertisement to deliver on its promise of enjoyment. It is the promise of pleasure in the advertisement that is key, not the pleasure derived from the product itself. As we saw in Chapter 3, material aspiration, "having things," is far less important to people than the emotional states of well-being so often promised in advertisements. Ads evoke authentic desires and pleasures, but fulfillment of emotional needs simply cannot be bought for the price of the product. Although authentic yearnings are addressed by the admittedly well-crafted, often aesthetically pleasing images in effective advertising, these images need to be seen fundamentally as emotional persuasions. After all, advertisements have been designed not to fulfill their promises but to sell products.

Postmodern theory, applied uncritically, encourages us to be dazzled by the shining surface of the world of consumer culture. It does not go beneath to decipher the strategies and false promises hidden by that surface. Certainly some pleasure is derived from consumption, but the profound and authentic new sensations and liberating experiences that advertisements associate with products cannot be fulfilled. The dissonance created by this aesthetic of consumption leads inevitably to dissatisfaction and emotional poverty. If one looks too closely at such details, the shining commercial surface begins to crack. Beneath is an opaque wall into which authentic human desires and satisfaction eventually crash.

Advertising has come to the attention of psychoanalysts who assert that its images are indeed invested with meaning—meaning that emerges from the language of unconscious desire or avoidance. Advertising creates a world in which psychocultural symbols promise that a pair of shoes will alleviate psychological fears and a car stereo will make an unbearable world bearable. As Haineault and Roy (1993, 110) argue, "The fullness of advertising presents itself . . . as a stopgap against authentic desire, as a blinder, but above all as a perversion," ultimately of the self. Again, as noted in Chapter 3, ads evoke needs and desires to sell products, not to satisfy those needs and desires.

Consumer culture contains the search for human well-being within the simulational world of consumption. The promotion of product solutions to social and economic problems has become not only the easy way out, but the only way out. As consumer culture increasingly comes to define social life, the rupture between personal well-being and political and economic forces makes appropriate participation seem impossible. Compared to the pleasing discourse of advertising, the political and economic worlds appear ugly, corrupt, and impenetrable. Within this context, advertising has become a kind of national pseudotherapy, making people feel better about increasingly intolerable conditions. And this therapeutic discourse, the primary practice of advertising, now also penetrates every aspect of commercial television.

∾   ∾   ∾

Observations by Baudrillard (1983) and others regarding postmodern culture are accurate and sensitive descriptions of what consumer culture *looks* like. However, when postmodernism goes beyond a description of cultural phenomena to attempt a theoretical explanation, it fails to understand and explain what underlies that appearance. By rendering superficial glamour and dislocation a positive aesthetic, description of the surface is believed to be a theoretical explanation. And so theory, rather than being an attempt to understand, becomes a proud mystification. Scannell, et al. (1992, 3) have referred to postmodern theory as a "retreat from reason." They point out that "the possibility of rational social inquiry producing valid knowledge of the workings of the social world . . . is incompatible with the philosophical basis of postmodernism." It is true that material meaning has been lost. Or, rather, it has been supplanted, not by the absolute absence of meaning but by a set of arbitrary psychocultural meanings that must be examined and reconnected to the material world. By accepting depthless, surface images as meaningless but real, analytic postmodernism relinquishes the quest to understand the forces, power, motivations, and processes that underlie those symbolic surfaces.

Advertising, and the wealth of resources and technologies applied to selling, has become so sophisticated that postmodern theory now seeks to evaluate the products of promotional culture primarily from an artistic/aesthetic point of view. In doing so, it takes cultural analysis down a path distinctly less critical of consumer culture than one might expect to be appropriate given its problematic nature.

The nature and meaning of the associational techniques of advertising are still being discovered. Associative language has demonstrated its ability to wield enormous social power. At the same time, little is understood about the precise nature of such techniques. This is cause for concern to Haineault and Roy (1993, 97), who assert that associative logic "is one of the most complex [subjects] our modern knowledge has had to consider." Its persuasive abilities has devastating consequences for the self, as "the (global) strategy leads to the everyday apprenticeship of the perversion of self. It is there, it seems to us, more than in the market economy, where analysis should remain extremely vigilant" (Haineault and Roy 1993, 106). Understanding the advertising mechanisms that undermine the authentic self is key to understanding advertising. But our assessment should not stop there. If a truly global and complete picture is to emerge, the analysis of advertising and consumer culture in general must be reconnected to the "market economy." Only then will such an analysis be capable of explaining how the strategies of advertising and consumer culture operate to prevent a social and economic context within which the public might achieve subjective well-being. As we have seen in previous chapters, the perversion of self, the market economy, and advertising are intimately connected.

And now the associative language of advertising has been fully incorporated into a variety of television programs, including nonfiction forms. In Chapter 7, for instance, we will see how the discourse of advertising, when applied to "reality"-based programming, obscures social, economic, and political processes. But before that, in the next chapter, we will turn our sights toward television program design and discover how it has been affected by advertising and the ethos of consumerism. Lifestyle marketing was a significant force behind the creative design of the baby-boom series *thirtysomething*. As we shall see, reinforcement of the consumer imperative led to the program's embrace of advertising's culture of therapy and to Hope's role as a "new traditionalist."

5

Thirtysomething, Lifestyle Consumption, and Therapy

In Chapter 1 I examined the unity of purpose between programming and commercial messages. Throughout the 1980s demands on programmers to provide appropriate vehicles for advertising messages influenced creative strategies in profound ways. As audiences became more closely defined demographically, programming and advertising campaigns dovetailed. Marketing strategies and the design of programs themselves together now fulfill the consolidated purpose of commodity presentation.

The television program *thirtysomething* was developed to target baby boomers, demographically defined as those people born in the immediate post–World War II period between 1945 and 1955. By the 1980s they made up the largest segment of adults at the height of their income-earning years. A spate of programming was developed to reach this audience, and in the process a generation was transformed into the largest and most significant target in the history of market segmentation. *Thirtysomething* illustrates a creative process heavily influenced by the marketing imperatives that propelled it. The defined audience was a target market, and the show itself conformed to consumer logic. Even though *thirtysomething* never achieved higher than a 25 rating, the majority of its viewers had incomes of $60,000, making them a highly desirable market. These were not just boomers but well-off boomers. Many others outside this target audience were also invited to engage in imaginary aspirations of the lifestyle depicted.

Between Community and Lifestyle Enclave

One of the most intriguing aspects of *thirtysomething* was its appeal as *community*. Even though the story of Michael and Hope was a contemporary ode to a newborn nuclear family—an electronic realm in which Father really does know

118

best—the parent-child relationship was mysteriously unimportant and virtually absent from their lives. (It did, however, become a subtheme of the breakup of Nancy and Eliot.) Instead, seven main adult characters with various relationships to one another interacted, at what appeared to be a deep emotional level, as a community. Family, marriage, and children were talked about between these friends far more than they were dramatized. It was the drama of adult friendship and the struggle for a sense of meaning, acceptance, and belonging that captured the imagination of its baby-boom viewers.

These images were intoxicating to a generation of people whose youthful experimentation included a variety of alternative communal living situations. Their relationships often extended beyond the boundaries of traditional family life, much to the dismay of their parents. The boomers' continuing need for a sense of community (and the loss of that community in the 1980s) was recognized by the creators as one of the defining themes of *thirtysomething*. As program producer Marshall Herskovitz told *Philadelphia Magazine* (Fried 1988, 202–204), he was reaching out to a generation who felt "cut off from the institutions of their youth, [and thus experienced] the lack of community."

The portrayals of adult relationships on *thirtysomething* were reflected in numerous advertisements that punctuated and reinforced the program's main themes. One ad for Gallo wine depicted an upscale kitchen full of party guests. A male chef cooks a gourmet meal, with salmon as the main course. A woman with long blond hair, bearing a stiking resemblance to the actress who plays Nancy, is in charge of supplying the wine. The kitchen, lavish in the style of Pottery Barn or Pier 1 Imports, is crowded with adults sharing the good feelings of one another's company, with no children in sight. Every aspect of the ad's depiction is reminiscent of the program. Accordingly, the product—Gallo wine—is incorporated into the cultural attitude of the program, representing the unity of entertainment with product promotion.

What looked at first glance like a depiction of community on *thirtysomething* was actually what Robert Bellah and his colleagues (1985) have defined as "lifestyle enclave" masquerading as authentic community. The characters on the program never seemed to connect in any genuine sense, remaining always a phrase away from mutual understanding and peace of mind. The term *yuppy angst* became a derogatory catch phrase for the program, as week after week the characters' struggle for meaning and intimacy seemed to descend into a nagging whine of spoiled discontent. This was no accident. Ultimately, as we shall see, the representation of a lifestyle enclave is incompatible with a more genuine portrayal of communal relationships. According to Bellah et al. (1985, 335), a lifestyle enclave is a group of people whose common identity is forged through "shared patterns of appearance, consumption, and leisure activities." This definition is also recognizable as a set of marketing categories. With media marketing as the starting point— defining a generation through the rubric of lifestyle—the program was doomed to fall victim to the numerous contradictions of marketing logic.

Lifestyle as Programming Strategy

Lifestyle marketing is not about designing advertising campaigns that provide information about the benefits of using any particular product. Rather, lifestyle images always speak about social relationships. The products displayed signify the distinction of shared good taste, and the images of group conviviality confer a sense of belonging on those wise enough to select products that communicate to others what type of people they are.

The strategy of lifestyle marketing incorporated within *thirtysomething* accounted for much of the program's content, and especially its contradictions. Lifestyle messages promise a sense of group membership, but membership earned through commodity consumption. It is this logic of lifestyle that, as a set of marketing relationships, is incompatible with the authentic needs of human relationships. The "yuppie angst" of *thirtysomething* was the failure of community denied by the lifestyle epitome that drove the program.

The construction of lifestyle images was particularly influential in determining the *look* of the show. The art direction and set designs provided the defining space for dramatizing the culture of lifestyle. The carefully accessorized backgrounds were full of eye-catching art, design objects, and furniture, depicting a professional lifestyle in which good taste was continually on display. As one reviewer, Roberta Smith (1990, 35), noted, the Steadmans' furniture "could have come entirely from stylish shops in SoHo." The dining room featured a "Stickley-type breakfront . . . that Barbara Streisand probably wouldn't mind adding to her Mission-furniture collection." An antique wicker set was noticeable in the sunroom, and setting the stage in the bedroom was "a blond wood bed that says French (or maybe Swedish) Country and a black-and-chrome lamp that says high-tech." Careful attention was given to visual details, because as Scott Winant, the supervising producer, observed, "What may be perceived as a small point may actually register subconsciously with the audience" (Smith 1990, 40). Because of the these and other "artistic" references the program was praised for its creative innovations, which reviewers claimed set a high standard of quality for television. But as Smith (1990, 40) admits, "The art here leans toward the commercial variety, just as the creative dilemmas take place in unusually cushy surroundings."

Lifestyle messages constantly tell the consumer to scan the social landscape for the latest indicators of self-worth and social distinction. The social identities of those on the cutting edge of trend require "avant-garde" taste (albeit a de-clawed one) and the economic wherewithal to express that mark of distinction. Style says "success," the ultimate indicator of social standing.

The Steadmans' house is a veritable display case ("a Noguchi lamp here, a Christo poster there") of what can be referred to as "positional goods," defined by Robert Leiss et al. (1988, 249) as "things that allow us to detect social status differences among individuals; their chief value lies in the fact that some persons have them and others do not." Even though the Steadmans never express an interest in collecting, such rare items as a "heavily framed Frank Lloyd Wrightish architectural drawing was glimpsed in the stairwell" (Smith 1990, 35). Yet all this merchandise, laden with social meaning, arrives mysteriously. It would be gauche for people as hip as Hope and Michael to be seen queuing up at the department store or boutique making purchases and discussing mundane material acquisition. But their hipness is a particular brand of 1980s hipness. It is not the marginal anti-establishment cool that defined the 1960s. By the 1980s baby boomers were being asked to redefine their notion of hip, to abandon out-of-date marginality and use new categories of *consumer taste*. The material context expressed an attitude of economic privilege and commitment to a lifestyle in which immense value is associated with expensive possessions.

The world of lifestyle is a world in constant flux, inasmuch as today's product indicators are soon meaningless relics of yesterday's fad—or, worse, embarrassing reminders of outdatedness. Taste must always change. Acquisition can never be complete because style dictates taste—the primary indicator of social place—and, as Stuart Ewen argues (1988), changing styles propel consumer society. Consumer society always "recognizes an open-ended set of competitive situations, . . . new symbols of success to be striven for" (Leiss et al. 1988, 250). And, indeed, Hope and Michael were on their way up. The task of art director Brandy Alexander was to keep the Steadman house "in a constant state of renovation" (Smith 1990, 40). Consistent with the logic of consumption that propelled the program, the set of *thirtysomething* was continually reworked to reflect the culture of consumption it validated.

But taste expressed through consumption is expensive and can be sustained only through an ever-increasing corporate income. Maintaining the viewers' admiration for the Steadmans by means of carefully accessorized backgrounds kept Michael Steadman doing the long-term jog on the corporate treadmill. His steady climb up the ladder is a main source of drama and tension in the latter part of the series. He and Eliot, after the financial failure of their own agency, give up on small business and start working for an unscrupulous corporate powerhouse, Miles Drentell (played with cool irony by David Clennon). DAA, an advertising agency in the Franklin Furnace architectural style of historic Philadelphia, is also rich with decor—as often explicitly remarked upon in various episodes. At DAA, Michael's star just keeps on rising. Winning his samurai battles with Miles gains him income, status, and increased spending power. But Michael's economic conquests come at the expense of his own need for community. At various points, Gary, Hope, Eliot, and Susannah all have trouble dealing with Michael's newfound wealth and corresponding corporate power.

Michael's corporate quest, rewarded by status and income (often achieved by neglecting his family), is a drama informed by the commercial values of consumer culture. The program dramatizes the contradictions embodied in consumer culture inasmuch as the hopes for any real sense of community are quickly dashed by the drive to express self-worth through monetary success. In short, the message of lifestyle embodies a set of market relations with negative social consequences. As Fred Hirsch (1976, 109) puts it, "To the extent that marketing and advertising appeal to individuals to isolate themselves from . . . groups—to get ahead or to protect their positions—they are socially wasteful." The expression of social status through the continual acquisition of expensive products is antithetical to cohesive social relationships, because getting ahead means leaving your community behind. Social-status mobility exists within a set of hierarchical relationships that are counter to cooperative community practices. The social relationships of community are egalitarian and supportive. They demand solidarity and a united struggle against forces that undermine such unity or the integrity of any one of its members. The loss of authentic community is inevitable when upscale lifestyle becomes the fundamental creative principle.

Indeed, if "all are urged to get ahead, many are likely to have their expectations frustrated" (Hirsch 1976, 109). As Michael rises, he leaves Eliot behind. Eliot's inferior corporate position strains, and almost destroys, their friendship. There is never a hint that Michael and Eliot should approach Miles together and bargain for equitable pay for both. Michael refuses to discuss his promotion with Eliot; he even tries to hide it from him. When Michael gets his raise he does not tell Eliot, but not out of any sense of social injustice or economic disparity about the arbitrariness of corporate salary scales, nor out of a sense of loyalty to a member of his community. He doesn't tell Eliot because he remembers his own jealousy as a boy, when a friend of his got a better bicycle than he did. He doesn't want Eliot to express that same jealous response. Michael's actions are detrimental to community because, according to Bellah et al. (1985, 335), they are "undertaken in the interest of the self at the expense of commitments to others." Once again the distinction between community and lifestyle enclave is significant: "Community is a group of people who are socially interdependent, who participate together in discussion and decision making and who share certain practices that both define the community and are nurtured by it" (Bellah et al. 1985, 333); but Michael's actions follow the primary logic of lifestyle enclave, in which its members "are not interdependent, [and] do not act together politically."

The Defining Role of Character

"Subject comes from character and only from character; that was our group mantra," explains Richard Kramer, one of the show's producers (Cole 1991, 568). Even though the producers insisted that their work was informed by a creative artistic process, it is clear that the depictions of the *thirtysomething* characters were primarily informed by the program's commercial requirements. These characters are confined to a world in which complexity and contradiction finally capitulate to the commercial world. As the main character, Michael holds the dominant perspective. We are asked to see the world through his eyes, as he struggles to adapt to a 1980s world with a set of 1960s values—an undeniably painful process. The show's disingenuousness emerges, however, when Michael, placed in such dilemmas, compromises his values without fail. With every move he glides from an old life into a new one, but it is the facile depiction of his transformation from social liberal to corporate conservative that renders the depiction a counterfeit. Michael, no matter what he compromises or how he capitulates, is always portrayed as morally correct.

Between jobs, Michael delves into the world of noncommercial creativity and takes a writing class. His writing is stilted—the themes stolen from the experiences of other people's lives. After this failed attempt he succumbs to Drentell and starts working for DAA. Through an artful but dishonest script his creators turn his defeat into a personal triumph with these words to Hope: "I could wear down enough pencils to make a forest," he intones, "but I could never come up with a sentence that'd be worth as much to me as you are." He is a master at rationalizing his compromises, often made of a result of his own failings. Michael's character flaws are thus ignored; and worse, as critic Lewis Cole (1991, 569) has rightly observed, "all his shortcomings are portrayed as ennobling attributes. . . . His desire for other women proves his fidelity to Hope—not his simple fear of having an affair; his contempt for his younger brother demonstrates his peerless grasp of reality—not his childish wish to beat his sibling."

In a similar vein, Cole describes Ken Olin's character as "emotionally remote"; he is "a coward" who "emulates a boss he despises and excels at a job he believes unworthy of his artistic talents." At least Steadman has the "good sense to surround himself with friends more interesting than himself." Michael accepts his quirky friends, but, as Cole suggests, he does so "only to feel superior to them." Michael Steadman, then, is recognizably a brooding, snobbish, condescending corporate climber, willing to compromise his values at the slightest twist of the plot—but the program never presents him as such. As the main character, Michael is portrayed as the "good guy," which has come to mean that anything he does is acceptable—not that his actions are good.

Mark C. Miller's (1990) insightful discussion of character depiction in American films during the 1980s is relevant here, because a similarly unsettling rendering is notable in the filmmaking of that period. Miller argues that because films are required to be vehicles for "product plugs," a practice that dominates the big screen, "the happy ending" is now a governing principle. In a surprising number of contemporary films, no matter how contradictory, sad, or disturbing the plot or characters, all problems melt away in the filmic device of the feel-good grand finale. Nearing the conclusion, we are left with "just the star himself, famed face transfixed in a wide, phony smile . . . as if posing for a series of publicity shots." Then the "movie finally dead-ends into a promotional photo, an image that—all at once—extols (some) celebrity [and] . . . invites you to identify with that bright entity—like any ad that features someone famous" (Miller 1990, 244). Just as film endings descend into convenient harmony for commercial purposes, *thirtysomething*'s endings present a false unity as problems neatly resolve. Neither the characters nor the viewers feel good after an episode of *thirtysomething,* but for all the messiness of the situations Michael grapples with—many of which challenge his conception of himself as a principled individual—he nevertheless accepts, with great aplomb, a new life based on materialism, acquisition, and some of the worst avarice of corporate culture. In the process, the decisions he makes are usually tacked on as endings to drawn-out struggles that seemed irreconcilable. Cole (1991, 568) points to this inconsistency in noting that "the resolutions of *thirtysomething* episodes constantly confound the characters."

In one sequence, Gary visits Michael in his new, vast office. Gary's character is the last vestige of the critical outsider by virtue of his 1960s worldview, symbolized by his long hair. A university professor denied tenure, Gary was forced to take an inferior position at a lesser-known institution. His personal crisis continues as Michael's star rises. During his visit with Michael, Gary's discomfort and backward thinking about corporate America dissolve as they decide that their friendship is too important to let Michael's success interfere. Gary's unease, following his admission to Susannah that he is jealous of Michael, is defined not in terms of a principled objection to corporate advertising, arbitrary notions of status that imply inequality, or unjust salary scales between corporate and educational work, but rather as an expression of personal insecurity. In *thirtysomething,* conflict is never social; on the contrary, it is of a personal nature, worked out through a discourse of therapy (as discussed below). Once Gary's unhappiness has been defined as the ignoble emotion of childish jealousy, he must overcome such petty indulgences and gracefully accept Michael's good fortune as an adult.

The theme that the criterion for assessing friendship has nothing to do with shared social or moral concerns is underscored in many episodes. The message asserts again and again that choosing friends or judging peers (or anyone else) cannot be accomplished using a standard based on integrity. The experience of the world of private feelings is posited as isolated from any commonly held set of shared values or social responsibilities—which would exist if *thirtysomething* were a community.

In commercially dominated popular culture, it is hard to find characters made powerful by the force of their own convictions. Characters modeled, for instance, after the judge in the film *The Music Box* are all but nonexistent. A Jew, this judge nevertheless remains impartial during the trial of an accused Nazi. He is truly a mythic character who, as objective arbiter, cannot be swayed by personal feelings. His judgment, removed from narrow private interests, will render an unimpeachably just decision. An interesting exception on television was the lawyer, in *Shannon,* created by independent filmmaker John Sayles. Shannon actually quits a high-paying corporate job because of the company's unscrupulous business practices. In fact, the character is also explicitly emotional and personal; he is even allowed a depth of character, with principles. The series was short-lived.

Michael, by contrast, is the "new-age sensitive guy" who justifies all the concessions he makes to what he considers a corrupt social and economic world by claiming that his behavior is motivated by commitment to a force greater than himself—his family.

Family

Most of the intimate conversations that dominate *thirtysomething* emerge from a very limited set of motivations defined strictly in terms of private desires and familial relationships. When the characters do express a desire for social connectedness, it is quickly channeled through a dialogue that relentlessly presents private family life as the only meaningful realm of existence, the last hope for happiness and self-fulfillment. In one episode, Gary contemplates his life as a teacher; distraught by his lack of "success," he stays up late, falls asleep on the couch, and dreams. A vision of Emily Dickinson appears. Having earlier struggled to untangle her poetry, he asks her for an interpretation:

GARY: Uh . . . could you . . . could you . . . I'm in big trouble here. . . . Could
  you explain this to me, please."
EMILY: Explain what?
GARY: (*holding up the book*) This . . . This . . . all of this. I mean, you wrote
  it, you're Emily Dickinson. You must understand it. God knows I don't
  and I have to.
EMILY: Why?
GARY: Because I have to explain it to my class. I have to be able to explain
  myself to my friends.
EMILY: Why?
GARY: Why? Because if I can't explain what you wrote, then I'm not even a
  teacher. And if I'm not even a teacher, then I'm nobody.
EMILY: You? You seem so confident.
GARY: Yeah, well that's an act. That's all an act. I feel like a total failure.
  Everyone I know is more successful than I am. . . .
EMILY: You have no sense of perspective. Just look! You have this beautiful
  poem right under your nose and you're not even grateful.
GARY: (*pointing to the book*) Which poem? Show me.
EMILY: It's not my poem, it's yours.
GARY: (*whispering as Emily leaves*) Emma.

Emma is Gary's baby daughter. In this sequence, Gary is compelled to shift the focus of concern away from his need to be an educator and toward that age-old enterprise—reproduction. What had been important to him, his sense of identity and social purpose as a teacher, he now accepts as inconsequential. His daughter Emma is his poem, the most beautiful poem of all. Private triumphs are defined as the only ones that matter. The message: Forget social purpose and learn to appreciate your existence within the emotional realm of the family. Battering down the walls of ignorance is for baby-boom television an old-fashioned, outdated enterprise, something that one leaves behind during the "maturing" process.

By virtue of their unity of purpose in placing family interests above all others, Michael and Hope occupy the central position in the lifestyle enclave. The other characters follow their example, striving to occupy a similar space because Michael and Hope "make it look so easy." But theirs is a solitary quest that pulls them away from their friends, and from the world:

> MICHAEL: We're working on a family here. Maybe that is being selfish. Maybe we should spend more time worrying about what's around our family. You know what I realized the other day? Janey is going to be fourteen in the year 2000. . . . That is plenty old enough to ask us why the world is the way it is. What are we going to say, 'Sorry about the ozone layer, sweetie, but we were a little focused on your preschool'?
> HOPE: Maybe Gary and Susannah are entitled to hate us.
> MICHAEL: I don't think they hate us. I think they are afraid.
> HOPE: Afraid of what?
> MICHAEL: Afraid of the kind of intimacy required to be a family. And some people avoid it by doing work, and some people avoid it by doing good deeds. But that's not life. I mean, life isn't only the things you do. It's also who you do things for.

The real meaning of life, then, can be found in the nurturing cradle of private sensations. This skillful dialogue has turned singularly personal interests into altruism—"It's also who you do things for." Consideration of the common good or the environment is not only secondary but antithetical to the true meaning of life—intimacy. Family becomes a wedge of separation between the individual and society.

Thirtysomething exists at the crossroads of a historical transformation in political culture. At the close of the twentieth century, the breakdown of any sense of personal connectedness with the larger social world has become very nearly complete. Incapable of representing that historical shift in any meaningful way, the program transforms the process into a biological phenomenon. Characters simply grow up. Political history is thus transformed into a maturing process in which the "natural" thing to do is finally to take on adult responsibility, defined strictly as family commitment. For *thirtysomething,* becoming an adult is a matter of making whatever political and social compromises are necessary in order to ensure one's existence within a set of narrowly defined parameters of the nuclear family.

Concern for any other issues that might affect the characters' lives is abandoned in favor of that privileged realm. Growing up hinges on the eternal return to domesticity, a private world made problematic in youth and considered too confining to be totally fulfilling. Interestingly, the makers of the program knew that its target audience did not view family as the sole measure of their lives; indeed, one critic observed that, "as a group, they [baby boomers] tend to be introspective and alienated from the familial values of an earlier generation" (Gerard 1988, 28).

There is no doubt that nurturing familial relationships can be an essential aspect of a fulfilling life, but on *thirtysomething* such relationships are presented as the single most important measure of life. By diligently separating the family itself from any broader social context, this measure also divides private preoccupations from social formulations of the common good. Characters are constantly asked to choose between social interests and private ones. They invariably choose the latter.

The dream of intimacy fulfilled through the promise of a nurturing nuclear family is obviously a compelling one. Its continual recurrence in popular cultural representations makes that clear. But interpersonal feelings do not exist in a social void. When social and economic conditions worsen, so do relationships. What belies those representations are current rates of infidelity, divorce, domestic violence, and incest, which in real human terms mean broken lives and misery. In actuality, the nuclear family cannot be the sole provider of personal happiness in the midst of economic degradation. Nor can it shelter its members from the sickness and disease caused by environmental degradation or the loss of the ozone layer.

Reference to social participation or social goals—or even the realization that social conditions might have an impact on the quality of life—remains at the level of what Stuart Hall (1986) calls the "repressed."According to *thirtysomething*, social concerns and family values are mutually exclusive. The program is not kind to activists who retain their ideals of social commitment, connectedness, and "good deeds." In the end, Gary, who has expressed ambivalence toward and even criticised conventional values, is simply eliminated in a car accident. Meanwhile, his partner Susannah, a full-time community-service worker who cares for the homeless and supports shelters for battered women, is never accepted by the lifestyle enclave. Utterly cold when Gary dies, she is portrayed as heartless, disconnected, and insensitive. Michael shows more grief over Gary's death than she does. On *thirtysomething*, even a beard, once the outward sign of a critical stance toward the given social order, symbolically condemns the character who is socially connected. One bearded man, an environmental activist, is portrayed as a home wrecker; another bearded man makes Ellyn's life miserable. In case the show's first message—*that it is always necessary to compromise your values for your family*—did not make the point, the second one will—*people who are socially committed have no families and are therefore immoral.*

But *thirtysomething* directed its worst diatribes against women's struggle for independence. In its reassertion of "family values," women were to assume singular positions within the home and to be defined solely by their roles as wife and mother. This relentless message was manifest in the sympathetic treatment of married life, as contrasted with the perilous struggle to exist as a single woman. In her eye-opening work, *Backlash,* Susan Faludi (1991) documents the harsh treatment women received in the media during the 1980s. In media themes promoting everything from the "man shortage" to the "misery of the single woman," from "working-mom burnout," to the "empty-womb syndrome," women bore the brunt of trend stories. Through meticulous documentation, the Pulitzer prize–winning journalist demonstrates the origins and mythic nature of these themes. She also demonstrates that they do not reflect the lives of American women. Yet each and every one was thematically depicted on *thirtysomething.* It is in this context that the program most notably betrayed the goals, aspirations, and sensibilities of the generation of women it claimed to represent. Clearly, marketing strategies overpowered viewer preferences. Even in the face of audience research that demonstrated viewer dissatisfaction, especially with Hope's role, the producers hammered home their message: Get out of the public sphere and back into the (fashionably accessorized) kitchen.

Marketing's "New Traditionalism"

Thirtysomething exists in the cultural ether of the widely reported "cocooning" trend of the so-called new traditionalists. In the late 1980s the media announced that "traditional family values" were once again warming the hearts of cold career women. Now disillusioned with corporate America and the public sphere, they were retreating in large numbers to the domestic "cocoon," preferring to labor full-time nurturing their children and serving their husbands, as their mothers once did. *Thirtysomething's* Hope held the banner of retreat high, in the role of the female lead, as popular cultural portrayals relentlessly induced a return to the safe constraints of domesticity. In episodes ranging in subject matter from day care to pregnancy, to the possibility of career employment, and even at the expense of adult friendships, Hope reconfirms her commitment to family above all else. Indeed, this commitment becomes Hope's only identity. Even though occasional episodes depict Hope as a part-time consumer affairs writer, the program's mini-biographies of characters described Hope Steadman with these words: "Hope is married to Michael." For the men, they listed career goals, hobbies, and convictions.

This new emphasis on traditional women's role is very much a product of media marketing. "Cocooners" inhabit an imaginary domain conjured up by the visions of marketeers and politicians. As the creative director for one of the largest advertising firms in the country explained, new traditionalism "is a nostalgic image of a past that never existed." In advertising, there is no "linear connection" to people's lives. "We sell fantasies."[1] A woman named Faith Popcorn, a former advertising executive who is now the head of her own marketing research firm, BrainReserve, coined the term *cocooning.* A "prophecy" she admitted had no basis in actual behavior, "it just popped into my head. . . . It was a prediction. . . . It hadn't happened" (Faludi 1991, 83). Popcorn proposed that American women were, in large numbers, leaving their jobs, going back to the home, and engaging in something akin to nesting behavior. According to Faludi (1991, 83), "She managed to attract hundreds of corporate clients, including some of the biggest Fortune 500 names in the packaged food and household goods industries"—the largest advertisers on television. Popcorn promised her corporate clients that her "retrotrend" themes would reinvigorate "mom foods" and ensure "brand renewal" for old-fashioned staples. The Campbell Soup Company used the new traditionalism to sell chicken pot pies, but it was the success of the Quaker Oats campaigns pitch—"It's the right thing to do" (i.e., the right thing for mothers to provide their families hot meals in the morning)—that helped convince many in the industry that neotraditionalism was real, because it worked as an advertising pitch. Popcorn's "foodmaker clients were more than happy to back her up on that. As one enthusiastic spokesman for Pillsbury told *Newsweek,* "'I believe in cocooning'" (Faludi 1991, 84).

Another advertising man, Malcolm MacDougall, vice chairman of Jordan, McGrath, Case & Taylor, advised the publisher of *Good Housekeeping* to use the new traditionalism pitch to boost his dwindling ad revenues. Circulation of traditional women's magazines had dropped precipitously and the total number of *Good Housekeeping*'s advertising pages was down by 13 percent. The new traditionalism campaign responded by promoting "deep-rooted values" of now trendy women who "find their identity" in nurturing husbands, and children. From their inception, however, the "new values" emerged as a symbolic invention tied to consumption. Ad copy made it clear that motherly nurturing meant providing families with highly accessorized homes stocked with all the right products. As Faludi (1991, 92–93) points out, "The New Traditionalist ads presented grainy photos of former careerist cuddled in their *renovated Cape Codder homes,* surrounded by adoring and *well-adorned* children" (italics added).

But the "trend" toward neotraditionalism has yet to manifest itself in any tangible way in the lives of real American women. In one ad for *Good Housekeeping* the copy referred to a poll that "proved" women were returning to a traditional lifestyle and embracing their neo-identities. But researchers for the *Yankelovich Monitor* poll said *Good Housekeeping* had misrepresented their findings, pointing out that "neither study shows any sign of women leaving work or even fantasizing about leaving work. The percentage of women who want to work in the Yankelovich poll is as high as ever" (Faludi 1991, 94). Thus did the new traditionalist phantasm gain a foothold in marketeers' imagination, even in the face of evidence contradicting their assertions that women no longer wanted to work. The neotraditional trend is illustrative of the blinding feedback mechanism that tricks the media into believing its own constructions. As programs and advertisements mirror the same themes, each points to the other for confirmations of their declarations. The creators of a Canada Dry commercial featuring "cocooning" couples claimed they were following a trend—one authenticated weekly by the show *thirtysomething*.

In fact, *thirtysomething* wholeheartedly adopted the neotraditional theme, hitting its viewers week after week with the message that married women who ventured into the world of work ended up with deprived children, unhappy husbands, and above all an unrelenting sense of guilt. Popcorn's prediction of cocooning had indeed captured the program's collective imagination. But the theme was neither creative nor original—it was simply a reflection of the media itself. *Newsweek* (March 31, 1986, p. 47) insisted that "today the myth of Supermom is fading fast—doomed by anger, guilt and exhaustion. A growing number of mothers have reached the recognition that they can't have it all" (Faludi 1991, 90). Desperate to find these dropout mothers, the magazine comissioned a poll in search of evidence to support its claim; however, the poll did anything but confirm the assertions. Few women felt as content as Hope did about the virtues of the "cocoon." Most claimed that work was an important part of their lives: "71 percent of mothers at home wanted to work, and 75 percent of the working mothers said they would work even if they didn't need a paycheck" (Faludi 1991, 90). "And contrary to the press about 'the best and the brightest' burning out, the women who were well educated and well paid were the least likely to say they yearned to go home" (Faludi 1991, 88). Nor do figures from the U.S. Bureau of Labor Statistics support the claim that women retreated to the home in the 1980s. In fact, women's representation in the work force increased over the decade "from 51 to 57 percent for all women, and to more than 70 percent for women between twenty-five and fourty-four" (Faludi 1991, 84).

Yet for women depicted in the media, happiness became cemented in the home. From advertisements to TV themes, the utopian images of the new traditionalists beckoned married women to a cozy retreat from loneliness and the harsh world of work. The sad irony is that the actresses hired to perform these narrow-minded roles on *thirtysomething* themselves have children, marriages, and careers. As Mel Harris, who plays Hope, told Faludi (1991, 167), "I think I'm a better mother and a better person because I work." And Patricia Wettig (Nancy) felt the same way: "From my perspective all three things are extremely important and I'm not willing to give up any one of them."

But the worst distress of all was set aside for those who lacked husbands and therefore had no identity and no sense of place—single working women. For such women the age of media discontent began in the 1980s. They were supposedly as miserable as their neotraditional counterparts were happy. From the Glenn Close character in *Fatal Attraction* to Ellyn and Melissa on *thirtysomething*, unwedded females were thought to be suffering any number of unhappy maladies—hence their portrayals as being "man hungry," career driven, just plain neurotic, or downright icy. Consider the character of Ellyn, a stereotype of the miserable, unfulfilled career women who suffers from empty-womb syndrome—and we rarely see her bleak apartment. Always desperately seeking a relationship but never capable of having one, she perpetrates an imprudent relationship with a married man, only to become more unhappy. Actress Polly Draper, who played Ellyn, was told that her character should be portrayed as "so irritating that she made people walk out of a room." She was directed to worship Hope, to behave as though she wanted to be just like her. Draper objected to the good/bad dichotomy and the fawning characterization. But the producers pressed ahead, thinking it might be a good idea if Ellyn had a drug problem as well. Always stressed out, Ellyn cannot even bear to hear Hope's baby cry. Ultimately, *thirtysomething*'s lifestyle choices— portrayed as the be all and end all of human existence—pit one woman against another, shattering any hope for a sense of community.

Melissa is equally miserable, but her anguish is literally visible, writ large under her eyes in the dark lines of streaked makeup that flow with her constant tears. The show's producers described this character as "man hungry." Even though actress Melanie Mayron, who played Melissa, also objected to her role and offered critical input (in fact, she succeeded in making the character less neurotic and less juvenile), Melissa, too, is portrayed as desperately seeking Mr. Right. A single woman herself, Mayron resented the message that to be single was to be miserable: "That's not like me or any of my friends" (Faludi 1991, 165).

In one episode, Melissa, thirty-five, tries a relationship with a twenty-three-year-old man. Despite graphic depictions of their extremely gratifying sex life (a ratings draw), the teary conclusion contends that such an arrangement simply will not work. All the other "couples" are also experiencing sexual problems—lack of desire, no time to make love, and so on—but in the end they are still together whereas Melissa is left isolated and lonely. (Of course, television's double standard allows men to have fulfilling relations with much younger women. The pairing of seventeen-year-old Shelly with sixty-two-year-old Holling on *Northern Exposure* is only the latest and most extreme prime-time example.)

Interestingly, when real women's voices replace those of their fictional (or commercial) counterparts, they tell a different story about what makes them happy. A 1985 Virginia Slims poll reported that 70 percent of women believed that they could have a 'happy and complete' life without a wedding ring" (Faludi 1991, 15). A 1989 New Diversity poll pushed that figure to 90 percent. And another Virginia Slims poll taken in 1990 found that nearly 60 percent of single women felt that they were much happier than their married friends and that their lives were easier. While *thirtysomething* and the media in general were portraying marriage and home life as a utopian escape, fourteen years of U.S. National Survey data charted the opposite—an 11 percent increase in happiness among 1980s-era single women, and a 6.3 percent decline in happiness among married women. In 1985 *Woman's Day* asked 60,000 women if they would marry their husbands again if they had it to do over. Only half said they would (Faludi 1991, 15).

Thirtysomething assiduously asserted that the mature adult of the 1980s had to stay within the confines of familial walls or else bear the brunt of social derision, pain, and financial disaster. Its vision of "yuppie angst" was a hell from which there is no escape. (Yuppies supposedly find it nearly impossible to derive pleasure from their relationships, but they will stay in them.) One critic has pointed out that the program revolves around "a structure of disavowal, in which the acknowledgement of critiques of the family somehow renders them unimportant" (Torres 1989, 102). When Hope and Michael have problems with their marriage, they reunite while attending Hope's parents' anniversary celebration. For this unhappy couple, returning to tradition is life's only alternative.

Characters who transgress familial boundaries are always made to suffer the consequences. They become even more miserable than Hope and Michael—or, worse, they feel it financially. For example, when Hope is thinking of having an affair, her dreams conjure up an "infidelity club" where one of the most notable members (because of his infidelity to Nancy) is a dejected and miserable Eliot. Earlier in the same episode, Michael remarks that "all the good things are happening to us, and all the bad things are happening to him." Roberta Smith (1990, 35) sums it up well: "Ultimately, the show's terrific visual form seems to exceed its content. The air of culture works primarily to give a smart, informed gloss to extremely conventional values."

Hegemonic Masculinity

At first glance, through its depiction of male roles, *thirtysomething* appears to represent a move toward gender equality. Michael, Gary, and Eliot are all sensitive, caring, and at times even nurturing men. They listen to the women in their lives and verbally express themselves at an emotional level. These "soft men" have come a long way from the violent, aggressive "macho men" once prevalent in popular culture. But as Robert Hanke (1990) argues, although the depiction of "soft men" in *thirtysomething* seems to represent a more modern, less sexist role model, this depiction actually functions hegemonically—in that it is used to subordinate women and others to the patriarchal order. In particular, it serves "to defuse crisis tendencies in gender order by using counter and oppositional discourse for its own purposes" (Hanke 1990, 231–32). Through portrayals, of "soft men," "patriarchal ideology is voiced and effaced" and the hegemonic process "is able to express and contain elements of liberal feminist ideology while remaining complicit with dominant gender ideology." Illustrative of women's subordination to such "soft men" is the episode in which Eliot, following an epiphany that redeems him as the consummate father, rebukes Nancy for forgetting her responsibilities to her children (especially her son) and brings her back into the patriarchal family. Beset by cancer (which she contracted after contemplating a career as a children's book illustrator), she has begun to think too "selfishly" about her own life. And her relationship with a single woman (who, in turn, is coded as unfeminine and unstable, is considered unhealthy and unmotherly). In short, the encroachment of men into what has traditionally been the nurturing role of women reasserts male dominance—one way of casting a 1980s sensitive man in an unchanged patriarchal order. As *thirtysomething* producer Marshall Herskovitz admits, he was trying to reclaim masculine ground lost: "Manhood has simply been devalued in recent years and doesn't carry much weight anymore" (Herskovitz, quoted in Faludi 1991, 167).

Hope and the Backlash

One episode places Hope on a trip to Washington to interview for a job with the Environmental Protection Agency. As it turns out, she's not really serious about the job but is simply contemplating an affair with a political activist. In short, her motives stem not from concern for the environment but, rather, from romantic fantasy. Hope's journey only reinforces the stereotype that women have jobs outside the home for all the wrong reasons.

Another episode, notable for its excesses, portrays Hope as struggling to arrange a surprise birthday party for Michael in the midst of domestic chaos—the kitchen is being remodeled. The specter of her *old* women's studies teacher relentlessly follows her about the house making disdainful comments. In the final sequence—a dreamlike segue (see Figure 5.1) that allows her to walk from the original narrative into a women's studies seminar—Hope confronts her teacher:

TEACHER: You're late, Ms. Murdock.

HOPE: I know, I threw my husband a surprise party for extra credit.

TEACHER: Extra credit, for a seminar in women's studies? I don't think so.
   Let me ask you this: What are you planning to do with your life?

HOPE: Well, I still don't know. All the women we studied in college, well, ei-

FIGURE 5.1 Hope Confronts Her Women's Studies Seminar

In this dream sequence from *thirtysomething*, Hope confronts a women's studies seminar from her college days. She tells her professor, "All the women we studied in college, well, either they never had children or they killed themselves, or both." She adds accusingly, "You were teaching us to be rigid and driven and judgmental, and completely insane!" These exaggerated, inaccurate lines isolate Hope within the confines of a narrowly defined domestic sphere by severing her ties to the larger community of women.

ther they never had children or they killed themselves, or both. It makes it
difficult to have a plan.

TEACHER: Let's throw it open for discussion. Yes, Amy.

AMY: Where are your priorities? I might have children and a sunroom some-
day, but I know it won't define me.

HOPE: How do you know?

FEMALE STUDENT: My career will definitely come first. And if and when I get
married, my husband will definitely be the kind of person who can han-
dle that.

HOPE: You don't understand. Anything can happen. The ceiling can come
down at any minute.

TEACHER: That's not applicable, Ms. Murdock.

HOPE: What were you teaching us? You were teaching us to be rigid and driven and judgmental, and completely insane! You were teaching us to be
exactly like the men we supposedly despised.

TEACHER: You're wasting your education.

HOPE: No, no, I've just begun it.

JANEY: (*from the narrative Hope walked out of*) Mommy!

HOPE: Excuse me, my daughter's crying.

The assertion that all women's studies role models are either childless or suici-
dal is of course ridiculous. Most feminists, past and present, have been mothers,
and only a few killed themselves. The assertion is a rhetorical flourish that serves
to condemn the entire enterprise of struggling for women's rights and independence. Hope's words are metaphorical, delivered with an uncertainty that implies
an open mind, whereas the teacher and students sound dogmatic. The language
belies the extreme assertion that Hope is actually making. Every one of her statements presents a set of rigid dichotomies: That studying women's history means
one despises men. That it is impossible and undesirable to have a career and a
family, and impossible to find a man to marry who will accept a woman's career.
But these are false dichotomies; they do not reflect the aspirations of real women.
Indeed, a Harris poll found "adult women increasingly more determined to have a
career with a family (63 percent versus 52 percent a decade earlier) and less interested in having a family with no career (26 percent versus 38 percent a decade earlier)" (Faludi 1991, 84).

The implications of Hope's assertion are as harsh as her words. Hope has been
set up with a husband whose single income can support an upscale lifestyle. She is
insulated from economic want. But in actuality, most single incomes could not
possibly support such a lifestyle; on the contrary, a double income would be required. Still, according to Hope, motherhood will define you. So if you work,
which most mothers do, your motherhood will be first and foremost. In the real
world this has come to mean the "mommy track," a situation in which women are
supposed to be content with less challenging jobs that have no possibility for promotion because their roles as wife and mother come first. But happily, most

American women are shrewder than Hope and understand "mommy tracking" for what it is—a way to keep women out of challenging, high-paying jobs. According to a research report on "Women Who Work" done in 1984 by *Newsweek,* "more than 70 percent of women interviewed said they would rather have high-pressure jobs in which advancement was possible than low-pressure jobs with no advancement" (Faludi 1991, 91). By 1990 women had not changed their minds. When asked about "mommy tracking," 70 percent of the women in a Virginia Slims poll said they found it discriminatory and "just an excuse for paying women less than men" (Faludi 1991, 91). Unfortunately, opting out of a career while still having to work means accepting the pink-collar secretarial positions and the low and unequal salary scales of traditional women's work.

It is most definitely true that the hopes and dreams of baby-boom women, who were in college at the height of the women's movement, did not pan out. Considerable gains have been made by some educated women, but many others are unemployed or remain in nonchallenging, low-paying positions. These failed expectations are a consequence of steady economic decline, society's inability to accept women's equality, and, of course, media portrayals such as those discussed here. But, as Susan Faludi documents so compellingly, in the age of the 1980s backlash, it is the struggle for women's independence itself that is blamed for women's unhappiness. Given the dichotomy between motherhood and career, the episode's message is clear: You were duped into raising your expectations by the women's movement. You never should have tried. If you still desire a career, you are selfish and will end up like the worn-out old professor. Indeed, the episode was designed to arouse an overwhelming sense of guilt in all women who have not given up the balance of their lives to stay home full time with their children and cater deferentially to the needs of their husbands. For women thus denigrated, the possibility of connectedness to any larger community is foreclosed. The sad conclusion is that Hope can find happiness in the home only by breaking all community ties.

In short, it is nonsensical to claim that the portrayal of character, rather than the depiction of social issues, indicates artistic purity on commercial television. The *thirtysomething* characters were cardboard representations, significant only as shadows of the social positions they occupied. The program did not reflect real people's lives. Those in the "right" positions were rewarded; those outside conventional boundaries suffered. Characters used blatantly in this way simply cannot represent the far more complex nature of social subjectivity; what they constitute is the quintessence of persuasive communication, not artistic creativity. Even though the producers claimed that they were dealing with character and not issues (a false distinction to begin with), the show had a moral for literally every issue. Liberty Godshall, the writer of the "Weaning" episode, admits that she was trying to make a point. In fact, she would have liked to convey the message—that mothers should stay home—even more strongly: "I think I probably wanted it to be more a celebration of staying home" (Faludi 1991, 163). And even over the objection of viewers who said they would rather see Hope working, the producers kept her in the house. At one level, the show can be thought of as little more than very cleverly constructed propaganda.

Ultimately, *thirtysomething* was unable to offer any solutions to the painful life choices to be made from the given range of alternatives. Characters and viewers alike were left with a sense of uneasiness in the face of unending concessions made to an inauspicious world. And such disquiet can be alleviated only through an endless therapeutic process. Ultimately, *thirtysomething* was a melodrama of intimacy with a flare for the sort of pop psychology that provides a kind of solution/resolution, one that at least temporarily seems to ease pain and justify spurious choices.

The Program as Soap Opera

Thirtysomething was admittedly a soap opera, but it expanded the definition of that format. Traditional melodrama is characterized by heightened emphasis on the emotional impact of events on characters' lives. Through close-ups that draw out the pain etched on the faces of familiar characters, the suffering caused by infidelity, disease, death, divorce, illegitimate offspring, betrayal, and a host of other traumas is felt by the viewers—not because all these events could possibly have happened to them in a lifetime, but because the emotional moments are familiar to some of the viewers through their own experiences. In the book *Watching "Dallas,"* author Ian Ang (1985) describes this format in terms of "emotional realism." The format is not realistic in its depiction of events (far too many traumas are portrayed as occurring in one life span), but it is true to the emotional makeup of lived experience—at some point *everyone* has felt that way.

The "New Intimacy"

In pushing the boundaries of "emotional realism," *thirtysomething* went beyond the worn and sometimes laughable exaggerations of the soap opera format. It pressed on toward a realism that combined emotional empathy with the pacing of real-life experience or, in the producers' words, "life as we know it." Not satisfied with exaggerations that call attention to themselves, the producers struggled for a totally believable slice-of-life drama that none dared to call fiction. "We're interested in the stuff of real life," they said. "Small moments examined closely, showing the way people really talk, and dream, and even fantasize ... The kind of show that people might look to and say, 'That's my life, I said that last night'" (Cole 1991, 567). This attitude defines the new television intimacy.

The Language of Therapy

Thirtysomething took a quantum leap from the conventional forms of the soap opera genre, and with that leap entered a dimension where no dramatic series had gone before. The new intimacy between characters carried them out of the world of melodrama and into a new world of television therapy (a terrain simultaneously explored on daytime talk shows and in much of advertising copy). The "real-sounding" dialogue of the new intimacy was quickly recognized as the language of therapy by the American psychological establishment. And that made great business sense: As one survey discovered, people were more inclined to try therapy after watching (Faludi 1991, 161). A spate of magazine articles lauded and appropriated the program for therapeutic purposes. A *Psychology Today* article entitled *"thirtysomething* Therapy" announced that "real-life" therapists were using the program in their work (Hersch 1988, 62). Some even tried to get videotapes of the program for their patients. Another writer asserted that "Americans are looking to the ABC dramatic series *thirtysomething,* not only for entertainment but for insights into interpersonal and psychological problems" (Pearce 1988, 12).Therapists noted that the psychological problems depicted in the show were characteristic of a generation "struggling with feelings of uncertainty and alienation while pursuing visions of the American Dream" (Hersch 1988, 62). But as argued above, the pursuit of the American consumer dream is carried out at the expense of the equally compelling need for community. What remains to smooth the pain of that loss is therapy. Therapy "is a private space, a refuge where the individual, suffering the insults of life without adequate community support, can go for healing" (Kovel 1989, 106). There is no doubt that the program was intended to be used in this fashion. "Self-analysis" was, as actor Ken Olin recognized, one of the main elements of the show (Fried 1988, 149).

The Construction of Social Reality

> *The feelings of three little people aren't worth a hill of beans in this mixed-up world.*
>
> —Rick, *Casablanca*

If the writers of *thirtysomething* had had anything to do with it, Rick would never have uttered those lines. Instead, the *thirtysomething* crew would have conveniently eliminated Ingrid Bergman's husband by having Louis kill him. Because Rick is the only one who can "make her happy," she would have gotten pregnant. He would have sold Rick's Place to a multinational resort consortium (which in turn would have destroyed local culture) to buy her (now his wife) a house in suburbia. No one would have been left to fight Fascism, but that would not matter—for intimacy is the only thing that does matter.

Thirtysomething was heavily invested in getting a generation to forget the types of sentiments expressed in *Casablanca*. To the baby-boom generation, the social world did matter. But recollection of that fact occurs only in small-audience art forms, or in documentary films like *Berkeley in the 60's*. This film recounts activities now portrayed as utterly foreign to the very generation that participated in them. In one sequence, students who have become involved in community politics are pressing local businesses to stop discriminatory practices and hire African Americans. Then the University of California administration retaliates. The ensuing conflict results in heightened political activities on campus, bringing up larger issues of democracy and participation. In the film, a member of the free speech movement, Michael Rossman, describes the impact that these activities had on members of his generation; "People started talking, bringing in the Greek philosophers, bringing in the French revolution, talking about all the ideas, constitutional liberties, as if they had meaning." It was this connectedness with social issues and historical practices that gave the 1960s generation a unified sense of purpose with the larger social and political community.

But by the 1980s *thirtysomething* was teaching the same generation "a new language," in terms that no longer challenged social reality but, instead, revealed ways of adjusting to it. Within *thirtysomething*'s discourse, the quest for solutions to the larger political and social issues of the 1960s is obliterated. In short, *thirtysomething* redefined the meaning of life and what matters. A key word in this new discourse was *feelings*. The program essentially provided the baby-boom generation with a language for framing their problems and for discussing "the day-to-day unhappiness." As Robert Hanke observes, *thirtysomething* characters used a therapeutic language "to find themselves" and "get in touch with their feelings" (1990, 243). Theraputic intimacy gave a clear, if painful, voice to this new practice.

In criticizing the therapeutic project, psychoanalyst Joel Kovel (1988, 94) addresses the narrow focus of the language of therapy. Psychological "bad faith," he explains, arises less in "what is said than through the creation of a way of speaking in which certain things are simply not capable of being thought, because all the words for them have been given other meanings." This resetting of the boundaries of the social world is what Anthony Pratkanis and Elliot Aronson (1992) have called "pre-persuasion." When the social limits are set and the world is redefined, the argument can be more naturally directed toward the position we are being asked to accept. The function of the language of therapy is to redefine social issues, to telescope into the personal realm a whole range of discourse once thought of in purely social terms. In Hanke's view, *thirtysomething* did exactly this "by representing social, economic, and political issues in affective terms" (1990, 243). But the therapeutic dialogue characteristic of *thirtysomething*, as Kovel argues, is also "a kind of shadow life, a marionette theater about which people can prattle as a way of evading life, and its real political choices" (1988, 95).

The American Psychological Association gave the television program its annual award for promoting "inner thinking." But inner thinking has its consequences. In therapy, when people "work it out" the social world is interiorized, through a process that transfigures emotional reactions. Psychoanalyst James Hillman explains this mechanism by describing the following scenario. On the way to therapy, driving on the freeway, a man becomes outraged. The "trucks almost ran me off the road. I'm terrified, I'm in my little car, and I get to my therapist and I'm shaking." In talking out his problems, he discovers that "my father was a . . . brute and this whole truck thing reminds me of him. . . . Or we talk about my power drive" (Hillman and Ventura 1992b, 11). During the session, emotions evoked in a social context are turned inward. Fear is converted into anxiety, which is an inner state. And outrage at the pollution, traffic, or urban chaos is converted into rage and hostility, again an internal condition. Along the therapeutic way the social connection is lost, because we do not work on "what the outrage is telling [us] about potholes, about trucks, ... about burning oil, about energy policies, nuclear waste, that homeless woman over there with the sores on her feet " (Hillman and Ventura 1992b, 12). "Dealing with it" has come to mean a type of interior self-reflection that allows subjectivity to cope with a hostile and painful world. When we retreat into our homes or therapists' offices to "work it out," we deal with our feelings about the homeless, but we do nothing to change the social and economic conditions that cause it.

This process of interiorization is the mechanism for a process of capitulation to 1980s values; it is also the way social issues in general are dealt with on *thirtysomething*. Michael, once critical of Miles Drentell, learns to appreciate the latter's unscrupulous corporate power plays by realizing his own ambition to be a "boss." In the series, as Hanke notes, "issues of power and control, winning and losing, are played out in terms of individual initiative and feelings of fear" (Hanke 1990, 236). As Michael discovers that he has feelings (some of which are rather dark), his preoccupation with self-reflection helps him adjust to corporate America. His behavior is consistent with Kovel's assessment of therapeutic preoccupation as "a way of social being which reflects the domination of consumer capitalism and the breakdown of community which accompanies this. That is to say, the structure of our whole society entails self-preoccupation, and the more so as society is unchallenged" (1991, 209).

This social obscurity is the fault line that runs the length of the therapeutic project. And the failure is not only a social one; it also obstructs the individual's search for peace of mind. As James Hillman points out, therapy's basic premise "has not connected with the world, and without that connection it's incapable of treating the whole individual" (Hillman and Ventura 1992a, 60). Kovel argues along the same lines, insisting that the idea of "neutral mental health" is a meaningless construct because it defines subjectivity in a vacuum, positing the possibility of a "healthy" self outside of a social context.

On *thirtysomething,* as on many 1980s television programs, private life exists in a bubble, pretending to be untouched by its surroundings. *Thirtysomething*'s quest for meaning and well-being is directed down a lonely road that deposits a generation of people at the gates of their own private world. Once they enter, the social terrain implodes behind them. The continual contemplation of the *self* in a void leads only to a dead end. As Kovel argues, "There is no such thing as mental health. There are only various degrees of conformity and unconsciousness on one side of a divide, and on the other, revolution or madness" (1988, 95).

Thirtysomething chose the path of conformity and unconsciousness, simply voiding the social world. Social issues, along with the urban problems of its Philadelphia setting, were unimportant to the lives of the lifestyle enclave.

Therapy's refusal to acknowledge the detrimental effects of social problems causes the internalized individual to become politically passive. Understanding social problems as a part of individual and group ill health necessarily leads to a desire for social change. As Kovel points out, after one acknowledges the existence of atrocious social conditions, "the only morally adequate response includes feeling pain and then doing something about it" (1988, 95). Active participation is the salvo for the grief experienced by the awareness of the social suffering around you. This point was clearly made by Jackie Goldberg, another student activist interviewed for the film *Berkeley in the 60's*. In one sequence, students have successfully persuaded bay-area businesses to end discriminatory practices and hire African Americans. Goldberg describes the meaning of that success:

> It was historic, and it was very elevating, and it really pumped us all up to think that, my god, we really could have an effect on history. We could have an effect on lives of people we'd never known, we'd never meet. And it was simply by taking seriously the words of the Constitution and the Preamble and the Declaration of Independence, and all that stuff that we believed in, you know, with great vim and vigor, and here we just saw it happen and it worked.

But social involvement as portrayed on *thirtysomething* is antithetical to well-being, not elevating as Goldberg remembers. By pitting the righteous (private) "family man" against the malicious (public) "social activist," the program invalidated social and political action that would lead to a better life for the greatest number.

Therapy focuses on the past, not on present causes of abuse and victimization. People feel victimized by any number of everyday experiences—humiliated by superiors and institutions that exert power over them. But the parameters set by therapeutic discourse evoke an interiorized past as the cause of unhappiness, not a social present. The familial power relationships that victimized us then become more significant than the present powerlessness caused by job woes and an unresponsive government. The preoccupation with interior life removes a significant number of citizens (those with economic means) from political connectedness, taking a serious toll on democracy. Indeed, Hillman contends "that psychotherapy—by turning us inward, away from the world and its problems—is actually causing our social breakdown, not healing it" (Hillman and Ventura 1992a, 60). Abandoning the broader political and social world leaves out the possibility of social change. Therapy's inward gaze obscures an outward critique that would bear in mind that "the buildings are sick, the institutions are sick, the banking system's sick, the schools, the streets—the sickness is out there" (Hillman and Ventura, 1992b, 61). And as Kovel argues, the individualized therapeutic process "obscures the real social nature of the mind. And by keeping people in the dark about this, while diverting them with its illusions of self-fulfillment, [it] confirms the passive acceptance of an atrocious society" (1988, 95).

Family Fills the Void

Michael is not angry because (as finally acknowledged on the front page of the *New York Times,* of March 5, 1992) a great portion of the affluence of this country was handed over to the wealthiest few in the 1980s. He is not upset about the fact that the politicians elected by "popular vote" have allowed private business to continue environmental degradation unabated. And he's certainly not concerned with the continuing cuts in social services as massive numbers of his fellow citizens (even Gary) became underemployed and unemployed. Instead, he blames his parents, whining, "They taught us we could have everything, they taught us to be spoiled." Hand in hand with the message that *the baby-boom generation should not have raised its expectations for positive social change* is a focus on the family of the past.

For American culture, as everyday life is ruptured from the political context, the family has become the site of a struggle for meaning that embodies all the contradictions of the discourse of persuasion. Presented as utopian fantasy, it is simultaneously the source of all dysfunction. Even if pleasure is to be found within its confines in the present, family structures of the past are responsible for our dysfunction. The pop psychologist, John Bradshaw, now a constant fixture in the media, has announced that 97 percent of American families are dysfunctional. As the flashpoint of our culture, family life backs us into a corner, trapping us in a search for happiness within a fantasy built from the fragments of the shattered dreams of our childhood. It is a Sisyphean search.

On the one hand, evocation of the dysfunctional family diverts attention from the social causes of pain. On the other, presentation of the family as utopian fantasy blocks participation in the quest for social solutions. Therapy, as practiced in American culture, is doomed to fail. As Hillman argues, there remains a sense of cultural gloom, whose cause is well beyond the family dynamic: "The depression we're all trying to avoid could very well be a prolonged chronic reaction to what we've been doing to the world, a mourning and grieving for what we're doing to nature and to cities and to whole peoples—the destruction of a lot of our world" (Hillman and Ventura 1992b, 45).

Of "Family Values" and Morality

As Michael struggles to reconcile himself to abandoning his 1960s social concerns for the "good" of his family, his father comes to him in a dream and reassures him that he's doing the right thing. Michael learns that it is not selfish to abandon social and political involvement, and in doing so he finds solace in a patriarchal order he once rejected. With this episode, *thirtysomething* redefined values and morality for a generation struggling with the changing political configuration of the 1980s. It preached adjustment, insisting that the measure of one's character could not be based on social integrity, or social responsibility, or any type of non–self-interested altruism aimed at promoting the common good. The lesson of the episode is that no one who chooses selfish interests or economic gain at society's expense is immoral, even those who, like Michael, work in advertising, creating misleading and socially destructive illusions (enumerated in Chapters 2 and 3). Morality, then, cannot be defined through any criteria involving the public sphere but, rather exists in the private realm of "family values." In short, social responsibility is annihilated by the weight of family responsibilities.

But here again we have a false dichotomy, inasmuch as moral and social relations have to be included in the measure of a "good life." If being a conscientious family man who feels good about himself is now the criterion of morality, we need only think of Adolph Eichmann and remember Hannah Arendt's admonition on the banality of evil to realize that moral and social relationships must be taken into account when assessing morality. As Kovel also points out, Eichmann, the man who sent Jews off to gas chambers with Nazi efficiency, functioned well and felt just fine about himself. A more contemporary example is illustrated in *The Official Story*. Based on an Argentine family, this film was constructed out of the broken lives of people who "disappeared" at the hands of the military. As the plot advances, a woman unravels the details of the origins of the child she raised, brought to her by her husband because of his connections to the military apparatus that killed the child's parents.

The Series' End

As *thirtysomething* came to a close, the consuming sense of discontent it had generated was not alleviated. Its contradictions did, however, finally reach a crisis point. Through therapeutic discourse, Michael learned to adapt and even to function well within corporate culture. But the sacrifices he made for the benefit of his family—all the compromises necessary to survive within the exploitative relations of DAA—ultimately failed. His dedication to work alienated him from Hope, and with his marriage on the rocks he chose work over family. However miserable, they stay together. Eliot and Nancy move their nuclear family to Los Angeles, doomed to live in isolation, beyond even the lifestyle enclave.

By the end of the 1980s, American collective culture had become adamant in its blanket denial of any sense of responsibility for social problems. But such denial did not block the uneasy sense of guilt that remains: "We talk about our parents having shamed us when we were little, but we've lost our shame in relation to the world and to the oppressed, the shame of being wrong, of messing up the world. We've mutated this shame into personal guilt" (Hillman and Ventura 1992b, 45). Indeed, what hides barely under the surface of *thirtysomething* is a desperate attempt, on the part of "well-off boomers" (especially those working in the media), to alleviate their own sense of guilt. Guilt, combined with an increased sense of fear; and fear being the inevitable result of the social abandonment of an unsafe and inhospitable world that has now become a threat. The message of *thirtysomething* was to not worry about the abandonment of, for example, the desolate inner city—until it became dangerous. It was up to filmmaker Lawrence Kasden to deal with these issues after *thirtysomething* was canceled.

Grand Canyon, *the Movie*

Aside from the producers of *thirtysomething,* no one articulates the constellation of guilt, justification, and moral superiority better than filmmaker Lawrence Kasden. His first film, *The Big Chill* (featuring sequences brazenly stolen from John Sayles's deeper *The Return of the Secaucus Seven*), introduced the generation to navel contemplation, of which *thirtysomething* was undoubtedly a TV "spin-off." But it was his later film, *Grand Canyon,* that drew this inauspicious beginning to its ultimate conclusion. In it he chronicles the spiritual quest of a group of well-off boomers—the jogging professional/technical turtle-neck-wearing, mini-van-driving set—who are looking for "higher meaning." This quest quickly moves into a discourse on personal morality, as a function of individual good deeds. Kevin Kline's character befriends the character played by Danny Glover and helps his family, while his wife gives shelter to an abandoned (Hispanic) baby she has found while jogging. These actions are admirable, of course, and would even have positive meaning in a different context. But the characters are not motivated by an altruistic desire for social change; what drives them, rather, is an overwhelming sense of fear, which they must "deal with."

Kevin Kline has a close encounter with black rage, from which he is rescued by Danny Glover. The "good black, protector/bad black, threat" dichotomy posits race, not environment, as *the* factor responsible for the degradation of the inner city. Indeed, the movie seems to disavow the role of socio-economic conditions in the deterioration of city life. In short, *Grand Canyon* contends that society (of which the yuppy characters are a part, after all) has no responsibility for the economic and social degradation of the inner-city poor. Instead, in a vicious depiction now common in the media, the movie blames the victims, those whose lives have been diminished by lack of employment opportunities, discriminatory banking practices, real estate scams, and political abandonment.

Like *thirtysomething* and much of media discourse, *Grand Canyon* denies that concerted political and community action are needed to "fix things"; the movie looks instead to individual good deeds performed by those occupying positions of privilege. The development of the political theme of "family values and morals" is deliberately designed to obscure that connection and to confirm the rupture between the understanding of the social world and private life. But to define morality in terms of those who do good deeds is to forget that it is active social participation that leads to positive social change. Morality becomes the realm of those who have the luxury to carry out those good deeds (if only to appease their guilt). Those not able, or not inclined, to do so—enraged by circumstances of economic oppression and degradation—are condemned as "immoral." But the notion of an immoral society is deeply repressed.

The problem for the more affluent sectors of society is that they cannot keep their humanity and spirituality in a society that marginalizes the poor. No matter how far they drive or how long they gaze out over the the Grand Canyon, that majestic transcendence of time and nature, an immoral society is still a spiritually deadening place. The movie translates this sense of spiritual death into middle-class fear through the Steve Martin character, a filmmaker who is shot down by a punk who wants his Rolex. Although this character (the most self-serving character in the film) experiences an epiphany, his understanding of his own role in societal violence as a maker of cheap exploitation movies is quickly forgotten during his convalescence. Limping back to the studio, he justifies his profit-making at society's expense with the old media argument that he is only reflecting the declining social fabric, not creating it.

The portrayal of homelessness as benign is even more insulting. During her habitual jog past a homeless man, the Kline character's wife imagines that she hears the man say, "Keep the baby." In this scene, homeless people are portrayed as having attained a transcendent quality; now that we are invited to pretend that their suffering has left the realm of material want, it becomes spiritual. Pop spirituality is defined as blissful fantasy, where simply wishing makes it so.

It is useful to compare the pseudospirituality presented as fantasy in *Grand Canyon* to Kovel's description of a spiritually fulfilling encounter with another unfortunate individual:

> The spiritually realized person, the person of soul, breaks across the class barrier. He or she not only becomes open to the Other but actually appropriates the Otherness of the oppressed. That is, the spiritually realized person makes this Otherness his or her own, through an act of protection. This act also constitutes a risk to the normal, egoic self—hence the element of courage. The result is a mutual empowerment of the person who had been Other and the person who has made the leap. (Kovel 1991, 95)

Filmic wish fulfillment is a sad substitute for a sense of the spiritual. This theme, now so prevalent in popular culture, is one born of the confused emotional response to a society so clearly on the way to a spiritual void. As Kovel points out, quenching the thirst for the inner self is done not just by looking inward but also by taking action in an outward direction. That is the message and the remembering deliberately obscured by *thirtysomething*, which portrays a culture selling accumulation at the expense of community.

Community and Spirituality

As the rupture from the political world becomes more complete, the spiritual quest implodes. At least it seems that inner life is one area in which the individual can assert control. Consumer spirituality, like therapy, demands that radical alternatives to the existing social order be ruled out. Once this hope is denied, people begin to pay heightened attention to themselves, and "their desire for a radically different existence—which had traditionally taken the shapes of heaven or revolutionary utopias—[becomes] diverted into the hole for a radically different self" (Kovel 1988, 95).

But the failure of this formula is nowhere more apparent than in the mass media visions of community and spirituality of the 1980s, which fell victim to the contradictory demands placed on them. The need of advertisers to create vehicles for consumption and the need of viewers for meaning and a sense of well-being were reconciled at the expense of the viewers. But such a format is incapable of presenting authentic community of the kind that Kovel (1991) articulates in *History and Spirit.* The truly spiritual community must overcome an interlocked set of problems arising from the existing relations of power and domination:

> It must decide how it will sustain unalienated production and reproduction, avoid gurus and other remnants of patriarchal domination, advance internal democracy and self government, and relate to the larger society, the increasingly devastated earth, and the oppressed upon it. In a word, the task is to develop communalism. This is a fantastically difficult challenge, but one of the few really worth taking today. (Kovel 1991, 211)

ᴏᴠ   ᴏᴠ   ᴏᴠ

Thirtysomething sold 1980s consumer values by harking back to the social values of the 1960s. It sold baby boomers nostalgic images of a nonconformist past that were now incorporated within a 1980s consumption ethic. In advertisements for entities ranging from Coors beer to the phone company, they were invited to bask in the memories of their anti-establishment youth—a culturally dominant aesthetic retreat but one from which all meaning had been drained.

The themes of family, therapy, and personal morality developed by the producers of *thirtysomething* were emblematic of media trends in the 1980s. They were offerings made to a public increasingly unable to make sense of the social and political decline of the decade. They offered an entire generation of people a state of mind divorced from the political acumen of their youth. These themes were compatible with a cultural and political discourse that tenaciously asserted that the quest for personal well-being must be made alone, and that the social, political, and economic terrain must be abandoned.

These themes exist in a culture that claims all the rotten things that happen to people have nothing to do with political processes, social pressures, or economic disparities. Posing all problems as individual means denying their social and economic determinants. That the themes developed for *thirtysomething* served a political agenda was clearly demonstrated in the 1992 presidential election campaigns. Whereas the Republicans, through Vice-President Dan Quayle, formulated a platform around "family values," the Democrats adopted the mantle of therapeutic well-being to formulate their "new covenant."

But it was the rise of the talk show as the dominant forum for public discourse that further defined media pseudotherapy as the model for American political culture. As we shall see, talk shows quickly appropriated the culture of therapy—a narrow view that telescopes all problems into personal faults.

6

The Television Talk Show: From Democratic Potential to Pseudotherapy

---

The Crisis of Information

In the mid-1980s television talk shows shattered the conventional wisdoms guiding nonfiction television programming. Before then it was hard to imagine a daytime schedule featuring such a profusion, in the morning as well as the afternoon, of people talking. After all, the dreaded "talking heads" had been avoided for so many years on news programs, covered up at every opportunity with what industry people refer to as "wallpaper shots"—anything visual to insert over someone talking. Critics of visual communication and the fragmented fast-paced video editing style of televisual news lamented the lack of serious discourse. If only thoughtful people were allowed to speak about important issues, the public would be better informed instead of mindlessly entertained. News managers themselves claimed that there was no alternative to what had become visual sensationalism, because a sophisticated audience simply would not watch static shots of talking heads, especially noncelebrities. Since the days of Edward R. Murrow, Sunday morning had been the ghetto of talk and public affairs, at a respectable distance from weekday scheduling. One critic (Postman 1986) went so far as to say that video technology itself was incapable of holding a coherent thread of logical discussion that the audience could follow.

The new cheap formats of tabloid television, the news magazines, and "reality" dramatization formats featuring "real" people, together with talk shows, marked one of the most dramatic shifts in programming design in the history of the medium.[1] "Slick" had been the operative concept. American TV news and information programming was nothing if not polished and state-of-the-art. But during the 1980s even prime time began to display an excess of grainy home video–style programming, often shot deliberately at night, making audiences strain to see and hear the "ordinary" people they featured. The daytime *service*[2] talk shows that feature ordinary people (and "therapists") are now so numerous it is difficult to keep track of them.

A number of factors must be considered if we are to understand such transformations in nonfiction programming techniques. Hour-long formats of people talking from the same minimal studio sets each day and amateurish tabloid magazines featuring cheap dramatizations are, first and foremost, cost effective. In a word they are cheap. Escalating production costs and the accelerated drive to make nonfiction programming profitable (as discussed in Chapter 1) account for the willingness of broadcast executives to give the new formats a chance.

But the public must also tune in. Advertising revenue must be maintained through viewers, and tune in they do—in very large numbers. The popularity of the talk-show formats indicates a genuine appeal. But how and why do these programs appeal to the public? What needs are they addressing? Answering these questions will lead us to two others: As they have come to be practiced, do the new formats fulfill the needs they address? And, finally, in the larger sense, can the overarching need for profitable nonfiction TV formats coexist with a medium that is capable of furthering democratic practices and human well-being?

Talking Heads Are Back

Using the visual language of "objectivity" developed during the medium's infancy, Dan Rather and Ted Koppel sit planted behind their desks.[3] These TV anchorpersons and others control banks of monitors and a vast array of official information sources from around the country and around the globe. They relay the factoids from "experts" and government officials who hold sanctioned positions of power and influence. Up against this broadcast news establishment the new generation of "hosts" take their mobile microphones into a live studio audience, composed of ordinary people who enter into public discussions on national television. Oprah dashes between the aisles of participants, visibly trying to give everyone who wants to speak a chance. Dan, Tom, and Peter, on the other hand, switch to video hookups from professional correspondents who have carefully chosen and rehearsed every word. Official news selects, composes, and digests word and image, assembling them into pleasing consumption bits. Talk shows appear to do the opposite, relying not on professionals but on the random and unrehearsed participation of the audience. The discussions they feature hinge on audience involvement and on the willingness of ordinary people to tell their stories on national television.

Oprah appears noticeably upset as a guest recounts the details of a painful experience. Tom and Dan sit unmoved as they report excruciating human suffering across the globe. Phil wrinkles his brow and chews his knuckle in response to people's stories. Objectivity of style demands that serious news anchors express no emotions that could influence the information received. But talk shows are the epitome of advocacy journalism. The stated purpose of talk-show information is to help those who receive it. Both formats, news and talk, however extreme their differences of style, profess to do the same thing—to bring information to the public. The real differences lie in the nature of that information and its possible use to the public.

Experience, Knowledge, and the News

News reporting has become increasingly incapable of providing information and knowledge that can be incorporated into peoples lives in meaningful ways. As Paolo Carpignano et al. (1991) have pointed out, the development of news as a social construct poses various problems for information and its legitimacy. Other authors (Shudson 1978; Meyrowitz 1985; Postman 1986) have also observed the movement from information communities to mass-marketed journalism has created an estranged media environment with little relevance to everyday life. The rise of talk television and its continual expansion as a TV format should be viewed as a repercussion of the continuing crisis of information in postindustrial America. Talk television offers viewers something more than what has become decontextualized reporting of events. It offers them information wrapped in a now more legitimate context: human experience.

By the 1980s the inability of traditional news formats to speak in meaningful ways to the lives of people had reached a crisis point. As John Fiske (1989, 186) points out, public discourse as presented on national television news fails to have meaning at the level of lived experience. The disjuncture between people's lives and national TV news coverage discourages the use of news as information:

> If there are no relevances between a text and the everyday lives of its readers, there will be little motivation to read it. . . . News may well be watched out of a vague moral sense that we ought to know what is going on in the world, but if it lacks these microconnections, it will be watched half-heartedly and will be rapidly forgotten—which, indeed, is the fate it frequently suffers. (Fiske 1989, 187)

The frustration and sense of irrelevance with which the public has come to view traditional news reporting is confirmed by an in-depth study entitled *Citizens and Politics: A View from Main Street America,* supported by the Kettering Foundation and carried out by Richard Harwood (1991) of the Harwood Group, a public issues research and consulting firm. During 1990 and 1991, ten focus groups were carried out in different regions across the country. Those interviewed "consistently complained that current discussions on policy issues do not resonate with their deeply held concerns. They say they are unable to see themselves—their perspectives and desired choices for action—reflected in the way in which issues are discussed" (Harwood 1991, 13). In short, the study confirmed that many Americans feel that "all the jargon, statistics, and other forms of 'professional speak'" do not "resonate with citizens' concerns and the realities of life they experience and see around them" (Harwood 1991, 14, 22).

The constructed interpretations of TV's view of the world as a swirl of disconnected events stand in striking contrast to the lived experiences of everyday life—the microlevel. Issues of public concern are characteristically represented in one of two ways: at the decontextualized, individual human-interest level (Bennett 1988) or at an abstract sociopolitical level—the macrolevel (Calhoun 1988). Either way, news representations obscure the relevance of public issues to people's lives.

The experiences, actions, motivations, and explanations of statecraft formulated through news-as-information can no longer be understood within the realm of common sense. There is no longer an apparent connection between the public world and private life. Because of this rupture, the public's involvement in political debate and in the process of government has been diminished.

Sound-Bite Media

The short bursts of de-linked news fragments (Bennett 1988) now so characteristic of the sound-bite media have further obscured the various ways in which macrolevel social forces affect everyday life. The people interviewed by Harwood indicated that media coverage of politics and policy issues did not leave them informed but, instead, led to a "sense of frustration and dismay." One man from Richmond put it this way: "The technology of the media and communication controls [politics]. It's sound bites. It's quick. . . . It has distanced every one of us from what's really going on, and has distanced all our political leaders from what's really going on with us" (Harwood 1991, 23). The Harwood study concludes that people do not need *more* information in order to make political choices but, rather, that "the issue may be [that] they need different kinds of information" (1991, 3).

News can no longer be turned into knowledge—especially a type of knowledge that can help people understand their world and country, knowledge that can help them plan courses of action intended to make the changes needed in public policies. Sound-bite statecraft has rendered politics impenetrable. According to Harwood, "This emphasis on conveying short quick pieces of information appears to have disconnected Americans from the substance of politics" (Harwood,

1991, 23). As the political world becomes increasingly opaque and irrelevant to people's lives, the result has been "to push citizens away from participation in the political process" (Harwood 1991, 14).

The Edited Public

Citizens are indeed given little voice on official news, except as the "edited public." This is the term used by Carpignano et al. (1991) to describe the few interviews with individuals that are shown. Participation in the news has come to mean being selected for use in a sound-bite that serves as a slice of authenticity. The "man-on-the-street" interview is usually inserted to make the desired point or to affirm the thrust of a story. Take the example of a southern California woman walking in the park with a friend the day after Christmas. She was approached by a TV journalist doing a story on the therapeutic benefits of exercise to overcome depression. The journalist asked if the woman was walking because of some post-holiday melancholy, to which she replied, "No. I had a great Christmas. I'm just taking a walk in the park." Nevertheless, with some dismay she saw herself that night as the "edited public"; her picture was used to confirm the benefits of exercise as an antidote to post-holiday depression.

The Crisis of Representation

The news as a social construction has also reached a crisis of representation at the political level.[4] The Harwood study itself was a response to the growing sense of political malaise so evident in this country. Its objective was to understand the depth of public dissatisfaction, and its findings were dramatic. The people interviewed demonstrated a "widespread public reaction against the political system" and expressed the feeling that "politics has been taken away from them." The authors stressed that this response was not merely the usual discontent with big government, party politics, and corruption but, rather, "a reaction against a political system that is perceived as so autonomous that the public is no longer able to control or direct it." Ultimately they found that people believe "that representative government has failed" (Mathews 1991, iii).

Citizens believe that they have been squeezed out of politics by a system "dangerously spiraling beyond their control, a system made up of lobbyists, political action committees, special interest organizations, and the media" (Harwood 1991, 5). One woman from Des Moines lamented the failure of representative democracy in this way: "The original concept was for elected representatives to represent your interests." But that is no longer true, she continued. "It is now [the case that] who ever has the most money can hire the most lobbyists to influence representatives" (Harwood 1991, 22).

Another respondent expressed frustration with the government's failure to represent the public: "I know everyone in the state of Virginia is against drilling for oil in Chesapeake Bay. But just because every man, woman, and child doesn't want the drilling and Exxon does, you can bet your life there will be drilling. This makes me feel helpless" (Harwood 1991, 20).

Instead of acting for the common good, politicians are perceived as servants to the special moneyed interests that donate hundreds of thousands of dollars to campaign funds for both the executive and legislative branches. Because of this influence and political action committees (PACs), government has come to serve the interests of corporate America almost exclusively; it cannot regulate capital in such a way as to function in everyone's best interest.[5] Indeed, as David Mathews notes:

> People believe two forces have corrupted democracy. The first is that lobbyists have replaced representatives as the primary political actors. The other force, seen as more pernicious, is that campaign contributions seem to determine political outcomes more than voting. No accusation cuts deeper because when money and privilege replace votes, the social contract underlying the political system is abrogated. (1991, v)

The Harwood study discovered that Americans are keenly aware of the way in which government has come to function, and that "they are hopping mad about the situation!" (Mathews 1991, v). Americans are also expressing "outrage at the disproportionate influence of the wealthy" (Harwood 1991, iii). The general lack of economic justice in American life is sharply perceived by the public.[6] Throughout the 1980s the news media habitually reported the government's justifications for an economic policy that failed miserably.[7] In March 1992 even the *New York Times* admitted in its headline, "The 1980s: A Very Good Time for the Very Rich." It went on to detail in a subheading that "Data Show the Top 1% Got 60% of Gain in Decade's Boom" (Nasar 1992, A1). Clearly, corporate profit margins were assiduously valued over the country's need for an employed work force.

Citizen apathy is not a consequence of the public disinterest. It results from the belief that even if one did become involved, this action would have no effect. People have dropped out of the present formulation of political life because it has become clear that politicians do not speak to their needs. As economic conditions worsen and solutions to social and economic problems become further out of reach, feelings of anger and helplessness are evoked among those viewing the nightly displays of news-as-fragmented-statecraft.

Continued economic stagnation, unemployment, the lack of proper health care and day-care facilities, and the persistent decline of urban America can no longer be explained by traditional news formats. The realization that government and public officials are increasingly incapable of solving social problems only adds to the crisis of public discourse and news reporting. News reporting of political issues obscures rather than illuminates political practices. The result is cynicism and the feeling that, as the Harwood study found, there is no room for the public in the political process: "Citizens feel cut off from political debate: they neither see their concerns reflected in the way current issues are discussed nor believe there are ways to participate in discussion on those issues" (Mathews 1991, 11). National political debate discourages public involvement because it has become impossible to carry out the will of the people.

Political Uses of Sound-Bite News

Numerous critical approaches to media studies imply that some quality inherent in video technology renders it incapable of producing segments longer than about 20 seconds. The popularity of the long-form talk-show format is evidence enough that there is nothing intrinsic about the medium's fragmented textual strategies. Indeed, the short dramatic visual and audio bursts of news infobits have historically resulted in ratings boosts; but other formats can also be profitable. The short format must therefore serve an additional purpose, which it most certainly does. That purpose is to deliberately obscure the means by which the political and social worlds function. Speaking in sound-bites has become popular among politicians because it allows them to avoid detailing their political intentions. Audience effects are also far easier to predict and accommodate with the short format. This point is graphically illustrated by reference to the media strategies developed for former President Bush. Marketing research found that Bush was perceived as insincere if he uttered more than seven words in a row. Positive effects could not be achieved with longer phrases, thus accounting for his staccato bits of vague locution: "a thousand points of light," "a kinder, gentler America," "stay the course," "read my lips." The strategies developed for the use of video itself determine its ability to serve, or not to serve, the public. It is therefore the use of the medium that determines its social value, not an evil inherent in the technology.

The Shape of Political Discourse

The rupture between life experienced at the microlevel and the dubious macrolevel discourse of statecraft has raised questions about media credibility and legitimacy, accelerating the crisis of news as reported event. As Mathews (1991, v) notes, "People know exactly who dislodged them from their rightful place in American democracy. They point their fingers at politicians . . . and— this came as a surprise—at people in the media." Mathews's point should not come as a surprise: The unity of discourse between the government and news reporting does call media legitimacy into question. Since the two entities have come to speak with the same voice, government failure now translates into media failure.

During the 1980s government and the media did indeed reach an accord, and numerous studies have demonstrated this point. In one research project, "The News Shapers," performed at the University of Minnesota, Lawrence Soley (1989) found that the analysts, experts, and consultants featured on network news programs were drawn from a pool of former and current government officials.

When Republican presidents were in office, more than 62 percent of news interpreters described as former officials were ex-Republican officials. The study also found that 34 of the 177 news shapers were responsible for 45 percent of all appearances and, further, that 7 individuals accounted for 20 percent of all appearances. This is a small group of friends indeed.

Government officials, together with a number of politically conservative "experts," constitute those interviewed most often by media organizations. As Soley (1989, 40) points out, "There is strong evidence that the network news organizations repeatedly interview these individuals, who can deliver usable, but not necessarily profound, sound bites." Moreover, these people are often presented as neutral. For example, Soley's study logged William Schneider from the American Enterprise Institute as having made the most network appearances of any of these sources—58 during 1987 and 1988. Yet all three networks described Schneider as a political scientist, political analyst, expert, or spokesperson for the Institute, which was never identified as a conservative organization.

D. Charles Whitney and his colleagues (1989) examined the sources and types of news included on weekday network newscasts aired between May 1982 and April 1984. They found that government officials were more often cited than any other source. Nor did the press present perspectives from a wide variety of viewpoints. Individuals from public interest organizations were rarely seen. Representatives of human rights, civil rights, women's, and labor groups, when combined, accounted for only one-twentieth of all news sources.

Another set of studies was done by the public-interest organization known as Fairness and Accuracy in Reporting (FAIR), which examined the guest lists of the ABC program *Nightline* and public broadcasting's *MacNeil/Lehrer News Hour*. FAIR's 1989 study came to similar conclusions about who shapes the news and from what perspective: Three-fourths of the individuals who appeared on *Nightline* between January 1, 1985, and April 30, 1988, were "elites," defined as former and current government officials and "professionals." Women, minorities, and the vast majority of the American public were excluded from participating in any meaningful way on *Nightline*.[8]

As William Hoynes and David Croteau (1990, 12) point out, FAIR's 1990 study of the *MacNeil/Lehrer News Hour* found that when this program "covered Washington politics, 60 percent of its guests were government officials." They also note with some dismay that coverage of the "inner workings" of the nation's capitol "serves as a veritable press agency for the views of U.S. officialdom—one that excludes the views of critics" (Hoynes and Croteau 1990, 12). The FAIR studies concluded that both PBS's *News Hour* and *Nightline* "fall far short of being politically or socially inclusive." Because of their limited political scope, Hoynes and Croteau note, both programs "generally exclude critics in favor of voices of the powerful" (Hoynes and Croteau 1990, 13). In their view, when the media "regularly exclude significant views within the U.S. population—the voices of women, people of color, environmentalists," democracy and a free press that should "present multiple perspectives on issues" are undermined.

The documentation of the elite nature of public discourse is especially disturbing in the context of public broadcasting. As Hoynes and Croteau (1990, 4) note: "The Carnegie Commission Report, from which the Public Broadcasting Act of 1967 was derived, suggested that public television 'should be a forum for debate and controversy' and called for public television to 'provide a voice for groups in the community that may otherwise be unheard.'" The discovery that the *MacNeil/Lehrer News Hour* does not live up to that goal demonstrates that the interest of the vast majority of the American public is not being served.

The exclusion of the public voice, and the overall lack of inclusive public debate from a broad range of perspectives, is readily apparent to those who are asked to consume news coverage. Public dyspepsia over these restrictions further accelerates the crisis of the news and accounts, to a large degree, for the crisis of media legitimacy. Citizens are indeed aware of the insincerity of political discourse and feel that "policy issues are framed in ways that actually prevent them from participating in political debate" (Harwood 1991, 13).

The flagship network news programs no longer hold the monopoly on information programming and have lost the revered position of legitimacy they once had. Recognition of the crisis of news legitimacy grew out of years of research and documentation of the news media's inability to represent the world, in all its complexity, in a way that created meaning or led to public knowledge. As it became evident that the professional canons of journalism could not ensure disinterested representations (Tuchman 1978; Bennett 1988) and that the press could not distance itself from those in power, the model of "news as representation" (i.e., the belief that the media can portray nonfiction events with any degree of veracity) lost salience.

More recently, as we saw in Chapter 1, the commercial pressures on and corporate ownership of the media prevent journalists and producers from bringing to light a vast realm of information, especially news that could provide an analytic or critical perspective on the business practices that drive the American economy and affect the general quality of everyone's life. Restrictions on information critical of corporate practices—but crucial to the public's understanding of economic issues—has been systematically expunged from the news agenda.

Media mergers and economic forces have rendered the press incapable of fulfilling its First Amendment mandate and the public's right to know. Even more important, information regarding environmental destruction, public health issues, and corporate labor practices are reported, in the vast majority of cases, from a perspective favorable to corporate America. Unfortunately, as discussed in in Chapter 2, what is good for corporate America, especially in times of economic recession, is not always good for the American public. The ideas, opinions, interests, and concerns of the public are not represented, primarily because we are not given a voice on the narrow spectrum of corporate-owned media. As the media move closer to perspectives that represent the powerful in the political, or corporate, and financial spheres, they create a formidable block that obstructs the public's understanding of material and social forces, thereby restricting public expression about and interaction with the process of history.

The Rise of the Talk Show

The new forms of TV programming that have emerged within the last decade—especially the talk shows and other types of "tabloid" television—should be understood as the consequence of a medium that, mired in official statecraft, has been unable to speak from the perspective of microlevel discourse in any satisfactory way. The new talk formats, by contrast, struggle to position members of the public as participants, not only because those formats are cheap to produce but also because people are hungry to see themselves represented in a medium they have been historically, and in recent times increasingly, excluded from.

Talk shows address the need for information that relates to people's lives, and their method has been to provide the public with narrative representations of lived experiences. "If you don't talk I can't grow," Phil Donahue cajoles before a commercial break as a way of soliciting guests for the program. Talk-show "guests" are not experts or people in positions of power; rather, they are deemed legitimate sources of information by virtue of their experiences. They have "been there," and they come on television to tell their stories with the hope that others may learn from them.

Experience, then, becomes the source of authority. Talk television is formatted to present life experience as the now-legitimate author of information. Ordinary people recount their own experiences, which provide a perspective from the microlevel, and they are given ample time to do so. The new formats of tabloid TV have gained legitimacy through the proposition that they ring true to the average person's life activities. They appear to provide living knowledge useful to the everyday lives of people by retrieving human experience as a source of knowledge. Thus the stories of human experience are considered to be legitimate sources of information.

These formats have the appearance of being truly participatory and seem to provide an alternative to "official" news presentations. Many believe them to be a valuable democratic tool, one that promotes an engaging participatory discursive practice. But as we shall see, the talk show's democratic appearance does not provide an alternative discourse that leads to public knowledge. Instead, it promotes a pseudotherapeutic discourse that fails to explain social and economic forces.

Talk Shows and the Public Sphere

With the rise of talk shows and the crisis of legitimacy of traditional news representations, media scholars have focused analytic attention on the communications model known as the public sphere.[9] Inspired by the translation into English of Jurgen Habermas's (1962/1989) book, *The Structural Transformation of the Public Sphere*, such scholars have begun to emphasize the relationship between the media and democratic public life. Key to the formulation of the public-sphere model is the assumption of the need for an inclusive public debate on issues of common concern. From this perspective, the role of the media is to provide a forum that facilitates a participatory, democratic public discussion.

According to Habermas (1962/1989), the emergence of a public sphere was essential to the development of democracy.[10] The public-sphere model posits the media as the place where equality of judgment and equal access to discussion are encouraged. These practices, in turn, assume that individuals, even those of unequal social and economic status, participate effectively, ensuring their mutual influence on issues of common concern. The public sphere is essential to the ideal of a democratic system because it functions to give everyone a voice.

Democratic public life exists only when active citizens "critically" participate in communication practices. A vibrant public sphere assumes the public's participation, even when the focus of public discussion lies outside the realm of purely personal or "private" economic interests. A philosophy of discourse characterized by an open forum for debate is the main criterion for public involvement in political processes and, indeed, defines the practice of public life.

The talk shows offer the public an engaging participatory format, which has the potential to be what Habermas terms "a philosophy of discourse essential to democracy" (1962/1989). This format engages the public by providing the space for a potentially egalitarian public discussion—one that evaluates contribution and allows participation to the debate, based not on expertise, power, or wealth but on civic involvement. Experience at the microlevel is examined, described, and shared.

This kind of democratic discussion is exactly what Americans express a desire for. Indeed, on the basis of his findings, Harwood (1991, 15) concluded that "Americans seem to be yearning for open, public discussions among themselves and between themselves and public officials." The virtues of public discussion are clearly articulated by a Richmond man quoted by Harwood: "When you hear what others have to say, your views tend to broaden" (1991, 15). People want equality of access to discussion and they look to the media to provide that; "citizens seem to want a media that challenges them to think, that engages them in politics. As a Dallas man put it: 'I think we need a public interest developed in order for people to participate. And maybe this is where our news media come in'" (Harwood 1991, 24).

The public's desire to hold meaningful discussions with elected officials is also clear. As Harwood says, "It would be nice to have a politician come in and ask *us* what we want as opposed to coming in and telling us, 'This is what I want to offer you.'" One Philadelphia woman emphasized, "It would be ideal just to have a forum that is a discussion" (1991, 16). Through the communications practices of a public sphere, members of the public are able to formulate an understanding of issues of common concern to them. This should be the practice of opinion formation in a democratic system. Public opinion, formulated at the microlevel by incorporating individual experience within the larger understanding of public life, should then be brought to bear on the state. In other words, open debate allows citizens to understand and articulate their interests. It allows them to express those interests at the level of policy debates. Through this process, opinion formation takes into consideration the common good because perspectives are shared and views are expanded.

An early Oprah Winfrey program illustrates the potential for wide-ranging discussion in which a variety of perspectives are debated in a public forum. The topic in this case was employment. The guest was a woman who had been fired from her job. Sitting next to her was her ex-boss. The audience was made up of employees and employers (on opposite sides of the studio) with similar experiences. The credibility of each narrative was based on the individual's ability to respond to the questions and accusations of the other. People were subjected to close questioning of their motivations, intentions, and justifications for actions. A length of time was provided during which numerous points and counterarguments could be made. During the debate the authority of the expert was replaced by the authority of a narrative informed by lived experience. This process counteracted endless news reports that imply that the public cannot understand or affect the world and must therefore leave it in the hands of the experts.

The talk show is altogether different from the traditional nonfiction format in which the credibility of the speaker is based on official power or is visually coded, as, for example, when the expert sits in front of bookshelves. Within conventional news texts, the word of the official is left to stand, rarely called into question with the kind of intensity with which it is judged on the talk show. Official political discourse of news reporting is most often presented at face value, so it is lacking in authenticity and integrity. The talk show allows the public to question, point up contradictions, and engage in critical discussion. Therein lies the potential of the discursive practice of talk show, and of its public appeal.

Hungry for such discussions, the public tuned in to talk shows during the 1980s in large numbers. As they did so, the format proliferated, and competition for ratings increased. Functioning under the same economic constraints of information programming detailed above, talk-show discussions were directed toward themes and narrative practices that dominated the existing media environment. As we shall see, it is because of these presures that talk shows have been unable to meet their potential as a meaningful public forum. The primary reason is that talk-show discussions are directed away from contextual understandings of private experiences. Instead, the emotive narratives of personal life featured on these television fixtures are translated into the same privatized language that constitutes the therapeutic themes of television itself, in the age of advertising dominance. Within this framework, talk shows have proven to be incapable of connecting individual life experiences and human needs to larger macrolevel political and social forces. A closer look at the language and themes of talk shows will illustrate these points.

The Talk Show's Lost Potential

What is immediately apparent, even from a cursory glance at talk-show titles, is a selection of topics so bizarre that they verge on the absurd.[11] This is now a routine observation, easily explained by the need to compete in a media environment crowded by one talk show after another. The punchy "teasers" programmed throughout the day have to be provocative and grabby, and the shows themselves, in this age of remote-control technology and intense ratings wars, must hold the viewer's attention. Any potential that the participatory discourse of inclusion might hold is wiped out by the commercial imperative. The demand for ratings creates an escalating sensationalism that jades the public, made eager for tomorrow's displays only by the most titillating exhibitions. The joke about talk shows these days is that a guest must be more than a nymphomaniac prostitute. She needs to be a nymphomaniac prostitute with HIV-infected children who was abused by her Satan-worshiping stepfather.

But it is not only the demand for ratings that drives producers to find topics so extreme in their sensationalism. Added to the necessity for freak shows that leave the eyes bugged and the jaw slack is the requirement that topics defy rational explanation. This is the logical outcome of a routine cultural practice, influenced by the discourse of consumption, that presents human phenomena disconnected from the larger social and political context. If the topic cannot be held within the pop-psychology discourse of media therapy, it must enter the realm of the utterly fantastic. For instance, by the 1990s a number of talk shows detailed the horrors of Satan worship.[12] Appropriately supernatural, this problem is presented as a manifestation of the forces of evil and its solution requires the intervention of higher powers.

Therapy and the Devil

Sometimes the narratives of therapy and the supernatural meet to produce a unified discourse that is more determined than ever to deny social connections. One talk show dealt with the case of a woman who, abused by a family of Satan worshipers, had developed multiple personalities. The show's narrative began by explaining that one of the woman's less dominant personalities had gone to a minister for help. The dominant personality was now suing the minister for performing a forced exorcism. Of course, once the discussion hinged on the issue of exorcism, it entered the realm of predictably hideous spectacle. The minister brought with him a videotaped exorcism that included gruesome visual details of what appeared to be blood spewing from a "possessed" man's mouth. The sticky substance also flowed from his eyes. The grotesque display and the claim of possession by the devil became the focus of the show. In effect, the devil himself was assumed to have occupied the center of a clinical discussion about multiple personalities, with exorcism presented as a therapeutic cure for the disorder. The discussion revolved around unexplainable forces of good and evil.

Real-life clinical cases indicate that the creation of different personalities provides some victims with the distance needed to cope with the pain of abuse. An understanding of this phenomenon as the effect of extreme childhood abuse might well be helpful to some viewers. It could even further an understanding of the larger public issue of mental health. But the injection of the supernatural only prevents a meaningful social discussion. The dimension of Satan worship draws the discussion away from an understanding of social phenomena and into the realm of bizarre ratings-boosting curiosity. What does it mean for a culture to publicly display grotesque depictions of spirit possession as entertainment, and then to assert that such possession is the cause of child abuse?

Of Personal Culpability and Public Responsibility

The July 15, 1992, broadcast of the *Sally Jessy Raphael* program on the subject of "Mothers Who Have Bully Sons" is illustrative of a discourse that exploits the misery of painful problems, backing the participants into a corner of blame, hopelessness, and self-loathing. This exploitation is accomplished through equal measures of accusations of individual irresponsibility, social decontextualization, and traditional gender formulations.

The mothers testify to the brutality of their young thugs, who are of course extreme in their delinquency, having broken bones and bashed heads with gleeful malevolence. Sobbing, the mothers recount years of helplessness, detailing the first time he banged his head against the wall and the first of many humiliating complaints of his ruthlessness. Then the "understanding" begins.

As the mothers sit crying, bewildered as to "what went wrong," desperate for reasons, grasping for solutions, a "therapist" planted in the audience, with hand waving, glibly offers the explanation. It is the mothers' own fault. In fact, the therapist has written a book on exactly this topic, and if only the mothers had taught their recalcitrant offspring discipline and respect, this never would have happened. The obedient audience follows with "If only you had set boundaries," as they no doubt would have done. Mythic themes, planted in the media ether, emerge as the social, institutional explanation for delinquency. In the process, motherhood is devalued by the notion that traditional families, which once raised wholesome offspring, have been torn apart by women's selfish desire for liberation.

This explanation hinges on the assumption that mothers are the sole influence on their children's behavior, ignoring a sweeping range of social influences that affect teenage behavior. In the absence of any social context for understanding a problem that seems so formidable, and no doubt strikes fear in the hearts of mothers everywhere, the mothers of the bullies themselves become the scapegoats.

This "therapeutic" deciphering directs audience sentiments down a discourse not of empathy but of distance—a distance bred by fear and lack of understanding; a distance that prevents the audience from having to accept any mutual blame, as members of a shared culture, for the prevailing social practices of power gained through force and physical domination; a distance designed to obscure an analytic understanding of the way in which the bullies' aggressive subjectivity fits within the distorted belligerent power brandished by the "heroes" of morning television and celebrated in the big-screen action adventures. A week after this show aired, a rock-and-roll radio station in New York, targeting teenage listeners in the largest market in the country, held a call-in contest to see who could propose the "most creative way" of breaking Saddam Hussein's fingers.

Private Life in the Public Forum

Most talk shows are concerned with relationships. Revolving around topics made titillating by taboo, such as "Daddy's Girls", and "Newlyweds at Each Other's Throat," they engage in marriage counseling and relationship therapy of every persuasion; from psychoanalysis to the more pedestrian group counseling. Audiences around the country tune in, trying to "work it out" with their loved ones.

These programs are much more than mass cultural curiosities. They are taken very seriously as helpful forums to which people—guests, studio audiences, and home viewers—go for help, expression, and sharing. And on talk shows just about everything is shared. From murder to incest, crime and punishment, almost no boundaries exist between what can and cannot be said in public. No revelation, confession, or disclosure is so personal that it cannot be exposed by a talk-show host. In this atmosphere of total exposure, no secrets are allowed. For instance, the aforementioned victim of Satan worshiping described the most intimate details of what her parents did to her and how it made her feel. On display, no question was inappropriate; so the audience was not embarrassed to ask her to switch personalities on command: "Can we see Jenny now?" Men who cross-dress but have hidden this fact from their families sit in full regalia, entrusting a mass audience to their innermost passions for a behavior that has isolated them from their closest relatives. And many people—mothers and children, brothers and sisters— are reunited for the first time after years of separation over some deep hurt—on national television.

During one show a husband complains that he's not getting enough sex from his wife; during another, couples learn sexual arousal through public kissing. The TV talk format represents a profound transformation in this country's formulation of what used to be valued as the right to privacy. Clearly it appeals to a public whose most intimate needs are not being met by other means. But what types of needs are met on talk shows? How are problems defined and solved through exposure in a public forum? And what are the implications of the shift in positioning between public and private life in this age of TV therapy?

"Don't Tell Me, Tell Her"

Relationship therapy is, of course, about *communicating*. "Don't tell me, tell her," the therapist enjoins. After all, people go on talk shows to talk about their problems. On an *Oprah Winfrey* program entitled, "Newlyweds at Each Other's Throat," three couples bring their marital problems to the small screen. One couple, Stephen and Christy, have a problem that cannot be solved within the realm of private life. Nevertheless, even in this public forum, private solutions are the only ones offered. As Christy puts it "He didn't work for four months, and it's hard. I cannot support the three of us, me and him and our daughter." Throughout the program, both consistently assert that their problems stem entirely from Stephen's inability to find a job. Stephen offers reasons—Christy takes their only car to work and he is forced to stay home with their small child. Nevertheless, his wife has come to resent his unemployed status: "She seems to think there's a standing job for me at Burger King." Christy, meanwhile, believes that her husband has not tried hard enough to get work.

> STEPHEN: I've tooken [*sic*] jobs picking up garbage out of parking lots from 11:00 at night until 5:00 or 6:00 in the morning, and I hated it.
> OPRAH: So, the problem, you're saying, is not that you're just waiting on a construction job. You can't find anything.
> STEPHEN: No, I'd take any job that's offered to me, but there's 28,000 construction workers out of work in Palm Beach County, and they're all looking for every job there is that's available.
> OPRAH: Oh OK. Well, coming up, we're going to find out why John thinks Dawn has put his sex life on the skids. We'll be back.

Absolutely incapable of discussing the impact of economic hardship on a relationship, the show simply ignores it. To acknowledge it as a fundamental problem would foreclose the possibility of offering a pseudotherapeutic solution. In fact, a therapist, Dr. Gray, is brought on midway through the discussion to tell everyone what their problems are and how to solve them. After all, he has written a book entitled *Men Are from Mars, Women Are from Venus*. Dr. Gray explains, "What they're really—the issue is—what you were talking about, Oprah, is—the underlying problem in every one of these cases is communication. Nobody's hearing the other person."

But Christy and Stephen are definitely not being heard above the therapeutic din. They continue to ground their discussion on the issue of employment:

CHRISTY: All I want is—

DR. GRAY: He gets the message that you want to change him, and that hurts a man. That's the most painful thing.

CHRISTY: I don't want to change him. I just want him to work.

The participants talk at cross-purposes throughout the program because the doctor simply cannot discuss unemployment. He is locked in a therapeutic mode that views the world and its problems solely from an interiorized perspective. Oprah and the doctor translate everything Christy says into a subjective affect devoid of social context. She must "get in touch with her feelings" and "work them out":

OPRAH: . . . What she's really saying is, "I'm scared. I'm scared that whatever expectations I had that you were going to be there to take care of me—I am scared that you are not going to be able to fulfill. . . .

DR. GRAY: But she's terrified. She's terrified. . . . What she needs is for him to understand and hear that and give her reassurance.

Christy does not seem terrified at all. In fact, she feels confident enough to leave her husband. This is where the therapeutic discourse really goes wrong. An understanding that unemployment is structural leads to the realization that not everyone who looks for work will get it. Viewing her situation from an economic context, Christy might have been more inclined toward patience. Together, she and Stephen might even be able to develop a strategy with which to deal with that situation and thereby alleviate their marital problems. But in the absence of such a discussion, the conventional wisdom that blames the individual is simply presumed. In a culture that continually asserts that anyone who looks for a job will get one, those who do not are considered failures. Those out of work are blamed, just as Christy blames Stephen.

As high-paying skilled jobs are lost and replaced by low-paying service-industry (Burger King) jobs, young couples like Christy and Stephen feel its impact on their personal lives. The injustice of economic disparities and of corporate practices that have taken jobs out of this country by the thousands go unmentioned and therefore unrecognized as significant factors contributing to Christy and Stephen's problems. In addition, a focus on the general social and economic need for day care might have made this couple's problems seem less individual, and more manageable.

But to include the social and economic context would direct the discussion toward an entire set of contingencies with which the therapeutic discourse is incapable of dealing. That context becomes a Pandora's box, and talk shows strain to keep the lid firmly in place. If they were truly a forum for discussing issues of public concern—for a participatory discourse that would further the goals of democratic practice—they would have to include at least a small range of social, cultural, and economic connections to the human suffering they so effectively exploit. But discussion of such connections would lead to the realization that, in many cases, only economic improvements can ameliorate personal problems. The further discovery might be made that only social participation and citizen involvement in the political process will lead to change. But the amazing talk-show phenomenon prevents literally thousands of people from making those connections, offering self-reflection, instead, as the solution to all our problems. The solution is to work on ourselves rather than on the social problems that render us increasingly miserable as a society.

The therapeutic solution offered to cure Stephen's employment problem is so deficient that the dialogue verges on the absurd.

> DR. GRAY: That's what men want to do, they want to solve the problem.
> They want—instead of listening—
> STEPHEN: That's right. I want to solve the problem.
> DR. GRAY: She doesn't want the problem solved. She wants you to understand, empathize. Here. Give her a hug. This lady's starved for a hug. She can't give sex until she gets affection and love and touching and all that stuff. That's what she needs.

John and Dawn are another newlywed couple who are "at each other's throat":

> JOHN: I work six days a week. I'm up at 7:00 every morning to go to work, OK. Dawn, that's the only thing you have to do, is take care of the baby and clean the house. I go to work and make the money—

TV therapy focuses on private relationships, but as Hillman and Ventura (1992a, 63) point out, "Work may matter just as much as relationship." John's bitter complaint is as much about his work as it is about his wife. Six long days make for an unreasonable schedule, and "in a world where most people do work that is not only unsatisfying but also, with its pressures, deeply unsettling . . . we load all our needs onto a relationship or expect them to be met by our family. And then we wonder why our relationships and family crack under the load" (Hillman and Ventura 1992a, 63). But no one on *Oprah* asks John about his job or his working conditions. Instead, all problems are assumed to hinge on the couple's relationship.

As the discussion continues, John openly belittles the domestic work his wife does. But he does not want her to work outside the home. Rather, he wants more attention from her and clearly would like her life to revolve around his needs: "She takes care of the house, she takes care of the baby, OK, but what about—when is it time to take care of me?" he asks. These demands elicit a negative response from the audience, but Oprah insists, "That is a legitimate—may I say this? Everybody's yelling at him, but that is a legitimate concern."

For Oprah it is a legitimate concern because it is about *feelings*. On talk shows the expression of any feelings is legitimate, even if they are feelings molded by a society in which relationships between men and women are structured in domination. John's devaluation of his wife's domestic work reflects a society in which the sexual division of labor remains dominant. Work in the public sphere is valued and rewarded, whereas domestic labor is "free" and not highly regarded. In addition, John's demand that his wife pay more attention to him exists within a social context that expects women to defer to the needs of their husbands.

But blaming John personally (which is what the predominantly female audience would like to do), without examining the social and economic origins of his attitudes, will do nothing to change his outlook. In her desire to accommodate all feelings (according to the rules of TV therapy), Oprah goes so far as to tell John, "It's not wrong that you think that way, John."

But Dawn certainly thinks it is a problem and has become uninterested in John as a consequence of his manifest disrespect. And that is the real tragedy of people's lives. Relationships based on inequality are not happy ones. Just as Hope and Michael could never find happiness on *thirtysomething* because they had accepted a patriarchal structure that accommodated Michael's needs at the expense of Hope's, these newlyweds play out the unhappy relations of domination. A young woman on the *Oprah* program came close to making such connections: "In my opinion, he's not treating her with respect, and people want to hug and kiss and love when you feel respected." But without a context, her remark fell into a void of no response.

Dr. Gray offers John another nonsolution, similar to the one he had offered Stephen. Simply think of women as different and learn to "deal with it":

> And we are different, and so a nice, light way of looking at it is men are
> from Mars. . . . It's a whole different world. That's why we're that way.
> Women are from Venus. They're just that way. I used to think my wife was
> off the wall. Now I know she's from Venus and I—and instead of judging
> her, I said, "OK. I need a survival guide for how do you survive on Venus."

What Herbert Marcuse (1966) once referred to as "repressive tolerance" is offered on the talk shows as a solution to problems with relationships that lack equality. Such shows also reassert the biologistic notion that the sexes are different (a notion that has served to justify women's second-class status for centuries). And the vast implications of the social definitions of gender—which include disparities of all sorts—are reified into mystified categories from outer space. Admitting that some expectations could be considered unreasonable because they are based on assumptions of social inequality is beyond the ken of TV therapy. Thus the social impact on the formation of human subjectivity is further eclipsed.

To enter into what Marcuse (1966, 301) termed "truly personal relations," the socially formed character must overcome "modes of universal alienation." The inequality of socially defined gender positions causes a whole range of conflicts and discontentments in relationships that cannot be alleviated until they are recognized. Only by acknowledging and understanding the existing social relations of hierarchy will couples be able to overcome the negative impact these relations have on their relationships. If we were to judge talk shows on the basis of their own rigidly defined individual/psychological terms, they would fail to satisfy. The reason, as the women's movement pointed out so long ago, is that the personal is political. That point is incomprehensible in a discourse where there is no "political." Without a context, personal feelings and behavior can never be understood.

It is not surprising that by the end of the *Oprah Winfrey* show, the newlyweds are more confused than ever. John, especially, hangs his head in puzzlement and frustration. In the end, the confusion between public and private space, and the continual encroachment into private life, means that nothing gets solved. As with the "new intimacy" of *thirtysomething*, talk-show therapy ruptures the connection between societal conditions and emotional peace of mind. When that link is broken, paths to well-being become more obscured than ever.

This conspicuous inability to offer solutions that ring with even a modicum of veracity leaves talk shows in the unhappy position of having to offer their audiences a different set of emotional dynamics for enjoyment and entertainment. Unfortunately, the programming strategies used to maintain these audiences in an increasingly competitive environment have taken an unhealthy turn. TV talk therapy's lack of explanation and understanding has led to strategies that evoke— not empathy—but ridicule, distance, and moral superiority. *Sally Jessy Raphael's* "I Stole Money to Get Married" show demonstrates talk-show tactics in this age of emotional discontent.

Small-Town Pathology

On *Sally Jessy Raphael* we are introduced to a young couple from a small town in Kentucky, Danny and Jeannie, who recently ended up in jail on their wedding day. Before the ceremony, they had embarked on a greedy grab, stealing everything from bridesmaid's dresses to jewelry, ring cushions, and lingerie. A huge bag filled with what the audience believes to be the stolen merchandise sits next to Sally. The girl's cousin, Bobby Ray, is also introduced. These people are talk show choices, not simply by virtue of their criminality, but because they have turned on one another. Cousin Bobby is telling a different story than Danny and Jeannie. They say he stole everything. He says they did it. They have not spoken to one another since giving the police different stories. They meet again today for the first time.

From the start, Sally asks probing questions, trying to pin something on each of the guests by catching them in an inconsistency. The audience members follow suit, and the program turns into a harsh inquisition. They ask Jeannie's dress size and shoe size, and the sizes of the stolen clothes; then they try to find out whether Bobby knew her sizes. When someone from the audience asks if he had any "idea the trunk was being filled with merchandise?" Bobby says "No." His implausible denial results in an audible sigh of disbelief from the audience. From their confused narratives of denial the realization emerges that none of them is innocent. They are simply trying to blame each other, causing one audience member to

FIGURE 6.1 Sally Jessy Raphael with Wedding Dress
This program, entitled "I Stole Money to Get Married," illustrates the staged nature of talk shows. Sally Jessy Raphael pulls a collection of items from a large bag. The audience believes them to be the actual articles stolen by her young guests. "I'm going to take it this is the wedding dress. But I can hardly—This is very heavy. You know shoplifting is one thing. It has a long train. Whoa. . . ." Another guest later reveals that the dress Raphael pulls from the bag is not the stolen dress, and that the actual dress "wasn't near that size."

announce, "If any of these people stood here and told me that Sally's glasses are red, I wouldn't believe it from any of them." A growing sense of disgust and impatience with the guests causes Sally to respond with "What do you want from me?" But she continues on, encouraging everyone to play detective by asking, "If you were the police, who would you believe and what would you do?"

The audience is provided with a dramatization of the theft. From a rack of wedding dresses Jeannie is asked to pick the one most like the one stolen and to try to fit it under her jacket. Bobby Ray objects, saying, "All these is too long. . . . This was a short dress, come to her knees, and she knows it."

The audience is led to believe that the items in the bag next to Sally were the actual ones stolen. Sally says, "This is a kind of reenactment of what the police found when they looked in the trunk of Bobby, the best man's car." (See Figure 6.1.) She pulls the merchandise out, one item at a time; playing the scene for maximum impact, she displays each item and makes comments. With exaggerated artifice she finds the wedding dress: "Now, this—Oh my goodness, this—(*straining to pull it out of the bag*). This is enormously heavy. This is—I'm going to take it this is the wedding dress. But I can hardly—This is very heavy. You know shoplifting is one thing. It has a long train. Whoa . . . ." Then, and a few items later: "Here is the one that somebody said their mother made. No way. This is the ring-bearer thing, right?" Because of the way the items are presented, the audience believes them to be the real ones. Much later, however, during the audience interrogation, one questioner responds with disbelief at Bobby's claim that he did not see Jeannie carrying the wedding dress out of the Bridal Boutique under her coat. The viewer, incredulous, says, "You couldn't see *that* dress?" BOBBY: "The dress wasn't near this big. The dress wasn't even near that size. It wasn't near that size." To this revelation the audience responds with loud grumbles of disapproval for having been misled. SALLY: This is not the—this is the—We didn't take that dress because it's stolen merchandise." This explanation is accepted. No one bothers to ask why a dress so much bigger than the real one was chosen. The next comment comes from someone in the audience: "I think they're all involved in this . . . ." But the show's producers, staff, and Sally are all involved, too. Their exaggerations have caused confusion and made the guests look even more mendacious then they really are—and just plain stupid for thinking anyone could believe such nonsense.

As the story unfolds, copious details of different accounts of the theft are argued over. All of the guests refer to police reports they say would verify their claims. Accusations are followed with denials such as "The cops never said no such thing." We find that eight people (all related) were involved in the robbing spree, continuing a drunken episode that had begun the night before. The argument descends further into a bickering harangue between family members when Jeannie's sister Betty Jo is brought out. The transcript reads as follows:

BETTY JO (*jailed before her sister's wedding for stealing*): No, I didn't take a damn thing.
SALLY: Nothing?
BETTY JO: Not a (*expletive deleted*) thing. And if he wants to sit here and tell me I took (*expletive deleted*).
BOBBY: —damn piece—(*cross-talk*)[13]
BETTY JO: Yeah, sure, Bobby, sure.
BOBBY: Why did you sign the papers for it?
BETTY JO: I didn't sign no (*expletive deleted*) damn papers. Because you (*unintelligible*).

We also find that cousin Bobby is awaiting trial for driving a bus while drunk; one girl is hospitalized with injuries. Bobby counters with the information that Jeannie's "daddy" robbed a department store, and that Danny and Jeannie have stolen $100,000 worth of merchandise in the past. In addition, someone has tried to burn down the couple's trailer—they blame cousin Bobby for it.

The growing sense of disgust compels Sally to detach herself from these miscreants. To do so she corrects their grammar and mocks their Kentucky drawl. When she asks, "What has this done in the family?" Danny responds that "it's caused peeyur hail."

SALLY: Caused what?
DANNY: Peeyur hail.
SALLY: (*sarcastically*) Pure hell.
DANNY: Peeyur hail.

Sally rolls her eyes to create distance between her guests and decent people everywhere. They squirm like insects under a microscope. They have been turned into the Other, strange aberrations of the kind created by David Lynch for the cult TV series *Twin Peaks*—itself a view of the unhealthy underbelly of small-town life.

The final insult to the guests comes at the very end as Sally returns from the commercial break, saying, "You talk about reality television." She announces having just received a fax from the Ramada Renaissance Hotel (promotional plug), where a hair dryer is missing from the couple's room. All deny having taken it, saying they had their own. The hotel's mini-bar was also "wiped out"—the bill came to $116. As Danny protests, "No, no, no, no, they got that. . . . That ain't right now," Sally corrects, "That isn't right?"

In a gross violation of privacy, during the next commercial break, the show's staff members rifle through the couple's luggage (or say they have done so) and come up with a hair dryer. (The hair dryer shown has a cord, not like the wall-mounted kind hung in hotel bathrooms.) Sally brandishes the dryer, saying, "There's a hair dryer in the suitcase. Give me the hair dryer. OK (*she says to Jeannie*), you said you used her—." Danny comes to Jeannie's aid, claiming, "That was my fault. I packed the suitcase."

Sally finishes with irritation in her voice: "I don't know what they do in Kentucky, but in New York, this is trouble. I mean, you just can't do this." She continues sternly, "I want the hair dryer back in the hotel. . . ."

As the credits roll, Jeannie and Bobby hang their heads, and we are left with a sinking feeling of disgust, having been exposed to the banality of some senseless malfeasance perpetrated by unhappy miscreants. We have no idea what has gone wrong in their small town and with their lives.

The pathology so blatantly demonstrated on this talk show exists in total contradiction to the mythic political themes developed during the Democratic convention, which was televised nationally that very same week. In fact, the *Sally Jessy Raphael* program aired the same day that presidential candidate Bill Clinton gave his acceptance speech at the convention. Clinton stressed (as dictated by focus groups) his upbringing in the small town of Hope, Arkansas, an upbringing he said had instilled moral character. In short, the political myths developed for public consumption at the Democratic convention stand in striking contrast to the representations of small-town pathology developed on *Sally Jessy Raphael*. But this contradiction remains at the level of the repressed; no conscious connection is articulated. Instead, it registers in the deep collective unconscious as the cultural contradiction of marketing culture. The clash of myths is observed, but it remains just below the level of comprehension that would delegitimate the discourse. Indeed, it sits hidden, creating a sense of uneasy awareness that something is desperately wrong—but ever illusive. This awareness, of course, breeds the cynicism so apparent in American culture today.

Of Authenticity and Artifice

In the face of Sally's claim to be doing "reality television," it is immediately apparent that everything about her talk show—from the planning stage, to the search for victims, to the development of the gimmicks of the format, to the audience preparation and its group dynamic—is fraudulent. The story of Jeannie, Danny, Bobby Ray, and Betty Jo was formulated and staged. The resulting disgust and hostility on the part of the audience is no accident.

Even though the program is structured as a detective intrigue, and Sally compels the audience to cross-examine, no real attempt is made to understand what went on. Such an attempt could have been summarized easily at the beginning of the program. All of the guests had already told their stories to the police, and a review of those reports could have been presented. That would have cleared up the majority of contended assertions. But the arguing and lying are ruses—they are the entertainment. The show was deliberately set up to provide toxic fun for an audience invited to play detective, police, and moral arbiter all at the same time.

The Discourse of Confusion

The shouting, confusing, (expletive deleted) bluster of talk-show "debate" is the formula to which everyone must adhere as a requirement for participation. In *I'm Dysfunctional, You're Dysfunctional*, writer Wendy Kaminer (1992, 39) explains the preparation she received before appearing on the *Oprah Winfrey* show:

> "Just jump in. Don't wait to be called on," one of Oprah's people told us when she prepped us for the show. "You mean you want us to interrupt each other?" I asked; the woman nodded. "You want us to be really rude and step on each other's lines?" She nodded again. "You want us to act as if we're at a large unruly family dinner on Thanksgiving?" She smiled and said, "You got it!"

This format is antithetical to authentic understanding. When the volume is turned up on a cacophony of noise calculated for its dramatic entertainment value, the "debate" is reduced to grunts and shouts: "I'd never call what goes on over the turkey a debate," says Kaminer. She points out, "The trouble with talk shows is that they claim to do so much more than entertain; they claim to inform and explain. They dominate the mass marketplace and help make it one that is inimical to ideas" (1992, 39). This is the most detrimental aspect of the format, whereby the potential for inclusive discussion of public issues is lost. The wedding day program was a stereotypical drama featuring a feuding backwoods clan. It engaged the audience at the level of elitist voyeurism. No one left more informed; self-righteous superiority is not edification.

The credits at the end of the program that name the professionals who have fixed Sally's hair and designed her clothes are symbolic of the process by which she has been created. The discourse, too, has been created. The producers seek people out and provide the hosts with the notes they have taken. Hosts and the guests alike are thoroughly "prepped." Strategies are developed to frame the discussion itself. Other guests are introduced according to a predetermined narrative pace and progression. And questions initiated by the host direct the audience to the appropriate topics.[14]

With contrived spontaneity, they talk to one another, these hosts and their allegorical representations of social pathology. These hosts will often pretend shock or surprise at some revelation after asking a question they most certainly know the answer to in advance. The same practice is now apparent on the morning news/talk programs, where, for example, Regis and Cathy Lee act out a preplanned discussion. From *Home Show* to Dan Rather's dialogue with a correspondent after a segment, "reality television" asks itself "Did you know?" and feigns surprise at the prearranged answer.

The audience members, too, have become actors. They play along, following both the implicit and explicit directions. Indeed, professionals prep the audience as well as the hosts. Before a *Geraldo* show featuring "homeless couples," Rivera told studio guests to ask questions about homeless *relationships* only, not about the causes of homelessness or any other "general" aspects of the topic. And before the *Phil Donahue Show* gets under way, a coach "revs everybody up a couple of emotional notches," according to one staff member. Applause, used to indicate approval, encourages viewers to ask the toughest questions, or compels guests to reveal the most intimate details of their private life.

Therapy or Exploitation?

Such is the sad exploitation for ratings of a daytime parade of human anomalies; but these shows claim to be helping people. By providing information and letting people know "they are not alone," they claim to dispense wisdom about life, along with specific techniques for negotiating adverse situations. Unfortunately, many people, particularly the guests, are not finding help.

Many times, late at night in their hotel rooms, the anxiety of exposure overcomes these would-be guests, and, as one staff member put it, "they try to bolt." Talk show producers have devised a strategy to prevent their guests from backing out. Employees of the show are "planted" in hotels to deal with precisely this eventuality. Taking an adjoining room, they are on-site if a guest tries to leave before going on the air. The job of these employees is to "talk them down," and they do so by telling the guests how much they will be helping other people—people with problems just like theirs, who have no one to talk to, nowhere to turn for help. Most of the time this strategy works. But as the *New York Times* (July 18, 1993) reported, an increasing number of people are finding that they feel worse after exposing themselves on national television, and support groups for these people have sprung up.

The devices used to create the smug aloofness with which hosts (Raphael especially) approach their sensational topics offer a convenient way to avoid having to take the blame for setting up these public spectacles. This aloofness denies responsibility for the exploitation of people's pain and distress for ratings. As the topics become more vile and grotesque, everyone involved is compelled to distance themselves from the freakish guests. Despite constant assertions that information is being provided to help others heal, TV therapy is often as much about ridicule as it is about empathy.

In its healthiest manifestation, the talk show *is* about emotional empathy, a hope held out for understanding. But what has become apparent is that it functions predominantly as a public confessional. In short, the distinction between confessing and testifying has been effaced. As Kaminer (1992, 30) points out, "The tradition of testifying in court, church, or the marketplace for justice, God, or the public good is a venerable one." Talk shows claim to be engaging in public testimony—for the betterment of all. But when that testimony is gathered within a social and political void, the once-honorable practice amounts to little more than public humiliation and exposure.

Public testifying for the common good is very different from confessing in the pseudotherapeutic context offered on talk shows. As therapy, talk shows are also fraudulent. A genuine theraputic process involves years of private struggle to attain self-knowledge and come to terms with emotional configurations. It is sometimes argued that talk shows provide a catalyst for healing, by prompting the realization that emotional problems are not unique; but as such shows have devolved into spectacle, any positive gain is canceled out by the formatting strategies employed to contain the discourse within the realm of entertainment.

That ratings matter more than "healing" the guests is evident from the amount of time the show's producers allot the teletherapists. According to a study done by Vicki Abt, the average amount of time therapists spend on the show is about 2 minutes per guest (cited in Berger 1995, A9). After almost an hour of conflict and cross-talk, these narrative spectacles demand some type of closure. This is when the "tube-shrinks" make their appearance, at the very end of the show. One particularly popular TV therapist, Dr. Gilda Carle (who actually holds a Ph.D in organizational studies) appeared on almost 100 shows in 1994. Dr. Carle is considered one of the best because of her ability to cajole antagonistic guests into hugging just before the credits roll. The quick clichés promoting self-esteem offer dubious therapeutic content, but they do serve to legitimate the TV-talk spectacles.

Therapy as a spectator sport belittles the healing process and serves a different purpose altogether. When the format does not elicit sympathy, it become a destructive public spectacle invoked to confirm, for example, the moral righteousness and superiority of the audience. These formatting strategies produce results that are antithetical to social justice and also to psychic well-being.

Like the ad for Evian that claims to "Refresh Your Inner Self," talk shows exist within the culture of therapy, forming part of the heart of a heartless world, where a lost public seeks to find a transcendent *self* in a society offering few alternatives. The vast landscape of therapeutic culture promises healing, pleasure, and psychic well-being in a world, it proclaims, that has gone terribly wrong. The therapeutic talk-show discourse of sharing, trust, and disclosure has even taken on spiritual overtones, and is often presented as a way of surpassing the mundane needs of life. But, for the most part, talk shows degrade the emotional and spiritual life of the viewer. In the end, we are left with a profound sense of disgust; viewing other people's pain for our own enjoyment leaves us, at best, feeling empty; at worst, feeling soiled.

On talk shows, the graphic descriptions of abuse turn into grotesque public displays of obscenity—a process that is antithetical to spiritualism, to say the least. The discourse of blame and the individual culpability of the victim create a morality of condemnation devoid of empathy and magnanimity—and explanations of social cause. Audience engagement at the level of elite voyeurism leaves little but the residue of despair.

The Failure of the Talk Show

The talk show emerged at a time of increasing ossification of traditional news reporting, public dissatisfaction with the interdependence between the media and the state, and the restriction of a multiplicity of voices so apparent on news and information programming. At first, talk shows held out hope as an alternative space for discursive practice. They seemed to give voice to a public straining to make sense of its own experiences and hoping to take action in its own best interests.

In the final analysis, however, talk shows—like advertising and entertainment programming—address real needs but do not fulfill those needs. Talk shows respond to the need for a public forum on issues of common concern, but, like traditional news formats, they fail to connect personal experience with the larger socioeconomic context. Therefore, they cannot help individuals understand their own lives in relation to the social, political, and economic forces that shape them. The TV therapist has come to replace the expert (or political official) as the voice of wisdom. Talk shows speak with a therapeutic language that examines only a privatized landscape of human experience, further rupturing individual needs from collective solutions. Instead of understanding and knowledge, television talk offers its viewers the voyeuristic pleasure of gazing into the private lives of society's victims. In essence, television's therapeutic discourse prevents the public from understanding social issues and participating in the search for answers to social problems.

In Chapter 9 we will examine Bill Clinton's use of the language and themes of talk shows in designing a media campaign for the 1992 presidential election. Indeed, both candidates for president responded to and reflected the dominant media environment. Once again, the language of persuasion and that of information were merged in such a way that the candidates could resonate with existing cultural themes and attitudes.

These themes and attitudes were, of course, determined through the same research techniques that guide advertising campaigns. Even focus groups were employed to develop the candidates' speeches to the public during the 1992 election. Candidate Bill Clinton was particularly successful in his use of powerful and contemporary media themes, those that appear to address issues of human experience and well-being—those from television talk shows.

In the next chapter, meanwhile, we will examine another nonfiction format— "reality"-based crime programs—so as to determine how the dual influences of advertising language and the demand for cheap programs have affected TV discourse.

7

Cops on the *Night Beat*

"Reality"-Based Police Shows, Urban Community, and Criminal (In)Justice

Cops

Opening a segment of *Cops* is a view of a room stocked with electronic equipment. Text at the bottom of the screen identifies the room as the Communications Center. The audio of a recorded phone call plays. "10:42 P.M.: Dispatcher Call" then appears on the screen. We hear of a shooting and see the needle registering sound levels on an open-reel tape recorder. These ambient details serve as orientation to the event we are about to experience but not understand. In the next instant we are on the scene, pulling up to a house. The cop is out of the car, asking, "They shot you in the head?" A young woman mutters incomprehensibly as the cop darts after her, saying, "Come here and talk to me."

"My head is bleeding," she responds.

"Who shot you?" he insists, following her.

As the cop and the camera move behind her, into the house and out again, blood soaks her neck and has begun to saturate her Yankees' shirt. Inside we discover another wounded girl; this one, with more serious injuries, is lying on her stomach. Blood stains the floor under her. The officer immediately shines a flashlight into her face and begins interrogating her. "Do you know the name of the guy who did this?" Her shaky voice responds, "It was females." She tells him they were in a Malibu. We cannot make out the words of the other family members inside the house. Only the cop's voice is audible, and he seems to be answering a question when he says that an ambulance is on the way: "They're real busy tonight." The scene becomes more chaotic as various family members with dazed expressions come into view. A child crosses from left to right in front of the camera with a look of incomprehension. The girl we saw in the opening sequence is now being dragged into the house and across the floor. We hear her moan; then magically she is on a stretcher outside being lifted into the ambulance. Suddenly we are looking into a car with blood on the dashboard as the cop explains that a car was following them for a while, and as "they were driving down Cleveland, five girls in a Chevy Malibu opened fire on them with a 12-gauge shot gun." We have not seen or heard him retrieve most of this information.

"Obviously there's some bad blood between these girls and the other girls," he says, driving away from the "scene of the crime." He emphasizes the girls' uncooperative attitude, even though we heard a seriously wounded girl answer his questions under obvious duress. He continues:

> Younger kids like this are highly excitable, and their concern at that time was revenge. Not caring for their injuries, not caring for their other family members' injuries, it was getting revenge on these people who had done harm to them because they know 'em. This situation is far from over.

The cop is white. The girls are black. With that fact established, we move on to the next segment.

The Style of Reality

The "realism" of *Cops* tells us that we have been present, as witnesses, even though we do not really know what happened. The frenetic pacing of the editing creates confusion. It is unclear from the start what is going on. We are taken to a scene, but whether it is the scene of a crime we cannot say, because in most cases we have little or no information about what the people there have done. The commotion at the scene leaves the event indecipherable in its actual details. We are relieved of the burden of knowing what has come before or after the incidents we race in on.

Our limited camera perspective does not provide a complete view of the whole scene, as fictional compositions do. We hear the cops speak in a one-way dialogue that omits most of the other voices. The editing hangs only the most exciting pieces together, and the jumps in place and time ensure a heightened level of excitement. Indeed, the program makes no effort to explain all that is happening—this is not the point. Instead, it simulates the most exciting on-screen experience of a situation in crisis. Things happen so fast that a blur of activity is the result. Understanding is inappropriate.

The exciting *verité* denies the enormous gaps in time and space that do not register consciously. The entire incident is condensed into a few minutes, but the cops and camera must have been on the scene for a much longer time. The excitement of video realism is created through a taping and editing process in which time is contracted into jerky abbreviations that transform reality into a blur.

The claim that *Cops* is "reality" hinges on several formatting strategies: live-action shot with extensive use of a hand-held camera, the absence of reenactment or dramatizations, and the lack of a narrative voice. Yet these now nightly representations of cops pursuing drug dealers and "criminals," and intervening in various other crisis situations—including a staple diet of "domestic disturbances"— are actually social constructions. The chaos of crisis is given meaning through the use of narrative structure.

Masquerading as "reality," the selected sequences are drawn from the immediacy of live events; but the story of *Cops* is nevertheless just that—a story. A contrived order provides a plot progression and a sense of resolution, even though the events themselves are not usually resolved. The narrative is structured with a beginning—with the viewers positioned in the police car, and an end—with the viewers in the same position. This arrangement provides the skeleton upon which the on-the-scene chaos can be hung.

As we drive away with the cop in the police car, he makes sense of it for us. He articulates the story's resolution and, in doing so, assumes the multiple roles of social worker, therapist, prosecutor, judge, and jury. All-knowing, he tells us what the people at the scene were feeling, what motivates them, and how this dangerous world of the street works. The distance between "us and them" is increased by the cop's insinuation that the shooting was somehow gang related—although we have been given no information that would confirm this interpretation. He says the girl's brother (whom we never see) knows the shooters and understands the background to the incident but would not tell the police. Clearly much of the action that took place during this incident, including a good deal of interaction between the cops and those involved, is missing. But one thing is certain: No detail that would reflect negatively on the cops is incorporated into the program.

One editor's working experience at ABC's docu-cop show *American Detective*, a prime-time competitor of *Cops* before being cancelled, illustrates the fabricated nature of "reality-based" narratives and their sympathetic stance toward law enforcement. Debra Seagal (1993, 4) explains that the brief segments aired were

> squeezed out of hundreds of thousands of hours of raw footage and significantly edited. This footage, before it's transformed into an acceptable episode, features cops and detectives at their uncensored "best," which invariably includes slander against every minority under the sun, as well as numerous acts of excessive physical and verbal harassment.

It is through the process of inclusion and exclusion that such narratives (as with any narrative) are constructed.

"Video realism" convinces us that we've "seen with our own eyes," yet we depend on the cop's sources, perspective, and judgment to make sense of the world he defines as criminal. All we actually *see* in the segment described above are badly injured victims of gunfire. But our sympathy for the wounded girls is foreclosed by the cop's lack of empathy. Interrogating the victims is apparently more important than seeing to their injuries, and, after all, if the girls do not care about their own wounds (as he asserts), why should we?

Listening to the cop, we find that the entire criminal justice system is being condensed into his law-enforcement perspective. The wounded girls are no longer victims, having become criminalized in the process of being "explained." They now exist as part of a dark criminal world, inhabited by those on the other side of the law—and on the other side of the lens of video realism.

These cheap state-of-the-art tabloid forms influence other programming formats, even "serious" news, and affect public perceptions. Survey and focus group research done by Times Mirror (1993) reveals that the public regards "reality" shows as informational programming. Such research demonstrates a higher public tolerance for the violence depicted on "reality" programming than for the violent depictions of fictional fare. Fictional violence is viewed as gratuitous, whereas reality shows are viewed as real and are said to "make a point." But what kind of point do they make?

Force Without Justification

In one sequence we arrive with the cops at a restaurant, where a man is sitting quietly at a table. By all appearances he is simply a customer. The police insist that he leave. He sees no reason to do so and refuses. He does not fight, but he also does not move. What ensues are images of a brutal arrest. The man is thrown on a sofa, his head twisted and jammed down while his arms are wrenched behind him. The sounds of struggle render any words incomprehensible. We hear only guttural animal-like noises from the criminal/victim as he is overpowered. He is then dragged out the door by his hand-cuffed arms; which are lifted up, almost to the back of his head, in a position where, it appears, they will surely break. Outside on the sidewalk, he is once again thrown down on his stomach and the cop sits on him. One side of his face flattens into the concrete, twisting his neck in a gruesome anatomical distortion. Another cop shackles him. He is forced into and then out of a police van, which has appeared from nowhere. In the next instant we are at the police station. The receiving officer asks his name, and when he refuses to cooperate, the officer says, "You wouldn't be here if you hadn't done something."

The docu-cop formula reduces conventional crime narratives to denuded fragments. Crime drama traditionally presents police force, and especially direct violence, as retaliatory.[1] In conventional narratives, police pound on criminals only after viewers have had the benefit of seeing the crime or its bloody consequences. As Doug Kellner (1976) argues, this narrative structure evokes an emotional response, which explains why the audience cheers when Kojak shoots the criminal who then falls ten stories to his death. Disgust has been aroused to justify police force. Uncooperative suspects can be roughed up and houses broken into (and civil liberties violated) if it helps get the dangerous (and, by this time, dehumanized) criminal off the streets.

But *Cops* offers no such justifications. We have no idea as to what the hapless restaurant patron may have done, yet we see brutal force employed in his arrest. He continually asks what right the cops have to take him away, but they feel no obligation to explain anything. His resistance becomes the justification for their action. The message is clear: Anyone resisting arrest, even if there is no explanation for that arrest, is guilty and deserves the most brutal treatment.

Content analysis confirms that the excessive and predominantly unjustified use of police force is a defining characteristics of these programs (even though the most extreme and unacceptable brutality and slander are removed). A study of *Cops, Top Cops, America's Most Wanted, FBI: The Untold Story,* and *American Detective* has found that these programs "tend to portray police officers as more aggressive than criminal suspects, and especially when the criminal suspects are black or Hispanic" (Oliver 1993, 18).

Without a doubt, these programs "make a point." Any actions taken by the police against the public, even if brutal, are considered acceptable. (The four officers who beat Rodney King explained that he was resisting arrest, and this explanation was accepted by a jury.) Police force is justified purely on the basis of the cops' own judgment and assertions. But then, telling their side of the story is the whole point of *Cops*.

The Camera Perspective: Through the Eyes of the Police

On *Cops* we are positioned with the officer as his partner, privy to the hidden dangers of the world of police work.[2] We ride "shotgun" in the car, in the front seat next to him. Significantly, no reference is made to the reporter/photographer who never speaks. Therefore, the cop speaks to us. Our eyes see through the camera. The subjective position pulls us directly into the action. Our format of *Cops* and other tabloid crime shows develops a point of view vastly different from that of previous nonfiction programs. Clearly sympathetic to one position only, these crime shows make no effort to create even the appearance of what were once called "rituals of objectivity" (Tuchman 1978). The perspective of the docu-cop shows has transformed nonfiction TV formats. As Richard Campbell (1992, 1) observes, the point of view of conventional news moved during the 1980s "from the appearance of disinterested and dispassionate reporters to shots that identify strongly with police."

Cops *are* sympathetic characters. Even if the politicians and bureaucrats do not care, they do. They want to protect us from the mean streets that they—along with the criminals–must negotiate on a daily basis in the line of duty.

We are not threatened by the celebration of police force against the public on *Cops* or any of the other programs that feature these now formulaic representations. Instead, through our privileged position as part of the police action being featured, we are empowered by it. When cops force their way, shouting, into a house, throwing the occupants down on the floor and tackling "suspects," we feel a surge of excitement at the moment of confrontation. We are on the side of state-sanctioned power. The grainy black-and-white video shot at night communicates increased danger and anticipation. We could be attacked at any moment as we follow cops out a window onto a rooftop, tracking someone who (we have been told) is high on crack and therefore dangerous. Just like the cops on these programs, we always win. Those we confront on the other side of the lens threaten us as well as our chaperons, the police officers/heroes. We are not positioned as the "public." Rather, we identify with the cops. This constructed perspective excludes considerations of our own civil liberties and of constitutional rights in general.

So, the basic elements needed for narrative constructions are complete: suspense, conflict, and clearly defined heroes and villains. *Cops* depicts real events, not dramatized ones. But it tells stories about reality; it does not present reality itself. Ascribing meaning to the chaotic events presented on "reality"-based shows is done through the interpretive structure of a story—a story told not from the multiple perspectives of all involved but, rather, from a singular point of view—that of law enforcement.

The construction of reality depends on whose story is told, and on who does the telling.[3] What does it mean to tell stories about cops, criminals, and drug dealers, even about people who simply find themselves in the wrong place at the wrong time, over and over again from the point of view of law enforcement? Throughout the 1980s we became accustomed to looking collectively at the world of criminal justice through the eyes of police officers. This law-enforcement version of reality is now the dominant media canon, even if it contradicts the interests and experiences of a good portion of the viewers it excites. What are the meanings of these narratives that never speak with other voices? And whose narratives are never told because the same ones get recounted over and over again?

The "reality" formats have had a dramatic impact on the public's perceptions of a range of criminal justice issues including crime, drugs, violence, and imprisonment. This impact can best be illustrated through a closer look at one of these new hybrid forms of nonfiction shows. A good example is the program *Night Beat,* which, though produced by the Fox network news division, was aired as entertainment during prime time in December 1992. In the style of *Cops,* journalist Penny Crone, of channel 5 news, followed police narcotics officers as they patrolled the streets of Newark, New Jersey, providing viewers with an hour-long dose of law enforcement.

Night Beat

A police siren screams as a patch of red flies at the viewer, expanding on the screen, ripping through a blue border. Jagged images hurl into and out of view as they cut across the wall of blue. Everything moves; images flicker behind the blue and inside the red. Pulsating excitement, they obscure what they promise to reveal. A police car hangs suspended for an instant, camera angle askew; then it bursts through the tear in the screen. We look through the knife-cut openings at the quick flashes of motion to grainy video of cops in hot pursuit. The jerky camera runs behind blue jackets, made large by the tight shots; on their backs the word *Sheriff* wiggles into and out of view. This frame gives way to the image of a black man, hands cuffed behind his back. Another black man is forced to lie in the street and is then rolled onto his stomach by a white cop.

Through the continuous wail of the siren are shouts of "police . . . police . . . search warrant . . . hands up . . . right there . . . on the wall . . . on the wall . . . on the wall," the latter growing louder with each repetition. The noise of police-car radios is layered over the sirens. On another layer of audio, the words "drugs involved" can be heard. Images of city streets flash past the window of a moving police car; then from a camera view outside the car we see it race by—siren still blaring. A sheriff beats down a door; cut to a black man cuffed on a couch; cut to a white hand holding a plastic bag: "We found this in the apartment. It's a rock—cocaine." Out on the street another black man is pushed by a white cop.

After this furious introduction, the words *Night Beat* pulsate over the red blotch that continues to struggle against the blue wall. The image immediately cuts to an interview segment in which a black official says, "What we have here in Newark is 300 kids, or 300 *thugs,* holding 270,000 people hostage, and what we have to be about is getting rid of those 300." We are swept from the talking head back onto the street as two white cops force five people of color up against a wall, creating an image almost identical to those that appeared in TV stories of El Salvador during the 1980s—guards or death squads holding guns on peasants up against a wall. One cop says, "Bitch and I'll put a bullet in your head."

Finally Penny Crone delivers her opening remarks:

> The heart of Newark seems to beat faster at night. It thumps at a frightening pace. It's surrounded by drugs, danger and often death.
>
> For whatever reason, be it excitement, dedication, or just living on the edge, the men and women behind the badges are trying to make Newark a safer place to live.
>
> Tonight your heart will beat faster when you see what it takes to divide and conquer.

Crime and the Media

Night Beat, Cops, Top Cops, American Detective, America's Most Wanted, and the many other TV programs that now follow the lurid "reality"-based formula are products of the media's reliance on the entertainment value of the law enforcement establishment. This reliance extends from police officers as sources, to the "mean streets" as settings, but, most important, to the themes, issues, and definitions of crime provided by the police. The alliance of government policy and media representations is one of mutual convenience. The police allow cameras to follow officers in return for the valuable public relations provided by the favorable portrayals and characterizations. As Seagal (1993, 4) has observed, police "have a tacit agreement with the producers that they'll be shown in a positive light." Including anything negative would amount to "jeopardizing their (the producers') livelihoods." The crowd-pleasing drama and excitement of the raw formula, as well as the demand for cheap programming, make these shows irresistible to an industry brought to its knees in many ways by the bottom-line concerns of the 1980s.

In fact, the increasingly profitable alliance between law enforcement and television parallels the disastrous period in television history that led to the quiz show scandals of the 1950s. Cheap and highly rated in their day, quiz shows such as the *$64,000 Question* proliferated. And like the docu-cop programs of today, TV quiz show were promulgated as real—until it was discovered that ratings-obsessed producers were coaching contestants and rigging questions to keep the most popular contenders on the air.

Producers of "reality"-based programming, like their earlier quiz-show counterparts, are similarly concerned that their ratings remain high. Now, producers coach cops rather than contestants. As Seagal (1993, 4) learned while working for *American Detective,* producers were more than willing to prod police officers to repeat certain lines, to play to the camera, or to recap events in a televisually appealing "tone." But in the cynical age of lost innocence characterized by postmodern culture, outrage is not the contemporary response to faking the real.

The mutually dependent relationship between cops and TV has had a profound impact on media representations of crime and the general discussion of those issues within the public sphere. Especially popular are episodes about drugs and related crime, in which cameras follow cops as they engage in street-level narcotics enforcement. The alliance between cops and TV means that media discourse has failed to negotiate an independent stance that would reflect the complex and contradictory nature of drugs and drug-related crime. Instead, given their position of dependence and their emphasis on market priorities, docu-cop shows have reproduced, very nearly verbatim, the existing government policies on crime and drugs. But these policies are coming under increasing scrutiny and criticism from a broad spectrum of policy analysts, politicians, lawyers (prosecutors as well as defense attorneys), judges, public-interest organizations, scholars, and many law-enforcement officials themselves.

With their eerie visuals of the nighttime urban drug trade and their electrifying images of the cops who hunt down the dealers, these television "documents" celebrate the "war on drugs" initiated during the 1980s. They air nightly in seeming affirmation that public funds are being spent in the most productive ways to rid the streets of drugs and crime. They purport to confirm the rightness of police actions taken in inner-city communities; and, most of all, they define drugs and the dealers themselves as the sole dimension of the problem. What they conceal are much deeper social, economic, and political failures (including police corruption) that, if unexamined, guarantee that the problems will never be solved.

The War on Drugs

In 1989 the Bush administration's "drug czar," William Bennett, laid out the National Drug Control Strategy, commonly referred to as the Bennett Plan.[4] The plan stated that, "The typical cocaine user is white, male, a high school graduate employed full time and living in a small metropolitan area or suburb" (Office of National Drug Control Policy 1989, 4). In spite of that identification, the Bennett Plan continued a policy, begun in the early 1980s, to fight the war on drugs in the most densely populated urban areas, primarily in black and Latino neighborhoods, communities characterized by high levels of unemployment and poverty. The Bennett drug-control strategy directed more than 70 percent of total resources to law enforcement, focusing on street-level narcotics operations such as New York's Tactical Narcotic Teams (TNT), Memphis's Operation Invincible, Chicago's Operation Clean Sweep, Los Angeles's Operation Hammer, and Atlanta's Red Dog Squad. The rationale behind this "war" strategy was the assertion that hard-core drug use among white suburbanites was declining. Although numerous reports documented the prevalence of crack addiction throughout the country (including white middle-class suburbs), urban and minority neighborhoods were nevertheless to be the strategic targets of Bennett's war.

As TV cameras brought stark surveillance images of black street dealers and raw video of police sweeps, the drug crisis came to be defined as urban and black, even though white drug use continues to predominate. By the end of the decade, the conservative *U.S. News and World Report* acknowledged that "76 percent of those who use illegal drugs are white" (Gergen 1989, 79). Indeed, separate studies by the FBI and the National Institute for Drug Abuse report similar findings: "Blacks make up only 12% of the nation's drug users. Studies of those who consume drugs, in fact, show slightly lower percentages of blacks and Latinos than whites in every age category" (Harris 1990, A1).

The target, then—the street-dealer, usually young, black, and male—came to be the media icon of the drug crisis, the news-at-11 criminal image. Emphasizing urban street-level enforcement, the main strategy of the war on drugs became the "buy and bust" operation in which plainclothes officers purchase drugs from urban street dealers who are then arrested. The prime-time news special *Night Beat* features cops cruising city streets in search of those dealers. Suddenly cops and camera tear out of a police van, pursuing a daring foot chase that ends with a flying leap as one cop tackles a young black suspect to the ground and wrestles his hands behind his back. The youth lies cuffed in the street as the cop, breathing heavily, surges with adrenaline from the thrill of the chase. Pulling the boy to his feet, the cop screams, "Don't put your nasty head on me . . . you ain't my brother and you ain't my friend. Don't lean against me, my shoulder ain't for you." Seconds later, the cop, presenting the boy for the camera, is shown with his arm around the boy's neck.

Two vials of cocaine with a street value of $20 are found on the youth, who is taken away to jail. Penny Crone and the cop exchange cheerful banter about how he learned to "tackle like that" in high school football. The cop says something reassuring to the effect that the streets are now a little safer.

These fast and furious street arrests are easy to make and give the public the (false) impression that the war on drugs is making an impact. Nabbing the major suppliers, however, requires long-term investigation that may result in only a couple of arrests. Explaining this situation, Atlanta police investigator Ed Brown noted that two "suburban" arrests may "shut down five or six crack houses" (Harris 1990, A26). But such arrests do not make impressive media spectacles. As discussed, the saturation of air time with cheap "reality" programming that spotlights street-level narcotics enforcement conveys the impression that blacks are the major purveyors of drugs in America. Yet law-enforcement officials around the country are beginning to understand that urban street-level enforcement does not solve the problem. In Memphis, County Sheriff Jack Owen, who uncovered a drug-dealing ring in an upper-income white community, points out that "the worst offender is the functional user, the BMW guy, the guy who goes to work every day. That's who's fueling the drug industry. It's not the people in the projects" (Harris 1990, A27). White suburban demand is fueling the drug industry, but the violence and community disruption caused by the trade are felt most sharply in poor urban neighborhoods where the war on drugs is being carried out.

To date, street-level narcotics operations, such as the one that Fox publicized for the Newark police department, have been wholly unsuccessful. For the most part, apprehension of street dealers and the "buy and bust" operations serve only to disperse street corner drug trade temporarily.[5] The ineffectiveness of street-level drug enforcement is most clearly illustrated by the continued availability on the streets of crack and cocaine. Despite "vast sums being spent on the police saturation techniques," carried out in urban areas, "no one has been heard to claim that police operations have resulted in any decline in drug abuse" (Letwin, 1990, 807). As the chief judge of the New York Court of Appeals put it "the cocaine market, . . . particularly in New York, is as healthy now, or healthier, than it ever has been" (Letwin 1990, 806–807). A 1988 Senate report on national drug availability also confirmed "a greater influx of cocaine than when the war on drugs was declared in 1983, and a cheaper, higher quality product."[6]

Even though the majority of those who deal drugs are white, and up to 76 percent of those who use drugs are also white, it would be folly to ignore the increase in hard-core drug use in inner-city communities. Also, there is no doubt that the drug trade during the 1980s led to increased urban decline and violence. But after a decade's worth of waging the war on drugs, drug dealing and drug-related crime continue to thrive in urban communities. TV uses the "reality" of that violence as entertainment, to keep audiences tuned in, listening in disbelief as the latest innocent victim is caught in the cross fire.

Associative Discourse Versus Narrative Explanation

The media portray violent urban crime as incomprehensible, existing in a world apart that no longer makes sense to the public it engages. "So heinous a crime, so senseless a death." The dark images present drugs, violence, and criminality at the level of deep associational subtext, even as the causal links between them (the links necessary if we are to understand the dynamics) are broken. What we do understand is simply the coupling between drugs and violence, and from that connection emanates our sense of the barbarism of young black men. That is all the audience needs to know.

A narrative discourse examining the multiple factors responsible for the situation, one that intends to explain, is replaced by images evoking waves of revulsion that wash over the audience. *Drugs, criminality, young black men*—the words go together like a media mantra. The fragmented associational narratives are divorced from the economic and social dynamics that explain them. As discussed in Chapter 3, these are the narratives of advertising discourse, visual juxtapositions that create emotionally laden associations. In an era driven by the influences of advertising, associational language has become the language of nonfiction programming as well. The fast-paced, MTV-styled fragments of excitement create atmosphere and tone at the expense of explanation.

There are essential connections among drugs, poverty, and violence that can be understood. In fact, they're fairly simple to comprehend, once the cultural, political, and economic causes are brought to light. But doing so requires a narrative intended to explicate, not one intended to evoke fear, fascination, and spectacle. Michael Letwin (1990, 798), New York public defender and president of the Association of Legal Aid Attorneys, rightly points out that the drug trade can be understood only within the "context of the interaction between drug prohibition and oppressive social conditions."

The Economic Void

Over the past two decades the conditions of inner-city life became increasingly unbearable. As urban communities were faced with the flight of stable blue-collar jobs, federal funding for social services was cut dramatically. Between 1981 and 1987 the federal government cut $57 billion in aid nationally, including $6.8 billion from the food stamps program and 5.2 billion from child nutritional services (Letwin 1990, note 90, 810).[7] Many sociologists agree that the economic and social gains made by the black community in the 1960s were effectively rolled back through unemployment, assaults on affirmative action, and the fiscal austerity programs of the 1980s. Letwin (1990, 810–811) explains:

> As a result, twenty-five years since the Johnson Administration launched the War on Poverty, thirty-five years after the Supreme Court outlawed school segregation in *Brown v. Board of Education,* and 127 years after the Emancipation Proclamation, the

communities which TNT and other such programs operate suffer growing poverty and intolerable conditions in, and shortages of, housing, childcare facilities, schools, transportation and decent employment opportunities.

As economic opportunity was foreclosed in the inner city, many young people turned to drug dealing as a viable means of support. Now, as Letwin notes, "The retail street trade is conducted largely by teenagers, some of whom earn up to several thousand dollars a week and are thereby the primary source of income for many poor families" (1990, 813). David Meyers, assistant director of the Los Angeles County Public Defenders Office understands that the problem is systemic: "For a lot of these guys, that's the only way he has of addressing his economic problem" (Harris 1990, A27).[8]

The assertion that "reality"-based crime programming uniformly eliminates social context[9] was dramatically articulated by Seagal (1993, 6), who, as an editor, was involved in systematically excluding the "depressing memories" of the people on the other side of the lens of video realism:

> Before the raw footage of reality-based TV ends up on the proverbial cutting room floor, we in the production trenches watch . . . stories that the viewer doesn't—about women who fall into prostitution because they can find no other work, about teenagers who live below the poverty level and sell marijuana to the same white middle-class couch potato who watches reality-based cops shows . . . These stories and thousands like them will never be shown on reality-based TV because they question the very system that has created, on some level, the misery of its victims, suspects, and criminals.

But the violence of poverty—too real for "reality"-based shows—is excluded from those narratives. Telling the story of crime exclusively through the eyes of law enforcement ensures that outcome. The themes of prevention and education, and the elimination of conditions of poverty, are indeed antithetical to the content of such programming.

At present, few economic alternatives to the underground economy of drugs exist in the inner city. Minimum-wage service jobs such as those at McDonald's do not constitute economic hope for the future, much less provide a living wage. Sociologist Terry Williams (1989), writing in *The Cocaine Kids,* points out that, in the inner city, the desire for status and prestige (which in wealthier communities would be acquired through high-paying jobs or the promise of such through upward mobility) can be fulfilled only in the underground economy. And anthropologist Phillipe Bourgois (1989 note 117, 65), who spent five years studying street culture in East Harlem, observes that it is often the most aspiring, determined individuals who are drawn to the drug trade:

> Ambitious, energetic, inner-city youths are attracted to the underground economy precisely because they believe in the American dream. Like many in the mainstream, they are frantically trying to get their piece of the pie as fast as possible. In fact, they

follow the traditional model for upward mobility: aggressively setting themselves up as private entrepreneurs. Without stretching the point too much, they can be seen in conventional terms as rugged individualists on an unpredictable frontier where fortune, fame and destruction are all just around the corner.

Yet the social and economic conditions propelling the drug trade are lost in the contextual void that surrounds crime narratives. As David Altheide and Robert Snow (1991, 46) point out, the excitement of video realism is presented "without any overlying sense of value or justice. Put another way, there is little attempt to provide an explanation or framework that would make it socially redeeming." In short, there is no narrative space available in which to include any social or economic contingencies when all the stories are about cops chasing dealers.

Drug Prohibition

On *Night Beat,* Crone tells viewers that Newark is a place of "decaying neighborhoods and record-breaking car thefts." Then an official explains that "drugs are at the core of a lot of these things. A lot of these young people are getting high and they're stealing the cars and vice versa—stealing the cars first, getting high during and after." The next cut takes us to the scene of a car theft. As the two black men being arrested get up from a prone position (having been kept on the ground until the camera arrived), we see that they are clearly not young, nor do they appear to be in any way intoxicated. Yet the segment purports to demonstrate the all-encompassing explanation for crime and urban decay—the intoxicating effects of being on drugs. Again, a narrative of association implies that getting high is the cause of crime.

But the urban crisis has not been caused by the use of drugs; rather, it is the consequence of their prohibition. As Greg Donaldson (1993) points out, most inner-city kids do not use drugs themselves.[10] It is the potential to make huge profits that propels the drug trade. There are money, power, and prestige in drug dealing, which is all the more alluring in light of the dearth of alternatives. In the atmosphere of poverty and hopelessness that pervades inner city life, drug dealers are often perceived by children as heroes and role models; indeed, "they often stand out as symbols of success to children who see no other options" (Nadelmann 1989, 942). Nathan Riley, legislative Director for the New York State Senate, also understands that "the existence of illegal drug profits is one of the few alternatives that promise a way out of poverty."[11] Many young people begin dealing drugs well before they have ever used them.

As drug-trafficker violence has escalated into a major criminal justice issue, scholars such as Ethan Nadelmann have focused research on understanding the consequences of prohibition. Most law enforcement authorities agree that the dramatic increase in inner-city murder rates during the past few years "can be explained almost entirely by the rise in drug dealer killings, mostly of one another" (Nadelmann 1989, 942). So the current connection between the drug trade and violence is not difficult to explain: "Illegal markets tend to breed violence." Because they are illegal they are defended with weapons, and black marketeers "have no resort to legal institutions to resolve their disputes" (Nadelmann 1989, 942). Nathan Riley also notes that urban drug wars of the present bear a striking resemblance to the prohibition era of the 1920s, when "our cities were also buffeted by gangland violence."

In addition, drug prohibitions contribute to inner-city crime by imposing risks on distributors. As Letwin (1990, 811–812) argues, "Drug prohibition raises the street-price of crack to well-above what it would cost to produce and distribute legally. The resulting price rise has contributed to an explosion of street crime, fueled in large part by crack-users seeking to finance their habit." Yet getting tough on dealers has proven ineffective because they have come to accept being arrested as part of the cost of doing business. As attorney James Ostrowski points out, a well-publicized arrest actually stimulates enlistment to the trade: "By instantly creating a vacancy in the lucrative drug business, [it] has the same effect as hanging up a help-wanted sign saying, 'Drug dealer needed—$5,000 a week—exciting work'" (Ostrowski, quoted in Letwin 1990, 816).

Possession as a Crime

Hundreds of thousands of arrests are made each year for violation of drug laws—not for selling and producing, but "solely for possession of an illicit drug, typically marijuana" (Nadelmann 1989, 941). As of 1992 the number of federal prisoners convicted of a drug offense had more than doubled since the 1980s to 59 percent of inmates. These arrests are hopelessly ineffective in stopping drug use, representing only about 2 percent of the 35 to 40 million Americans who use illegal drugs. Yet they "have clogged many urban criminal justice systems: in New York City, drug law violations in 1987 accounted for more than 40% of all felony indictments, up from 25% in 1985" (Nadelmann 1989, 941). The *Night Beat* segment demonstrates, if nothing else, how easy it is to make a drug arrest. Cops need only drive past street corners in urban centers, run down a few of those hanging around, and display their catch for the cameras. These visuals assure viewers that the police are doing an important job for their safety. However, by focusing so much time and money on what usually turns out to be nothing more than drug *possession,* the police neglect to pursue the criminals who are committing more serious robberies and assaults against people—a much more difficult law-enforcement task. As Nadelmann (1989, 941) argues, by emphasizing drug possession, such practices have actually "distracted criminal justice officials from concentrating greater resources on violent offenses and property crimes." In 1993 the American Bar Association (ABA) issued a report analyzing criminal justice for the years 1986 and 1991. It found that drug arrests had increased by 327 percent, and that the rate of arrest was ten times greater for minorities than for whites: 57 percent compared to 6 percent. The report concluded: "While drug use is decreasing and violent crime is increasing, the criminal justice system is directing more of its attention to drug offenses and less to violent crime."[12] (The proportion of juveniles in custody for serious property offenses decreased from 33 percent to 27 percent during the same period.) And as Sklar puts it, "The racist war on drugs has become so out of control that violent offenders—including killers, rapists, and child molesters—are being released early to make way for incoming prisoners in systems bursting with nonviolent offenders convicted of drug possession" (Sklar 1993, 60).[13]

The War on African Americans

Ron Harris (1990, A1) writing in the *Los Angeles Times,* emphasizes that "the War on Drugs has in effect become a war on black people." As we have seen, law enforcement has proven ineffective in stopping, or even slowing down, the drug trade. What it has accomplished, however, is an increased police presence in urban communities that has led to abuse and harassment. Senate aide Riley agrees, asserting that drug policy has amounted to anti-urban policy.

"Buy and bust" operations are difficult to perform with any degree of accuracy. They are often done at night, making identification difficult. Often back-up teams move in and make arrests with little more to go on than "Young black, wearing jeans, T-shirt and sneakers." And descriptions are frequently written only after the suspect is sitting in front of the officer at the precinct. Letwin (1990, note 153, 823) points to the "inherent problems" in these arrest methods: "Precinct identifications are inherently suggestive and unmonitored and an identification may occur hours after the transaction."

Discussing a particular "buy and bust" operation that was litigated by the defendant, one court found that "the back-up team . . . swept through the block and lined up, against the wall, any male who happened to be in the vicinity and since the defendant was in the vicinity he too was ordered out of his van" (Letwin 1990, note 153, 823–824). In fact, these practices are often portrayed on "reality"-based programs. On *Night Beat* the police are shown ordering everyone on the street up against the wall. At one point Penny Crone admits: "This attempt to buy and bust was a bust. Despite a search outside and inside this apartment building, no drugs were found." To fill in air time, however, the officer plays to the camera and continues to search in a "hollow" door and in hallway light fixtures. These visuals are accompanied by a running commentary from the cop that serves to demonize all the people being held: "They don't care where it is, they put it anywhere. They don't let their friends know about it 'cause their friends will rip them off. They trust no one but themselves." He finds nothing. Eventually, all the individuals are released, but they have now been criminalized by the cops and the cameras. The program again makes the point that if the cops suspected them, they must be guilty of something. Constitutional assumptions about due process, and civil liberties such as the protection against unwarranted search and seizures, and the presumption of innocence, are antithetical to the docu-cop formula, which does not conceal its approval of the abuse of police power.

In addition to the false arrests made during "buy and bust" operations, there are arrests made when police tactical units sweep neighborhoods that have nothing to do with the drug trade at all. Ron Harris (1990) has documented cases of police harassment of inner-city residents across the country. During a sweep against drugs and gangs in Atlanta, for example, the police targeted public-housing units that accommodate about 10 percent of the city's residents. Within a month, the people living in those units had received more than half the city's tickets for minor traffic violations.

Because of the highly politicized atmosphere of the war on drugs, police officers are often under pressure from superiors to produce sufficient "body counts." Letwin (1991, 822) quotes a former high-ranking NYPD official, who admits that "pressures to produce 'good cases' have resulted in flacking [planting evidence], dropsy, perjury, entrapment and framing, by cops anxious to please demanding superiors." Moreover, street-level narcotics enforcement leads to a disproportionate number of arrests of minority members. In Los Angeles, a crackdown on drug dealing around schools resulted in the placement of officers "at predominantly minority schools, despite federal studies showing more drug use among white youths than among both black and Latino juveniles" (Harris 1990, A26, A27). Minorities constituted 97 percent of those arrested—this in spite of a number of Health and Human Services reports documenting that white high school kids are more likely than their black counterparts to use illegal drugs and alcohol (Sklar 1993, 55).

The widespread and systemic nature of police abuse is an unfortunate and toxic side effect of the war on drugs. In Boston, an ACLU lawsuit charged that police randomly stopped young black men, threatened them with guns, "pushed them to the ground, physically and verbally abused them and often forced them to pull down their pants and underwear in public. One man was shot accidentally by a police officer during a search; no charges were filed against the shooting victim" (Harris 1990, A26).

One assistant U.S. Attorney in Memphis admitted that increased drug enforcement resulted in abusive behavior in minority communities: "They start hassling people they suspect to be drug dealers. Some of them are. But they also hassle kids who just want to play ball, kids who want to court, people who just want to walk around the neighborhood" (Harris 1990, A26). This type of indiscriminate harassment is actually shown on the *Night Beat* program, presented as legitimate police work (see Figure 7.1). Without a word of introduction, two white cops select a black man walking on the sidewalk and begin a body search while his girlfriend looks on. As they pat him down, we hear one cop say in a belligerent tone, "Touch my hand one more time, you're going to go to the hospital. Understand me?" The "suspect" says he works at a hospital and the cop says, "Good, you'll be right there." The cop is wearing plainclothes and the "suspect" asks, "Where's your badge at?" Pulling it from under his shirt, the cop replies, "Right here." He repeats that two more times and continues with, "And stop getting cute, OK?" This he also repeats several times, each time more loudly. Finally, near shouting, he warns, "And stop getting cute in front of everybody, all right?" After finding nothing, the cop walks off, leaving the contents of the man's pockets strewn about. When the man asks him to put these items back in his pockets, the cop replies, "You got a better shot of seeing Jesus Christ, you got." Such rude harassment is presented

FIGURE 7.1 Cop Harassment
The docu-cop shows often extol police belligerence. Indeed, they regularly present the curtailment of civil liberties as the norm. One episode of *Night Beat*, for instance, shows two white cops targeting a black man for doing nothing more than walking down the street.

within a program which has established police work as heroic but, in actuality, extols police belligerence and presents the curtailment of civil liberties as the norm.

The Capacity for Violence

Street-level law-enforcement officers forced to carry out the war on drugs find themselves placed in "grossly unsafe buy operations in order to achieve a high body count and the resulting headlines" (Letwin 1990, 808). Many officers now realize that the personal risks they take on the street are not worth it. "We're getting shot out there and the drugs don't seem to go away. . . . I'm never going to make a buy again" (Letwin 1990, 809). Assistant Chief Francis Hall, who helped design New York's TNT, now admits that the policy is destructive. He compares urban drug enforcement to the Vietnam war: "We lost the Vietnam war with half a million men. We're doing the same thing with drugs" (Letwin 1990, 808). The analogy to the Vietnam war is fitting. Soldiers fighting in Southeast Asia became disillusioned as their noble motivations turned to perceptions of injustice and defeat. The war on drugs breeds the same type of pessimism. When operations are perceived as politically motivated, rather than directed toward the higher, more ennobling goals stated, the result is cynicism. That lack of social legitimacy also breeds corruption. Just as GIs began to use and sell drugs in Vietnam, a series of disclosures of police involvement with the drug trade have emerged in New York City.[14] The best-known case involves former officer Michael Dowd, arrested with five other officers, who "received weekly cash payments—typically between $5,000 and $10,000—from members of a Dominican drug gang" (Wolff 1993, B3).

The frustration and hostility generated by the drug trade is often unleashed on the community at large. Police corruption occurs in the very precincts where the war on drugs is carried out. According to the Mollen Commission (1993, 5) report, "While greed is still the primary cause of corruption, a complex array of other motivations also spurs corrupt officers: to exercise power; to experience thrills; to vent frustration and hostility; to administer street justice; and to win acceptance from fellow officers." And as Letwin (1990, 819) has observed, "Police abuse in the minority communities, which has often resulted in the deaths of civilians under questionable circumstances, is a chronic epidemic in New York City."

Police force has not been successful in stopping either the drug trade or crime. Instead it has had the opposite effect. Nathan Riley argues that the war on drugs has resulted in bringing more violence into neighborhoods, not less. Indeed, many critics now understand that the drug war has escalated the level of violence in inner-city communities by "increasing the capacity for violence."

The rage produced by police harassment and corruption perpetuates the spiraling cycle of violence that is now openly understood to be the nation's "domestic Vietnam war." The misguided policies of the war on drugs and the abandonment of the inner city has resulted in a cynical sensibility on all sides, such that justice and fairness have been almost totally eclipsed. The so-called gangster-rap music of Ice T and Ice Cube, which contains lyrics promoting violence against the police, is the cultural expression of that rage. These lyrics should be understood as counternarratives to those that celebrate the police on "reality"-based crime shows.[15]

Blacking Out White-Collar Demand

One of the significant aspects of the drug crisis lost in the rush of hot pursuit is an uninhibited discussion of demand. Rarely asked, and never adequately answered, is the question as to why so many Americans turn to drugs. The largest segment of drug users are the ones least frequently talked about—the affluent white users of powdered cocaine.

As documentation on drug use confirms, the demand for drugs exists not only in depressed inner-city communities but also in expensive flats and at sophisticated cocktail parties. Yet discussion of the causes of drug use among whites is infrequent indeed. The issue was picked up in fictional form by media critic–turned–novelist Todd Gitlin (1992). In *The Murder of Albert Einstein*, Gitlin creates a female TV star who works for a tabloid "news" magazine show called *In Depth*. The world of tabloid television is illustrated through the eyes of the heroine Margo Ross, a woman constantly engaged in a mental process that translates the world into grabby electrifying visuals that arouse but never explain. After producing a piece on the dangers of "designer drugs," the latest yuppie craze, she realizes the shallowness of her piece and the key issue of *demand* it fails to explain, as expressed in the following internal dialogue:

> The designer-drug piece runs smooth as an electric carving knife. Two teenagers uncontrollably shaking, faces obliterated by the digitalizing process. Hand-held authenticity. ... The piece is not wrong, not at all. Dead right as far as it goes, which is about six inches. *In Depth,* the lazy man's guide to the lower depths. Indignation washes over America. We never ask: Why do people want to shoot up with this shit? (Gitlin 1992, 189)

To deal with the issue of demand, news narratives would have to bear the discomfort of expanding the abbreviated conventions of the drug/crime formulas. They would have to confront the reasons for which more than 30 million people in every sector of American society use drugs. Including a discussion of demand might lead to a critique of American social and cultural life.

Fast-paced, hectic lifestyles, together with increases in overtime work (as discussed in Chapter 2), have led to highly stressful social conditions. As Johns and Borrero (1991, 82) put it, modern urban life is "linked to excessive competition and consumption," which elevate "psychological and physical demands. In response to these demands, cocaine is a panacea. [It] keeps a person awake, functioning, striving, and competing–in short, in sync with the accelerated rhythms of postindustrial life."

Blue-collar work, often repetitive but physically demanding, also accounts for a considerable amount of cocaine use. As journeyman carpenter Guy Robinson, editor of the construction newsletter *Hard Hat News,* commented, "It helps people do repetitive, mindless hard work and not get tired or bored." On one particularly stressful job, into overtime and past deadline, "the foreman started using cocaine. It helped him overcome a lot of the stress. You don't get upset when people yell and scream—it doesn't get to you."[16]

The increase in hard-core drug use in urban centers is not hard to understand, either. As both Nadelmann (1989) and Letwin (1990) contend, drugs provide a temporary escape from the hopelessness and degradation of inner-city living conditions.

But these issues of demand are not part of the drug/crime story told by the media. An authentic critique of working conditions, poverty, and American social and cultural life in general is simply not possible in a medium embedded in the world of consumer advertising. Television's deferential attitude toward the commercials that sustain it requires that it not contradict those promotional messages—messages that continually assert that this is the best of all possible worlds, and that the products offered will fulfill every conceivable fantasy. If American consumer culture really did provide the sense of fulfillment and well-being promised by the makers of the likes of *Nike* and *Reebok,* why do people look elsewhere for escape or pleasure?

Also absent from media representations is the pervasive and growing use of legal drugs such as psychotropic mood adjusters and tranquilizers among more affluent people. The exorbitant pricing by drug companies affects the nation as a whole. Apparently it is difficult to live in this culture without a fix of cocaine, scotch, Prozac, or new shoes.

Introducing the question of demand, especially with respect to affluent white users, would also confuse one of the media's key assumptions—that anyone who uses drugs is either immoral, threatening, or criminally inclined. That assumption stems directly from the political formulations of the 1980s, which were used to justify the increased criminalization of drug use. But early in that decade, before the war on drugs, media narratives did include references to white-collar users of cocaine. The media's treatment of these users was quite distinct, however.

Television Depictions of White Users and Black Criminals

In their book, *Cracked Coverage: Television News, the Anti-Cocaine Crusade, and the Reagan Legacy,* Jimmie Reeves and Richard Campbell (1994) trace the shift in television crime narratives that occurred in the 1980s under the Reagan and Bush administrations. Prior to the war on drugs, television news stories focused primarily on white-collar cocaine users, who were characteristically portrayed with a degree of empathy. These early stories evoked a sense of compassion, holding out a kind of therapeutic hope that, "through some combination of self-discipline, treatment and religion, the drug abuser may again become 'one of us,' restored to the terrain of middle ground" (Campbell 1992, 6). Reeves and Campbell (1994) note that the therapeutic metaphors used during the early 1980s in reference to the decadent (white) users of cocaine were "rituals of inclusion." But by the mid-1980s as the cocaine crisis became defined as an urban, black problem "the cocaine/crack narrative shifted from the therapeutic to the pathologic—from treatment stories in the early 1980s about middle and upper class . . . users . . . to gangster and race narratives in the late 1980s" (Campbell 1992, 1). When the drug narrative turned to pathology, abusers became sinister "Others" with virtually no prospects for becoming "one of us." These rituals of exclusion have criminalized black drug users and, indeed, remain the dominant media interpretation. Inner-city dealers, suspended on the other side of the police perspective, are oddities of the human condition—to be loathed and, above all, feared.

The dehumanization of "suspects" is clearly reflected in the language used by the cops. Richard Campbell (1992, 6) reports that LA police officers referred to an inner-city domestic scene as "gorillas in the mist," and that police described Rodney King by using animal analogies such as "bear-like" and "grunting." In the program *Night Beat* the white officer in charge of narcotics units tells his assembled officers, not once but twice, "Remember, you are dealing with the scum of the earth." The next sequence shows two white officers stopping and searching a black man, and being rude and belligerent. After finding nothing, they walk away.

By association, this man too becomes "the scum of the earth." Throughout the program, every opportunity is made to dehumanize everyone the cops select for treatment. Yet the cops themselves are given every opportunity to appear human, kind, and fair, thus further legitimating their belligerence toward "suspects."

The media's propensity for telling drug stories that feature young blacks is not hard to explain. Watching black youths being hunted down is cheap, exciting, and convenient entertainment, and their demonization has become acceptable. Given the emphasis on associational portrayals of blacks, criminality, and drugs, the inclusion of white users would require presenting them as criminals. Hence the predominance of black faces associated with drug use. One can hardly imagine *Cops*, with camera crews trailing, busting into affluent homes where professionals have gathered to "network," (as often depicted in expensive lifestyle advertisements) to make brutal arrests of cocaine users. Their class status, income levels, and race afford professional users the privacy that keeps criminalized depictions of them off the television screen.

In allowing themselves to become public-relation tools for the war on drugs, the media have generated a distorted view of black versus white drug use.[17] This view continues to fuel misconceptions and racial tensions.

Lack of Judicial Justice

The national atmosphere created by the war on drugs and the climate of opinion promoted by the media have facilitated judicial inequalities that are beginning to be acknowledged. White users of cocaine have consistently been given less severe sentences than blacks for the use of crack. As federal appellate judge Stephen Reinhardt (1992, 17) notes,

> There are other aspects of our laws and sentencing procedures that have undermined the faith of minorities in the judicial system: the disparity between sentences for possession of crack, a substance used principally by minorities, and possession of cocaine, a favorite of wealthy Caucasians; the harshness of some of our other narcotics laws and their disparate impact on young, unemployed black males.

In particular, Reinhardt notes a drastic difference in the treatment of offenses most frequently committed by minorities as compared to those of which Caucasians are most often the perpetrators—lenient sentences for white-collar fraud or theft of millions of dollars versus harsh punishment for more traditional crimes involving far smaller amounts of money or property (Reinhardt 1992, 17).

In December 1991 the Minnesota state supreme court ruled state drug laws unconstitutional. It found that crack users received, on average, four-year sentences for first-time use whereas users of powdered cocaine received probation. The main distinction was racial: 79 percent of the cocaine users were white and 96 percent of the crack users were black. In *Unequal Justice*, Coramae Mann (1993) cites a study based in California, Michigan, and Texas that found that "blacks and Hispanics were more likely to be sentenced to prison, with longer sentences, and less likely to be accorded probation than white felony offenders."[18]

Violent Crime and White-Collar Crime

On television, "crime itself is defined in most shoot-'em-ups as something that happens in the street and not the suites" (Parenti 1992, 123).[19] The portrayal of violent street-level crime to the exclusion of white-collar malfeasance has long been television's tendency. The easy visual translation of violence into graphic images was described early on as a ratings grabber by TV analyst Eric Barnouw (1975). And the lack of white-collar bad guys on the small screen was defined as a characteristic of classic crime narratives by Craig Haney and John Manzoloti (1981, 129). The new "reality" formats, which find their roots in television fictions of crime, push the exciting portrayal of street-level violence to new heights of distortion.

The harmful social effects and national expense of a broad range of criminality, including corporate crime,[20] have been and continue to be downplayed in the media. The absence of white-collar criminality is apparent on news programming as well. One need only think of the absent discussions of the S&L debacle to confirm this tendency.[21] The financial crime involved in drug trafficking is also neglected. Congressman Charles Rangle of Harlem, who chairs the House Committee on Narcotics Abuse and Control, has criticized drug control policies for disregarding enforcement strategies that would prosecute drug-money laundering by the financial sector (Letwin 1990, note 12, 797). Affluent white-collar criminals, a great proportion of them Caucasian, are indeed treated far differently in the media and in the court system. Social ills are blamed on poor people, blacks, and other minorities, not on the affluent lawyers and bankers who bilk the country out of literally *billions* of dollars, causing extreme financial distress that reverberates throughout the economy. Nor do white-collar criminals end up in prison as often as poor blacks do.

The High Cost of Mythic Solutions

We're in the business of tricking people into thinking that spending hundreds of millions for new prisons will make them safer.

—Daniel O'Brien, assistant to Minnesota's commissioner of corrections.[22]

The docu-cop shows usually wrap up their artificial narrative fragments with an image of the cops pushing the head of the suspect—hands cuffed behind his back—as he bends awkwardly into the back seat of a police car. This resolution is presented as the solution to crime, the answer endlessly promoted by political and media discourse: Get the criminal (suspect?) off the street and into prison.

During the 1980s the war on drugs led to the prosecution, conviction, and incarceration of large numbers of drug offenders. The highly visible drug operations around the country, featured through the live camera work of the "reality" shows, have resulted in impressive arrest records, especially when police swept highly populated urban communities and housing projects. These massive numbers of arrests, together with longer mandatory jail terms for drug crimes, including possession, resulted in an explosion of the prison population. Because of the law-enforcement focus of the drug war, prison overcrowding is now at an all-time high. Before Ronald Reagan announced his "bold, confident plan" to curb drug abuse and crime in 1982, "most convictions for drug-related crimes had . . . meant substance-abuse treatment, community service, or a short jail stay; most now carry mandatory prison sentences" (Horn 1991, 14). As Laurie Garrett notes, "By 1990 more men were in federal prisons on drug charges alone than had comprised the entire 1980 federal prison population for all crimes combined" (1994, 509).

The war on drugs has led to the disproportionate imprisonment of people of color. As Patricia Horn points out, "Nearly one in four black males between 20 and 29 is in prison or jail, on probation, or on parole—a higher rate of incarceration than that of black South Africans. More American black men go to prison than to college" (1991, 14). These figures caused Atlanta's police chief, Eldrin Bell, to ask, "If we started to put white America in jail at the same rate that we're putting black America in jail, I wonder whether our collective feelings would be the same, or would we be putting pressure on the President and our elected officials not to lock up America, but to save America?" (Harris 1990, A26).

Incarceration is not the solution to crime, because, as discussed, "most crime is rooted in social and economic discontent" (Horn 1991, 12). Drug dealing, and the crime associated with the trade, is also rooted in poverty. As one Los Angeles public defender put it, "If your chances are no chance at all and five years in jail, you're probably going to choose five years in jail. If that's the best of your options, that's no choice at all" (Harris 1990, A27).

Many people involved with the criminal justice system believe that because most crimes are rooted in economics, the threat of imprisonment does not act as a deterrent. In fact, imprisonment often turns drug users into hard-core criminals, thus exacerbating the problem of crime. According to the National Council on Crime and Delinquency (NCCD), incarceration makes people "more alienated, more prone to violence, and less capable of re-entering productive society" (Horn 1991, 13). Those faced with the greatest lack of economic opportunity suffer additional setbacks after they emerge from prison with felony records, further lessening their chances for legitimate employment. Todd Gitlin, through his fictional character Margo Ross, has also commented on the nonsolution of prisons. As a TV producer, Margo is disturbed by her own complicity in creating a more dangerous world: "What I really want to say is that when the jail terms wind to an end, there's more net wickedness in the world than before, and the fallen angels can kill you as they fall, and I don't understand the world, Tony, I swear I don't" (Gitlin 1992, 189).

Drug crimes account for almost half of the total prison population. Increasingly, those on the front lines of criminal justice are coming to understand that treatment and prevention, not incarceration, constitute the solution to drug abuse. According to Colleen Roach, spokeswoman for the New York Division of Criminal Justice, there is no social value in turning drug offenders into convicts.

"The 16-year-old who is addicted to crack, who is otherwise OK," should be given an alternative such as going to a treatment facility. "Don't throw him in jail."[23] And the head of narcotics enforcement in Seattle complains that "we've arrested more people than the prosecutors can prosecute, than the judges can convict, more than the jails can hold. Until there's a demand reduction—and that means education and treatment—you're not going to see any change" (Harris 1990, A27).

In April 1993 two of New York's most prominent federal district judges, Jack B. Weinstein of Brooklyn and Whitman Knapp of Manhattan, refused to preside over drug cases as a protest against national drug policies and federal sentencing guidelines. Both judges felt that the emphasis on arrest and imprisonment rather than prevention and treatment had been a mistake. Many other federal district judges are refusing to take drug cases as well. As Judge Weinstein argues, "The penalties have been increased enormously without having any impact. It's just a futile endeavor, a waste of taxpayers' money" (quoted in Treaster 1993, 27).

Many are beginning to realize that drug abuse must be viewed as an economic, educational, and medical problem. As one official from the narcotics and special investigations division in Atlanta explained, "There must be treatment; we have none. There must be education; we have none. The problem is that for years everybody has viewed this as a law enforcement problem" (Harris 1990, A27). Moreover, as money is poured into law enforcement, it is taken away from exactly the programs needed for prevention. Between 1982 and 1992 federal spending on drug control strategies increased from $1.7 billion to $12 billion. But as Holly Sklar notes, "Despite the proven success of intensive treatment for addiction, the portion of the federal drug budget going to treatment has dropped from 25 to 14 percent" (1993, 56). Fewer than 15 percent of those needing publicly funded treatment are able to get it.

As punishment, prison time is also tremendously expensive. Spending on prison budgets blocks more cost-effective alternatives to incarceration. In California, for example, the 1991 prison budget[24] was boosted 11 percent, whereas Aid to Families with Dependent Children was cut by 9 percent and the state's university system was forced to raise fees by 20 percent. Continuing cuts are devastating California's once exemplary system of higher education.

One objective the war on drugs has not met is to curb drug use. The harsher penalties instituted by the drug war have resulted in increased hard-core drug use in the inner city. But in middle-class communities, which, unlike their urban counterparts are not criminalized, drug and alcohol use actually declined during the 1980s. Marc Mauer, executive director of "The Sentencing Project," attributes this finding to various social and economic factors.[25] Middle-class people have greater access to education and treatment, and are generally more concerned with health issues. Most important, "this group feels they have a future," exactly what inner-city drug users and dealers lack.

This sense of hopelessness is no doubt confirmed every time a camera crew follows cops into an inner-city neighborhood to glorify the police force, celebrate violence, and demonize young blacks. In this atmosphere, social and economic connections are obliterated. Public approval for the misguided policies that exacerbate the problem of drug abuse and crime continues to be secured by the "reality" crime programs that champion law enforcement to the exclusion of any discussion of education and prevention. The public's "understanding" of the issue is reduced to fear and racism. The words of the *Night Beat* program have an ominous ring: "What we have to be about is getting rid of those 300 [thugs]." Calling for the virtual elimination of young black men, a course America actually seems to be taking, is not only the most immoral route; it is also clearly ineffective. It has not worked so far, nor will it work in the future. Documentation shows that most men in prison have no job training, have not finished high school, have never held a steady job, and were unemployed at the time they were arrested. In California as many as 63 percent of released inmates return to prison within two years. Taking on the difficult task of dealing with poverty and the foreclosure of economic opportunity is the only solution that will work.

Issues of Social Control: Voyeurism, Privacy, and the Culture of Surveillance

---

The media fascination with the "hidden camera" blossomed during the 1980s. *Candid Camera* introduced hidden camera programming long ago, but infrared cameras capable of capturing surreptitious nighttime images facilitated the emergence of the surveillance culture of the 1980s and 1990s. At the same time the move toward the grainy, "authentic" look of home video created a tolerance for what would previously have been considered crudely unsophisticated visuals. When camera crews scurry behind cops on the beat, adding live unpredictable action, the excitement becomes irresistible. The multiple dimensions of live action, mystery, and authenticity produce a compelling programming formula. But, as noted, these formats have been highly structured and stylized to appear "real." The very crudeness of the images is therefore a sophisticated visual technique, and an effective one, interpreted as real by the audience.

This acceptance of the low-quality look and of electronic surveillance exists within a changing social and political environment. In this context, too, the war on drugs has exacted a social cost. Surveillance is the cornerstone of police methods used in the war on drugs because "drug law violations do not create victims with an interest in notifying the police, [so] drug enforcement agents must rely heavily on undercover operations, electronic surveillance, and information provided by informants" (Nadelmann 1989, 943). In 1986 almost half of the 754 court-authorized orders for wiretaps in the United States involved drug trafficking investigations. Propelling the use and approval of intrusive and often secret cameras that prowl the nighttime landscape is the public's fascination with electronic surveillance. The media's celebration of such surveillance has gone hand in hand with viewers' acceptance of the crude visual style.

Media Violations of the Right to Privacy

The social acceptance of surveillance practices and the overuse of undercover strategies threaten and undermine the right of privacy to which Americans are constitutionally entitled. With astonishing frequency "reality"-based shows violate the privacy of the "real people" they feature. Intrusive cameras not only spy on drug dealers, they also invade the homes and privacy of law-abiding individuals.

Watching "reality" shows, viewers can best be described as voyeuristic. We jump out of the car scurrying after our partner, following just behind, looking over his shoulder. We enter peoples house's and survey whatever we can find. We tromp though living rooms into bedrooms, looking under beds, often after the occupants have been ordered to stay outside. In short, we routinely violate their privacy, now that we are allowed the privilege of the worst kind of voyeurism—detached.

The World of Domestic Violence

Viewers are invited to peep into the intimate, often tragic affairs of strangers. We experience the thrill of being made privy to private lives in crisis. Take, for example, the food-fight incident in Kansas City featured on *Cops.* The police pull up to a low-income housing complex. The door is answered by a black man dressed only in his underclothes, which are covered with food. In a high-pitched voice, one cop says, "What's going on," as he muscles past the man and into the house. We move in right behind him as the food-covered kitchen floor and walls come into view. But we find that no physical violence has occurred. The man, who made the call, says his wife is trying to provoke him into hitting her. The cops say there is nothing they can do, and we all leave. An hour later, after another phone call, the cops return and take the husband away handcuffed. The couple is black; the cops are white.

This fragmented view of personal tragedy unfolded for the viewing pleasure of the audience. Little was explained, but one thing became apparent: the cops' inability to cope with a human crisis situation. They offer no help or social solutions to the people they visit. Indeed, they have no positive effect whatsoever. This program demonstrates a set of misguided social priorities whereby television cameras are sent to deal with interpersonal tragedies. When the poor call for help, they must now contend with the display of their personal lives as entertainment on national television before an eager public. The legality of such questionable media fare has seldom been pressed, but certain court decisions reveal its unconstitutional nature.

The Case Against CBS

The first significant case involving the issue of privacy was brought against CBS before a federal court in Brooklyn, New York. On March 3, 1992, a CBS *Street Stories* crew accompanied secret service agents as they searched the home of Babatunde Ayeni, a man accused of credit-card fraud. The tape was not aired, but a *New York Times* article described the search as a "ransacking," with federal agents "strewing furniture and the contents of drawers and closets about" while Mrs. Ayeni looked on. The CBS crew arrived shortly after the agents and began taping "without disclosing their journalistic identities." The camera crew moved through the home "as agents," focusing on everything from clothing, bedding, and furniture to photographs, pictures, and letters, as well as banking documents and paycheck stubs, including "a trunk full of Christmas ornaments." The suspect, Mr. Ayeni, was not home, but "Mrs. Ayeni, clad in a dressing gown and evidently unaware that the camera crew was not part of the official search, asked that she not be filmed and cowered on a couch with her child while the camera took close-ups of them" (cited in McFadden 1992, B3).

The search was legal—a warrant had been obtained—but the judge ruled that allowing CBS to go along (explicitly against the orders of the prosecutor) was a "failure of public trust" and violated the constitutional protection against unreasonable searches. The judge reasoned that it was one thing to have one's house searched, but another to have it displayed on national television, an action that constituted government abuse of the right to privacy. A lawyer for the defense called the ruling "the first step in barring reality TV from joining in raids on private homes" (McFadden 1992, B3). If the poor whom the media prey upon had resources with which to litigate, there would undoubtedly be more such rulings.

This case also demonstrates a profound historical reversal of the tradition of press protection of news sources from the state. In this case, CBS refused to release the *Street Stories* tape—not to protect the privacy of the individual defendant but, rather, to protect the identities of the secret service agents. Mr. Ayeni requested that the tape be released to his defense lawyers because it demonstrated that no evidence was found in his home.[26] The network's refusal to release the tape demonstrates the degree to which the media have allied themselves with the forces of law enforcement, regardless of individual rights.

This alliance of state and media in violating defendants' right to privacy was noted in another case brought against NBC. Convictions were blocked in an Oakland drug raid because custom agents had invited an NBC news team along. The judge ruled that "NBC acted as a government agent in the bust, a relationship that showed potential for 'abuse and corruption'" (Weinberg 1993, 6).

Formatting Participation

With the enlisting of the public's help to solve crimes, a participatory strategy made popular on programs such as *America's Most Wanted* and *Prime Suspect,* another threshold in American society has been crossed. Aided by the media, the public is now asked to engage in law enforcement, a practice associated with the war on drugs. According to Nadelmann (1989, 943), "Disturbing are the increasingly vocal calls for people to inform not just on drug dealers but on neighbors, friends, and even family members who use illicit drugs."

On television, helping catch the bad guy is now generally promoted as a fun and exciting way to do one's civic duty. When *America's Most Wanted* (April 11, 1992) proclaimed its 197th successful "capture," host John Walsh lauded the public on a job well done: "Last week the LA County Sheriff's Department asked for your help in finding the accused killer of one of their own. Deputies feared he might head for the border, but you answered the call. Three thousand miles away, and 48 hours later, the manhunt was over."

Walsh was referring to a case the program had featured entitled "Cop Killers" (April 4, 1992). Cesar Mazariego-Molina, a twenty-six-year old undocumented agricultural worker from El Salvador, was a suspect in the March 1992 shooting death of a Los Angeles County sheriff's deputy. *America's Most Wanted* portrayed him as a convicted rapist and a member of a Salvadoran death squad. It also told viewers that he had murdered his uncle. He was described as "armed and dangerous." One police officer being interviewed added, "He has no value for human life. Killing to him is like a hobby."

Two days after the broadcast, Molina was killed by a New York State police officer with a shotgun blast to the back of the head. He had been working picking apples in Ulster County, New York. The owner of the orchard recognized him from television and called the police. Reports that Molina was "armed and dangerous" helped prevent the filing of criminal charges against the state trooper who killed him. District Attorney Michael Kavanagh said, "I don't know if any of that is accurate, but that is what these police officers were told" (quoted in Gordon 1992, 21). Although the orchard was searched for two days, no weapon was found "either on the grounds or among Cesar's possessions" (Gordon 1992, 21).

George Ducoulombier, spokesman for the LA County sheriff's department, could not confirm any of the alleged charges against Molina aired on *America's Most Wanted,* but he said, "We had a very good relationship with the media out there, and we went from there" (Gordon 1992, 21). Meanwhile, the program's spokesman, Jack Breslin, claimed that the information had came from the LA County sheriff's department. Justifying the program, and making an unusually candid remark about the relationship between all such programs and law enforcement, Breslin noted, "As any media outlet would do, we report what the police tell us" (Gordon 1992, 21).

Molina's family insists that he was never convicted of a crime, had no connection to the Salvadoran death squads, and would never have carried a weapon. They contend that he was in New York State at the time of the LA shooting. But this case did not go to trial so that evidence could be proven true or false. On the contrary, the alliance between the media and state effectively tried, convicted, and executed a man who was never found guilty of a crime through the criminal justice system. Not only was the case never investigated for possible violations of civil liberties, but *America's Most Wanted* received an award for Meritorious Citizenship from Ulster County.

Participation in a democracy should mean a public informed (with the help of the media) and actively involved in debate leading to equitable social policy. But the information needed by the public in order to understand the social causes behind criminal justice issues is absent from the docu-cop format. Without such a perspective, the public is prevented from participating in the establishment of fair and effective crime prevention policy. Indeed, television's "reality"-based crime programming has redefined participation, turning the democratic model into a neototalitarian surveillance model. It has goaded the public into watchful suspicion, encouraging viewers to supply information (through the media) to an increasingly repressive state apparatus. The result of "citizen surveillance" is an environment in which democratic tolerance and constitutional rights are undermined. The very notion of citizenship has been transfigured.

Public Attitudes and Social Control

American democracy is fueled by the consent of the people, a delicate agreement that is achieved through trust in government and the legitimation of social and political institutions. This social contract is one by which we as citizens essentially agree to be law abiding; but if it were to break down, the population would so outnumber the police that they would have no hope of maintaining order through force. This was one of the lessons relearned during the Los Angeles riot/rebellion of 1992.

The presidential election in that year was a profound demonstration of the crisis of legitimation. Ross Perot's meteoric rise from obscurity was pure symbolism; a metaphor for the public's disillusionment with "the folks in Washington." The slide toward public cynicism continues; if anything, it is exacerbated by the loss of economic well-being felt dramatically among the middle class as real income levels continue to decline.

The crisis of legitimation is directly felt with regard to law enforcement. Consider the Gallup survey published in *New York Newsday* (July 9, 1992), which featured a front-page headline reading "Half Think Cops Are Often Corrupt." A majority of respondents linked cops to drug sales, and 45 percent believed that cops were soliciting bribes. Local and federal investigations were conducted regarding allegations that "some officers in at least 10 precincts are involved in stealing from drug dealers, extorting [from] business owners or selling drugs themselves" (Ladd 1992, 3).[27]

The formulation of perceptions about law enforcement is exactly what the "reality"-based crime shows expect from viewers. The following summary remarks made at the end of the *Night Beat* program illustrate the positive rhetorical stance taken by "journalists" as they follow behind cops: "Rarely do cops complain about their jobs, but as you just saw, it's a very tough life. Every day they see conflict, anguish and poverty—the pay barely compensates for their depressing memories."

Frequently inserted between images of cops harassing suspects (even though the most revealing details are often left out) are pictures of them helping people. In *Cops,* officers assist motorists, return lost dogs, and distribute baseball cards to inner-city youths to demonstrate their concern for the community. As Debra Seagal's production experience has led her to conclude, the "highly edited TV shows . . . communicate two primary reality-based messages to the viewer: 1. The streets are dangerous—be fearful. 2. The cops are out there—be thankful" (1993, 4).

Indeed, the content of such shows paints a picture of a very dangerous world in which violent crimes are successfully resolved by police. Because a majority of these crimes are depicted as "cleared," TV cops enjoy a success rate of 61.5 percent. But as Mary Beth Oliver points out, the overrepresentation of police effectiveness is apparent when TV resolutions are compared to FBI statistics, which indicate that only 18 percent of crimes are actually resolved (1993, 12). Oliver further notes that content analysis of "reality"-based crime shows "revealed an entertainment genre that typically portrays a great deal of violent crime . . . and a plot which most often features the 'restoration of justice,' though often through aggressive behaviors" (1993, 20–21). The message is clear: The aggressive behavior displayed by cops toward suspects, especially those who are black and Hispanic, is necessary and effective in protecting law-abiding citizens from dangerous minorities.

That these formulations have had a significant impact on public attitudes toward drugs, crime, race, and criminal justice can be illustrated from a number of perspectives. Despite the fact that drug use by whites far exceeds that by blacks, the impression that drug abuse is the exclusive domain of young blacks is so pervasive that, in May 1992, the Office of Health and Human Services carried out a national media campaign to dispel misconceptions about alcohol and drug use among African Americans.

In an early study of crime programming, Haney and Manzolati found that people "do indeed appear to internalize the belief system that television crime drama provides for them. 'Heavy viewers' had theories about crime that reflected almost perfectly those that television presented to them" (1981, 131).[28] For example, in about 90 percent of the cases presented on crime dramas, the first person to be picked up by the television police turned out to be the actual perpetrator. The authors argue that this illusion of certainty in police work leads to the presumption of guilt rather than of innocence. "We found that 'heavy viewers' were significantly more likely than 'light viewers' to believe that defendants 'must be guilty of something, otherwise they wouldn't be brought to trial'" (Haney and Manzolati 1981, 132).

The historical overrepresentation of violent crime (Parenti 1992) accounts for the early findings of George Gerbner and Larry Gross (1976) that television inflates people's estimate that they will become victims of crime. Continuing "cultivation analysis" also demonstrates that public attitudes are affected over time as a consequence of cumulative television viewing. Heavy viewers of television's dangerous world, in which five to six acts of physical violence occur per hour, "overestimate their chances of being a victim of violence; they are also more mistrustful and suspicious and more likely to demand protection in their neighborhoods" (Morgan 1989, 248). This should be viewed in light of the related finding that "the more people think that crime is on the increase and the more they fear victimization themselves, the more likely they are to favor harsh punishment for criminals" (Haney and Manzolati 1981, 127). Although crime rates have declined slightly in the 1990s, fear of crime continues to accelerate.

Fear has been the cornerstone of TV crime dramas, and the "reality"-based shows have taken that tendency to extremes by adding a racial component. In addition to the racial coding of villains, television images of black criminality intensified during the 1980s and into the 1990s (Campbell 1992). This emphasis has historical significance. In the 1950s as the cold war took hold in American society, TV villains were most frequently depicted as sinister foreigners (MacDonald 1985). Spies with dastardly accents reinforced public perceptions of the communist threat. In the 1970s, as Haney and Manzolati (1981) have observed, TV criminals were not racially or ethnically coded;[29] crime was characteristically thought to be caused by personal/individual motivations, either greed or insanity, not by economic or social circumstances. In contemporary programming, however, when the issue of race is embedded within the traditional genre formulation (which holds that crime is caused by individual motivations) and when those individuals are predominately black (as seen on television today), the resulting equation concludes that blacks must simply be more violent than whites. What "reality"-based crime programs have done is to make visually manifest the public's existing fears of African Americans.

Fear of blacks has been an enduring aspect of American culture, as graphically demonstrated in a study cited by R. L. McNeely and Carl Pope (1981) in which "subjects were shown pictures of a white man holding a razor during an argument with a black man. When the pictures were described to others, the white subjects recalled the black man as wielding the razor!"[30] Ten years later, in *Deadly Consequences,* Deborah Prothrow-Stith (1991) examined the widespread perception that when murder takes place during a crime, it is usually committed by a stranger, and that the victim and perpetrator are racially different. In fact, both assumptions are incorrect. Homicides are most frequently carried out after violent arguments between family members, and 90 percent of murder victims and their killers are members of the same race. Historically, blacks have exhibited higher homicide rates than whites, but as the Center for Disease Control reports, "when socioeconomic status is taken into consideration, racial differences in homicide mortality rates all but disappear" (Sklar 1993, 57). Poverty, unemployment, and urban density are the key factors in violent crime. And African Americans are more likely to live in such conditions than are poor whites.

A study by Robert Entman (1990) has examined the degrading images of blacks on local news shows, connecting those images to what the author defines as "modern racism." The habitual portrayal of blacks in degrading positions, physically held down by cops, implies that blacks are more dangerous and threatening than whites—an implication that can be associated with anti-black affect, a "general emotional hostility toward blacks" (Entman 1990, 332).

The cultivation of fear legitimates and reinforces repressive law-enforcement measures directed against African Americans. And as we have seen, crime-program viewing is correlated with favorable attitudes toward law enforcement. Exposure of such shows to adolescents is significantly associated with higher rates of perceived effectiveness of law enforcement officials, less support for civil liberties, and a greater degree of compliance toward the criminal justice system (Carlson 1985).

"Reality"-based crime TV takes the position that both law enforcement and the curtailment of civil liberties are necessary for public safety. This attitude is also evident in American culture, a tendency reinforced, in turn, by depictions on television. The correlation between fear and criminal justice was described in an eloquent statement by Abraham Blumberg (1979, 358) many years ago:

> So acute has the fear of crime and disorder become that many Americans would welcome the savage repression of some version of a garrison state, and the scrapping of the Bill of Rights, if it would free them from the problems of living in a modern mass society. [But] the mass of Americans is deceived by the law and order ideology, for it promises that one can achieve "peace of mind" and the "good life" without addressing such underlying issues as poverty, racial conflict, education, health care, population pressures, and the allocation of resources.

Social and economic problems require social and economic solutions. But the correlation just drawn is precisely what crime programming seeks to obscure. Scholars (e.g., Gitlin 1983; Kellner 1976) have long noted that television crime dramas are rituals intended to maintain the status quo. Positive attitudes toward increasingly repressive law enforcement tactics, bolstered by TV's criminal depictions, help direct public funds away from *the allocation of resources* that would alleviate conditions of poverty. Because these funds are spent on law enforcement instead, the status quo persists.

The failure to fund drug education and treatment, and to address the underlying economic conditions in the inner city, is "justified" by the nightly images of black drug criminality so popular on American television. Someone must be held responsible for the contemporary decline of urban America; evidently the black community has been spotlighted to play that role.

The complex of media attitudes regarding crime translates directly to political power and criminal justice practices. As Michael Morgan (1989, 245) has observed, "Those who protect us from crime and other risks of life—law enforcers, attorneys, judges, doctors, . . . are vastly overrepresented and dangerously overidealized. . . . Furthermore, the power relationships repetitively demonstrated in television drama help maintain the positions of various groups in the real world power structure." In fact, there are few better examples of the relationship among media misrepresentations, public misconceptions, and misguided political and economic policies than depictions of criminality on television.

Candidates running for office on law-and-order platforms have the advantage. Indeed, they are well-advised to avoid projecting a political image that is not perceived as tough on crime. One need only recall the 1993 Los Angeles mayoral victory by Richard Riordan—the law-and-order candidate—to confirm that media portrayals coincide with dominant attitudes about issues of criminal justice. One *New York Times* article read, "Illustrating a sharp ideological divide, Riordan voters said by a 2-to-1 ratio that the problems of minorities and the inner city are problems of personal responsibility rather than problems of racism and economic imbalance" (Mydans 1993, 24). Given this atmosphere it is not surprising that public spending on law enforcement continues to increase, whereas in April 1993 the Republican architects of the war on drugs successfully filibustered a jobs spending program that would have provided more than 100,000 summer jobs for New York City youths alone.[31] As one unemployed fifteen-year-old commented to the *Daily News* (New York), apparently with greater insight than is shown by many public officials, "It's upsetting. There are a lot of people who need jobs. If you don't have a job, you can end up hanging out in the streets" (Seagal 1993).[32] Even in the wake of numerous arrests of New York City police officers on charges of corruption, the police department's budget was not cut, though social crime-prevention strategies such as "Safe City" youth programs were dramatically reduced.[33]

Television and Violence

Violence on television has long been of concern to parents, teachers, public interest groups, politicians, and even some broadcasters. The fear that television violence increases violent behavior, especially in children, has prompted more discussion on the effects of television than any other issue. Many scholarly studies have connected aggression in children to violent TV fare. In addition, numerous major government-funded studies have been carried out by such organizations as the National Commission on the Causes and Prevention of Violence (1968); the Surgeon General (1972); the National Institute of Mental Health (1982), and the U.S. Attorney General's Task Force on Family Violence (1984). The National Institute of Mental Health (1982) summarized the consensus that watching TV violence does lead to aggressive behavior by children and teenagers.[34]

Young people, especially males, are attracted in greater numbers to "reality"-based crime programming. Times/Mirror Media Monitor (1993) has found that those under thirty were more accepting of television violence and less concerned about its effects on society. Maryann Banta, a member of the National Coalition on Television Violence, connects the popularity of such programming to the fact that the current generation grew up watching extremely violent television: "This is the generation that we were concerned about 10, 15 years ago when we looked at Saturday morning television. . . . We called it Saturday morning school for violence."[35] For example, between 1982 and 1988, after Saturday morning children's television had been deregulated, "television time devoted to war cartoons jumped from 90 minutes to 27 hours a week" (Sklar 1993, 58). It is not surprising, then, that televised violence of all sorts is more attractive to the generation who grew up watching it. Not coincidentally, the same generation supported the Gulf war in greater numbers than any other demographic group. Certainly television violence proposes that conflict, whether personal, social, or international, can be solved with a gun—or a patriot missile.

But many still point to mitigating social factors that preclude drawing a direct causal link between TV violence and social aggression. These factors, which include inadequate gun control, family violence, individualism, and patriarchy, suggest that American TV violence is an insufficient cause for violence on its own.

This debate is important, but so is the narrative context within which images of violence are placed. Yet the contextualization of violence is rarely brought into the debate. Studies of TV violence have historically assumed a behavioral model, whereby graphic violence compels those who view it to engage in acts of aggression. However, as television is primarily a cognitive medium, the relationship between TV and violence must be conceptualized in a more complex, mediated way.

As demonstrated earlier, television helps mold and reinforce opinions and attitudes about crime. Those attitudes are then acted upon. The theories of crime derived from television, rarely contested in any other public forum, can influence real-world political decisions. For instance, when television programming consistently frames criminal justice issues by focusing on certain crimes but not on others, proposing exclusively personal motivations for violence, and offering incarceration as the sole solution, the "common sense" understanding of crime and violence that results may be translated into political power and social policy. Politicians who confirm these attitudes will be elected, and criminal justice policies will follow.

Violence escalated in American society during the 1980s, fueled by the war on drugs, which in turn was reinforced by television. In this sense, television, as a historical player, has led to increased levels of violence and aggression, not simply because the public has imitated the violent acts it depicts but also because it sanctions formulations that reflect a misunderstanding of the causes of crime and are therefore incapable of producing viable social and political solutions to crime.

In short, we find ourselves incapable as a society of solving social problems, because we no longer have a discourse of understanding. Rather, we are entertained by crime formulas that use the associational discourse of persuasive communication. Television's jarring visual imagery, which associates criminality and drugs with race, insinuates false assumptions that, in turn, lead to feelings of retribution and fear. Such public attitudes lead to political policies that are unjust as well as ineffective. Docu-cop shows are only the latest and most extreme additions to this violent arsenal we call television, but they have proven themselves to be powerful and effective weapons against society as a whole.

Distopian Images

Get me the Justice Department, entertainment division. . . .

—from *The Running Man*

In the futuristic distopian fantasy *The Running Man,* criminals are invited to "pay their debt to society" as contestants on a game show. The film stars Arnold Schwarzenegger as the "Butcher of Bakersfield," who is pursued by wrestling-style "stalkers" with names like Iceman and Thunderball. Huge outdoor TV screens bring the spectacle to the "margins," where the impoverished population is controlled by an Orwellian system of state control, censorship, video manipulation, and surveillance. Personal privacy has become a thing of the past, and people are routinely encouraged to spy on their neighbors. The shining star in this media system is the live three-hour television show called *The Running Man,* the number one–rated program in the world. As depicted in the film, audience members are routinely manipulated by video documents of the crimes allegedly committed by the contestants. (Arnold is of course innocent, but doctored videotape shows him as a brutal mass murderer.) Waves of emotions wash over the viewers as the criminals' villainy is replayed to set the mood. Stunned by the dastardly deeds, they are easily whipped into a vengeful frenzy of emotional contempt. Thus aroused, they cheer as the stalkers hunt down their criminal/victims during the Gladiator type games set in a derelict part of the city once devastated by an earthquake. As the stalkers move in for the kill, the studio audience—as active participants in the game, choosing which stalker to send after the criminals—jump and scream with excitement as they win prizes.

The populist host of *The Running Man,* Richard Dawson (from the "real" game show *Family Feud*), is a contemptible opportunist; merely by giving the home audience "what they want," he generates high ratings for the network. The government, however, uses the program as social control. Together, the Network "ICS" and the Department of Justice's Entertainment Division have designed a media environment that offers sex, violence, fear, and revenge, instead of social justice, to a population continually on the verge of food riots. As Dawson advises a nervous Justice Department official, "You want ratings, you want people in front of the TV set instead of the picket line, you ain't gonna get that with reruns of *Gilligan's Island.*"

The Running Man is a violent entertainment spectacle and an appropriate vehicle for display of Schwarzenegger's physical prowess, but it is also shrewd social commentary. Distanced from the present by its futuristic setting and exaggerated portrayals (and perhaps by the fact that Schwarzenegger is white), it nevertheless nods with a certain wisdom toward the current relationship among television, crime, social policy, and political power. The film was made in the mid-1980s, at the same time the "reality" crime shows were emerging full-blown on American television. By then, the war on drugs was also well under way, providing the themes, violence, suspects, and cops to be featured on television. Cheap and highly rated, the crime shows have become a nightly event, provided for entertainment purposes by a broad spectrum of media outlets. Viewers ride in the passenger seat as the cops on *Cops* stalk their criminal/victims. And when the TV is off, they are warned to be on constant vigil against dangerous criminals and to turn in anyone they suspect. Social indicators register increasing disparities between rich and poor, while drug-related crimes continue to exact increasing social costs. Political demands for more cops and more prisons are main features of American public discourse, but as the war on drug continues, even government statistics make it clear that it is little more than a war on black and poor neighborhoods. Hopelessly ineffective in solving the problem of crime, the war on drugs continues to be fought, propelled by a relentless media environment that nourishes a mythic understanding of criminal justice issues. Drugs, violence, and poverty—and the political policies that fuel them—have created a fearful society. Punishment—getting tough on criminals—is offered to appease a frustrated and vengeful public. Social problems have become the stuff of entertainment, and "suspects" are displayed as social retribution. Increasingly preoccupied with issues of personal welfare, the "middle class," feeling under siege from the margins—the inner cities—not only condones the harshest punishment but is increasingly willing to trade civil liberties for the false sense of security offered by tougher law enforcement. As the main victims of the violence, large segments of the urban communities themselves feel the same way. As of the 1990s the United States leads all other countries in per capita incarceration, now exceeding even South Africa and China.

∾   ∾   ∾

The cultivation of fear as social control cannot be discounted, given what we know to be the programming strategies of "reality"-based police shows. The fact that these shows emerged in an era of economic decline and urban decay is also significant. It is not an exaggeration to say that the media portrayals of blacks-as-criminals, patterned after the criminal justice definitions that proliferated in the 1980s, serve the classic scapegoating function of inciting fear and deflecting public sentiment away from an understanding of the economic and political context.

The programming strategies used by these shows address the frustration of people living in a society that is incapable of solving crime, precisely because of the policies so positively promoted by the same programs. "Reality" crime narratives leave the false impression that the war on drugs helps eliminate drugs and related crime, when in fact the drug war's policies have done nothing but exacerbate the problem. In place of solutions to crime itself, "reality"-based shows evoke voyeuristic pleasures by allowing the public to watch "criminals" in the act of getting caught. Often the criminals hang their heads, squirm, and beg not to be taken away. In place of discussions about political and economic causes of crime that would have relevance to the social dynamics of real life, "suspects" are offered up as cathartic entertainment fare in a modern-day bread and circus spectacle. Without doubt, these programs are escapist fare—"a few minutes of manipulated magisterial retribution," as Seagal (1993, 6) puts it.

The degradation of blacks presented nightly by "reality" crime shows only promulgates fear and further polarizes society while mystifying the causes and prevention of social and urban problems. As the media's war on the black communities continues, the nation becomes less capable of understanding and therefore solving the problems of drugs and drug-related crime. A simple verity has been lost in the deluge—that the quality of American life depends on the well-being and freedom of everyone.

8

Advertising and the Persian Gulf War

As soon as the war in the Persian Gulf began, television advertisers made it clear that they were disinclined to sponsor news coverage of the conflict. Executives at all three networks complained that "advertisers' skittishness about war coverage was costing them millions of dollars" (Carter 1991a). War specials received high ratings, but only about 20 percent of their commercial time had been sold. Richard Dale, an executive at Deutsch Advertising, told Bill Carter (1991a) of the *New York Times,* "Commercials need to be seen in the right environment. A war is just not an upbeat environment." Advertisers worried that the "tone" of most commercials was vastly different from that of war news, which could contain tragic images. Indeed, as William Croasdale, a senior vice-president at the Backer Spielvogel Bates ad agency, points out, "Commercials are full of music and happiness. They have a lot of comedy in them. Everything is upbeat." Advertisers were generally reluctant to place such upbeat commercials for items such as soup, soda, and cereal on programs about the war. And the Campbell Soup Company in particular decided to minimize its commercials in news programming during the war. The decision was part of a trend among advertisers to "stay away from programs involving heavy controversy" (Carter 1991a).

The reluctance by advertising CEOs to buy time on war-related programs highlighted two important points. On the one hand, it signaled the degree to which advertisers had become accustomed to programs which they considered appropriate vehicles for advertising messages. But on the other, it indicated the degree to which broadcasters were willing to accommodate the needs of their sponsors. Pressure from advertisers led to the proliferation of upbeat "home front" stories of the war as network executives sought to assuage the worries of their sponsors. For instance, CBS executives "offered advertisers assurances that the war specials could be tailored to provide better lead-ins to commercials" with "patriotic views from the home front" (Carter 1991a).

211

Such advertising imperatives were to have a profound effect on the media representations of the Gulf war. Very early on, the war coverage became so exaggeratedly positive that it seemed a caricature of news reporting. The embellished reports of the accuracy and effectiveness of America's high-tech weaponry employed adjectives so inappropriate for nonfiction programming that they seemed a burlesque. The maudlin narratives of hardship endured by those involved seemed a parody of the victims and heroes of tabloid news. Saddam Hussein, scripted as "the enemy," hence the embodiment of evil, resembled a cartoon character rather than a head of state. And the ubiquity of the flag-waving images rendered an unmistakable impression of the lack of media independence. In other words, the discourse was not one of information, knowledge, or understanding—or of any of the social purposes usually associated with news reporting. Instead, it was the simplified, exaggerated, upbeat, and exciting discourse of persuasion and advertising.

This type of coverage is indeed suitable for the promotion of products. It utilizes a language borrowed from advertising. Controversial reports full of disagreements and qualifications would have represented a public-sphere debate among informed citizens seriously considering the necessities and consequences of going to war. That the coverage of the Persian Gulf war seemed to be a commercial for American involvement did not go unnoticed by at least one journalist, ABC correspondent Beth Nissen (1991), who by this time had become disillusioned with the media. To her credit, she went on record as saying she did not like the idea of working for an advertising agency. "Coverage of the war was like an advertisement for the U.S. military: the bombs always hit the targets, the U.S. government always scored perfectly. The pictures were like pentagon commercials and we just played them." (Interview with the author, January 1995.)

Many journalists were surprised by the results of opinion polls that measured the response of the American public to the war coverage. David Colton (1991), deputy managing editor for *USA Today*, said that numbers like these had not been seen before:

> 85 percent who want to start a ground war, 88 percent supporting Bush. I mean, you ask somebody their correct name and you don't get those numbers. . . . And Saddam Hussein, who was known by nobody on August 1st, suddenly was Hitler, and chemical weapons were known. . . . I'm still stunned by the support on a very complicated issue that isn't as black and white as the numbers are showing.

A University of Massachusetts study done by Justin Lewis, Sut Jhally, and Michael Morgan (1991), in which public opinion and public knowledge were measured, illustrated the power of persuasive modes of communication to generate support for a war the public knew very little about. The study found that "the more television people watched, the less they knew"—and the more they supported the war.

The effects of "news" reporting were overwhelming because, in coverage of the Gulf war, journalistic standards were replaced by the more persuasive logic of advertising. The fundamental assumptions of advertising, with its simplified and exaggerated language as well as its false promises of fantasy wish fulfillment and empowerment, inspired the design of Gulf war coverage. The war and its media representations met at a historic crossroads where advertising communication practices converged for the first time with international conflict.

The transformation in nonfiction reporting did not occur overnight. As we saw in Chapter 1, economic pressures encountered by the media during the 1980s and 1990s brought advertising influences more clearly into news programming. In essence, the definition of news has changed. Direct modes of address, subjective camera techniques, dramatization, and video graphics were once excluded from the repertoire of nonfiction representation. Journalistic practices that once attempted to provide balance and accuracy have been replaced by those answering the demand that news excite and engage. Now, the grabby, stimulating, evocative formats lead to a single sensibility and, ultimately, to a nod of agreement. They stimulate a type of unspoken consensus characteristic of the world of persuasion.

In addition to these changes in the modes of nonfiction representation, the Pentagon imposed severe restrictions on the press that successfully excluded a great deal of information about the war from press reports.[1] Together with advertising influences, this military censorship created a powerful form of contemporary propaganda. A close look at one of the many TV war specials will illustrate this point.

The War on *PrimeTime Live*

Diane Sawyer hosted a *PrimeTime Live* segment that clearly demonstrates how the language of advertising employed in war coverage became a strategy of persuasion that influenced public opinion (see Figures 8.1 and 8.2). The segment features the tank being used in the Gulf at the time. Sawyer begins by explaining that "the Army let us use their tank simulator so we could take you to the battlefield inside a tank." The unity of the military/press perspective is notable, but the language of this story is even more striking. The adjectives and nouns used throughout the segment were chosen not to describe or inform but to convince and persuade. Almost from the first utterance we are invited to leave the world of information and to enter into the realm of illusion, into "a rolling hi-tech fantasy." And in the exaggerated language of advertising, Sawyer intones: "The U.S. says when it comes to mobility, your tank is the best in the world." None of these superlatives convey information about the design or construction of the tank or its appropriateness for desert warfare. Instead, we are given the soft sell: "This is it the M1A1. It's called the king of the killing fields." It's "the fastest" in the world and in it "you go head to head" with the enemy.

FIGURE 8.1 Diane Sawyer with Tank

Experience the News

This mode of address is fundamentally different from that of traditional news formatting. The segment speaks directly to the viewer throughout. But it goes beyond simple direct address—the camera is used extensively to incorporate the viewer into a prescribed subjective position. Indeed, the viewer is invited *to experience* the tank. The visual language conveys a sense of danger and anticipation. We follow Sawyer, looking with the camera over her shoulder as she climbs onto the military vehicle. As if following a tour guide through an army theme park, we enter right behind her. This subjective perspective gives the viewer the experience of entering the tank as the camera descends through the narrow compartment on top. The camera lens is our eyes. Inside, we move toward the tank's view finder to survey the battlefield, the blurred image coming into focus as if our eyes themselves had approached the lens. The image then turns to video simulation as "we" start driving. The tank vaults over hills. The visual frame shoots up into the sky and then bounces back down as we hit the bottom of a rut.

We do not see someone looking through the lens into the simulated battle space. Rather, we look through it ourselves, and as we do so any remnant of analytical detachment is lost. No longer allowed to sit on the sidelines and to watch or contemplate, we become participants in the battle. Our tank is under attack. From the cockpit we are aware of being fired at. The military video simulation shows explosions coming dangerously close. As we traverse the rough terrain through ditches meant to stop our trajectory, we continue on, under fire. The camera perspective tells us that our fingers are on the buttons, and we are directed that "how fast you sight the target and fire on the enemy can make the difference between life and death, and death can come very quickly. . . . You made a mistake, you're dead."

FIGURE 8.2 U.S. Army Computer Simulation
On the ABC program *PrimeTime Live,* Diane Sawyer explains that "the Army let us use their tank simulator so we could take you to the battlefield inside a tank." The viewer is invited to leave the world of information and enter into the realm of illusion, into "a rolling hi-tech fantasy." We follow Diane as we might a tour guide through an Army theme park. No longer allowed to sit on the sidelines and watch or contemplate, we become participants in the battle. The military video simulation shows explosions coming dangerously close. As we traverse the rough terrain through ditches meant to stop our trajectory, we continue on, under fire. The viewer is invited to *experience* the tank. The visual language conveys feelings of danger and anticipation.

Positioned within the action, we now know what it feels like to push the buttons that control the most modern and efficient hi-tech "killing machine." We have experienced the thrill of power and the threat of being the enemy's victim. We have been given control of the technology and the justification for its use. The position is one that assumes total engagement and therefore complicity. By watching we have come to participate in the war—quite literally, from the point of view of the military.

Feel the Power

As advertising drives media culture, its modes are embedded at every level. The evocation of feelings and excitement through jarring visuals and associational techniques characterizes that sensibility. Media constructions take us with them. They invite us to ride shotgun beside the driver, then to jump out at the site of action and follow just behind. There is no time for reflection. The action is live. It is exciting, and we experience the tension of anticipating what (or who) will come at us around the next corner. We are taken to places we have no business being, adding intensity to the titillation. Clearly the exciting subjective positioning that characterizes the "reality" shows discussed in Chapter 7 has been adopted to other forms of nonfiction programming.

Techniques that convey immediacy, excitement, and highly charged emotional experiences are now acceptable as "serious" news. They are also evident in contemporary filmmaking practices. Drawing on Mark Miller's (1990) analysis of transformations in cinematic devices, we can see parallels between current news design and filmic techniques. Miller argues that movies "force our interest, or reactions, through a visceral jolt that stuns the mind and shuts the eyes" (1990, 209–210). He describes film techniques that are inherently "non-narrative and subvisual." Depictions of violence now routinely place us within the action in a "rapt gaze of wondering assent" (Miller 1990, 209). Films such as *Cobra, Rambo,* and *Mississippi Burning* (to name only three) position the viewer in an intense experiential relationship with the hero and, by doing so, extend an "open invitation to *become him* at that moment—to ape that sneer of hate, to feel the way it feels to stand there tensed up with an Uzi" (Miller 1990, 210).

In the *PrimeTime Live* segment described earlier, we feel the thrill of the battle. We furiously dodge the explosives threatening to blow our tank off the killing field. This feeling of tension, of being under attack and fighting back in a hi-tech killing machine, is created by the same technique used for depicting the type of film violence that Miller describes. Even though *PrimeTime Live* was ostensibly offering informational programming about a war the public was being asked to support, the visual and textual rhetoric of the segment allowed no space for thought, contemplation, and especially "ambivalence" about the war. Instead, it offered "virtual reality." The act of viewing constituted participation as the format actively worked to deny any distance from the action, thus making us *feel the experience.* Miller argues that the filmic portrayal of violence is now also experiential. In "the movies of Sam Peckinpah, the violence was, however graphic, muted by a deep ambivalence. . . . Now, by contrast, screen violence primarily invites the viewer—man or woman—to enjoy the *feel* of killing, beating, mutilating" (Miller 1990, 210).

Such depictions exist within an increasingly commercial medium. The rise of "product placement" has "damaged movie narratives . . . through the fundamental shift of power that the practice has wrought within the movie industry: the transfer of creative authority out of the hands of filmmaking professionals and into the purely quantitative universe of the CEOs" (Miller 1990, 198). Product placement demands that movies become vehicles for the display of commodities, and film language follows the logic of advertising. Such representations come at us head on: "The whole selling project now depends on moves that are less rhetorical than neurological" (Miller 1990, 206). As advertising has inserted itself into broadcasting, these effects have become evident in nonfiction forms as well.

Patriot Magic

As we discovered in Chapter 3, the foundation of advertising culture is the intoxicating assertion that for every problem or need there is a product solution. And, indeed, the Patriot missiles, "smart bombs," and a vast array of other hi-tech weapons were "incanted" as product solutions to the war. What we see here is advertising that promises magical outcomes from products. Consider, for example, the ad for Oreo cookies that features a boy and his bedroom. The room looks like a cyclone hit it; the boy's mother tells him to clean up the mess. He reaches for a bag of Oreo cookies and, as he opens it up, all his clothes fly back into the drawers and closets. Oreos, we are told, "unlock the magic." In another scenario extolling the magic powers of products, a mother listens to the cacophonous noise of her son's piano practice. Then she prepares herself a cup of tea. As she drinks it, her son's playing becomes expert and melodious.

Products routinely perform impossible feats of magic in advertisements. As Sut Jhally (1989, 217) points outs, "All normal physical and social arrangements are held in abeyance." So accustomed is the public to this mode of discourse that singular, exaggerated, one-sided claims, almost magical in nature, seem plausible.

Weapons became the magical objects that, in the most simple, clean, and easy way, would solve the problem in the Persian Gulf. As Judith Williamson (1978, 140–142) has observed, "Magic . . . creates a never ending exchange between passivity and action, a translation between technological action and magical action" (1978, 142). Advertising offers the individual compensation for inactivity and, in the case of the war, exclusion from public debate and participation: "The only thing we can *do* in fact is to buy the product, or incant its name—this is all the action possible as *our* part of the excitement offered" (Williamson 1978, 142). The excitement offered by the "smart bombs" and missiles constituted the public's participation in the war.

Air Superiority

On the night that the bombing of Baghdad began, "unconfirmed" reports from the Pentagon claimed that the Iraqi air force was "decimated." Of course, these reports would prove to be false; but even though they were described as "unconfirmed" they served to set a simple, exaggerated, and positive *advertising* tone. On CBS the "rolling thunder air war" was described as "staggering" and "fantastic." Images of cruise-missiles, "electronic warfare," and planes that could "see" for 300 miles confirmed one pilot's assertion that "we dropped some excellent bombs." The night footage of the bombing of Baghdad, presented as a thing of beauty, became the visual reference for the destruction of the city.

The Nintendo War

As the bombing continued, animation footage was used on every network, presenting the war through the visual icons of the video game. The incorporation of video-game entertainment and visually graphic formats created a unity of expression wholly distinct from traditional nonfiction. Views from cockpits showed direct hits fired on imaginary targets. Yet snippets of infrared video footage released by the Pentagon, taken from cameras mounted on the noses of bombers, were strikingly similar to the animation. Pentagon pictures aired incessantly and were enthusiastically described as "riveting visuals" showing the "astounding accuracy" of a "smart weapons system" with "computer brains." Each of the pilots became a "Top Gun," just like the movie of the same name.

The visuals provided by the Pentagon were convenient one-way images, familiar to a generation brought up on video games and commercial television. The assumption behind these visuals was that real people do not inhabit the interior space of video monitors, so there would be no need to give one moment's thought to the consequences on the ground. The seductive visual perspective invited the viewer in, and this engagement created a type of complicity with the "operation."

No one spoiled the fun by pointing out that these were only a few of thousands of "sorties" flown, and maybe they were not all so accurate—meaning, of course, civilian casualties, or "collateral damage." But such negative information would not have been appropriate to the upbeat, simple, positive advertising environment. Rather, the coverage of the bombing of Iraq and Kuwait fit the common definition of persuasion, the repetition of one powerful message to the exclusion of all others.

Utterly absent from this media discourse was concern for the people of Iraq. Although the media engaged in endless scenarios depicting how the war was being fought, speculation about Iraqi casualties was conspicuously absent—nothing said or shown to dampen the mood of celebration of firepower unrivaled since the movie *Top Gun* (which was also a commercial vehicle). The coverage certainly created the desired impression that this war was accurate and, above all, clean—just like the world presented in commercial messages. And the celebration of the modern technology of war gave the bombing a kind of moral justification. The "smart bombs" were accurate, we were told, and there was "no intention" of targeting civilians, so those worries were easily set aside. No messy pictures of the estimated 100,000 civilian casualties in Iraq muddled the picture, with the exception of those provided primarily by CNN's Peter Arnett. His efforts were met with accusations of disloyalty and sympathizing with the enemy—accusations that, once again, were meant to poison the debate about America's moral responsibility for the death of innocent people. Arnett incurred such criticism because he provided a consistent view of the other side of the war, a view dangerous to the legitimacy of the media as a whole. The celebration of firepower depended on the blacking out of its consequences, so as not to contradict its representations of magic and fantasy.

The generational appeal of this "video war" was clearly demonstrated by findings indicating that people between the ages of eighteen and thirty-two supported the war in greater numbers, but knew less about it than any other age group (Lewis, Jhally, and Morgan 1991).

Meanwhile, most journalists described the incessant bombing in exultant terms like "a marvel" and "picture-perfect assaults." Some publications went to great lengths to cavalierly abdicate moral responsibility. For instance, *Time* magazine defined "collateral damage" as "dead or wounded civilians who should have picked a safer neighborhood." It is at this point that news reporting becomes a cartoon, defined mainly in terms of its commercial viability.

"Smart bombs," successfully disassociated from human costs, became the heroes of the war. But it was primarily dumb bombs that wiped out the Iraqi forces. Over a period of six weeks, old-fashioned terrorizing B-52 carpet bombing destroyed "Hussein's war machine." And as British analyst Paul Rogers asserted, old-fashioned weapons were also effective in wiping out the Iraqis in retreat. "There was systematic carpet bombing with B-52's of fleeing troops . . . and persistent use of antipersonnel munitions such as cluster bombs, and I would guess that there was a level of carnage which we've probably not seen since the first world war."[2]

But war casualties, media representations of the real consequences of war, were absent, hidden by the overwhelmingly upbeat environment of persuasion.

Patriot Disappointments

Only after the war was the record of the Patriot missile revised. After examining videotapes and the record of damage done by Scud missiles before and after the use of Patriots, Theodore A. Postol, professor of national security policy at the Massachusetts Institute of Technology, found that the Patriot had been highly ineffective. Just as commodities disappoint when compared to the exaggerated and fanciful promises made in advertisements, so too the exaggerated claims of Patriot magic were unfounded. Before Patriot missiles were used, thirteen unopposed Scuds fell in Israel. These Scuds "damaged 2,698 apartments and wounded 115 people" (Postol 1991/1992, 140). After Patriot missiles were set in place to defend Tel Aviv and Haifa, there were fourteen to seventeen Scud attacks, as a result of which "7,778 apartments were reported damaged, 168 people were wounded, and one person was killed . . . by an impacting Patriot intercepter" (Postol 1991/1992, 140). Postol explains that the increased damage after the Patriots were used was a consequence of greater amounts of debris falling to the ground when Scuds were intercepted. Pieces of Patriots were added to the Scud debris. In addition, "it appears that in a high percentage of these cases, the Scud warheads fell intact and detonated, but the impact of the large pieces could do considerable damage as well" (Postol 1991/1992, 146).

The Acceptance of Contradiction

As Stuart Ewen (1988) argues, the logic of advertising promotes a unity of opposites, a milieu in which contradiction no longer evokes a sense of uneasiness. Because the quality of commodities is conferred through an associational discourse, advertising creates a geography of arbitrary connections devoid of internal coherence and material connections. Nonconformity is sold as a lifestyle, the adherence to which requires conformity. Reverence of nature is evoked to sell a plethora of products whose manufacture, use, and elimination destroy the serene beauty of nature depicted in those advertisements. Four-wheel drive vehicles appear on inaccessible mountain tops and tear up wilderness terrain, while being promoted in the context of environmental adoration. Within this postmodern landscape, contradiction is allowed to stand without having to bear the scrutiny of critical judgment.

The same discursive strategies allowed the enormous contradictions of Gulf war reporting to go unchallenged. How could Saddam Hussein be likened to Hitler? Was the history of the post–World War I division of the Middle East remotely similar to the history of Europe? How did the United Nations suddenly become the legitimate voice of world unity when previous U.S. involvement with this world body had been utterly contentious? How could the occupation of Gaza and the West Bank by the State of Israel not be part of the context for Iraqi occupation? Most telling of all was the justification that U.S. and UN forces would restore "democracy" for a kingdom with no electoral process. And, finally, we must ask, If the war was fought for human rights or humanitarian purposes, and not for the control of oil, why was nothing done later to stop the Serbian slaughter and dismantling of Bosnia?

In lieu of independent evaluation, the public was enjoined not to seek accuracy in these justifications for war but, rather, to enjoy the feeling of national unity, even if that unity was coerced.

Lifestyle and Belonging

Just as lifestyle advertising promises emotional security through a sense of belonging to the consumption group, the coverage of the Gulf war offered belonging as a psychological gratification. As William Fore (1991, 52) points out, media representations invited viewers "to share emotionally charged experiences with others, [and] to gain a sense of identity." In this way, too, the war representations resembled advertising rather than reflecting the complicated, confusing, often negative aspects of war.

Indeed, the public was enjoined in no uncertain terms to buy "the product." A proliferation of stories from the home front aired nightly. Opposition came to mean disloyalty, an assertion articulated consistently not only by the media but also at the highest levels of government. Patriotism was the last refuge for support of a war that was little understood by the public. The wave of yellow ribbons and American flags that swept across the doorsteps of America became testimonies to the power of the media to generate a mass psychology of uncritical national unity. As we have seen, this rhetoric of national unity applies the same promise of belonging as that asserted in lifestyle advertising.

Video News Releases and the Changing Discourse

As discussed in Chapter 3, advertising's purpose is not to inform but to evoke positive feelings that can be attached to products. Whether the products promise the alleviation of pain or the fantasy of wish fulfillment, advertisements work through affective states, not logical discourse. As an advertising consultant, Tony Schwartz regularly cautioned advertisers "not to make claims that could be proven false, but to concentrate instead on creating pleasurable experiences" (quoted in Jhally 1989, 225). The Gulf war coverage did just that as well. It created positive feelings, not public debate. Certainly many of the assertions made by the media about the war were subjects for debate, but that was not the point of the coverage. In the environment of persuasion, a visceral response becomes the substitute for such debate.

Most of the claims made about the motivations for the war—those concerning, for instance, the efficiency of the "smart bombs" and their effects on the people of Iraq—could easily have been proven false in an information environment. But the purpose of military control of the media during the war was to create a climate of opinion favorable to the war. Mechanisms of persuasion were set in place early on. The closing down of information left a void in media discourse that was filled with the feel-good strategies of advertising.

Among these strategies were video news releases (VNRs), advertisements masquerading as journalism. After President Bush sent troops into Saudi Arabia on August 2, 1990, the persuasive "news" contained in VNRs would become the cornerstone of a massive PR campaign set in motion to influence the American public and ensure U.S. military involvement in the Persian Gulf. In these advertising/news hybrids, persuasive discourse was merged with news coverage, setting the tone for the months to come.

In the early days of war preparation, video news releases figured prominently by promoting American intervention. Indeed, they became the centerpiece for the media campaign carried out by the public-relations firm Hill and Knowlton, in support of the war.[3] On October 10, 1990, Nayirah, a fifteen-year-old Kuwaiti girl, gave public testimony in front of the congressional human rights caucus. With tears in her eyes, and at times barely able to continue, she told of armed Iraqi soldiers storming hospitals in Kuwait, snatching premature babies out of their incubators, and leaving them on the floor to die. Adult men by her side cried as the testimony was given.

Nayirah's story was recorded by a camera crew hired by Hill and Knowlton, and the film was used to produce a video news release. Portions of the film were aired that night on NBC's Nightly News. The VNR was also sent to Medialink (a firm that serves some 700 TV stations around the country), eventually reaching a total audience of about 35 million.

Nayirah's story, and other reports of Iraqi human rights abuses in Kuwait, became the primary justifications for U.S. military intervention in the Persian Gulf. President Bush evoked Nayirah's story six times in one month while explaining the need to go to war: "Babies [were] pulled from incubators and scattered like firewood across the floor." And in another speech: "They had kids in incubators, and they were thrown out of the incubators so that Kuwait could be systematically dismantled."

By January 8, 1991, on which day the House Committee on Foreign Affairs held a hearing, the number of alleged incubator murders had risen to 312—a number also cited by Amnesty International in a human rights report widely circulated to Congress during the final months of 1990. No fewer than seven senators referred to the babies as justification for their support of the January 12, 1991, resolution authorizing war.

What many members of Congress and the American public did not know at the time was that Nayirah was the daughter of the Kuwaiti ambassador to the United States. She had been coached by Hill and Knowlton before giving testimony. The PR company was working for a group that called itself "Citizens for a Free Kuwait." As it turned out, the client was being financed almost entirely by the Kuwaiti royal family.

One Hill and Knowlton executive, when later interviewed on *60 Minutes,* admitted that the campaign had been designed to create public support for the war. Polls commissioned by Hill and Knowlton—utilizing the long-time Republican political consulting firm known as the Wirthlin Group[4]—showed a lack of support for intervention. Wirthlin then conducted focus groups in order to determine what persuasive strategy could change public opinion. What it found was that atrocity stories stirred anger and encouraged sentiments in favor of war. The babies-thrown-out-of-their-incubators tale was particularly effective.

As *Harper's* magazine editor John MacArthur (1992) observed, the baby incubator story was "successful, and false, propaganda." Journalists had accepted Nayirah's and other stories of atrocities without question, never seeking corroboration. The story was investigated, however, by Middle East Watch, a human rights group. Researcher Aziz Abu-Hamad interviewed doctors and staff at the neonatal wards of several different hospitals in Kuwait. He went specifically to the hospital at which Nayirah said she worked. Those interviewed either knew nothing of the story or said it never took place. In addition, Abu-Hamad found that many doctors had been employed by the Kuwaiti government to do public-relations work. Later, many of them changed their stories. After the war, ABC's John Martin also interviewed key Kuwaiti hospital officials. They acknowledged that some babies had died as a result of chaotic conditions, including shortages of nurses who had fled the country, but said that no infants had been dumped from their incubators. Nayirah herself later admitted that her written testimony prepared by Hill and Knowlton was not true. She had not seen even fifteen babies die.

Seemingly corroborating Nayirah's original story was testimony from a doctor who claimed to have buried fourteen newborn babies himself and to have supervised the burial of more than one hundred more. But Dr. Bebehani turned out to be a dentist, not a doctor, and later admitted that he did not know where the babies had come from, how they died, or exactly how many there were.

In the restrictive environment of persuasion that characterized media coverage of the war in general, journalistic newsgathering and critical skepticism gave way to the passive acceptance of persuasive messages. This dynamic had been set in place throughout a decade during which the news establishment learned to accept VNRs and to present them uncritically as news. The same dynamic applies today: Independent newsgathering and fact checking are rapidly becoming the old-fashioned techniques of a bygone era. Journalism is being replaced by media marketing techniques that target the American public with messages intended to persuade, not to inform. The same marketing machine behind product advertising now drives much of nonfiction reporting. As discussed in Chapter 7, these processes have foreclosed public participation in national debate, transforming an informed citizenry into the targeted consumers of persuasive messages.

Had the incubator story been proven a public-relations ploy at the time, the outcome would have been much different. Indeed, human rights reports, many of which were included in VNRs produced by Hill and Knowlton, tipped the balance toward war. Robert Dinlenschneider, president of Hill and Knowlton at the time, was very proud of the company's role in the war. Speaking in an Australian radio documentary, he said, "I believe we were able to target very precise audiences for a very precise message, and I think launch a communications campaign with an efficiency and economy that has never before been witnessed in the Western World."

The Hill and Knowlton company maintained its involvement in the media coverage throughout the duration of the war. Working for the Pentagon, it created VNRs using video footage from private companies in Kuwait that had been given access to the front. Broadcasting companies around the world bought the VNRs, as independent journalists were restricted from the fields of military operations. As Dinlenschneider boasted, "With one VNR, we reached 61 million Americans. . . . We found that the press kits were extremely important because the media couldn't get the information they needed."

From the beginning, the media environment could not be defined as informational; rather, it was characterized by persuasion designed to influence public perceptions. And under the influence of such "advertising," the public became a target, not a participant. But there was a reward for being kept in the dark. That informational void was filled with fantasy wish fulfillment. The war coverage offered the thrill of technological empowerment. Positioned in front of simulated control panels, viewers received a compelling summons, an invitation to control the technology. Media representations of state-of-the-art military weaponry—of tanks and Patriot missiles—evoked feelings of empowerment through such control. Yet all the while, real control and political power, through public awareness and debate, had been foreclosed by the military.

What substitutes for representations that offer distance and critical space is a type of voyeuristic pleasure, akin to what John Fiske has referred to as "empowering play." Television representations engage the viewer by offering "the power to play with the boundary between the representation and the real, to insert oneself into the process of representation so that one is not subjected by it, but, conversely, is empowered by it" (1987, 236). And indeed, the coverage of the Gulf war allowed the American public to feel powerful. William F. Fore (1991, 52) corroborates this point in noting that television representations of the war offered viewers psychological gratifications: "The War coverage met a number of deep-rooted psychological needs: to feel powerful and in control, to experience extreme emotions in a guilt-free and non-threatening environment." As "king[s] of the killing field," we ourselves could not be killed. The fantasy of hyper-realism protected us at the same time that it evoked positive feelings about war and its technology.

As noted, such feelings of empowerment have come to replace the actual political power that the public might have wielded by becoming involved in national debate from an informed perspective. Visual empowerment is truly a specious sense of power.

ɔᴎ   ɔᴎ   ɔᴎ

The media coverage of the Persian Gulf war marked a historic phase in the relationship between advertising and nonfiction programming. For a variety of economic and political reasons, that coverage adopted the logic of advertising messages. The merger of ads and news, then and now, has led to a profound lack of distinction between modes of communication intended to persuade and those intended to inform.

During the 1980s network executives became increasingly willing to accommodate advertising demands for a positive "programming environment." Programming strategies were designed to guarantee that both fiction and nonfiction television shows would be profitable—in other words, that they would more closely resemble the commercial messages within them. As a consequence, media representations began to incorporate the persuasive modes of communication characteristic of advertising. These practices, added to the severe political constraints imposed on the press by the military during the Persian Gulf war, dramatically changed the nature of nonfiction programs especially.

9

Democratic Talk-Show Strategies and the Competing Narratives of the 1992 Presidential Election

As Sally Jessy Raphael watched the final night of the 1992 Democratic National Convention, she felt a "shock of recognition" (Dowd 1992, A1). The testimonial revelations, delivered both in prepared videos and by the candidates themselves (live on national television), dealt with dysfunctional relationships, marital troubles, addicted family members, self-help, and recovery. "These people belong on talk shows," she reportedly told her husband. "They're the stuff we're made of. . . . They were pushing all the same buttons that we push on talk shows" (Dowd 1992, A1). Democrats became the party of disrupted families, unfaithful and abusive husbands, and single mothers. This is indeed the stuff of talk-show discourse. The video testimonials of lived experience recounted by Bill and his mother were standard Oprah fare. Vice-presidential candidate Al Gore's emotional rendering of his son's accident and subsequent survival and recovery was underscored by TV cameras that focused on the boy as he watched from the audience. Even before that, on *60 Minutes,* Clinton's repentance over the Gennifer Flowers affair and Hillary's forgiveness were pure public revelation—the new national symbols invoking trustworthiness and authenticity.

By the presidential election of 1992, the pseudo–self-realization and mock therapy of the talk shows had become fully incorporated into political discourse. Copying these thematic strategies, Clinton was propelled into the position of front runner throughout the race. He rode into the White House on the coattails of the talk-show hosts. With the help of the producers of the TV show *Designing Women,* who created the Clinton videotape shown at the convention, the Democrats fit themselves into television narratives that resonated with a large proportion of television viewers.

In the post–cold war economic recession, the mediated cultural environment no longer found it sufficient to slay the mythic dragons of the "evil empire."

225

Instead, the decontextualized psychological talk-show demons became the targets. These demons are the ones that haunt personal lives, that stop people from "getting in touch with their feelings" and from having fulfilling relationships. When it came to one of the greatest tests of contemporary television—personal intimacy—Clinton won hands down.

Images of Clinton night after night, deep in the crowd, a look of solemn concern crossing his face as yet another person told him about personal problems, created the impression that Clinton "really cared." As he sat in a diner with a single working mother, saying, "I'm really proud of you for raising that child on your own," Clinton became the "personal choice." Joan Didion remarked that Clinton had "personalismo," and Norman Mailer observed that Clinton had the capacity to "warm the country up."

Public television also embraced the talk-show format. Following the Democratic National Convention, Judy Woodruff hosted a call-in program on PBS that featured Bill Clinton answering questions via remote video. A Hispanic man called and, couching his question in the language of his own experiences, said that his son was on drugs. He asked Clinton what he planned to do about the national drug problem. Instead of offering a substantial political plan, Clinton assumed the talk-show mantle and began by congratulating the man for having the courage to talk about a member of his family, especially one with a drug problem, to a national audience. In the manner of an Oprah or a Donahue, he told the man that he was helping other people who have family members with drug problems. Clinton expressed concern for the man's problem and, using the discourse of personal testimonial, told him that he had "been there himself." After all, his own brother was a cocaine addict.

The discourse of TV therapy is now so pervasive that it penetrates the formulation and definition of public problems. And politicians have learned to stay within its parameters. For instance, the amount of time taken up with the talk-show testimonial style left Clinton no time to answer the question about drugs in broader political terms. In effect, the talk-show strategy allowed him to avoid relating the problem of drugs either to social or economic issues such as unemployment, poverty, and rage (the subject of Chapter 7) or to substantive policy proposals.

The political adaptation of talk-show discourse is a recent phenomenon, one that did not exist during previous elections. Former president Ronald Reagan, for example, was the son of an alcoholic father, but he did not use this fact to dodge political questions or to fashion his political persona. What he did use was the conventional formula for avoiding public questions: the appointment of "a blue-ribbon panel" to "study the problem." But by 1992 the public had grown weary of such evasive jargon.[1] People interviewed in the Harwood study (discussed in Chapter 6) complained about the language of avoidance used by politicians, citing such examples as "It needs further study" (Harwood 1991, 27). It had become obvious that "you ask them and you never get a straight answer."

Public awareness of this political language of avoidance had rendered it ineffective. The use of talk-show language in 1992 also allowed politicians to avoid giving a straight answer—but this time in a new way. Yet the strategy goes unnoticed, at least for the time being, because of the current cultural legitimacy of TV's therapeutic format. Phil Donahue indicated his understanding of the effects of the "new openness" of talk-show political language when he said, "This is the rhetorical equivalent of kissing a baby" (Dowd 1992, A10).

Sally Jessy Raphael was slightly uncomfortable with the political discourse that resonated with talk-show themes: As she put it, "For politicians to enter this grey area where it is neither news nor entertainment is a step backward" (Dowd 1992, A1). Her criticism clearly indicated her awareness of the contrived nature of the discourse. But it was inevitable that talk shows—as the dominant format addressing the needs of the public, and the only forum available for participatory discussion—would come to define political discourse. When applied to the electoral process, such discourse acquired an air of legitimacy.

It is equally evident that, with rare exceptions, the therapeutic mythography that constrains talk-show discourse has been incapable of addressing social and political issues in a meaningful way. Talk-show themes do provide an air of sincerity that addresses the public's lack of confidence in politicians, a distrust also revealed by the Harwood study. Citizens now perceive public officials as "inherently dishonest" because they "break promises, lie, and even sometimes cheat" (Harwood 1991, 33). The study found that "citizens believe that public officials no longer talk straight to them about issues; that public officials regularly dodge tough questions when they know the answers; and that public officials say one thing, only to do another" (Harwood 1991, 32). Some of the study's respondents stated simply, "I want representation." But they felt that politicians no longer care.

This bleak perception, held by many Americans regarding elected officials, is tempered only by the corresponding realization that it is the system that is responsible for the duplicitous actions of those once thought of as public servants. They know that "public officials are captives of lobbyists" and of political action committees, among other organizations (Harwood 1991, 29). As a Philadelphia man asserted, "The special interests and the lobbyists are in Washington 365 days of the year. They have no trouble getting the ear of the congressmen or senators." One woman added, "unless a politician feels threatened by the voting public, he will go with the lobbyist" (Harwood 1991, 29). In short, the legitimacy accorded those who govern has been undermined by a process in which politicians make electoral promises they do not keep. No better example exists than President Bush's famous campaign line, "Read my lips, no new taxes," which did not prevent him from raising taxes once in office. This syndrome that has created the perception that politicians cannot represent, and do not speak truthfully to, the public.

In 1992 talk-show discourse provided the Democrats with an effective set of strategies to deal with the themes of caring and trust that every pollster in America now knows are the key issues of any campaign. Clinton pollster Stan Greenberg underscored the effects of these strategies: "The campaign's polls showed that the 'sense of revelation,' the language of connecting and self-realization that is reflected in the political vocabulary, has reduced the impression of the ticket's being 'too slick and too political'" (Dowd 1992, A10).

But addressing the issue of public trust in a truly meaningful way would mean addressing the actual lack of political representation—the inability of elected officials to serve the needs of the people. Talk-show discourse addresses the theme of trust, giving politicians the appearance of sincerity—but it offers no substantial solution to the problem. Simply adapting the talk-show "trust through personal revelation" model does not make a politician more trustworthy. Only through changes in the system that allows the wealthy to buy political influence will the public be represented in an equitable manner.

The language of talk-show trust further obscures the reasons for the lack of political representation. The theme of trust reflects a systemic economic problem; it is not primarily a character issue. On the same day (July 27, 1992) that the *New York Times* noticed that political discourse was now identical to talk-show chatter, it ran an article on the success of the Democratic National Convention (see p. A10). Funds were pouring into Clinton's campaign. At the top of the list of contributors were "Lawyers and Lobbyists," who topped all other contributions with a combined total of $2,584,000. Nowhere in either article, however, did the press link the theme of trust with the political influence of wealthy lobbyists; nor did it point out the contradiction inherent in the use of the language of trust while business as usual continued.

On the few occasions that campaign designers attempted to have President Bush speak the language of talk-show therapy, the strategy failed. The problem was that Bush's efforts were such a dramatic change from his style (which was originally designed to overcome the "wimp" perception) that they appeared contrived and insincere. Spoken by Bush, the language of lived experience to indicate sympathy and caring seemed out of place. And the president's disastrous encounter with the families of MIA/POWs was not helped by his personal account: "When he was heckled by families of missing American service men the other day, he desperately tried to show them he understood sacrifice because he had lost his 3-year-old daughter to leukemia in 1953" (Dowd 1992, A10). Peggy Noonan, a long-time Republican speech writer, was clearly frustrated at the failure of the president's revelations, and went to considerable lengths to excuse them. For instance, she noted that Bush's "psyche" was sometimes very close to the surface: "His id jumps out of the box at inappropriate moments." Noonan was attempting to deny that his personal testimonial had been molded by political language. She was also frustrated with the Democrats' successful use of talk-show discourse: "When a beat-up President blurts out as a way of saying, 'Hey, I've lost someone, too,' is a lot different than the baby-boomer Democrats taking their focus-group information and ringing the childhood chimes in a prepared speech" (Dowd 1992, A10).

The "Talk-Show Debate"

Never was it more apparent how removed the Republicans were from the discourse of TV's primary discussion format than during the "talk-show debate" itself. The second presidential debate was indeed formatted as a talk-show discussion (an idea proposed by candidate Clinton not surprisingly). The public was invited to attend a public forum and to ask questions of the candidates. Unaccustomed to answering direct questions specifically, Bush used a vaguely encoded political language that was clearly out of date. Unwilling and unable to comprehend the needs, desires, and frustrations that had propelled the public talk-show phenomenon into existence, he was also unable to use its language.

The media imposed the sports metaphor of the "knockout punch," which Bush needed to deliver against Clinton. It was delivered instead to Bush himself—not by a journalist or opponent, but by an audience participant. One woman asked simply, "How has the recession affected your life?" Perot had spoken of a life disrupted, of having to leave his family, of having to endure hardship to answer the "call of the people." And Clinton had spoken about the pain of seeing the people of his state, many of whom he knew by name, suffer unemployment and hardship (see Figure 9.1). This was the language of the talk show, at its best. Both narratives expressed awareness and understanding acquired through personal tribulation, drawing the public into a shared experience.

But Bush's chances of staying in the White House narrowed with every word he spoke. When he answered, "You don't have to have cancer to know that it hurts," he demonstrated profound ignorance of the American cultural attitude. By using the delegitimated discourse of distance and expertise, instead of the "new news" discourse of life experience, he separated himself culturally from a public already lost to him both politically and economically.

The most significant result of the talk-show debate was that, for a brief time during the 1992 presidential election, the potential of the talk-show *format* was met: The public engaged in a participatory discussion with public officials, asking substantive questions that forced the politicians to answer in specific policy terms. For this moment of televised public discussion, the problems experienced at the micro-level of personal life were tied to broader economic and political policies aimed at alleviating those problems. Clinton, referred to as a policy "wonk"—meaning that he is conversant with the details of policy design and proposals—demonstrated his ability to draw these connections. His detailed descriptions of college loan repayment plans, national health care reform, and job retraining programs brought the felt needs of everyday life to the macro-level of policy discourse. In marked contrast, when Bush was asked a pointed question about retirement funds, he could not answer but, instead, referred to the audience member as "the expert" on that subject.

Now citizens were bringing their concerns not to a television pseudotherapist but to politicians with the potential to carry out the needs of a national con-

FIGURE 9.1 Clinton During the Talk-Show Debate
Presidential candidate Bill Clinton well understood the therapeutic style and testimonial
format of the talk show. Here, during the second presidential debate, he moves up close
and personal to answer a woman who asked how the recession had affected the lives of the
candidates. Although much of Clinton's success as a candidate was a matter of personal
style, the talk-show debate did allow the public to ask relevant political questions of those
running for elected office.

stituency. The politicians, in turn, were put on the spot by voters, not by the mediated and distanced perspective of journalists.

The most telling communication indicating Bush's discomfort with the format
was his repeated nervous gesture of looking at his watch. He gave the impression
that he was calculating, moment by moment, just how much more of the public
he would be forced to take. The *Nightline* program that followed the debate
recorded the public's perceptions of the candidates' responses. The show's producers had assembled a 125-member focus group, which had indeed responded
negatively to many of the president's answers. On the "pulse analyzer" to which
the focus group members were hooked up, the wiggly lines dove to the bottom of
the scale when the president revealed that the recession had not affected him, personally or emotionally (see Figure 9.2). This use of focus groups in election coverage marked another significant media development in the 1992 election, as detailed in the following section.

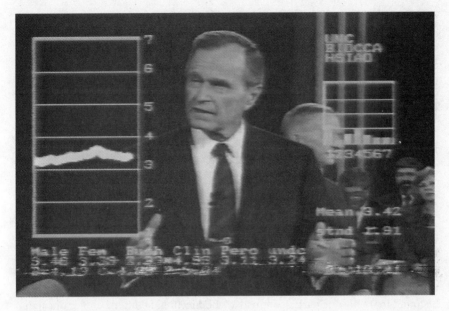

FIGURE 9.2 Bush with Pulse Lines
Following the second presidential debate, the ABC program *Nightline* assembled a 125-member focus group that responded to the candidates' answers. The wiggly lines on a "pulse analyzer" descended as then-President Bush revealed that the recession had not affected him personally. The use of focus groups and electronic perception analyzers was frequently referred to by the media, which presented them in a positive light. The ways in which such devices are employed to manipulate the public debate went unreported.

Measuring the Pulse of America

The news media's use of focus groups was not unique to *Nightline*. During the 1992 presidential election, political marketing techniques, especially those involving focus groups, became the subject of many news reports. Before the first debate, CBS news aired a story on such groups, inviting viewers into one of the sessions. We met the "typical cross-section" of people and were shown videos of the political advertisements they were evaluating. We even become privy to a small slice of their discussion. The group did not seem extraordinary in any way; in fact, the whole procedure was quite straightforward, amounting to just a more intimate way of taking a poll. As the group walked out of the building into the night, we felt better informed for having been exposed to the behind-the-scenes research techniques alluded to throughout the campaign.

The focus group procedure was also adapted as a news-gathering technique and incorporated into news sourcing. For instance, *World News Tonight* tracked its own group of real people throughout the campaign. And after the last presidential debate, ABC's *World News Tonight* began its coverage with the words *Pulse Poll*, which scrolled across the screen from right to left. The "pollsters" had gathered a collection of undecided voters, talking to them after every debate to see how their choices were developing. Their responses to events were presented even before media commentators had had a chance to interpret (or "spin") the results. Peter Jennings offered these words of explanation:

> Mindful of what Mr. Perot said about the press this evening, we have with us our focus group watching all the debates with us and we're going to hear from them . . . bearing in mind as we try always to do, your judgment at home is the essential one, and not to apologize at all for the wisdom of my colleagues like Jim Wooten who's out there in Michigan.

Throughout the election, many different broadcast news departments interviewed groups of people. Focus groups became the latest media format. In New York, Ernie Anastos, a channel 2 reporter for the 11 o'clock news, "got together with a cross-section for people from our area." And NBC's Dave Browde watched the debate with a focus group consisting of students at Rutgers University, where he found that only one participant had a "good feeling" about the choice of candidates.

The effect of this use of focus groups was to promote them as a familiar part of the political landscape. Indeed, they were presented as useful tools for evaluating public perceptions. Further, during the election they became the legitimate voice, more important than that of media pundits who "spun" their own interpretations. Focus groups were now thought to be significantly responsive to public concerns.

Yet the use of such groups had a negative impact on political discourse. When employed to determine public needs for the purpose of addressing those needs, as we saw in relation to the Harwood study (discussed in Chapter 6), they are a valuable democratic tool. But when used to manipulate public opinion, as occurred during the Gulf war (see Chapter 8), they are the antithesis of democratic practice. This latter description unfortunately characterizes their use in shaping public discourse.

The results of focus groups conducted before the 1992 election revealed keen public interest in NAFTA and the S&L bailout. Participants asked "tough, incisive questions . . . so you might think those issues would enliven the campaign" (Edwards 1992, 26). However, as one consultant put it while explaining how focus groups actually influenced the election, any issue that provokes intensive focus group debate is labeled a "negative referential." In the contained world of political handlers, an exciting issue provokes voters to ask unpredictable questions. So for the consultants this outcome is unmanageable, one to be avoided at all costs: "The point of focus groups or of any campaign research is to control the discourse, not enrich it. The point is to win" (Edwards 1992, 29). The media presentation of fo-

cus groups as beneficial sends out no warning signals explaining their actual political significance.

The ways in which political strategists determined what the presidential candidates would and would not say in the 1992 election illustrated the degree to which
focus groups (much like the marketing research techniques designed to sell products) are systematically used to "sell" political candidates by controlling electoral
discourse.

The Bush Team

Bush's political team fought an uphill battle after three years of economic recession that dogged the president in his bid for reelection. But when his handlers
rolled up their sleeves to take on the daunting task of the campaign, it was with a
sense of confidence—a confidence that stemmed not from their candidate's track
record but from their own ability to successfully define the public agenda. They
used the latest electronic technology combined with focus group research. But
what the Republicans failed to anticipate, after twelve years of superior political
design, was that they had met their match with Clinton's team, especially James
Carvel. The Democratic handlers had finally become as good as the Republican's.

Republican strategists began to design the reelection campaign by looking back
to the "emotional scores" recorded for President Bush's State of the Union address
given in January 1992. They also created a "values map" to determine which
themes from the speech were "media viable." They did so by assembling a "heart-
land focus group" of Chicago residents that consisted of what they considered to
be a demographically representative sample of Americans: five white male blue-
collar workers, four black and eleven white suburbanites, ten women, and ten
wealthy men. On January 21, 1992, this assemblage, arranged in demographically
distinct groupings, viewed Bush's State of the Union address while the president's
men, shielded behind a screen, looked on.

Each participant was given a miniature computer box equipped with a dial that
linked up to the central computer's "perception analyzer." By turning this dial
from 0 ("hate or/feel extreme discomfort") to 80 "love or/am very happy"), participants could register an immediate emotional response to everything the president said. Every element of the speech was then given an "emotional score," cate-
gorized along demographic "pulse lines," "which told, at each second, how the
blue-collar, suburban, female, and wealthy respondents scored each phrase"
(Edwards 1992, 25). At the same moment, the "average emotional response,"
(AER) was displayed on the screen.

Looking at these test results, the Bush strategists knew they had a serious problem. Very few of the fifteen different "moral and social values" to which the president referred in his speech were media viable. To become media viable, and thus
to have potential as a campaign slogan, a theme had to register above a 60 AER,
but "change" was the only thing that warmed the hearts of focus groups enough

for that score. "We learned change should be a campaign theme, which is tough if you're the incumbent," said a worried Fred Steeper, head of focus group research for the Bush campaign (Edwards 1992, 26).

When the president spoke of the "personal responsibility" necessary if people were "to seek work, education, or job training," a theme that in the past could have elicited a solid 60 ARE, it registered only a little over 45. Used so effectively by the Reagan and Bush presidencies to deflect attention from the harsh consequences of systematic cuts in social programs (e.g., by casting blame on "welfare frauds" for social ills), this theme, by 1992, no longer sounded plausible to a public whose jobs and quality of life were continuing to erode. Researchers also found that people did not want to hear about cuts in the capital gains tax once they realized that the well off had benefited from tax cuts during the 1980s while the income of the average American had fallen.

In short, Republican political analysts found the speech a dismal failure. Most of the slogans inserted to elicit a positive emotional response turned out to be "flatliners"—with very low emotional scores. The vague political phraseology of the Reagan/Bush years no longer rang with authenticity. Phrases such as "moods come and go, greatness endures," "the once and future miracle," and "the freest nation on earth, the kindest, the strongest" all plummeted. Trying to rekindle the flames of forceful leadership reminiscent of the Gulf war, Bush paraphrased his own words spoken during the war: "I look at hard times and make this vow: This will not stand." The phrase was a favorite of the strategists, and Bush repeated it twice—but twice it flatlined. When he called for an end to "pork-barrel appropriations," a tag intended to discredit the Democrats (usually a reliable tactic), the accusation hit the low 40s. Later, during interviews with focus groups, strategists found that it had backfired. The public wanted to know "who was paying for Bush's vacations."

In addition to change, the only theme still able to evoke a positive emotional response was the Gulf war. Feelings of power and patriotism remained salient, and marketers hoped to rekindle those feelings. Republican campaign managers worked with that single positive value, designing a number of trial commercials for the president that focused on the Gulf war. (One featured George and Barbara wearing fatigues.) Indeed, the argument could be made that Bush cared little about his campaign because of a false sense of confidence that had been inspired by his high approval ratings after the Gulf war only one short year before.

But such commercials did not test well. Strategists found that direct evocation of the Gulf war was an obvious election ploy that tended to cancel its positive power, so the war ads were not aired.

Only later in the campaign, after the failed themes of "family values" had rendered television coverage of the Republican National Convention ineffective, did the Bush consultants return to themes related to patriotism and the Gulf war. The artificial injection of political themes, evoked simply because they attained an AER over 60, illustrates the deleterious effects of political marketing on national discourse.

The Draft, Vietnam, Protest, and Patriotism

As the election moved into its final month, the Republicans made their last push to reverse the outcome. They hit Clinton hard with a negative campaign. Even in the face of national disgust with "mud slinging"—the degraded discourse of marketing strategies—their desperation and past successes left them with no alternative but to once again rely on what Kathleen Hall Jamieson (1992) terms "dirty politics." The intent of their carefully orchestrated campaign was to push Clinton's negatives up and to win swing voters who were disgusted with Bush but remained doubtful of a Clinton presidency.

The Trip to Moscow

By the end of September, Bush relied on surrogates to begin a campaign to discredit Clinton. Using the emotional-mythic theme of patriotism they had so effectively exploited during the Gulf war, Republican senators and representatives stayed late in the halls of Congress to call Clinton's patriotism into question for the benefit of C-SPAN cameras. They wondered about whom Clinton met when he traveled to Moscow in 1969, suggesting that the trip "was part of some obscure Kremlin plot" (Kolbert 1992, A9). As CBS journalist Susan Spencer noted, the conservative members of Congress had been musing out loud "about Clinton's antiwar past for days, implying KGB connections, hoping to entice press interest" (Kolbert 1992, A9).

The groundwork was laid in such a way that Clinton's Moscow trip would be picked up the media. By Wednesday, October 7, the anti-Clinton rumors had been circulated widely enough that CNN's Larry King saw fit to ask the president what he thought about Mr. Clinton's trip to the Soviet Union. "Larry," Bush replied, "I don't want to tell you what I really think because I don't have all the facts." His tone grave, he continued, "But to go to Moscow one year after Russia crushed Czechoslovakia and not remember who you saw—I think—I really think the answer is, level with the American people."

The wild accusations made by Senator Robert Dornan and others about Clinton's communist sympathies allowed Bush to use vague language—to make his point through association and innuendo but still have his meaning clearly understood. Similarly, the draft/Vietnam theme allowed him to make favorable connections to the Gulf war, the only Bush "accomplishment" that had tested as media viable in focus groups. At a rally on Thursday, the president made the link: "The sons and daughters of Louisiana that served in Desert Storm deserve our thanks and deserve our support. And so do those who served in Vietnam."

But as the week wore on, the media began reporting polls that demonstrated the public's unfavorable response to the issue. The public assumed, rightly, that the negative theme was deliberately intended to imply that something "clandestine" had occurred in Moscow; as one aide admitted, "The interpretation, frankly, bombed" (Wines 1992, A9).

The press began to report that the tactic had backfired, putting Bush on the defensive. On Friday the president appeared on *Good Morning America,* insisting that he was questioning not Clinton's patriotism but, rather, his "judgment." He tried to lay the matter to rest with: "Clearly, if he's told all there is to tell on Moscow, fine. I'm not suggesting that there's anything unpatriotic about that. A lot of people went to Moscow. And so that's the end of that as far as I'm concerned." Turning to *Good Morning America*'s Charles Gibson, he added, "I'd like to point out to you, Charlie, that the matter was not raised by me."[2] In other words, because the polls reflected a negative response to this issue, "plausible deniability" was invoked.

By this time, the Bush campaign had become frustrated with the media's refusal to follow it's lead and investigate the draft issue. A remark made by the president printed in the *New York Times* was telling: "I don't know why the press hasn't asked Clinton about his trip to Moscow."

It was then that the "liberal media" theme emerged. The press's refusal to pick up the theme of patriotism drew an irate response from the president. Later on Friday, as Bush was speaking in Cincinnati to the largest police union in the country, he said angrily, "You let the liberal elite do their number today trying to call me Joe McCarthy—I'm standing with American principle." Continuing with the speech, he backed away from the implications of treason but attempted to keep the issue of patriotism afloat: "It's wrong to demonstrate against your country when your country's at war, and I'm not going to back away from that one single bit" (Isikoff 1992).

The confused, volatile nature of Republican campaign themes revealed the relationship between political marketing discourse and its transformation as it reverberated within the public sphere. Such discourse created ways of speaking while not speaking, and it succeeded in promoting a sense of negativity and doubt effectively projected onto the opponent, while avoiding the blame for doing so. As the public responded, the twists and turns generated confusion, disgust, and a general sense of discontent into which Clinton was inexorably pulled.

Marketing strategies polluted the public dialogue at many levels, but they did just as much damage by preventing a more authentic discourse from occurring. The day after Larry King's interview, the Moscow story was featured on all the morning TV shows and appeared on the front pages of most daily papers. That evening the president's remarks and Clinton's response to them were the lead story on all three network news programs. Throughout the week before the debate, and on every public-affairs program the morning of the debate, the dialogue was consumed with the patriotism/trust issue. Journalists and pundits argue over its every wrinkle, predicting its effect on the outcome of the elections and directing the majority of their critical comments to Clinton's record, motivations, and political history.

Another example of political marketing strategies can be found on CNN's *The Capitol Gang.* Here, a group of syndicated columnists offers "insider chat" often removed from the concerns of the American public. In 1992, their discussion of the draft/passport issue was telling. The leader of the "Gang" opened the segment with a shot of a *Washington Post* article that, we were told, recounted the State Department's two-day search on Clinton's mother. Next, we saw footage of Clinton on the stump, saying that the State Department had investigated his mother, a "well-known subversive."

The camera then panned to the desk, where the leader of the "Gang" asked, "Is this a Bush Campaign Dirty Trick?" A segment from *CNN Newsmaker Saturday* featured Bush answering the question: "The State Department, if they did something out of the normal Freedom of Information Act procedures—that's wrong. But to equate that with the campaign, I'm sorry, I just think that's a stretch."

The host then directed a question directly at Vim Webber, the co-chair of the Bush campaign: "Campaign people have been telling the press for weeks, there's stuff in those passport files."

Webber answered: "I know it's out of character for this group—can we take a few minutes and talk about the facts? CNN polls show that we've narrowed to 8 points." He added that the themes of trust and taxes were working, and that the press was emphasizing the character issue, not the president. Conservative pundit Robert Novak then observed, "The pounding on Clinton" was also working:

> When they are that upset about this secondary story, about passports and John Sununu's protegé at the State Department doing something—that was kind of sleazy—but it isn't very important. But when the Clinton people make that their major effort, they're worried that the negatives against Clinton are beginning to hurt.

The host agreed, saying, "They should have handled it with some humor."

The Race

Those in politics who were interested in "the game" wanted a response. After the second debate, commentator David Broder, regularly featured on NBC's Sunday-Morning *Meet The Press,* made it clear that political journalists value the campaign-as-game over substantive issues or veracity. He noted that though the draft issue might not have been important to most of the public, the Republicans had successfully called Clinton's character into question. He went on to say that it was now up to Clinton to defend himself on the issue of character because Bush had succeeded in placing it on the agenda. Bush had thrown a punch, and it simply was not sportsman-like to refuse to retaliate.

The tendency of the press to portray presidential campaigns as if they were "horse races" (i.e., sporting events) has been observed frequently over the years (Jamieson 1992). Even though many strategies were put into effect during the 1992 campaign to improve media representations of "the race," the overriding themes were nevertheless "who was ahead" and "what were the other two doing to catch up." The story had become—what works. The one who was ahead in the polls, or was making a dramatic comeback, had succeeded in moving public opinion and that was the highest achievement. The media admired the Clinton campaign's successful handling of the Democratic National Convention. They judged the candidates by the ability of their handlers to create plausible images that the public could believe in.

As the 1992 presidential race wore on, the media began to disdain the mistakes made by the Bush team—mistakes that seemed so obvious, even to the press. Particularly damaging was the appearance of disarray: In the public eye, Bush's campaign strategists seemed divided and disloyal. But press admiration for the Bush team soared when, by the end of the race, the president actually succeeded in "coming from behind" and narrowing Clinton's impressive lead.

Competing Narratives

Long-time media analyst and practitioner Tony Schwartz (1973) first articulated the communication principle of "resonance." To resonate, persuasive messages promoting politicians or products must tap into themes already present in the hearts and minds of consumers/voters. (Thus we see why focus groups have become the research method of choice for marketers.) By probing the subjectivity and psychic makeup of the consumer/voter, marketers can design persuasive messages in such a way that they resonate with authentic needs, desires, and attitudes. Of course, this is not to say such needs will be met. Just as products do not fulfill the psychological longing that they evoke, persuasive political rhetoric all too often does not lead to public policies that carry out the interests of the voters.

Following Schwartz, Jay Rosen (1992) argues that political discourse, to be effective, must now make use of what is already being communicated on the "electronic commons." The point, he says, is not to attempt to sear a new message or political theme into the public mind, "but to somehow activate the layers of meaning already deposited there by the media." In this sense, the media, as "electronic commons," constitute a shared space "privately held but publicly traveled." With this formulation, Rosen has expanded the principle of subjective resonance to include what can be called "media resonance." He recognizes that viewers, as members of a shared media culture, possess a public subjectivity that holds in common the familiar visual codes, formats, and narrative constructions of the media. To be effective, then, political discourse must fashion itself according to these codes, formats, and narratives, which already define the media's "electronic commons."

As we saw in Chapter 1, the dominant aesthetic for the design of product advertising is to mimic, or copy directly, the programming genres and formats of television and film. In this way, advertising activates the layers of enjoyment and meaning already included in the familiar landscape of entertainment. By resonating with television narratives, the product and its message become embedded within the media environment. It is for this reason that the direct placement of product "plugs" in media content has become an advertising imperative. The persuasive message thus enjoys increased legitimacy. Accordingly, politicians must also be embedded within the larger media framework, not only to activate layers of existing meaning but also to become incorporated into the defining cultural landscape as a legitimate part of everyday life.

During the 1992 election, resonance with media narratives and formats became the effective strategy for the design of persuasive political discourse. Candidates fashioned their campaigns and advertisements according to the popular formats and genres already featured on television. As discussed, the Democratic language of self-realization, trust, and caring was molded to resonate with television's therapeutic culture, which dominates talk-show programming and much of television in general.

The Bush, Clinton, and Perot campaigns each resonated with a different set of narratives from the "electronic commons." In effect, then, the 1992 election became a referendum on the presentation of political discourse. It reflected a battle between television's various formats, and between the programming and marketing narratives of TV's popular culture. The media offered a choice among the various narrative vehicles of this political discourse but not a change in the substance of political content itself.

Perot

H. Ross Perot tapped into a long-standing American mythology. He was the hometown boy who made good, who made it from rags to riches. His story is etched indelibly in our collective culture. Perot embodied media narratives of past and present, narratives of a kind most recently (re)articulated in the movie *Rudy*. His message embraced the underdog. He was the lone hero fighting a Goliath government bureaucracy. Indeed, he fought City Hall, as so many American heroes have done and continue to do. Perot said he was in the political race to fight for the little guy.[3]

Perot's media themes reflected both legitimate public discontent with unrepresentative government and the tradition of populist politics. Yet his story exists at the level of pure symbolism. The contradictions between his mythic themes and his own life trajectory are glaring. Perot made his money on government contracts and worked as a lobbyist himself. His persona as an upstart outsider had nothing to do with his actual position as economic and social insider. In addition, his bid for the presidency was carried out through a TV campaign that only a billionaire could afford. If it weren't for television's economic exclusivity and its maintenance of the myths of popular culture, Ross Perot would never have had a campaign to begin with.

Fear and Negative Advertising

It doesn't surprise me. He's raised the flag of fear.

—Governor Clinton's response on Larry King Live (October 28, 1992),
when asked about his drop in the polls

In 1992 the Republican's political constructions were fashioned to resonate with yet another set of media narratives, also included among the media's multifaceted cultural representations. As the Clinton camp well understood, the Republicans were drawing on the discourse of fear, blame, and guilt, attitudes that had worked to keep them in the White House for the last twelve years. These narratives of exclusion exist as themes on many of TV's crime programs and tabloid formats.

Three weeks before the election, a clear win was predicted for the Clinton/Gore ticket. On October 19, *Newsweek*'s cover announced that the Bush campaign was "Running Out of Time." But by October 27, a CNN tracking poll found that Clinton's lead had narrowed from a maximum of 19 percentage points to a minimum of 2. Even though other polls showed varying spans of up to 10 percentage points, there was no doubt that, as Robert Novak asserted, the Bush campaign had succeeded in defining the theme of "trust" and in calling Clinton's character into question. This objective was met primarily through the use of negative television advertising.

One Bush/Quayle spot featured a split screen showing two views of Clinton side by side. Two large video blobs covered his two faces. Simultaneously a male voice charged, in low revealing tones, "He said he was never drafted. Then he admitted he was drafted. Then he said he forgot being drafted. He said he was never deferred from the draft. . . . " The ad consistently aired around 7 P.M. on NBC, just before the show *Cops*. The decision to buy time before that program was not accidental. Alteration of video images to blur the face is a technique commonly used to hide the identities of suspected criminals on television. And *Cops* was the most appropriate programming environment for the ad, helping to solidify the latent visual message that attempted to associate Clinton with criminality. Indeed, the introduction to *Cops* aired every night and featured similar blurred faces—the faces of criminal/suspects the cops aim their revolvers at and struggle to handcuff. The visual technique of blocking out Clinton's face tied Clinton, through image association, to the unsavory offenders on the wrong side of the law.

With the advent of negative political advertising, "resonating" has come to mean tapping into ambient feelings of fear and prejudice. Mythic themes of patriotism and glory also enter into these depictions, providing a foundation upon which to evoke and resolve the fearful anxieties. But it is no longer enough to rouse fear simply through traditional political rhetoric and campaign speeches. Emotional themes are most effective when they are fashioned on the basis of the familiar entertainment and visual techniques of television itself.

Media Resonance and Intertextuality

Consider, for example, the 1990 North Carolina senatorial contest between Harvey Gantt and Jesse Helms discussed in Jamieson's (1992) *Dirty Politics*. Two weeks before the end of the race, Gantt was ahead in the polls. He had defined education and environment as key issues. A solid one-third of the voters were tired of Helms, convinced that he did not represent the needs of the state. But in the final ten days, the Helms campaign ran a number of "race-priming ads" that focus-group testing revealed to be powerful and effective. Gantt lost his bid for the senatorial seat.

These race-priming ads were constructed through the use of visual "cueing." Jamieson (1992) defines cueing as a technique used to reach underlying prejudice and evoke visceral responses without openly verbalizing such messages. One ad she analyzed contains a subtext of racial prejudice that was elicited visually. Jamieson describes the effects created through this video manipulation: "In the rewinding image, Gantt looks out of control, his head bobbing from side to side." Then, when the image of him talking is slowed down, Gantt's voice is "slurred to a growling, drawn-out protracted drawl" (Jamieson 1992, 95).

Through rewinding and slow-motion editing, the ad simulates recognizable racial stereotypes. Focus group viewers who were asked to characterize these visual and audio effects used the words "stupid," "definitely black," and "growling" (Jamieson 1992, 96). One respondent characterized Gantt as "the kind of really dumb black you used to see in movies" (Jamieson 1992, 96). Through visual cues, the advertisement evoked visceral emotional responses, mediated through stereotypic imagery, and negative associations. Yet all this was accomplished without verbalizing racist attitudes as such. Visual cueing and media resonance are powerful persuasive tools indeed.

During the 1992 election, the themes of fear and guilt were rejected by viewers who picked up on them in speeches given at the Republican National Convention. The Bush interview with Larry King was also unsuccessful in calling Clinton's patriotism into question. Bush had failed to define patriotism as the overriding concern of the campaign. (Recall that the Pledge of Allegiance issue did succeed as such in 1988.) It was not until the Republican messages were dressed in the familiar visual styles of "reality" programming and advertising's associational techniques that they began to resonate with the public.

Other negative ads brought out near the end of the campaign succeeded in exacerbating Clinton's negatives, even in the face of public disapproval of such tactics. The *Newsweek* poll of October 19 showed that 72 percent of the public did not think Clinton's anti–Vietnam war activities and his Soviet trip were important campaign issues, and that 63 percent considered Bush's remarks about both issues to be unfair criticism. But Bush's handlers pressed on. They ran ad after ad pounding the "trust" issue home, and thereby set the media agenda from middle to late October.

The negative advertising began to succeed by affecting the public at a visceral level. Visual cueing and familiar TV constructions, with their corresponding assumptions, allowed the political advertisements to succeed where the Bush speech writers had failed.

Another anti-Clinton spot opened with a view of Clinton's face. The camera pulled in to a close-up so tight that it exposed only his eyes. The harshly lit black-and-white photo, cropped in this manner, revealed mostly eye wrinkles, making him appear old and ominous. It was recognizable as Clinton only when the camera pulled back slowly to a full view of what turned out to be the cover of *Time* magazine. Following fast edits on each word, the whole subtitle appeared: "Why Voters Don't Trust Clinton." The final frames again showed the magazine cover, but this time with the photo-positive replaced by an eerie X ray–like photo-negative. The background noise that had registered as an ominous low rumble throughout the ad ended with an abrupt and harsh "clank." The sound was similar to that of prison cell door slamming shut, conveying the message "You are trapped if you vote for Clinton." The visceral meaning, forged through advertising's associational techniques, was that Clinton himself is criminal.

Stylistically, the ad copied many aspects of *Time's* own promotional spot, which featured fast-paced edits of a series of magazine covers, ending with a loud clank. Use of the textual reference embedded the political advertisement within a broader media environment, this time in an attempt to associate the ad with legitimate journalism. *Time* disapproved of the implication that it had endorsed George Bush. Indeed, the ad was an implied endorsement by the media. The magazine filed a federal lawsuit against the Bush campaign for using its cover photo of Clinton without permission. But Bush's people left the ad on the air, waiting to pull it the night before the suit went to court.

The repeated airing of a series of negative ads, dark and fearful in tone and visually tense, moved public opinion. The Bush/Quayle attack strategies accelerated as the campaign came to an end. But the most effective *verité* ads were brought out after the final debate. These advertisements, too, copied the visual strategies used on *Cops* and other "reality programming." They gave the impression of having been shot by the same camera that follows slightly behind, looking just over the shoulder of the law-enforcement officers featured on *Cops.* The grainy, in-your-face visuals in these ads got up close and personal with "real people" whose faces were distorted from worry, reminiscent of tabloid style. They say, "Clinton means less food on the table, . . . fewer clothes on the kid's back. . . . I don't see how we can afford any more taxes. . . . I don't trust him. . . . He's a draft dodger. . . . I can't believe anything he says."

In both form and content, these ads plugged directly into the TV tabloid genre, the new "reality programming" of the 1980s. They also echoed the attitudes and themes of fear and criminality featured on *Cops* as well as *Top Cops, America's Most Wanted, Secret Service, FBI: The Untold Story, Unsolved Mysteries, Final Appeal,* and *I Witness Video.* These programs excited voyeuristic pleasures by allowing the public to watch criminals in the act of getting caught. The anti-Clinton ads evoked the same tense feelings of fear and loathing, directing those feelings toward Clinton. Instead of a coherent economic policy, Bush offered a criminalized Clinton, appealing to visceral anxieties.

Entertainment Metaphors

Even though many scholars and commentators criticized Larry King's "softball" lobs over the "punches" delivered by more serious journalists such as Ted Koppel, a look at the "politainment" discourse of standard press coverage reveals little substantive difference between Larry's style and that of hard-hitting journalists.

Compare, for example, the media commentary that surrounded the third presidential debate. After the debate, *Larry King Live* opened with "It was high noon in East Lansing tonight. The final shootout in the Presidential debates." King then turned to Lynn Martin, the secretary of labor, and asked her if the debate was a victory for the president. She responded with, "It was High Noon and this time Gary Cooper won. There was a nice slick gun slinger out there . . . but this was a victory." She went on to say that as a talk-show host Bill Clinton would have been the best, and that Ross Perot would have made a very good guest.

A news program that aired on ABC shortly before the final debate featured political correspondent Jeff Greenfield, who used a series of sports metaphors all at once: "Today they're telling Mr. Bush to . . . throw a knockout punch, to hit a home run, to score three touchdowns in the last quarter." After the debate, Greenfield was self-conscious about his overuse of the metaphors. Commenting on then-President Bush's performance, he said that this time the president was "up to it. He stepped up to the plate, to use one of those horrid sports metaphors, and really got into it for the first time."

Public broadcasting was also littered with the emotive language of fiction. Lee Cullum from the *Dallas Morning News,* which had endorsed the president, said the evening had belonged to Bush and Perot: They were "two gladiators who were having an amazing duel." The 11 o'clock news on CBS pushed the mixed metaphors to the extreme. Bush, Clinton, and Perot "all came out shooting from the lip in a final fiery showdown." The media uniformly spoke of the "contest" and of the "contenders" and their "crossed swords."

"Serious news" discourse has long incorporated such language. But the sports and entertainment metaphors have degraded election discourse and obscured rather than illuminated political issues. It was on the very serious public-affairs program hosted by John McLaughlin, *The McLaughlin Group,* which aired the Sunday before the final debate, that the inappropriate and obfuscating nature of such metaphors was most clearly revealed. McLaughlin's "exit" question was "Is the election over?" One member of his group said, "He's out of ammo." And syndicated columnist Jack Germond likened the rest of the campaign to a football game: "I think Clinton's ahead by 21 points in the 4th quarter. It's been done but it's tough. Very tough."

MCLAUGHLIN: Very tough. When has it been done? It's never been done historically.
GERMOND: 21 points. Yeah.
MCLAUGHLIN: This far behind, has it?
GERMOND: I'm talking about football.
MCLAUGHLIN: Oh. . . .

Ultimately, discontent with the media's focus on the "race" and with the general lack of political content pulled the public toward the "direct-access" formats. These formats offered a more direct dialogue with the candidates, unmediated by "serious" journalists.

"New News" and "Direct-Access Media"

The 1992 campaign was assimilated into what have been called "new news" venues.[4] Campaign '92 was carried into a wider variety of nonfiction formats than was the case with any previous campaign. And these new formats, in turn, reached a greater number of viewers than did traditional news. The now-famous appearances of Governor Clinton talking to teenagers on MTV and playing his saxophone on *Arsenio Hall* were matched only by Ross Perot's link with *Larry King Live.*

Clinton's appearances on these programs caused serious pundits of news and public affairs to lament the "degrading" influence that such appearances have on public discourse. Meanwhile, proponents of more traditional "serious" journalism argued that without the "journalistic filter"—the tough questions asked by experienced reporters and commentators—candidates could not be kept accountable to the public. However, Freedom Forum research demonstrated the value of bypassing that filter. A study that compared journalists' questions to those asked by the public on talk and call-in shows found that the latter were more serious and contained more social and political content than did those of seasoned journalists.[5] Lawrence Grossman also argued that the uses of "new news," also referred to as "direct-access media," indicated that "politics is moving into the mainstream of American life."[6]

The second presidential debate, which incorporated the questions of the public into its format, demonstrated that the public was capable of keeping the candidates accountable to its needs. The tense moment when a member of the audience pressed the candidates to make a vow that they would stop talking about themselves and instead address public needs was a defining moment for television's role as a public forum. This debate, which had borrowed its format from the talk shows, focused on the issues more than the other two debates because of the public's participation.

Expansion of the boundaries of political discourse, and of the public's involvement with that discourse, resulted in increased numbers of voters registering for the 1992 election. Advertising also took advantage of this electoral popularity by inserting the campaign into the promotion of products.

Insertion of the Campaign into Product Promotion

As the 1992 presidential campaign became defined as a major cultural event, it was incorporated within fiction and nonfiction programming. It also became a vehicle for product promotion as many advertisements started featuring references to the campaign, appropriating its themes to sell products.

In one commercial, an orange-and-green talking parrot mimics the most famous presidential line in a humorous French accent. "OK, kitty cats," he says, looking directly at the viewers. "Read my beak." The slow cadence and pausing are the same as in Bush's infamous line, "Read my lips." The parrot continues, "No more birds." Now the words are recognizable substitutes for "No new taxes." As the food falls into a pet dish, he explains, "For dinner, I mean. Try new recipe Whiskas."

Another commercial, for IKEA home furnishings, refers to the election by using sound-bite audio clips that mimic the words spoken by politicians and pundits. On the screen we read "Can politicians solve the recession?" The ad then cuts to a talk-show host who, while sitting in front of a bank of monitors, poses the question "How are we going to solve the recession?" Next, the ad cuts to another public-affairs program, as a politician repeats, "How are we going to solve the recession?" After a pause he begins to answer, but the ad cuts to another on-screen question: "Tough One, Huh?" Then it cuts to another politician, who says, "We have no solution to the problem, apparently." It cuts quickly back to the screen, which reads "IKEA does! Buy low. Live high." A picture of a sofa follows with the words "This Sofa $695." A pundit shrugs and a politician scratches his nose as more sofas are shown. One sells for $595, another for $1,495. Next, we see an African American pundit with headphones. The word LIVE appears in the upper-left corner as he says, "Americans will have to start spending much more wisely." The screen prints, "Hey, vote for that guy." Following the IKEA slogan/logo, the last frame reads "Come see our latest styles at recession-proof prices."

Then there was a Merrill Lynch advertisement that combined lofty images of past presidents flying through the heavens with the words "Every presidential election of the twentieth century has had enormous implications for America and the world. Through it all Merrill Lynch has understood those implications. . . ."

In addition, "change" became the advertising catchword during and after the election. MCI proclaimed, "In business, it is a time for change." And for its new line of cars, Chrysler Corporation announced, "This changes everything."

Finally, a spot done for the *Montel Williams Show* created a politician-like image for the talk-show host. First he is seen in military service, doing a physical workout; then he is talking to groups of people. The voice-over says, "No you can't vote for him, but. . . ." Clearly, the 1992 election and its political candidates were considered models for celebrities, thus indicating the unity of discourse between politicians and celebrities, as well as the rationale behind the parallel marketing of the two.

Just as advertising appropriated the campaign, the familiar punchy slogans of effective marketing were used to sell candidates. One Clinton campaign placard at the Democratic National Convention read "How do you spell relief? Clinton."

Advertising metaphors with negative implications were also used. A number of commentators noted after the vice-presidential debate that Dan Quayle was like the "Energizer bunny . . . he just kept going, and going, and going." After losing the race, Quayle surprised TV viewers by turning around and revealing himself in a Wavy Lay's Potato Chips advertisement during Super Bowl '94. With this 60-second spot, the circle of politician/celebrity/promoter was completed. The discourse was finally unified.

FIGURE 9.3 Quayle in Wavy Lay's Ad
After losing the race, former Vice-President Dan Quayle surprised TV viewers when he turned around and revealed himself in a Wavy Lay's Potato Chips advertisement during Super Bowl '94. With this 60-second spot, the circle connecting politicians with celebrity status and the promotion of products was finally completed. Political and advertising discourse are now indistinguishable.

Murphy Brown and the Vice-President

> *It doesn't help matters when prime-time TV has Murphy Brown . . . mocking the importance of fathers by bearing a child alone and calling it just another lifestyle choice.*
>
> **—Dan Quayle**

Murphy Brown and her friend/co-worker Frank hear Vice-President Quayle utter these words after they turn the TV on to watch the news. Frank had planned to look after Murphy's new baby while she takes a shower for the first time in days. He and Murphy are fictional characters, watching a fictional television news program on a Hollywood set. Yet they carry on a dialogue with a real vice-president concerning an issue raised during a real campaign. The vice-president's words are his own, contained in footage of a political speech given in California on May 19, 1992. This footage is featured on the fictional news that Frank and Murphy watch in her living room on September 21, 1992.

The American public also watches as the vice-president—who in slightly more than one month's time will either be reelected or leave the second-highest office in the land—appears in a situation comedy. When the vice-president refers directly to Murphy, she responds to his criticisms by saying, "I'm glamorizing single motherhood? What planet is he on? Look at me, Frank. Do I look glamorous?" After pausing for the laugh track, Frank replies, "Of course not, you look disgusting!" Peals of laughter follow.

The program itself is a comedic rendering of the very people who produce, direct, and write the scripts for prime-time television programming. It features reporter Murphy Brown, the star of a news magazine show called *FYI*. Dan Quayle's words could have been referring to the CBS program *Murphy Brown*, but as used on *Murphy Brown*, they applied equally to the fictional *FYI*. Thus television's self-referential system facilitated the words of the vice-president as viable fiction. He appeared to be speaking directly to a fictional character, criticizing her for setting an example for single motherhood on her prime-time program, *FYI*. His words could not have matched the entertainment narrative more closely if they had been scripted. (Television discourse has interconnected politics and entertainment so successfully that during the 1992 presidential campaign a new form of discourse was established. *Politainment* represents the lack of distinction made between the discussion of political issues in the public sphere and entertainment's fictional discourse.)

Frank tries to console Murphy by telling her that Vice-President Quayle is not important enough for her (a fictional character) to be upset about. He argues, "He's Dan Quayle, he's the one who said before the United Negro College Fund that it's terrible to lose your mind." (The vice-president really did say those words, intending to quote the actual United Negro College Fund slogan, "A mind is a terrible thing to waste.")

Murphy decides to ignore the story and starts off toward her shower when first the *Washington Post* and then the *New York Times* call on the telephone to get her response to the vice-president's criticisms. The fictional character refuses to comment, saying only, "What is it, a slow news day?" With this exchange, a television situation comedy has criticized the "papers of record" and assumed a position of superiority as the legitimate venue for the meaningful discussion of public issues. Traditional journalism is further delegitimated as the narrative unfolds. In events that follow, Murphy and her co-workers are hounded by members of the press, especially the print media, who camp out on her lawn and go through her garbage.

In her own time (at the end of the episode), Murphy Brown articulates a political position while defending herself. She sits behind her fictional news desk at *FYI* and begins her news story—directed not to a fictional public but to the American public. Murphy Brown, the fictional character, ends the story by walking over to join a collection of single parent families who are not fictional but, indeed, quite real. They are featured in direct critical response to the actual Republican campaign rhetoric about "family values." A short while later, pictures and information about the single parents who appeared in this last scene were featured in various real-life news reports.

Trying to undo the political damage to his campaign, the vice-president appeared in an advertisement that aired on television as a promotion of the episode. He also sent a handwritten letter to the fictional baby (the as-yet unnamed Avery), saying that he (the baby) had helped the country talk about an important national issue. The large stuffed elephant he included with the letter was eventually given to a real homeless child.

This dialogue between a politician running for elected office and a character who exists only in fiction became one of the most celebrated issues of the 1992 presidential campaign. It well illustrated the transformation in American media culture that has resulted in the erasure of boundaries between fictional narratives and the discussion of public issues. In this era of "politainment,"[7] the media, across the spectrum of fiction and nonfiction programming (and, as we have seen, in advertising, as well), no longer make a distinction between modes of discourse. In short, the 1992 political campaign became part of the shared discourse of television.

Another step into the *Murphy Brown* episode illustrates the ways in which contemporary political and social issues are discussed in fictional narratives. Murphy Brown is learning how to care for her newborn baby, and this fictional rendering is every bit as relevant to the electoral issue of "family values" as are the direct references to the vice-president. When the baby cries, Murphy holds it, in Frank's words, "like the main course at a luau." He shows her how to hold the baby close so it will feel secure. He even knows that "if you hold it on your left side it can hear your heart beat." Murphy, in awe, asks how he knows all this. He replies that he was the oldest of seven and "learned a few things" and, further, that "it just feels right." She retorts: "Oh great, Frank, your maternal instincts are better than mine." She tries to take notes, writing down "Pat, pat, sway, sway." Frank tells her, "You can't go at this like a reporter."

The portrayal of Murphy Brown as totally devoid of maternal instincts did indeed challenge the basic assumptions of the "family values" theme articulated by the 1992 Republican campaign. In effect, it asserted that motherhood is not instinctual; and it denied the naturalized framework of biology-as-destiny, which argues that because women bear children, they belong in the home. In fact, reporting comes more naturally to Murphy than does motherhood. She is willing to learn, however, just as anyone who desires to raise a child would be—whether a man or a woman.

Hill/Thomas and *Designing Women*

> *I'm sorry, I don't mean to be strident and overbearing, but you know nice just doesn't cut it anymore. Like a lot of women out there tonight, I'm mad. I'm mad because we're 51 percent of the population and only 2 percent of the United States Senate.*

These lines were delivered not by a candidate running for office but by an actress in an episode of the TV situation comedy *Designing Women*. The episode was used, with the help of its producer, Linda Bloodworth Thomas, to help raise

$1 million for Barbara Boxer, a candidate for U.S. Senate running in California. Women's anger over the treatment of Anita Hill by the Senate confirmation committee led to political activism that, in turn, prompted the placement of thirteen women on the ballot for Senate in 1992.

The televised Hill/Thomas hearings created the image of a panel of white men looking down with interrogating gazes on a black woman. That image was etched indelibly in the minds of incensed women voters, as it underscored the sexual imbalance in government. Paradoxically, the fact that the corresponding political activism of women was given voice through a fictional television program further illustrates the degree to which political and entertainment discourse have merged.

The Politics of Blame, Fear, and Guilt

Throughout the 1992 campaign, in one way or another, the Republicans consistently tapped into narratives of blame, fear, and guilt in an effort to blame individuals and groups for the failed political and economic policies of the Reagan/Bush years. The end of the cold war had left a void in the Republican camp that it filled by bringing the cold war home. The enemy within became defined as gays, women who do not know their place, African Americans, the poor, even people trying to protect endangered species.

The vice-president's attack on Murphy Brown was an attempt to reformulate women's desire for independence into anxiety and guilt. As commentator Molly Ivins (1992) pointed out:

> We have long been accustomed to hearing Republicans exploit racial fears, usually by talking about crime. The "family values" issue is a more subtle exploitation of the doubt, confusion and guilt felt by American women. Women are receiving so many conflicting messages from this society that no matter what choices we make, or more often what roles necessity forces on us—work, family or the difficult combination of both—we all feel guilty about what we're doing.

The American middle class, in particular, was made to feel guilty for its "lifestyle choices." And, indeed, the "family values" theme was an attempt to direct blame for the country's ills away from economic issues. Possessed of no positive "media viable" attributes himself, Bush was reduced to relying upon the negative narratives of exclusion characteristic of the Reagan/Bush years.

At no time was the underlying assumption of the "family values" theme more evident than when George Bush "explained" the problems of the inner city. When asked in the first presidential debate what "family values" meant to him, he took the opportunity to blame the problems in "the Ghetto" on a lack of such values. The "family values" theme was clearly a cue, a hidden code for racism. The assertion here was that what is wrong with urban America is the structure of the family, not the barriers to human improvement erected by economics and society. Accordingly, the public was directed to blame the ills of the inner city on its victims, the people who are forced on a daily basis to negotiate the conditions of poverty that exist there.

But the themes of fear and guilt did not resonate when associated with the television situation comedy *Murphy Brown,* a show created and designed by women, and expressive of their need for respect and independence. Quayle's attack openly confronted these desires and their familiar media representations. That was the strategy error made by his handlers.

Clinton's humanistic discourse was the final blow to the "family values" episode. For instance, on various occasions he spoke with compassion about holding a "crack" baby, an expression of inclusion and empathy. Indeed, the desire for unity was a theme the Democrats had detected in focus group findings. Meanwhile, the public had been looking for an end to divisiveness after twelve years of "wedge" politics. When Clinton answered Bush's character attack during the first debate by saying, "We've had enough divisions. I want to lead a unified country," he offered a dramatic change in political formulations.

The "personal responsibility" theme that blamed single mothers, "deadbeat" fathers, and crack-cocaine addicts for all the social and economic ills of the country was discredited, at least temporarily. This theme also pointed to Bush's refusal to take responsibility for his role in the economic decline of the country and the political delegitimation of the government. That was the specter that loomed even as the cameras were turned off. After twelve years of effectively diverting attention away from the exporting of jobs, the unfair tax burden on the poor, and the S&L bilking of the nation, the politics of blaming the public was no longer "media viable."

∾   ∾   ∾

Among the issues the media failed to impart to the American public was the profound negative impact that political marketing has had on public discussion. As we have seen, the same research strategies and marketing techniques that propel consumer culture have been applied to the political arena. In particular, focus groups have come to determine what will or will not become part of the public dialogue. Political consultants use them to define public issues, to set the parameters of debate on those issues, and to influence public opinion. Unfortunately, such information is not used by candidates to better represent the needs of constituents. Indeed, the discourse of "politainment" stems from the glaring difference between campaign promises and the candidates' political behavior once in office. Like the products that disappoint because they cannot live up to the emotional promises made by their advertisements, packaged politicians frustrate the body politic.

As Richard Goldstein noted during the 1992 campaign, "The trick is to choose the lies that are true." That statement in itself was not far from the choice actually made. The alternatives offered the public were mere narrative differences in TV formats and themes. It was *LA Law* against *America's Most Wanted,* and *The Oprah Winfrey Show* against *A Current Affair.* It even came to a choice in advertising strategies between the spunky little Stain Master baby tearing around in his walker and the Energizer bunny marching through a woman's pounding headache. The choice between Clinton and Bush became, in effect, the choice between *Murphy Brown* and reruns of *The Brady Bunch.* At some level, even President Bush understood narrative representation as political choice when he said, "We need a nation closer to the Waltons than the Simpsons" (Rosenthal 1992, A17).

The trick was to pick the narratives that most closely adhered to one's political perceptions. Each campaign used different themes from television culture, and those themes in themselves resonated with very different political choices. Clinton's talk-show discourse was about inclusion, consensus, redemption, and unity. Bush embraced the Republican-era narratives of exclusion, framing the nation's problems within the parameters of blame, fear, and guilt. The choice was between the talk-show host/repentant womanizer and his wife who had never learned her place, and the police officer on *Cops* who rids the streets of dehumanized "criminals" whose faces have been digitally removed from the image. Certainly the voyeuristic "reality" shows of the Reagan/Bush era represented the politics of fear. Bush advertisements featured the "real" people of "verité" formats—tense, anxious, and afraid. That kind of message won the battle in 1988. But by 1992 the more popular format had clearly become talk-show pseudotherapy. Using that discourse, the Democrats regained the White House.

Unfortunately, television narratives represented a more significant political choice than did the candidates themselves. In choosing the "lies that are true," the public made an authentic choice, but one that did not correspond to real differences in what can now be termed the "postmodern" candidates.

This point is best illustrated with Clinton's embrace of the North American Free Trade Agreement, which, in both design and execution, was a Bush-era trade agreement. Favorably disposed toward the mega-corporate structures, NAFTA will negatively impact employment opportunities, the standard of living, the natural world, and the general well-being of the American public (as discussed in Chapter 2)—this in spite of Clinton's campaign, which promised a reversal of the upward economic distribution that occurred in the 1980s, at the expense of working Americans. The blueprint for Clinton's promises came from focus groups whose participants conceived of themselves as working people with "a sense that lost jobs and corporate ripoffs" (Edwards 1992, 27) had created a disillusioned public demanding real change in economic structures. The passing of NAFTA also made it clear that corporate political action committees continue to maintain their hold on public officials, and therefore their privilege, under the new administration.

Conclusion:
The Commercial Politics
of Postmodern Television

ONE OF THE MOST CELEBRATED advertising campaigns produced for television was the series of commercials created by McCann-Erickson for Taster's Choice. The advertisements featured actors Sharon Maughan and Tony Head, who became romantically involved with a little help from the product. In the first install-ment, entitled "Doorbell/First Meeting," Sharon invites guests to dinner, only to find that she is out of coffee. She goes across the hall to borrow some from Tony. "Would, uh, Taster's Choice be too good for your guests?" he asks as he goes to the cupboard. "Oh, I, uh, think they could get used to it," she responds coyly. Thus be-gan a romantic involvement that developed with each successive episode/com-mercial. The couple's fantasy courtship was credited with raising sales of the cof-fee by 10 percent (Maslin 1992, 9).

In another installment the two meet again with equal interest in each other, this time amidst a crowd of other guests who have just been served Taster's Choice at another neighbor's dinner party. Though short and fragmented, the narratives of these ads feature key elements of dramatic fiction. The abbreviated romance is conveyed through tight close-up shots of knowing and alluring looks. The sus-pense and anticipation they offer follow from one unresolved story line to the next. The sophisticated urban setting, furniture, flowers, and well-stocked pantry shelves add to the contemporary consumer lifestyle setting so prevalent on televi-sion. Her drop earrings and basic black dress, his suave English accent, depict characters almost indistinguishable from those who populate the fictional narra-tives of entertainment television.

In the fall of 1992, two years into the Taster's Choice advertising campaign and after five different commercials had been featured on American television (in England ten episodes had been aired by that time), the "Mystery Man" installment was shown. Tony rings Sharon's bell and is surprised to find another man in her apartment (drinking coffee, of course) while she is in her room dressing. When she comes out, Tony has gone and she asks her "mystery" guest, "And did you tell him who you are?" He is noncommittal, responding only with "Great Coffee."

After the "Mystery Man" episode aired, the advertising campaign began to be noticed by media commentators as a form of entertainment equal to other television fictions. Writing in the *New York Times,* Janet Maslin (1992) referred to the series as "Coffee Opera," and noted that the episodes were shorter than daytime soaps but "just as long on suspense." At the Museum of Broadcasting, Irwin Warren, McCann-Erickson's executive vice-president, compared the actors, Sharon and Tony, to Tracy and Hepburn (Maslin 1992, 9).

It is clear that the serial commercials were entertainment forms. They copied the style, characterization, themes, and serial narrative structure of other fictional formulas that appear on television. In fact, as William Leiss, Stephen Kline, and Sut Jhally (1988, 125) point out, from the early days of television, advertisements placed on the new mass media learned the "stylistic of imagery, patterns of attention, and programming format" that were "bent to advertising purposes." The "to be continued" Taster's Choice commercials carried that logic to its ultimate conclusion. The commercials themselves were presented and evaluated as entertainment, no longer distinguished in any significant form from other television fictions.

The creative inspiration for the Taster's Choice campaign was borrowed by another fiction—a situation comedy. On the ABC show *Coach,* the two main characters, Hayden and Christine, are chosen as the couple who will star in a series of romantic coffee commercials. But when Hayden tries out for the part, he fails utterly and, after dozens of takes, is dropped. Christine is teamed with another man, and the series of commercials is done without Hayden.

The main comic element of this "to be continued" series is the constant play and confusion about what is real and what is an illusion or, put another way, what is the real fiction—the commercials or the program itself. In *Coach,* this confusion is introduced in the initial twist of plot. Hayden's inability to act contradicts our knowledge as viewers that the character of Hayden Fox is played by actor Craig T. Nelson, who in actuality would not have a problem acting. But Hayden's lack of talent positions him not as an actor but as a real person, implying that the program is therefore "real" as well. This device also allows another actor to be introduced, the man who will play Christine's romantic partner in the commercials. Hayden's substitute is a suave and gracious man with an English accent, clearly patterned after the Taster's Choice character.

The coffee commercials in *Coach* have their own narrative structure, which is embedded within the program's narratives. These subnarratives tell the story of a "coffee couple's" romance (just as the "real" commercials do). The first advertisement begins with the couple meeting in a hotel, then going off together for a cup of coffee. Their relationship is symbolically facilitated through the pleasure of sharing their enjoyment of coffee. With each new scenario the couple's romantic involvement becomes more serious. (The commercials are shot in different locations, requiring Christine to go out of town.)

Back on campus, meanwhile, everyone watches the commercials as they air on national television. Luther confuses the couple's feelings with the fictional romance depicted in the commercials. He becomes convinced, and tries to convince Hayden, that the relationship developing between Christine and the actor (on the commercials) is real. Hayden resists, telling Luther that "they are only commercials."

As the plot thickens, the boundaries between what is real (the program) and what is fictitious (the advertisements) become fuzzier. On the night before the last commercial is to be shot, the English actor arrives at Christine's apartment and professes his growing love for her. Christine tries to convince him that their romantic interlude was a fiction, and that they were only playing the part of falling in love on a commercial. Incredulous, he cannot believe that she did not "feel it too." When he tells her how he felt dancing on the rooftop, she says, "We weren't really on a rooftop; it was the set for a coffee commercial." But in the end everyone is friendly, the commercials are a success, and Christine has gotten a career boost.

Few people seeing these coffee episodes on *Coach* would miss the fact that this story was inspired by the Taster's Choice campaign. So we might say that the (original?) Taster's Choice advertisements, which themselves were copies of entertainment forms, were then copied by a situation comedy. In short, the commercials, which copied story line, romantic character involvement, setting, and serial narrative from entertainment, became the creative motivation for another story told as entertainment.

Playing with the meta-layers of internal references, these episodes of *Coach* deliberately refer to the plot as a copy. And by confusing the advertisements within the program as real, they pose a loss of distinction between the original and the copy. Indeed, these episodes are consummate examples of postmodern television. As David Tetzlaff (1992, 51) characterizes postmodern theory, "The real has been replaced with a hyper-real: a series of simulations, models generated from other models, representations only of previous representations." Just as with advertising texts (as we saw in Chapter 1), postmodern TV fiction can be viewed as a series of quotations from other popular texts—as a kind of "bricolage." Writing about postmodern culture, Fred Pfeil (1985) argues that the aesthetic appreciation of postmodernism becomes an act of *deja lu,* the always-already-read.

According to postmodern theory, the cultural copies of previous forms have lost their creative coherence and no longer retain their initial significations. Torn from their original design and purpose, such postmodern mosaics become composites of lost meanings. They exist only to be appreciated for the novelty of yet another arbitrary set of jarring juxtapositions. From the postmodern view, past forms are identified as the pleasure of "estranged recognition" but are not comprehended in any coherent way. In fact, the confusion generated by the cultural chaos of endless new juxtapositions eclipses the pursuit of meaning. According to postmodernism, audiences "attempt to avoid both terror and boredom by refusing to look behind the surface. The only form of authenticity lies in acknowledging that everything is faked" (Tetzlaff 1992, 52).

Yet an overriding meaning does emerge from the union of *Coach* and Taster's Choice—namely, the loss of distinction between advertising and TV entertainment culture. And that loss has economic and aesthetic implications. The coffee-date scenarios of the "original" advertisements do not exist purely to entertain. Indeed, they were quite successful in achieving their intended purpose: to increase the market share of a particular brand of coffee. Though the element of persuasion was not obvious, these scenarios were designed to fuse emotional and sexual desire with the act of drinking coffee.

The coffee entertainments on *Coach* carried the message of the advertisements they copied. But as Maslin (1992, 9) questions, "How often does anyone actually extend a romantic late-night invitation to share several cups of coffee?" She goes on to say, "It's a terrible idea. Even if the scene is staged prettily . . . the conversation is liable to be something short of soothing once the caffeine kicks in. One party may fidget; the other may sweat; both will chatter on unstoppably." The initial association, coffee with romance, was arbitrary, an advertising invention. Yet the persuasive purpose remained, even when transmuted into entertainment. In *Coach,* when Christine became engaged with the campaign, advertising itself was celebrated and legitimated. In the totalizing world of integrated fictional and promotional narratives, where entertainment and advertising are one, persuasion and the commodity do indeed become the conclusive significations.

Seinfeld offers another example of the centrality of commodity promotion to postmodern television. In an episode aptly titled "The Junior Mint," the product is the key element that propels the story. *Entertainment Weekly*'s unauthorized "Seinfeld Companion" describes the show this way: "Jerry and Kramer fumble with a piece of candy and end up performing an unexpected assist as they observe Elaine's ex-boyfriend Roy's splenectomy from the operating room balcony" (Fretts 1993).

When the group visits Roy in the hospital, Kramer asks Roy's doctor, "What do you know about inter-abdominal retractors?" The dialogue becomes intertextual when Dr. Seagal responds, "Are you asking because you saw *20/20* last night? Kramer confirms, "I sure am."

The doctor assures Kramer that the report was about "one very specific type retractor . . . that we do not use in your friend's procedure." When Kramer remains skeptical, the doctor invites him to observe the operation.

While Jerry and Kramer watch the splenectomy from above, Junior Mints are introduced:

JERRY: What are you eating?
KRAMER: Junior Mints. Do you want one?
JERRY: No. Where'd you get those?
KRAMER: In the machine. Do you want one?
JERRY: No.
KRAMER: Here take one.

JERRY: I don't want one.
KRAMER: Here, they're good. Take one.
JERRY: I don't want any.
KRAMER: Just take one.
JERRY: No. Stop it.

Finally, Kramer tries to force Jerry to take one; but as Jerry pushes him away, a Junior Mint is hurled into the air. It flies, as Jerry later tells George, "into the patient."

GEORGE: Into the hole?
JERRY: Yes, into the hole.
GEORGE: Did they notice it?
JERRY: No.
GEORGE: How could they not notice it?
JERRY: Because it's a little mint. It's a Junior Mint. (*pause, laugh track, and clapping*)
GEORGE: What did they do?
JERRY: They sealed him up with the mint inside.
GEORGE: They left the Junior Mint in him?
JERRY: Yes.
GEORGE: Well, I guess it can't hurt him. People eat pounds of those things.
JERRY: Yes, they eat them. They don't put them next to vital organs in their abdominal cavity!

Jerry is worried, and when Kramer arrives he asks, "Why did you force that mint on me? I told you I didn't want the mint!"

KRAMER: Well, I didn't believe you.
JERRY: How could you not believe me?
KRAMER: Well, whose gonna turn down a Junior Mint? It's chocolate. It's peppermint. It's delicious!
JERRY: That's true.
KRAMER: It's very refreshing!

Elaine arrives with the news that Roy's prognosis is negative. Later, at the hospital, when they find out that Roy is going to make it, Dr. Seagal conjectures, "I have no medical evidence to back me up, but something happened during the operation that staved off that infection. Something beyond science. Something, perhaps, from above." The laugh track kicks in loudly.

Kramer pulls the box out of his pocket and asks, "Mint?" Dr. Seagal plugs, "Those can be very refreshing," and Kramer shakes one out for him.

This new generation of television advertising/programming creates a hybrid narrative of persuasion and entertainment. The product is so thoroughly embedded within the text that it serves as a plot device and, indeed, becomes the main theme of the entire program. No longer a singularly positive text, the product now has its ups and downs as well. It begins to acquire the attributes of character. This scenario is not unusual for *Seinfeld*; from Pez to Junior Mints, commodities are often foregrounded as significant thematic elements throughout the entirety of the show.

Seinfeld is said to be a show about nothing save the minutiae of every day life. It's full of "open-ended conversation among characters who have nothing to gain in terms of plot development" (Schwarzbaum 1993, 9). In lieu of plot, emphasis is placed on the "great, quirky, quotable riffs and para-diddles of dialogue and free association. Brand names matter: Dockers jeans carry a specific resonance" (Schwarzbaum 1993, 15). Just as products have become the stuff of everyday life, advertising's associational language has become the word-play of TV discourse. A show about life, copious with advertising and product details, is emblematic of the commercialization of the American landscape.

The intertextual reference to *20/20* that initiated the plot is not surprising given that product plugging and intertextuality go hand in hand. Together they create a seamless environment in which the commodity form can be incorporated within the naturalized geography of postmodern culture. Meta-fiction is also characteristic of *Seinfeld*. One episode featured a show within a show. Jerry and George pitch a sitcom pilot called *Jerry*, a show about "nothing," to NBC executives. "Larry David, on whom the character of George is closely modeled, used the same description to pitch the real-life *Seinfeld* concept to real-life NBC executives" (Schwarzbaum 1993, 14). Both Sun-Maid Raisins and Pledge are featured on the hour-long episode.

The show's commercialization has become the measure of its success, as Lisa Schwarzbaum (1993, 10) observes: "Its offbeat cast members have become full-fledged celebrities whose faces sell hair-care products and credit cards." (In one episode Kramer poses in his underwear for a Calvin Klein ad.)

Bits of dialogue, including product names, serves as coded words for knowing viewers. As Schwarzbaum (1993, 9) asserts, "Fans of *Seinfeld* have mysterious ways of finding each other [by saying] 'Snapple.'" An appropriate response from another member of the "sitcom sensibility" might be: "Junior Mints!" In fact, *Entertainment Weekly*'s companion volume is sold as a guide to *Seinfeld* insider talk. It describes the characters, their background, and each of the episodes. But the majority of the text is taken up with "This, That, and the Other"—a kind of dictionary of the program's trivia and, of course, the products plugged. Entries include "Drake's Coffee Cake; crumb-covered snack that Jerry uses to bribe Newman not to tell his neighbor Martin that Jerry dated his girlfriend when Martin was in a coma" (Fretts 1993, 35–36). We are also told that Chuckles is the five-flavored jelly candy that causes a brawl among members of the ambulance crew taking George to the hospital. Yet this book offers no insider information on either the business practices or the profit margins derived from product placement. Nor does it mention the consequences of advertising's influence on media content.[1] Instead, the book provides another venue for the show-featured products, with pictures of Johnson & Johnson Mint Dental Floss, Frookwich Sandwich Cookies, and Pez among others.

All this time for commodity trivia on the program is made possible by the characters' lack of employment. Jerry is an "underachiever," George is comfortable complaining about being unemployed, and Kramer has no visible means of support. The only 9-to-5'er is Elaine. Even as the program celebrates the ostensibly 90s attitudes of irresponsibility, it fails to recognize that, in "real-life," a lack of income means unpleasant hardship. TV offers only a hip carelessness in the age of permanent underemployment. *Attitude* becomes the media substitute for authentic criticism born of an understanding of the mechanisms by which actual corporate and economic policies affect the lives of the unemployed and underemployed. It's the media refrain of the 1990s—everyone is very clever, but no one is getting anywhere. Not because there is no where to go, but because they like it that way.[2] The fact that *Seinfeld* is humorous and endearing illustrates the unbounded capacity of commercial television to absorb creativity and talent within its domain.

To further illustrate the centrality of the commodity in media culture, no better metaphor exists than the Budweiser advertisement that features a full-color glossy photo of the product, centered in the middle of the page. The ice-covered brew is proportionately larger than the text and images that encircle it. In orbit around the bottle is a narrative slice of a young man's life. He is watching television. Just past an arrow indicating that the reader should "start here," the text reads: "I'm at home watching the news." (Here we are shown a picture of a comfortable chair.) "Then that weird Bud commercial comes on." (Now we see a television set with an image from the MTV commercial.) As the narrative winds its way around the bottle, the young man gets up, goes to the refrigerator, grabs a Bud, and gets back in time to watch the "game" on TV.

The ad asserts that media culture and everyday life revolve around the central constellation—the product for sale. In doing so, it demonstrates the high degree of industry awareness about exactly what it is advertisers are trying to accomplish. The media exist as background props for the magnification of products now constantly in promotion. The products themselves are now fully incorporated, indeed central to, cultural expression.

Meta-Television

As we have seen with *Coach* and *Seinfeld*, television self-consciously comments on the nature of its own constructedness—in this case, as a copy. Scott Olson (1987) finds the literary equivalent of this practice in "meta-fiction," and he refers to the adaptation of postmodern textual strategies within television as "meta-television." As he puts it, "Metafiction undermines the illusion of realism, because it draws attention to the very devices used to create the illusion" (Olson 1987, 284).

Postmodern textual strategies have been distinguished from the false naturalism of realist texts. The latter hide the nature of their construction, presenting a seamless narrative that denies their own artifice (Fiske 1987).

Postmodern self-conscious texts, by contrast, continually refer to their constructed nature. The makers of television refer to the medium itself, its entertainment strategies, its generic constructions, even its production and scheduling practices. In a particular episode of ABC's *Growing Pains,* for example, as the Seaver children vie for their father's attention, one child speaks up: "Dad, when are you going to help me with my problem?" Alan Thicke responds, "Every Wednesday, 8:00 P.M., 7:00 central."

Another episode of *Growing Pains* does an exemplary job of deconstructing itself. Ben has taken the car out without permission. When his parents put him on restriction, he laments, saying, "I'm stuck here in the real world and not on television." Shortly after, his real (TV) life turns into a fiction. The remainder of the program portrays Ben as trapped in a situation comedy. He relives the experience of coming home late in the car and being caught by his parents; but this time, instead of restricting him, they accept his pathetic excuse. He finds that his parents no longer recognize him as their real (TV) son; they are simply actors mimicking the stale routines and tired lines of TV's conventional comedic formats—of happy people with happy problems. The crew and cast cannot understand what is wrong with Ben (and why he calls himself Ben and not Jeremy), as he discovers (like Hayden on *Coach*) that he cannot act.

Ben wants his "real life" back, pleading with his parents to punish him. But they respond, "Ben, this is television." He runs away in fright and is shown searching for his real (TV) family on stage sets made for the program. At this point he finds that his brother is also trapped in television's fake world. Then he discovers a director's trailer, which takes him further "behind the scenes." The director sits looking at monitors of the set. When Ben comes in, he attempts to hide his role as director and, referring directly to the "Wizard of Oz" as the creator of illusions, he says, "Pay no attention to that man behind the microphone."

When Ben pleads to have his real (TV) life back, the director tries to divest him of that desire by explaining life on television: "You're always happy. You don't get sick, and you never have to go to the bathroom." The episode ends with Ben waking up from the bad dream of this duplicitous world, back on the real situation comedy where his (TV) parents punish him and he is still on restriction.

In this narrative, television has exposed itself by revealing the conventions that govern it, unmasking its arbitrary formulaic representations. As the dominant aesthetic of contemporary television, meta-fictional textual practice is viewed by some analysts as a measure of TV's growing sophistication. As Olson (1987, 284) points out, "If self-reflexivity is one test of artistic maturity, there can be no doubt that television has matured." (Olsen 1987, 284)

But even though *Coach, Seinfeld,* and *Growing Pains* exposed their own fabrications, they also reaffirmed their authenticity—all at the same time. The three programs offered contrived narratives embedded within the now more authentic narratives of "real" programming. Compared to the Taster's Choice commercials, the sitcom Ben's original TV life is also real. Coach is real. And the sitcom pilot "Jerry" featured on *Seinfeld* is dull and derivative compared to the "real" show.

Cultural Literacy

According to Olson, meta-television "is the cultural expression of creators and consumers bored with and restricted by television's naturalness" (Olsen 1987, 284). Viewers are now historically sophisticated, steeped in the knowledge of TV genres and conventions and eager to see the rules broken. The pleasure of recognizing the transgression of genre boundaries and disrupted narratives depends on our being familiar with the conventions and on our understanding when they are being broken. We fill in the gaps of narratives told in fragments and comprehend the intertextual innuendos only fleetingly referred to. Certainly we recognize the exploded boundaries of genre convention when Doogie Howser finds himself on the Orient Express, Erkel becomes a gumshoe looking for clues in a piano bar where a sultry figure sings the blues, Kate and Allie turn into Lucy and Ethel for one episode, and *Perfect Strangers* is recast as *The Honeymooners*.

Television demands an active engagement with the text made possible by viewers' knowledge of the textual devices themselves. This cultural literacy demonstrates the intelligence of the audience. Indeed, meta-television fascinates by "putting readers in a powerful position and saluting them for their sophistication" (Olson 1987, 284). Postmodern theory asserts that in the absence of meaning and context, the deconstructed narratives themselves become the only meaningful set of interpretive categories.

As a culture we are now caught up in this system of TV self-reference. Intertextuality has become the dominant mode of communication. Through it we control and tame the medium by testing our knowledge against the endless set of quizzes that are no longer restricted to the domain of game shows. Tests of trivia are now the staple of television itself. Watching is a test of wits, a habitual game of trivial pursuits in which we are called upon to recognize all the references, and to nod knowingly at the intertextuality. At the end of a promotional trailer for the movie *Doc Hollywood,* the announcer says, "Buy two tickets and call me in the morning." We get it. The cute little boy playing "doctor" is retrieved as part of our cultural memory.

The medium is now, in its most defining characteristics, a vast network of visual and mythic connections to itself and other media forms, past and present. It is an inclusive system featuring a multiplicity of interconnections. Oprah Winfrey appears as herself on *Gabriel's Fire* in an episode in which Bird is a talk-show guest. Vanna White steps out of *Wheel of Fortune* to appear several times on *L.A. Law* as the senior partner's date. Connie Chung appears on the set of *Murphy Brown,* where Murphy continually makes references to "real" TV journalists such as Barbara Walters, Maria Shriver, and others.

FIGURE C.1 *Entertainment Tonight* on *Murphy Brown*
In this example of postmodern television, an episode of *Murphy Brown* begins on the set
of *Entertainment Tonight.*

Another episode of *Murphy Brown* (see Figure C.1) begins on the set of
Entertainment Tonight, just as that program is ending. The characters on *Murphy
Brown* are treated like "real" people, inasmuch as *Entertainment Tonight* provides
behind-the-scenes chatter about Corky's wedding. John Tesh receives a phone call
from Frank, who asks to speak to Leeza; but, not wanting to go out with him (a
fictitious character), she refuses to talk. The camera then switches to the set of
Murphy Brown, where Frank is talking on the phone to Tesh.

Television has become a totalizing medium; it is all-consuming with its seemingly endless references to every nook and cranny of the world—of television.
And that world appears to be a complete one; like an endless row of mirrors, it reflects back onto itself and incorporates the viewer within. The viewer-turned-
reader is thereby "foregrounded." As active readers of television we are indeed engaged in deciphering all its allusions and innuendos, and this becomes a full-time
job. The interpretive work of cultural literacy has made those texts our own. We
have worked on them and in them, and felt the pleasure of belonging, of being
part of a shared, unifying culture.

Lowest Common Denominator Revisited

For the members of the first generation to have grown up on television, the remembered history of television has now become their history. The cable show

Dream On, now syndicated on the Fox network, opens with a sequence of Martin, played by Brian Benben, growing up in front of television. First a baby, then a toddler, then a boy in a western outfit, the sequence ends as his face merges with the static of the TV screen. The program portrays a sensibility cluttered with all the old programs Martin has ever seen. As an adult, his feelings and thoughts are illustrated by quick edits to old films and TV clips. The black-and-white fragments often express his emotions better than he can himself. Michael Steadman of *thirtysomething,* undergoing a habitual bout of angst, daydreams while gazing at the television screen (looking for answers?). Beginning to fantasize, he sees himself and his fellow characters from *thirtysomething* on the black-and-white set of *The Dick Van Dyke Show.* The history of television is his personal history. He becomes the universal member of a lost generation whose diverse sensibilities and divergent life trajectories can at last be unified in the collective memory of the genres and formats of the mass media. By unifying this diverse audience, intertextuality serves a primarily commercial function. It keeps the ratings high and allows the TV to retain its claim to being the mass medium of a shared culture.

The Television Community

Erkel from *Family Matters* lands on the set of *Step by Step.* Cliff from *Cheers* appears on the game show *Jeopardy,* where the questions revolve around beer, bars, and the U.S. Postal Service. (In fact, *Cheers* made intertextuality a primary programming strategy.) Cliff and Norm also made appearances on the sitcom *Wings.* Members of the staff at the hospital on *St. Elsewhere* go out for a drink and end up at *Cheers,* where everybody knows their names. The fictional personae move outside the boundaries of their once-autonomous shows, expanding TV's world into a complex network of settings and characters. The result is a newly defined television community that bears no resemblance to the separate, isolated worlds of previous shows.

In the situation comedy *Blossom,* a teenage girl is raised without a mother. In one episode the girl deals with the problems and changes of adolescence. Television offers Blossom one of its most cherished mothers, Claire Huxtable, from *The Cosby Show.* Mrs. Huxtable appears to her in a dream, and thus it happens that TV's lost child finds a member of her own community.

In the 1993 season premiere of *L.A. Law,* a lawyer and a secretary from out of town join the firm. However, the characters were not new or unfamiliar to TV viewers. Eli and Denise were characters developed on *Civil Wars,* a program that probed the world of interpersonal conflict by featuring divorce lawyers and their cases. Often depressing, and undoubtedly difficult to watch week after week, it received particularly low ratings.[3] Postmodern programming strategies generated a solution by transferring the two characters intact. Eli became the (long-lost?) lawyer cousin of Stuart Markowitz on *L.A. Law,* where he joins the firm; and Denise remains his secretary. A history of Eli and Stuart as members of the same family is constructed as they talk about their memories of holiday gatherings. Once again, television has created a totalizing world in which everyone knows everyone else.

This world of television as vast community now extends into the world of non-fiction. When Murphy Brown refers to Connie Chung and Maria Shriver as if they were her colleagues, the effect is to affirm the authenticity of Murphy as an actual journalist. The strategy elevates the *Murphy Brown* program to the status of "real." By including news reporters, politicians, and celebrities within its realm, fiction incorporates the real world.

When the character who played Lenny's fictional wife quips, "Barbara Walter's just left . . . boy, is she nosey," the representation asserts that the character is experiencing the same world of nonfiction that is recognizable to viewers as real. In other words, viewers' knowledge of Barbara Walters as a TV journalist is incorporated within the entertainment. By association, Lenny, the working-class hero turned consumer, seems all the more genuine himself. In a self-conscious way, television thus declares its fictions to be not representations but the equivalent of life—indeed, the very definition of postmodern life.

As Roger Silverstone (1988, 27) points out, "We live in an empiricist culture, visibility and value are synonymous, our knowledge must be testable, its ambition is to control." We control the impressions and pleasures we get from television, and intertextuality helps us do so. It allows the viewer to engage, to participate. But what of the staggering amount of information that is excluded from television? The information we cannot see, and could not control if we did see it? On television, we still control the horizontal, and the vertical, through our knowledge and recognition of what we have seen for all the days of our lives. And this knowledge is so easily testable; it requires simply turning on the set and recognizing all the familiar protocols. The process is empowering; it entails a cultural empowerment accompanied by a sense of control in knowing.

But what kinds of knowledge and power are these, and what potential for human liberation do they provide? Much has been written about the interpretive powers of television readers, about the liberating potential of negotiating the television terrain by finding subversive meanings in it. But readers of television are invited to participate in negotiations only after the work has been completed. We read *what is there*, what has been given to us. It is the act of looking behind TV's reflecting mirrors that has become problematic. Television's self-contained logic is increasingly difficult to break out of. That task not only seems unnecessary, but it has become self-annihilating. As Tetzlaff (1992, 54) argues, social control is achieved through meta-television's superficial participation:

The form of cultural literacy necessary to appreciate deindividuation and deja lu requires only a recognition of familiarity of the image. Postmodern culture asks for no connection to be made between the text and the world outside the media. Being self-enclosed, it avoids the issue of social relations entirely. Its language, if it has one, is

apolitical. Time that might otherwise be occupied by subjects attempting to understand their position in the social system is taken up by fascination with depthless image fragments.

In this age of the commercial imperative, most things contradictory to the consumer view are absent from television. The amount of information barred from
TV's narrowing frame is indeed staggering. Certainly the nonfictions and fictions
critical of the corporate practices that dominate the media and the lives of most
Americans are omitted. As television becomes more of a vast reference to itself,
the world of production, corporate practices, and political and social forces becomes more obscure and out of reach. As we negotiate television's terrain, the
world outside its boundaries is lost. And as that world is lost, TV grasps for authenticity by relentlessly asserting its "realness." Ironically, authenticity is affirmed
through the techniques of meta-television, such as those used on *Coach, Seinfeld,*
and *Growing Pains.*

Viewers cannot engage in meaningful public life if much of the world cannot
be represented on television. As noted above (and as discussed at length in
Chapter 1), information excluded from media discourse covers a broad range of
topics, especially topics concerning corporate malfeasance (Jensen 1993). During
the 1980s the fine-tuning of television as an environment for product promotion
left the negative consequences of commodity production unacknowledged. Now
in the 1990s, as television moves closer to a unity of purpose with advertising and
promotion, its narratives lose the ability to represent anything outside that world
or critical of it.

Even as theorists of popular culture celebrate the new sophistication of postmodern television, those constrained within its velvet commercial ropes sometimes emit self-conscious criticisms. One *FYI* executive on *Murphy Brown,* responding to Myles's naive attitude toward TV, admits:

> Oh, grow up Silverberg. Television is nothing but a game of three card monte de-
> signed to keep the natives distracted while the nation goes to hell. They don't care
> what kind of garbage they put on as long as it sells product. They're greedy vicious
> miserable swine, and believe me I know. I've been one of them for 40 years.

Such criticisms by the real-life makers of TV actually serve to confirm the
medium's sincerity while relieving the writers of guilt and responsibility. To discover just how constrained the world of television is, let us look closely at one example of the variety of discourse systematically excluded from its purview.

GE and the Media

The restriction of information characteristic of the corporate/commercial media
environment is best illustrated by the case of General Electric. GE owns NBC, and
its prominent heartwarming advertisements frequently air on the media (including NBC's *Meet the Press*). With the help of focus group research (as discussed in

Chapter 3), GE maintains a humanistic, caring corporate image. Its underwriting of public broadcasting has brought the slogan "we bring good things to life" to noncommercial media as well. But an increasing body of evidence points to GE's unscrupulous control of media content.

One indication of GE's influence is the cautious way in which information critical to its corporate image has been presented on public broadcasting. The Academy Award–winning documentary "Deadly Deception: General Electric, Nuclear Weapons and Our Environment," which aired on PBS's *Independent Focus*, was introduced with careful wording such as "[the film makes] controversial claims regarding GE's alleged mismanagement at two government facilities." Unlike the producers of VNRs and other commercially sponsored broadcasting, those at PBS took pains to disclose who produced the film, Debra Chasnoff, and who paid for it: "Commissioned by Infact, a grass-roots organization advocating corporate responsibility, . . . [and] financed through donations from individuals and foundations." General Electric was given time to comment both before and after the half-hour program. In its statement GE accused Infact of "erroneous allegations," saying the film "propagandizes." Viewers were also told that the film will be followed by further comments from GE.

The film opens in Mesa, Washington. We meet Tom Bailie, who has lived on a farm next to GE's Hanford nuclear plant all his life. He was born with birth defects and is sterile. Tom drives along a street the downwinders call "death mile," talking about deformed farm animals, people with thyroid problems and leukemia, and babies born with no skull and no eyes. Severe health problems associated with high degrees of exposure to radiation affect twenty-seven out of the twenty-eight families in the areas.

As the narrator speaks, a picture emerges of enormous radioactive releases— some accidental, others deliberate—which GE continues to cover up. Over time, residents have been exposed to twice the amount of radioactivity released at Chernobyl. There, the Soviet government confiscated milk, evacuated the population, and cordoned off the area. No one told the U.S. residents of Mesa.

We are introduced to other people as well. Among them is a health and safety inspector who worked for GE and was fired after thirty years for submitting a report detailing unsafe conditions at GE's other atomic weapons facility, Knolls Atomic Power Laboratories in upstate New York. Next, a union business agent points out that a presidential order exempts Knolls from health and safety regulations and that radioactivity at Knolls exceeds OSHA limits. He says he is tired of informing workers' families that their loved ones have died of cancer. Then we see an emotional testimonial from one man's brother who worked at Knolls and died after cancerous tumors broke out all over his body. He was not able to get GE to release contamination levels before his death.

The narrator tells us that "GE has yet to take responsibility for its involvement in the nuclear weapons industry, choosing instead to keep making more commercials about the technology behind GE products." The film juxtaposes GE's life-affirming slogans—"People helping other people" and "We go hand in hand"—with stories and pictures of environmental destruction and workers who have died of cancer.

The film quotes from Environmental Protection Agency (EPA) data showing that the company still releases more cancer-causing chemicals than any other corporation, and that it has the largest number of superfund toxic dump sites in the United States. The health problems and birth defects are impossible to quantify. Whereas the government has acknowledged its own mismanagement, GE has not. So the company's research and production sites around the country continue to create pollution and health hazards.

In the film we learn that Infact has organized a boycott of GE. We are introduced to the owner of a chain of stores, More4, who has refused to sell GE products in his stores. The narrator tells us that the boycott is working. Especially effective is the refusal by religious and health care organizations to buy GE's high-tech hospital equipment because administrators have found the company's corporate policies to be inconsistent with public health.

As the credits roll, we hear, "Stay tuned for comments by GE about the film you have just seen." GE's statement begins, "GE is not the proper forum for debating U.S. defense or foreign policy. Those governmental decisions are not affected by whether or not GE is a defense contractor." But in the film, over an image of Capitol Hill, we've been told that GE is a "key player behind the scenes in determining federal nuclear weapons policy, thanks to the company's high volume of PAC contributions." (GE has a 150-person Washington lobby, the largest of any weapons contractor.) We have also been introduced to Rear Admiral Gene La Rocque, director of the Center for Defense Information, who informed us that the United States has "thirty thousand nuclear weapons. Far more than enough to defend ourselves." He also drew a connection between GE's military contracting and the U.S. government's weapons policy: "Industry exerts a lot of influence on whether or not we buy nuclear weapons. The American public ought to become aware of the fact that it is these companies that push the Congress into building more weapons than we need." So GE is, in fact, the most appropriate forum for such a public dialogue.

GE then says it has "a strong commitment to the environment" and that the film does not "represent the facts accurately." But the allegations made in the film are documented in further detail by investigative reporter Michael D'Antonio (1993) in *Atomic Harvest: Hanford and the Lethal Toll of America's Nuclear Arsenal.* And more allegations are featured in a *Newsweek* (December 27, 1993) magazine cover story. The article, "America's Nuclear Secrets," mentions a "witch's brew" of "notorious storage tanks at Hanford," adding that the Hanford nuclear facility was "regularly showering its neighbors with radioactivity" (p. 17). It ends by stating that the by-products of our cold war nuclear obsession have left us with "the single largest environmental and health risk in the nation" (p. 18). But no reference to GE is made anywhere in the article.[4] In failing to explain the company's role in the cold war nuclear industry, the article (unlike PBS's "Deadly Deception") denies members of the public an understanding of the forces that propel this industry, thus hampering their participation in future policy decisions.

In the aftermath of "Deadly Deception," GE went on to say that it wants peace as much as Infact does, but "we along with the overwhelming majority of the American people" believe in strong national defense. This is precisely the problem—GE's ability to influence public opinion through media control. Information critical to the company, and therefore to nuclear weapons production, has been withheld from the public. If the public knew of the disastrous environmental effects and health hazards associated with the nuclear industry, such information might temper public enthusiasm for a "strong defense." As a nation we might arrive at a different decision, believing that nuclear weapons are not worth the risks to health and environment.

For instance, we might consider a different set of priorities for public spending, especially in light of the amount of money that taxpayers must come up with after GE made its profits, an estimated $60 billion over the next thirty years. GE has left a toxic, radioactive legacy. At Hanford, two-thirds of the country's radioactive waste is stored in containers that leak. And the Columbia River is the most radioactive river in the world. Cost estimates for the total cold war cleanup amount to more than $1 trillion.

But the public has not been allowed to participate from an informed perspective on this issue. Through imaginative advertising GE generates trust, and through censorship it forecloses criticism. What the commercial media environment emphasizes instead of the horrifying nuclear reality is the fantasy of GE, with images of a young father working late on his computer, and of his sweet little girl who brings him something to drink from the refrigerator. These appliances, we are told, have provide the satisfying life depicted on the ad. GE "brings good things to life."

The Commercial View

The escalated use of television as a merchandising and marketing medium has dramatically influenced decisions as to what is and is not represented on television. The omission of much information and so many fictional themes from the media frame has exacerbated television's historical tendency to decontextualize. As a consequence, contemporary television seems incapable of depicting the political and economic forces that shape our world.

The media culture of consumption demands the obliteration of the other side of TV's images. Indeed, exploration of the territory hidden behind the medium's endless promotional fantasies has proven to be the single most difficult leap of critical judgment in consumer culture. Some information is eliminated through direct censorship, but far more is lost in the daily wash of advertising's persuasive messages, now an integral part of the media landscape. Even the entertainment narratives of commercial television have taken on the characteristics of advertising discourse and logic.

The Isolation and Magnification of Private Life

Because the media leave dark so much of the world, they must focus with heightened degrees of magnification on a particular portion of the interior landscape of individual experience. The universe of personal and private life is now explored in such detail that it alone has come to fill the void left by what has been omitted.[5] Just as soap-opera dramas survey the private world of personal sensibilities, the talk shows survey the private world of human experience. And advertising's focus group strategies mine the psychic landscapes of human desire, then promise the privatized wish fulfillment of innermost needs. Even the media representations of war take on a private view, with images of the trajectories of individual bombs tied to remote cameras on suicide missions. Such cameras are destined to blow up, but only after they have transmitted their video messages of hidden spaces.

The "reality"-based crime programs exemplify the worst commercial exploitation of private life. They have erased the direct linkage between social issues and the economic structures that must be negotiated on a daily basis. Instead of contextualized narratives, they present intimate images of a private world so as to titillate viewers from a voyeuristic perspective. If the 1994 court ruling against CBS (discussed in Chapter 7) were applied to all such programs, most would have to be ruled illegal violations of the right to privacy. As Judge Jack Weinstein puts it, "CBS had no greater right than that of a thief to be in the home, to take pictures and to remove the photographic record. ... The images, though created by the camera, are a part of the household: they cannot be removed without permission or official right" (1994, 12–13).

The stark views of the subjective world, amplified out of proportion through increasing degrees of magnification, tower over a public world reeling from underexposure. But the world itself can never truly be revealed. Even the private view, so amplified, but torn from the moorings that shape it, remains a mass of distorted reflections.

Television as Therapist?

As we have seen, TV's advertising culture is saturated with the intoxicating assertion that for every problem or need there is a product solution. As social, political, and environmental problems worsen and their solutions remain elusive, advertising offers escape into dreams of commodity fantasies. The world outside that mirage is lost amidst the dazzling images of television and becomes more difficult to imagine.

Because the media revolve around product promotion, they are unable to criticize or explain the systemic economic problems that so often account for people's pain. It follows that television therapy is inherently corrupt. Programs that purport to offer such therapy, as the vehicles for the promotion of products, are fundamentally incapable of presenting the viewer's perspective over that of sponsors.

Embedded within the logic of commercial messages is the urgency to persuade and manipulate. Fictional scenarios that pretend to reveal inner life present a template of conventional wisdom for solutions to problems, but they are solutions contained within the realm of consumption. How can guidance be offered in the absence of discourse about what really makes people miserable? Television at this point does not go beyond the logic of consumer culture. And that logic, at every step of the way, is ultimately invested in the pretense that there is no problem so large that a solution cannot be found in the satisfying world of commodity promotion. In short, television therapy can never work because of the commercialism that betrays its viewers. TV's privatized constructions assert that contradictions are to be lived with, and that what exists is the only possible world. But as Raymond Williams (1980, 188) has observed:

> Needs are social—roads, hospitals, schools, quiet—they are not only not covered by the consumer ideal: they are even denied by it. ... To satisfy this range of needs would involve questioning the autonomy of the economic system, in its actual setting of priorities. This is where the consumption ideal is not only misleading, as a form of defence of the system, but ultimately destructive to the broad general purpose of the society.

Conscious Consumption

Ironically, the most effective way for the public to be reincorporated into the realm of production (in its broadest definition) may be to intervene in the process through consumption. If consumers were to exert their considerable power, basing purchasing decisions not on product advertising but on the material conditions of commodity production, they would have a chance to participate in economic decisions. (Numerous books, currently available to consumers, detail actual corporate practices ranging from environmental policy to labor strategies.) Politicizing consumption would mean making purchasing decisions intended both to influence corporate policy and to reinforce existing socially responsible practices. In particular, consumers could bring their interests and needs to the attention of corporate CEOs. Past experience confirms that such action can be effective: Recall GE's fear of boycott threats. Indeed, consumers could impact the sources of power directly, bypassing the mediation of electoral politics so heavily influenced by corporate agendas through PAC contributions and lobbyists.

Doing so, however, requires that consumers take a critical stance toward advertising and its broad influence on the media. Specifically, they need to understand the destructive nature of the culture of consumption and its debasement of American media and cultural life. That culture of consumption has become openly and admittedly persuasive; its objectives are to change attitudes and promote acceptance, to present superficial solutions to problems, to establish and assert arbitrary associations, and to deny critical judgment. But it is only when we apply critical reason to the evaluation of the media that we can encourage the media environment to become more inclusive.

Meta-Television as a Dead End

Regarding theoretical conceptions of meta-television, analysts have asserted that because the text reveals its own constructedness, its formulations must therefore have less impact on public perceptions. The nonrealist text is one that reveals itself; therefore, its fictional conventions are perceived as just that—fictional. According to postmodern theory, either no meaning is derived from nonrealist texts, or such a multiplicity of meanings is derived from interpretations of them that the texts no longer influence public values, beliefs, or common-sense formulations of the world. But even meta-television texts contain social and political meanings. And those texts and their interpretations reverberate through the social imaginary with profound effects. The plethora of information left outside those textual frameworks also directs social forces along one path as opposed to another.

The critically sardonic intertextuality of *The Simpsons* is the best example of the playful aesthetics of meta-television. Every episode reveals the tired formulas of the medium's own artifices. When Bart takes a ride with cops who reveal their ineptitude by ignoring crimes in progress and viewing political corruption as ordinary, the conventions of police drama, both "real" and fictitious, are exposed as overused formula. But alternative representations, in addition to those that ridicule, are necessary to understand criminal justice issues. TV's view of crime, which is devoid of economic and political context, must be supplemented by these representations if it is to be revealed as inaccurate. Meta-television's textual strategies are by definition *self*-referential; they do not include such alternative views.

As we have seen with respect to *Coach* and *Growing Pains,* meta-television asserts its authenticity at the same time that it reveals itself as fiction. Defined, however, as a lucid consciousness of one's circumstances, authenticity cannot be achieved within television's constrained commercial view. Television itself, as a textual practice so informed by the medium, has lost most of its relevance to everyday life. But as a familiar Budweiser commercial reveals, the assertion of authenticity is a defense against that loss of relevance: "Why," the sponsor asks, "can't life be like a beer commercial? Why ask why? When all life's a stage, your beer should be real."

The "open" texts of postmodern TV exist in a contextual void. Only alternative representations of the world could expose what lies behind the screen. In their absence, meta-television is indeed a dead end, a monolithic world of self-references. And that world is imbued with the demand that programming facilitate the promotion of products. From infomercials to politainment, from advertorials to moviemercials, meta-television presents a unified discourse of commercialtainment. Product placement, and the general conception of programming as an environment of consumption, is transfiguring media content at the same time that television readers are being transformed into markets and sold as products to advertisers.

The reversal of the media trends imposed by advertising and economic imperatives will require a regulatory model able to reformulate public interest over private profit. A model of shared social wealth is a far more valid measure of public health than is the corporate monopoly of wealth.

Notes

INTRODUCTION

1. Kellogg was the only major cereal maker that did not lower its prices during the fourth quarter of 1993.

CHAPTER 1

1. The commercial structure of broadcasting was instituted during the development of radio in the 1920s. Leiss et al. (1988, 77–78) trace what they call the "bonding of media and advertising" to the print media at the turn of the century.

2. The style sheet and text of an article edited by the Sterling/Macfadden Partnership, representing the Macfadden Women's Group, were supplied to me by a member of the staff of *True Experience* who asked not to be identified.

3. Kessier explains the lack of articles about smoking even in *Good Housekeeping* (which does not carry cigarette advertising) by saying that the sellers of tobacco are part of corporate conglomerates, which also include major food companies; and magazines do not want to offend these companies because food items are also an advertising staple.

4. Interview with the author, May 1993.

5. Barter syndication, a practice whereby syndicators insert national advertising within programming in exchange for a reduction or elimination of cash payments, grew steadily in the 1980s. Both barter syndication and cable TV placed a significant restraint on the pricing abilities of the major networks in the advertising marketplace.

6. See Auletta (1991) and MacDonald (1990).

7. See Rapping (1987).

8. Zeyen spoke at the Donald McGannon Lecture on Communication Policy and Ethics, Fordham University, on April 21, 1994.

9. See the *New York Post* of May 6, 1993, cited in Fairness and Accuracy in Reporting (1993).

10. For example, many health and business "inserts" are purchased by stations to be sold to advertisers, who in turn sponsor those particular segments and receive adjacencies.

11. Interview with the author, April 1994.

12. InFact, cited in Collins (1992, 29) and Putnam (1991, 4–5).

13. For example, *Communiqué* (March 1994, 2), the newsletter of the Freedom Forum, observed that in the rush for ratings, the media (over)coverage of the Tonya Harding–Nancy Kerrigan case, the Bobbits, Joey Buttafuoco and Amy Fisher, Michael Jackson, and the Menendez brothers was characterized by "mere allegations and scurrilous rumors." And the spring 1994 "Mad at the Media" series sponsored by the Center for Communication asked, "Tabloid TV: Trial by Video? Where does privacy end and voyeurism begin?"

14. "Public Records/Private Lives," sponsored by the Deadline Club of SPJ, New York, March 31, 1994.

15. Interview with the author, March 1992.

16. Interview with an independent video producer in New York, March 1992.

17. A brief identification is usually given at the beginning of these programs, but as pointed out in the Center's (1992) lawsuit, it can easily be missed because of both the length of the program and the propensity of TV viewers to "graze" with remote control.

18. In actuality, an average of about 8 minutes per hour of commercials aired on adult programming, compared to an average of 14 minutes per hour on children's programming.

19. See "Addenda: Ad Spending Rise Forecast for 1994," *New York Times,* December 2, 1993, p. D21.

20. Illustrative of changing attitudes is the belief of Yoko Ono, owner of the rights to many of her husband's songs, that hearing these songs on Nike commercials will introduce his music to a new generation.

21. This observation was derived from a series of professional seminars given to Fordham University advertising students, funded by the *Radio Creative Fund* in the spring of 1992. After a long series of tryouts, one actor was short-listed with Kathleen Turner for a radio spot. Turner was finally chosen, after the company agreed to pay her price.

22. There is still some resistance to this practice, however. For example, Arnold Schwarzenegger and Sylvester Stallone turn down offers to do American commercials because they believe such ads would degrade their star quality. Both actors do consent to commercials in Japan.

23. Spike Lee's film production company, Forty Acres & a Mule Filmworks, is also looking for ways to get a stronger foothold in advertising. As reported in *Advertising Age,* he is "looking to nail a deal with an ad agency for an alliance to create commercials, just like Hollywood-based Creative Artists Agency does for Coca-Cola Classic" (Sloan and Magiera 1993, 1). The rap singer Hammer is looking for a similar deal.

24. For an intriguing revelation of the divergence between the Coors company's advertising images and its corporate ideology, see Bellant (1991, vii). Although Coors reaches out to new markets "among women, African Americans, Hispanics, gay men, and lesbians" with ad campaigns alluding to the tolerant values of the 1960s, "the Coors family uses their share of the beer sale profits to promote theories that would roll back the political and social gains made in the past 30 years by persons in these same social groups."

25. As Ewen (1988) points out, the appropriation of 1960s icons for advertising purposes results in a transvaluation of history—a loss of the political meaning of the times.

26. This feature is characteristic of the media's emphasis on the "character" of public figures. Recall, for example, the media's treatment of Oliver North during the Iran/Contra scandal, as discussed in Andersen (1991b).

27. I am grateful to Aaron Kaplan for bringing this episode to my attention.

28. Interview with the author, May 1993.

29. From a talk entitled "Hollywood in Europe: An Update," given by Janet Wasko at the International Association of Mass Communication Research (IAMCR) conference held in Dublin, Ireland, June 1993.

30. For example, Crichton writes: "Efforts to engineer paler trout for better viability, . . . square trees for easier lumbering, and injectable scent cells so you'll always smell of your favorite perfume may seem like a joke"; but, he continues, the fact that biotechnology is be-

ing applied to industries "subject to the vagaries of fashion, such as cosmetics and leisure activities," should be of concern to all (Crichton 1991, ix).

CHAPTER 2

1. Interview with the author, January 1995.

2. In this connection, note that in 1993 Indonesia shipped $620 million worth of goods to the United States for free.

3. With the newly elected Republican Congress in power as of 1995, Asia Watch also fears that the Generalized System of Preferences will not be renewed.

4. Interview with Jeff Ballinger, director of Press for Change, and publisher of the newsletter *Nike in Indonesia*, P.O. Box 230, Bayonne, New Jersey 07620.

5. From the transcript of an interviewed on *Street Stories*, July 2, 1993.

6. Cited in Corn (1995), pp. 117–118.

7. Schor (1992, 114) notes that because these surveys reach only the people who have homes and telephones, these numbers are understated.

8. These figures, along with explanations of the various methodologies used and evaluations of current and historical findings, were submitted to Congress in a letter to Tony Hall, chairman of the House Select Committee on Hunger, dated September 8, 1992. The letter was written by Larry Brown, director of the School of Nutrition at Tufts University.

9. Although it is true that the "Trade, Not Aid" policies were created during the Reagan/Bush era under the Caribbean Basin Initiative, which was responsible for this situation, Al Gore voted for those policies as a senator. Meanwhile, the Clinton administration has pushed through NAFTA, a trade policy that may result in the same job flight to cheaper labor pools that occurred during the Reagan/Bush years.

10. Discussion of the National Labor Committee in Support of Worker and Human Rights in Central America (1992) is included in *Paying to Lose Our Jobs*.

11. According to a 1991 funding agreement with the U.S. Agency for International Development (USAID), FUSADES was urged to pursue a "provocative, direct and systematic sales effort involving direct contact with targeted U.S. firms to convince them to explore opportunities in El Salvador" (Kernaghan 1992, 11).

12. As Uchitelle (1993, D3) points out, according to "a survey of 55 corporations, 64 percent reported that job-cutting had lowered company moral, even when the reasons given were buyouts, not lay-offs."

13. For an insight into the new model for American corporations, which are "lean and mean," with fewer workers doing increased numbers of tasks, see *Reengineering the Corporation* by Hammer and Champy (1993).

CHAPTER 3

1. The need for open and unrestrictive procedures is asserted in one company's internal report on focus groups entitled "An Overview of Qualitative Research. The report details the results of a professional marketing research seminar.

2. The practice of psychocultural appeals, as distinct from rational/informational or rhetorical approaches, has been delineated by Wernick (1991, 27–32).

3. Interview with Mrs. Ernst Dichter, executive officer of Dichter Motivations in Peekskill, New York, May 27, 1993. Dichter Motivations had been in existence for forty-eight years by this time.

4. See "Fashions of the Times" in *New York Times Magazine,* Part 2 (Fall 1993), pp. 30–31.

5. Ibid., p. 105.

CHAPTER 4

1. As Tetzlaff (1992) points out, the term *postmodern* is the academic vogue of our time, even though there are many postmodernisms.

2. This analyst appeared in "I'll Buy That," one of a series of Films for the Humanities and Sciences Inc. (Princeton, N.J.).

3. Research shows that women perceived as vulnerable (like the one in the B and B ad) are more likely to be sexually assaulted. In one study of college males, 51 percent reported that they might rape a woman if assured they would not be caught (Russell 1980). A closed hotel room with a "do not disturb" sign approximates such conditions. The alcohol use, female vulnerability, and date scene depicted also correspond to rape statistics. Among college students, more than 75 percent of victims knew their assailants and 57 percent of them were dates. In addition, 75 percent of the victimizers and more than 50 percent of the victims had been drinking before the assault. Cultural symbols, including such advertising images as those discussed here, reinforce our rape culture. Men who report a propensity toward rape are also the ones most likely to accept rape myths, such as the myth that women who are raped "ask for it" by dressing or behaving in a particular way. More than 44 percent of American women surveyed in one study reported being victims of attempted or completed rape. (See also Parrot 1991).

4. Marketing research did not invent the concept of lifestyle. Social subgroups first became an important sociological category in academic institutions. However, much of the research performed in those institutions was used and expanded by the media industry itself (Andersen 1992c). However, the notion of lifestyle adopted by postmodern theorists follows the industry definition: lifestyle as a consumption and taste grouping (see Chapter 5).

CHAPTER 5

1. Interview with the author, June 16, 1992.

CHAPTER 6

1. For an excellent discussion of the historical antecedents to daytime talk shows, along with a contemporary classification of the genre, see Munson (1993).

2. This term has been used by Munson (1993) to distinguish the daytime talk shows from other broadcast talk formats.

3. For a discussion of photography and the language of objectivity, see Andersen 1989.

4. Hebdige (1986, 83) speaks of the crisis of representation in terms of both the political and cultural realms, "where the term 'representation'—understood both in its everyday sense of 'political representation' and in the structuralist sense of a distortive 'ideological' representation of a pre-existent realm—is regarded as problematic. From this point on, all forms and processes of 'representation' are suspect."

5. For a detailed analysis of political action committees and the power they wield, see Sabato (1985).

6. For an in-depth look at the ways in which wealth floated to the top during the Reagan years, see Phillips (1990).

7. See Hertsgaard (1988), chapter 6.

8. According to the FAIR study, blacks accounted for only 6.2 percent and women for only 10.3 percent of *Nightline*'s guests.

9. Interest in the public-sphere model was also aroused by events in Eastern Europe that led to the dismantling of antidemocratic government practices. Many observers have noted that this outcome could only have come about through public participation outside centralized party politics. Thus "civil society" and the importance of participation within the public sphere gained renewed interest.

10. Habermas (1989/1962) formulated an "ideal" model of democratic, egalitarian public discussion in which the media play a key role as the forum for debate. However, as many critics have pointed out, this formulation was highly elitist, in that many people, especially women and people of color, were excluded from participating as citizens. For an excellent discussion of this issue, see Fraser 1993. Nevertheless, as an idealized model in the Weberian sense, the public sphere offers a valuable conceptualization of the potential role of the media in democratic systems.

11. The talk shows detailed in this chapter aired during the week of July 13, 1992, a randomly selected time period. I am indebted to Ellen Braune for my understanding of the discourse and dynamics of these shows.

12. For a fascinating discussion of the relationship between law enforcement and so-called satanic crimes, see O'Sullivan (1991), who provides a social and political understanding of this phenomenon. (See also Carlson and O'Sullivan 1991.)

13. "Cross-talk" occurs when one person's words overlap those of another.

14. According to one staff member on the *Sally Jessy Raphael* program, "Before the show is taped, the guests undergo several interviews where they meet and talk with producers about what they plan to say. They are told the types of questions the host will ask, and asked what their responses will be. If they give several possible answers, the producers will *suggest* that they use one (usually more outrageous) response rather than the others. Even the audience, which is peppered with a small number of people who will be able to relate to the topic, is not a completely random group of people. . . . For example, when they were doing a show about women who loved men who were in prison, the producers made sure that they had several women in the audience who would agree with the guests on this topic."

CHAPTER 7

1. See, for example, Haney and Manzolati (1973).

2. The vast majority of officers appearing on these programs are male.

3. For a comprehensive discussion of narrative constructions in nonfiction formats, see Bird and Dardenne (1988).

4. See Office of National Drug Control Policy (1989).

5. Often, after police sweep through a neighborhood, drug dealers move their operations from the high visibility of the streets to indoor locations. If drug operations are permanently broken up, they move to another part of the city—as in the case of the highly publicized Operation Pressure Point I (OPP-I). Launched in 1984 to rid New York's Lower

East Side of a heroin market that prevented gentrification, OPP-I was a massive effort, resulting in 46,903 arrests. It was declared a huge success by the creators of the Bennett Plan, who asserted that it "demonstrated how an area virtually overrun by drug traffic and use could be reclaimed by a persistent and well-coordinated police effort" (Letwin 1990, 799). But internal police documents later revealed that the drug dealers had not stopped but, rather, but continued "covert" operations carried out indoors. The decrease in drug trade and related crime merely reflected "displacement to poorer parts of the neighborhood and into adjacent or more distant neighborhoods, possibly as far away as Harlem" (Letwin 1990, 800).

6. See Senate Subcommittee on Terrorism, Narcotics, and International Operations of the Committee on Foreign Relations (1988).

7. One study, *Still Far from the Dream: Recent Developments in Black Income, Employment and Poverty,* performed in 1988 by the Center on Budget and Policy Priorities, found that government cuts affected single black mothers and their children the most (cited in Letwin 1990, note 90, 810).

8. Most street dealers aspire only to make large sums of money; however, the vast majority earn very little.

9. The lack of social context in crime narratives has historically been a dominant feature of the genre form. As Haney and Manzolati (1981, 128) point out, "The causes of crime on television are almost exclusively personal. . . . It is . . . never pathological social conditions that cause crime." Clearly, these "reality" programs have drawn their defining narrative elements from fictional constructions.

10. In *The Ville,* Donaldson (1993) documents the conditions of life in Brownsville, New York, an economically devastated, predominantly minority urban community. He notes that if the nation's wealth were measured by such communities, instead of the Dow Jones industrial average, America would not be considered a wealthy nation.

11. Interview with the author, December 1992.

12. American Bar Association report, cited in Sklar (1993, 60).

13. Police resources are certainly being consumed by the drug war. For instance, New York City no longer issues warrants for motorists who fail to appear in court for moving violations. The result has been an increased number of traffic fatalities involving people who should not have been driving.

14. Investigative reports done by the *Daily News* in March 1993 found a significant number of New York police officers involved in the drug trade. The revelations of officer Michael Dowd led to the Mollen Commission investigation of police corruption. See also Parenti (1992, 123) regarding earlier police corruption. From police programs, "one would never surmise . . . that entire police units have been on the take, systematically protecting organized rackets and drug cartels, railroading black community leaders into jail when they attempt to resist the drug trade in their communities . . . The Knapp Commission, for instance, found that the biggest drug pushers in New York City were the New York City Police" (Parenti 1992, 123).

15. This point was also made by Richard Campbell, in an interview with the author in December 1992.

16. Interview with the author, April 1993.

17. Content analysis of the "reality"-based crime shows clearly demonstrates this racial bias. According to Oliver (1993, 8), they tend to "portray whites as the heroes and people of color as the villains."

18. And a Federal Judicial Center study found that the "average sentence for blacks was 49 percent higher than for whites in 1990, compared to 28 percent in 1984" (Sklar 1993, 60).

19. Acknowledging this tendency and indicating a possible shift in federal policy, President Bill Clinton used virtually the same words in a public address.

20. See Clinard and Yeager (1986).

21. See Pizzo, Fricker, and Muolo (1991).

22. O'Brien, quoted in Horn (1991, 13).

23. Interview with the author, January 1993.

24. What can only be called the Prison Industrial Complex has now reached a degree of autonomy that is propelled by its own momentum. Some have called prisons the new outlet for Keynesian social spending in the post–cold war era. Others argue that prisons are a "clean" industry and therefore preferable to manufacturing.

25. Interview with the author, January 1993.

26. The head agent, connected to a microphone, can be heard saying that the house "looks clean."

27. For further discussions of police corruption and related issues, see Parenti (1992, 123–124) and Mann (1993).

28. The authors of this study recognize its methodological problems, acknowledging that "heavy viewers may have had attitudes consistent with television criminology before they began watching television" (Haney and Manzolati 1981, note 3, 131). The cultivation analysis conducted by the "Cultural Indicators Project" (see Morgan 1989) has overcome these methodological problems. Nevertheless, at the very least, television messages reinforce existing beliefs widely held by the public without offering alternative explanations more consistent with social and political actualities.

29. However, even when the villains were not racially typed, viewers supplied their own stereotypes. "Even though young, black males rarely appear on television as criminals, heavy television viewers were no less likely to identify them as the group most frequently involved in crime" (Haney and Manzolati 1981, 131).

30. This study was also cited by Mann (1993, 33–34), who points out that such prejudice impacts on the reporting of crime and, therefore, on the crime-rate statistics for African Americans. For example, one Oregon study on victimization that "matched crimes reported to the police by respondents with the retrieved original police reports found only 34 percent agreement on racial characteristics of suspects between the survey and police data. Further, the victims tended to overestimate the number of incidents including black suspects compared with police estimates of the suspect's race" (Mann 1993, 33–34).

31. The summer of 1993 New York City saw 48,000 job applications on file that could not be filled. Information supplied by New York City Community Group, Aliansa Dominicana. In an interview on July 9, 1993, Marvin Gerrero stated, "All these young adults are asking for is a chance to learn some skills so they can start thinking about careers."

32. The National Urban League's Hidden Unemployment Index indicates extreme levels of urban unemployment, especially among black youth. As Sklar (1993, 54) notes, "Black teenagers had a hidden unemployment rate of 57 percent in 1991 (36 percent officially) and Whites had a hidden rate of 30 percent (16 percent officially)."

33. See Myers (1994).

34. An ambitious longitudinal study performed by Leonard Eron in a semirural county in New York found that "the more frequently the participants watched TV at age 8, the

more serious were the crimes of which they were convicted by age 30; the more aggressive was their behavior when drinking; and the harsher was the punishment they inflicted on their own children" (*TV Guide* 1992, 3). The study was replicated in Austria, Finland, Israel, and Poland with similar conclusions. According to Eron, "Television violence affects young adults of all ages, of both genders, at all socioeconomic levels and all levels of intelligence" (*TV Guide* 1992, 3).

35. From the transcript of an interview on *All Things Considered* (National Public Radio), March 24, 1993.

CHAPTER 8

1. For a complete discussion of press restrictions imposed by the Pentagon during the Persian Gulf war, see Andersen (1991a).

2. Interview on WBAI-FM, Pacifica Radio (New York) spring 1991.

3. See Kellner (1992), Mundy (1992), and Rowse (1992).

4. For a profile of Richard Wirthlin detailing his influence in the design of contemporary political strategies and the role he played in Ronald Reagan's success, see Andersen (1992c).

CHAPTER 9

1. This evasive political language became the subject of political satire in a Doonesbury comic strip. (*Boston Sunday Globe,* February 18, 1990). The cartoonist, Gary Trudeau, created a parody of Ronald Reagan with the character Ron Headrest, who says to a group of kids he has been hired to entertain, "Heard the one about acid rain? It needs more study!"

2. Bush made this statement even though the day before he appeared on CNN he had held a breakfast meeting with four Republican senators, Robert Dornan and Duncan Hunter among them.

3. Perot does have a financial stake in many of the economic policies he proposes. For example, a reduced deficit would benefit Perot personally by increasing the value of a great proportion of his financial investments.

4. For a discussion of "new news" see Katz (1992).

5. See *An Uncertain Season: Reporting in the Postprimary Period,* The Freedom Forum Media Studies Center: The Media and Campaign '92, a series of Special Election Reports (September 1992), p. 23.

6. Ibid., p. 47.

7. "Politainment" refers to the lack of distinction made between the discussion of political issues in the public sphere and entertainment's fictional discourse.

CONCLUSION

1. Nor, finally, does it explain how audiences themselves are sold as products to advertisers who are well pleased with shows about nothing but the creation of funny environments for their products. Another aspect of the commercial media conglomerates is that books such as the present one are not widely available. In this age of cross-ownership among program producers, networks, cable, and publishing, media sections of stores are filled with

companion guides to programs. But books critical of media practices are much harder to acquire. I was shocked to find that one bookstore could not even order the present book, regardless of its possible notoriety. But, they said, since I was a local author, they might be able to avoid the usual constraints.

2. Although the *Seinfeld* characters are endearing for their rejection of middle-class values, the same attitude is often condemned when projected onto a more youthful generation. The media construct of people in their twenties (Jerry is in his thirties) as generation X, the "grunge" generation, is a convenient way of blaming the young victims of foreclosed economic opportunities and a lower standard of living. These youth are also referred to as "slackers," a term that implies they cannot get ahead—not because of corporate job-shedding and structural economic decline, but because they have a bad attitude and do not want to. (In this connection, see Cohen 1993 and Seligman and Strasko 1994.)

3. The much-publicized display of Mariel Hemingway's nude body, along with a number of other gimmicks such as extraterrestrials, provided only temporary ratings boosts.

4. As Gitlin (1983) has observed, the media often assume a critical stance toward government, but they do not venture into criticism of the actual economic practices and corporate policies that determine economic forces.

5. The outcome of this exploratory process has been described by Lukacs (1968) as a "partial totality."

Bibliography

Abbott, Rebecca L. (1991). "Selling Out Max Headroom." In *Video: Icons and Values*, edited by Alan Olsen, Christopher Parr, and Debra Parr. New York: SUNY Press. Pp. 109–120.

Altheide, David L., and Robert P. Snow (1991). *Media Worlds in the Postjournalism Era*. New York: Aldine De Gruyter.

Andersen, Robin (1992a). "Consuming the Persian Gulf War: Changing Modes of Nonfiction Communication." In *Proceedings: 9th Annual Intercultural and International Communication Conference*, University of Miami (May). Pp. 112–115.

——— (1992b). "Oliver North and the News." In *Journalism and Popular Culture*, edited by Peter Dahlgren and Colin Sparks. London: Sage. Pp. 171–189.

——— (1992c). "Media, Marketing and Politics in the Age of Fragmentation." In *The Ideology of International Communications*, Monograph Series No. 4. New York: Institute for Media Analysis. Pp. 47–68.

——— (1991a). "The Press, the Public, and the New World Order." In *Media Development—Special Issue: Reporting the Gulf War* (October). Pp. 20–26.

——— (1991b), with Paolo Carpignano. "CNN Covers the War: Iraqi Dupes or Pentagon Promoters?" *Extra: Special Issue on the Gulf War*, Vol. 4, No. 3 (May), pp. 12–13.

——— (1989). "Images of War Photojournalism, Ideology and Central America," *Latin American Perspectives*, Vol. 16, No. 61 (Spring), pp. 96–114.

Ang, Ian (1985). *Watching "Dallas": Soap Opera and the Melodramatic Imagination*. New York: Methuen.

Aronowitz, Stanley (1989). "Working Class Culture in the Electronic Age." In *Cultural Politics in Contemporary America*, edited by Ian Angus and Sut Jhally. New York: Routledge. Pp. 135–150.

Auletta, Ken (1991a). *Three Blind Mice: How the Networks Lost Their Way*. New York: Random House.

Auletta, Ken (1991b). "How General Electric Tamed NBC News." *Washington Journalism Review* (November), pp. 36–41.

Ballinger, Jeffrey (1992). "The New Free-Trade Heel. *Harper's Magazine* (August), pp. 46–47.

Barnouw, Erik (1975). *Tube of Plenty: The Evolution of American Television*. New York: Oxford University Press.

Baudrillard, Jean (1983). *Simulations*. New York: Semiotext(e).

Bellah, Robert N., Richard Masden, William M. Sullivan, Ann Swidler, and Steven M. Tipton (1985). *Habits of the Heart: Individualism and Commitment in American Life*. Berkeley: University of California Press.

Bellant, Russ (1991). *The Coors Connection: How Coors Family Philanthropy Undermines Democratic Pluralism*. Boston: South End Press.

Bennett, W. Lance (1992). *The Governing Crisis: Media, Money, and Marketing in American Elections*. New York: St. Martin's Press.

———— (1988). *News: The Politics of Illusion.* New York: Longman.

Berger, John (1972). *Ways of Seeing.* New York: Penguin.

Berger, Warren (1995). "Childhood Traumas Healed While-U-Wait." *New York Times* (January 8), pp. 2-33, 2-35.

———— (1994). "The Amazing Secrets of a Television Guru." *New York Times* (July 10), pp. 2-1, 2-25.

Bird, S. Elizabeth, and Robert W. Dardenne (1988). "Myth, Chronicle, and Story: Exploring the Narrative Qualities of News." In *Media, Myths, and Narratives: Television and the Press,* edited by James W. Carey. Newbury Park, Calif.: Sage. Pp. 67–86.

Blumberg, Abraham (1979). *Criminal Justice: Issues and Ironies,* 2nd ed. New York: New Viewpoints.

Bourgois, Phillipe (1989). "Just Another Night on Crack Street." *New York Times Magazine* (November 12), pp. 53, 62, 65, 86

Briggs, Barbara, and Charles Kernaghan (1993). "The U.S. Economic Agenda: A Sweatshop Model of Development." *NACLA Report on the Americas,* Vol. 26, No. 6 (July), pp. 37–40.

Broadcasting (1990a). "Network News: Changing as It Remains the Same" (September 24), p. 34.

———— (1990b). "Network News: Between a Rights Fee and a Hard Place" (October 22), p. 31.

———— (1988). "NBC Chief Discusses State of the Network, Fate of the Industry" (August 15), pp. 72–73.

———— (1987). "TV Networks Enter New Cost-Control Era" (March 2), pp. 70–71.

———— (1983). "Second 'Digest' Study Claims Network TV Erosion" (September 26), pp. 44–45.

Calhoun, Craig (1988). "Populist Politics, Communications Media and Large Scale Societal Integration." *Sociological Theory,* Vol. 6, No. 2 (Fall), pp. 219–241.

Campbell, Richard (1992). "No News, Old News or New News?" *QS News* (Spring/Summer), pp. 1, 6–8.

Carlson, J. M. (1985). *Prime Time Law Enforcement: Crime Show Viewing and Attitudes Toward the Criminal Justice System.* New York: Praeger.

Carlson, Shawn, and Gerry O'Sullivan (1991). *Satanism in America: How the Devil Got Much More Than His Due.* El Cerrito, Calif.: Gaia Press.

Carmody, Deirdre (1991). "Magazines Feel Pinch as Advertising Drops." *New York Times* (July 29), p. D6.

Carpignano, Paolo, Robin Andersen, Stanley Aronowitz, and William DiFazio (1991). "Chatter in the Age of Electronic Reproduction: TV Talk Shows and the Public Mind." *Social Text,* No. 25/26 (Summer/Fall), pp. 33–55.

Carter, Bill (1991a). "Few Sponsors for TV War News." *New York Times* (February 7), pp. D1, D20.

———— (1991b). "TV Networks, in a Crisis, Talk of Sweeping Changes." *New York Times* (July 29), pp. D1, D6.

Center for the Study of Commercialism (1992). "Petition Before the FCC for Declaratory Relief Regarding Sponsorship Identification Announcements for Infomercials Which Do Not Comply with the Requirements of the Communication Act" (January 3).

Clinard, Marshall, and Peter Yeager (1986). *Corporate Crime.* New York: Free Press.

Cohen, Andrew (1993). "Me and My Zeitgeist." *The Nation* (July 19), pp. 96–100.

Cole, Lewis (1991). "The Stuff of Real Life." *The Nation* (April 29), pp. 567–572.

Collins, Ronald K. L. (1992). *Dictating Content: How Advertising Pressures Can Corrupt a Free Press.* Washington, D.C.: Center for the Study of Commercialism.

Colton, David (1991). Panel on "The Media and the Gulf War," Suffolk University. (Aired on C-SPAN, February 23.)

Corn, David (1995). "Retiring Newt." *The Nation* (January 30), pp. 117–118.

Crichton, Michael (1991). *Jurassic Park.* London: Random House.

D'Antonio, Michael (1993). *Atomic Harvest: Hanford and the Lethal Toll of America's Nuclear Arsenal.* New York: Crown Publishers.

Davis, Mike (1992). *City of Quartz: Excavating the Future in Los Angeles.* New York: Vintage Books.

deCourcy, Hinds (1992). "Workers Say U.S. Program Took Their Jobs." *New York Times* (October 19), pp. A8.

De Vinck, Catherine (1992). "The Third World Secret of Nike's Success" (letter to the editor). *New York Times* (August 15).

Donaldson, Greg (1993). *The Ville: Cops and Kids in Urban America.* New York: Ticknor & Fields.

Dowd, Maureen (1992). "O.K. on the Self-Realization: What About the Economy?" *New York Times* (July 27), pp. A1, A10.

Edwards, Lynda (1992). "The Focusing of the President." *The Village Voice* (June 23), pp. 25–29.

Elliott, Stuart (1993a). "A Newscaster-Turned-Spokeswoman Raises Issues of Credibility." *New York Times* (December 2), p. D21.

——— (1993b). "Coca-Cola's New Campaign Shakes Up Madison Avenue." *New York Times* (February 11), pp. D1, D22.

——— (1993c). "A Broadcaster and Publisher Plan to Reach Out to Consumers in Action—at the Mall." *New York Times* (February 4), p. D22.

——— (1992a). "More Scenes from Past Sell Products in the Present." *New York Times* (April 24), p. D5.

——— (1992b). "One Happy CBS Advertiser: Itself." *New York Times* (April 4), pp. D1, D22.

——— (1992c). "More Campaigns Are Taking a Less-Than-Perfect Tone." *New York Times* (March 6), p. D5.

Engelhardt, Tom (1986). "The Shortcake Strategy." In *Watching Television,* edited by Todd Gitlin. New York: Pantheon Books.

Entman, Robert M. (1990). "Modern Racism and the Images of Blacks in Local Television News." *Critical Studies in Mass Communication,* Vol. 7, No. 4, pp. 332–345.

Ewen, Stuart (1988). *All Consuming Images: The Politics of Style in Contemporary Culture.* New York: Basic Books.

Fairness and Accuracy in Reporting (FAIR) (1993). "Soundbites: Absolute Influence." *Extra!* (July/August), p. 4.

——— (1989). "Are You on the Nightline Guest List?" *Extra!* (January/February), pp. 1–15.

Faludi, Susan (1991). *Backlash: The Undeclared War Against American Women.* New York: Crown Publishers.

Featherstone, Mike (1991). *Consumer Culture and Postmodernism.* London: Sage.

Fiske, John (1989). *Reading the Popular.* Boston: Unwin Hyman.

——— (1987). *Television Culture.* New York: Methuen.

Fore, William F. (1991). "The Shadow War in the Gulf." *Media Development* (October), pp. 51–52.

Foucault, Michel (1986). "What Is Enlightenment?" In *The Foucault Reader,* edited by P. Rabinow. Harmondsworth, Ind.: Penguin.

Fraser, Nancy (1993). "Rethinking the Public Sphere: A Contribution to the Critique of Actually Existing Democracy." In *The Phantom Public Sphere,* edited by Bruce Robbins. Minneapolis: University of Minnesota Press. Pp. 1–33.

Fretts, Bruce, ed. (1993). *The Entertainment Weekly Seinfeld Companion.* New York: Warner Books.

Fried, S. (1988). "Phillysomething." *Philadelphia Magazine* (December), pp. 145–151, 198–204.

Gamarekian, Barbara (1989). "In Pursuit of the Clever Quotemaster." *New York Times* (May 12), p. 38.

Gans, Herbert J. (1993). "Making Jobs." *The Nation* (September 20), pp. 270, 295–296.

Garrett, Laurie (1994). *The Coming Plague: Newly Emerging Diseases in a World Out of Balance.* New York: Farrar, Straus and Giroux.

Gerard, Jeremy (1988). "TV Mirrors a New Generation." *New York Times* (October 30), pp. C1, C28.

Gerbner, George, and Larry Gross (1976). "The Scary World of TV's Heavy Viewer," *Psychology Today* (April), pp. 41–46, 89.

Gergen, David (1989). "Drugs and White America," *U.S. News and World Report* (September 18), p. 79.

Giddens, Anthhony (1993). Keynote address given at the International Association of Mass Communication Research (IAMCR) conference held in Dublin, Ireland (June).

Girard, René (1965). *Deceit, Desire, & the Novel: Self and Other in Literary Structure.* Baltimore: Johns Hopkins University Press.

Gitlin, Todd (1992). *The Murder of Albert Einstein.* New York: Farrar Straus Giroux.

———— (1983). *Inside Prime Time.* New York: Pantheon.

Goffman, Irving (1979). *Gender Advertisements.* New York: Harper.

Goldstein, Richard (1992). "Sweet William, Sex and Sensibility: The Clinton Touch." *Village Voice* (October 27), pp. 29–33.

Gonzalez, Juan (1992). "Free Trade Pact Zoned for Slavery." *Daily News* (New York, October 9), p. A3.

Gordon, Jim (1992). "America's Most Wanted Takes Credit for a Killing." *Extra!* (September), p. 21.

Habermas, Jurgen (1962/1989). *The Structural Transformation of the Public Sphere.* Cambridge, Mass.: MIT Press.

Haineault, Doris-Louise, and Roy, Jean-Yves (1993). *Unconscious for Sale: Advertising Psychoanalysis and the Public.* Minneapolis: University of Minnesota Press.

Hall, Stuart (1986a). "Cultural Studies: Two paradigms." In *Media, Culture & Society: A Critical Reader,* edited by Richard Collins, James Curran, Nicholas Garnham, Paddy Scannell, Philip Schlesinger, and Colin Sparks. London: Sage.

Hall, Stuart (1986b). "The Problem of Ideology." *Journal of Communication Inquiry,* Vol. 10, No. 2 (Summer), pp. 28–44.

Hammer, Michael, and James Champy (1993). *Reengineering the Corporation.* New York: HarperCollins.

Haney, Craig, and John Manzolati (1981). "Television Criminology: Network Illusions of Criminal Justice Realities." In *Readings About the Social Animal,* 3rd ed., edited by Elliot Aronson. San Francisco: W. H. Freeman. Pp. 125–136.

Hanke, Robert (1990). "Hegemonic Masculinity in *thirtysomething.*" *Critical Studies in Mass Communication* (September), pp. 231–248.

Harris, Ron (1990). "Blacks Take Brunt of War on Drugs." *Los Angeles Times* (April 22), p. A1.

Harwood, Richard C. (1991). "Citizens and Politics: A View from Main Street America." Prepared for the Kettering Foundation by The Harwood Group. New York: Kettering Foundation.

Hebdige, Dick (1986). "Postmodernism and 'The Other Side.'" *Journal of Communication Inquiry,* Vol. 10, No. 2 (Summer), pp. 78–98.

Herbert, Bob (1993). "No Job, No Dream." *New York Times* (September 8), p. A23.

Hersch, Patricia (1988). "On Screen: *thirtysomething* Therapy. *Psychology Today.* (October), pp. 62–64.

Hertsgaard, Mark (1988). *On Bended Knee: The Press and the Reagan Presidency.* New York: Farrar Straus Giroux.

Hillman, James, and Michael Ventura (1992a). "Is Therapy Turning Us Into Children?" *New Age Journal* (June), pp. 60–65, 136–141.

———— (1992b). *We've Had A Hundred Years of Psychotherapy and the World's Getting Worse.* San Francisco: Harper.

Hirsch, Fred (1976). *Social Limits to Growth.* Cambridge, Mass.: Harvard University Press.

Hitchings, Peter (1993). "Reeboks, Rappers and Losers." *New Internationalist & Amnesty* (June), pp. 24–26.

Hoberman, J. (1994). "It's the Mr. Bill Show: The Making of a Sitcom President." *The Village Voice* (January 25), pp. 23–25, 28–30.

Horn, Patricia (1991). "Caging America: The U.S. Imprisonment Binge." *Dollars & Sense* (September), pp. 12–15, 22.

Hoynes, William, and David Croteau (1990). "All the Usual Suspects: MacNeil/Lehrer and Nightline." *Extra!* (Special Issue, Winter), pp. 1–16.

Isikoff, Michael (1992). "Bush Softens Attack on Clinton Moscow Trip." *Standard Star* (October 10), p. 21A.

Ives, Kim (1994). "The Second U.S. Occupation." *NACLA Reports on the Americas,* Vol. 28, No. 4 (January/February), pp. 6–10.

Ivins, Molly (1992). "Notes from Another Country." *The Nation* (September 14), pp. 229, 248–249.

Jacoby, Russell (1989). "The Decline of American Intellectuals." In *Cultural Politics in Contemporary America,* edited by Ian Angus and Sut Jhally. New York: Routledge. Pp. 271–281.

Jameson, Fredrick (1984). "Postmodernism and the Consumer Society." In *Postmodern Culture,* edited by Hal Foster. London: Pluto Press.

Jamieson, Kathleen Hall (1992). *Dirty Politics: Deception, Distraction, and Democracy.* New York: Oxford University Press.

Jensen, Carl (1993). *Censored: The News that Didn't Make the News and Why.* Chapel Hill, N.C.: Shelburne Press.

Jensen, Elizabeth (1993a). "TV Dials and Viewers' Heads Will Spin as Networks Launch New Fall Lineups." *Wall Street Journal* (September 15), pp. B1, B7.

———— (1993b). "Corpses, Blood and Sex Put Miami TV Station at Top of News Heap." *Wall Street Journal* (July 30), pp. 1, 5.

Jhally, Sut (1989). "Advertising as Religion: The Dialectic of Technology and Magic." In *Cultural Politics in Contemporary America,* edited by Ian Angus and Sut Jhally. New York: Routledge. Pp. 217–229.

Johns, Christina Jacqueline (1992). *Power, Ideology and the War on Drugs.* New York: Praeger.

Johns, Christina Jacqueline, and José Maria Borrero (1991). "The War on Drugs: Nothing Succeeds Like Failure." In *Crimes by the Capitalist State: An Introduction to State Criminality,* edited by Gregg Barak. Albany: State University of New York Press. Pp. 67–100.

Johnson, Bradley (1993). "CAA Looking for Bigger Role in Advertising." *Advertising Age* (July 19), pp. 1, 32.

Kaminer, Wendy (1992). *I'm Dysfunctional, You're Dysfunctional: The Recovery Movement and Other Self-Help Fashions.* New York: Addison-Wesley.

Kanner, Bernice (1989). "Mind Games: How Advertising Agencies Use the Latest Research Techniques to Get You to Buy the Products They're Hawking." *New York Magazine* (May 8), pp. 34–40.

Katz, Jon (1993). "Covering the Cops: A TV Show Moves in Where Journalists Fear to Tread." *Columbia Journalism Review* (January/February), pp. 25–30.

———— (1992). "Rock, Rap and Movies Bring You the News." *Rolling Stone* (March 5), pp. 33–40.

Kellner, Douglas (1992). *The Persian Gulf TV War.* Boulder: Westview Press.

———— (1976). "Television Crime Drama: Critical Studies." Unpublished manuscript.

Kernaghan, Charles, ed. (1992). *Paying to Lose Our Jobs.* New York: National Labor Committee Education Fund in Support of Workers and Human Rights in Central America.

Kilbourne, Jean (1991). "The Tobacco Industry Targets Women." *Extra!* (March/April), p. 7.

Kolbert, Elizabeth (1992). "Out of Bush's Mouth, Old Rumors Draw Big-League Attention." *New York Times* (October 10), P. A9.

Kovel, Joel (1991). *History and Spirit: An Inquiry into the Philosophy of Liberation.* Boston: Beacon Press.

———— (1988). "Oh, Psy Can You See?" *Z Magazine* (October), pp. 92–95.

———— (1989). "Politics of Therapy; Therapy of Politics." *Z Magazine.* (March), pp. 106–110.

Ladd, Scot (1992). "Half Think Cops Are Often Corrupt." *New York Newsday* (July 9), p. 3.

Larson, Charles U. (1989). *Persuasion: Reception and Responsibility.* Belmont, Calif.: Wadsworth.

Lash, Scott (1988). "Discourse or Figure? Postmodernism as a 'Regime of Signification.'" *Theory, Culture & Society,* Vol. 5, pp. 311–336.

Lawrence, B. H. (1989). "Advertisers' 'Hit Lists' of Network Shows Grow Longer. *Washington Post* (June 22), pp. E1, E6.

Lee, Martin A., and Norman Solomon (1992). *Unreliable Sources: A Guide to Detecting Bias in News Media.* New York: Carol Publishing Group.

Leiss, William, Stephen Kline, and Sut Jhally (1988). *Social Communication in Advertising: Persons, Products, and Images of Well-Being.* Scarborough, Ontario: Nelsen.

Lesly, Elizabeth (1991). "Realtors and Builders Demand Happy News . . . and Often Get It." *Washington Journalism Review* (November), pp. 21–23.

Letwin, Michael Z. (1990). "Report from the Front Line—The Bennett Plan: Street-Level Drug Enforcement in New York City and the Legalization Debate." *Hofstra Law Review,* Vol. 18, No. 4 (Spring), pp. 795–830.

Lewis, Justin, Sut Jhally, and Michael Morgan (1991). *The Gulf War: A Study of the Media, Public Opinion and Public Knowledge.* Study performed for the Center for the Study of Communication, University of Massachusetts at Amherst.

Lieberman, David (1992). "Fake News." *TV Guide* (February 22), pp. 10–11, 13–14, 16, 26.

Liebert, Robert M., and Joyce Sprafkin (1988). *The Early Window: Effects of Television on Children and Youth.* New York: Pergamon Press.

Lukacs, Georg (1968). *History and Class Consciousness.* Cambridge, Mass.: MIT Press.

Lyotard, Jean-François (1984). *The PostModern Condition.* Manchester, England: Manchester University Press.

MacArthur, John R. (1992). *Second Front: Censorship and Propaganda in the Gulf War.* Berkeley: University of California Press.

MacDonald, J. Fred (1990). *One Nation Under Television: The Rise and Decline of Network Television.* New York: Pantheon Books.

——— (1985). *Television and the Red Menace: The Video Road to Vietnam.* New York: Praeger.

Mandese, Joe (1993). "NBC and Kellogg Co-Star," *Advertising Age* (July 19), pp. 1, 32.

Mann, Coramae Rickey (1993). *Unequal Justice.* Bloomington: Indiana University Press.

Marcuse, Herbert (1966). *Eros and Civilization.* Boston: Beacon Press.

Marx, Karl (1887). *Capital: A Critique of Political Economy, Vol. 1.* New York: International Publishers. (Reprinted in 1967.)

Maslin, Janet (1992). "Steamy TV: Coffee Opera." *The New York Times* (November 22), p. 9-9.

Mathews, David (1991). Foreword to *Citizens and Politics: A View from Main Street America.* Prepared for the Kettering Foundation by The Harwood Group. New York: Kettering Foundation. Pp. iii–vi.

McFadden, Robert D. (1992). "Federal Judge Orders CBS to Surrender a Videotape." *New York Times* (November 24), p. B–3.

McNeely, R. L., and Carl E. Pope (1981). *Race, Crime and Criminal Justice.* Beverly Hills, Calif.: Sage.

Meehan, Eileen R. (1990). "Why We Don't Count: The Commodity Audience." In *Logics of Television,* edited by Patricia Mellencamp. Bloomington: Indiana University Press.

Meyrowitz, Joshua (1985). *No Sense of Place.* New York: Oxford University Press.

Miller, Mark Crispin (1990). "End of Story." In *Seeing Through Movies,* edited by Marc C. Miller. New York: Pantheon Books.

Mollen Commission to Investigate Allegations of Police Corruption and the Anti-Corruption Procedures of the New York City Police Department. (1993). Interim Report (December), New York.

Morgan, Michael (1989). "Television and Democracy." In *Cultural Politics in Contemporary America,* edited by Ian Angus and Sut Jhally. New York: Routledge.

Mundy, Alicia (1992). "Is the Press Any Match for Powerhouse P.R.?" *Columbia Journalism Review* (September/October), pp. 27–34.

Munson, Wayne (1993). *All Talk: The Talk Show in Media Culture.* Philadelphia: Temple University Press.

Mydans, Seth (1993). "Los Angeles Elects a Conservative as Mayor and Turns to a New Era." *New York Times* (June 10), pp. A1, A24.

Myers, Stephen Lee (1994). "Administration Plans to Cut 'Safe City' Youth Programs." *New York Times* (May 1), p. 1–47.

Nadelmann, Ethan A. (1989). "Drug Prohibition in the United States: Costs, Consequences, and Alternatives." *Science.* Vol. 245 (September 1), pp. 939–946.

Nasar, Sylvia (1992). "The 1980's: A Very Good Time for the Very Rich." *New York Times* (March 5), pp. A1, D24.

Nissan, Beth (1991). *Ann Arbor News* (February 16).

Office of National Drug Control Policy (1989). "National Drug Control Strategy" (known as the Bennett Plan).

Oliver, Mary Beth (1993). "Portrayals of Crime, Race and Aggression in 'Reality-Based' Police Shows: A Content Analysis." Paper presented at the International Communication Association conference, Washington, D.C. (May).

Olson, Scott R. (1987). "Meta-Television: Popular Postmodernism." *Critical Studies in Mass Communication,* Vol. 4, No. 31, pp. 284–300.

O'Sullivan, Gerry (1991). "The Devil's Due: The Satanic Panic." *Lies of Our Times* (December), pp. 12–14.

Parenti, Michael (1992). *Make-Believe Media: The Politics of Entertainment.* New York: St. Martin's Press.

Parrot, Andrea (1991). *Acquaintance Rape: The Hidden Crime.* New York: John Wiley and Sons.

Pearce, K. (1988). "ABC Series Getting in Touch with Audiences' feelings." *Channels* (February), p. 12.

Pfeil, Fred (1985). "Makin' Flippy-Floppy: Postmodernism and the Baby-Boom PMC." In *The Year Left,* edited by Mike Davis et al. New York: Verso.

Phillips, Kevin (1990). *The Politics of Rich and Poor: Wealth and the American Electorate in the Reagan Aftermath.* New York: Random House.

Pizzo, Stephen, Mary Fricker, and Paul Muolo (1991). *Inside Job: The Looting of America's Savings & Loans.* New York: Harper Perennial.

Postman, Neil (1985). *Amusing Ourselves to Death.* New York: Elisabeth Sifton Books/Viking Penguin.

Postol, Theodore (1991/1992). "Lessons of the Gulf War Experience with Patriot," *International Security,* Vol. 16, No. 3, pp. 119–171.

Pratkanis, Anthony, and Elliot Aronson (1992). *Age of Propaganda: The Everyday Use and Abuse of Persuasion.* New York: W. H. Freeman.

Presley Noble, Barbara (1992). "Mapping Offshore Migration of Jobs." *New York Times* (October 18), p. F25.

Prothrow-Stith, Deborah (1991). *Deadly Consequences.* New York: HarperCollins.

Putnam, Todd (1991). "The GE Boycott: A Story NBC Wouldn't Buy." *Extra!* (January/February), pp. 4–5.

Rapping, Elayne (1987). *The Looking Glass World of Nonfiction TV.* Boston: South End Press.

Reeves, Jimmie L., and Richard Campbell (1994). *Cracked Coverage: Television News, the Anti-Cocaine Crusade, and the Reagan Legacy.* Durham, N.C.: Duke University Press.

Reinhardt, Judge Stephen (1992). "Riots, Racism, and the Courts." Commencement speech given in May at Golden Gate University, San Francisco. (Also published under the title "The Trickle Down of Judicial Racism," *Harper's* [August 1992], pp. 15–17.)

Rohter, Larry (1993). "It Might Be News, But It's Not 'MacNeil/Lehrer.'" *New York Times* (April 25), p. C34.

Roman, Kenneth, and Jane Maas (1992). *The New How to Advertise.* New York: St. Martin's Press.

Rosen, Jay (1992). "Playing the Primary Chords." *Harper's* (March), pp. 22–26

Rosenthal, Andrew (1992). "In a Speech, President Returns to Religous Themes." *New York Times* (January 28), p. A17.

Rowse, Arthur (1992). "How To Build Support for War." *Columbia Journalism Review* (September/October), pp. 28–29.

Russell, Diana (1980). "Pornography and Violence: What Does the New Research Say?" In *Take Back the Night: Women on Pornography,* edited by Laura Lederer. New York: William Morrow and Company, Inc. Pp. 218–238.

Sabato, Larry J. (1985). *PAC Power: Inside the World of Political Action Committees.* New York: W. W. Norton.

Scannell, Paddy, Philip Schlesinger, and Colin Sparks, eds., (1992). *Culture and Power: A Media, Culture & Society Reader.* London: Sage.

Schiller, Herbert I. (1989). *Culture, Inc.: The Corporate Takeover of Public Expression.* New York: Oxford University Press.

Schor, Juliet B. (1992). *The Overworked American.* New York: Basic Books.

Schwartz, Tony (1974). *The Responsive Chord.* Garden City, N.J.: Anchor Press.

Schwarzbaum, Lisa (1993). "Introduction: Something About Nothing." In *The Entertainment Weekly Seinfeld Companion,* edited by Bruce Fretts. New York: Warner Books. Pp. 9–17.

Seagal, D. (1993). "Cops and TV—And Reality." *Columbia Journalism Review* (March/April), pp. 4, 6.

Secunda, Eugene (1989). "Video News Releases: The Hidden Persuaders Revisited?" Paper delivered at the Annual Media Ecology Conference. Saugherties, New York (October 8).

Seligman, Miles, and Aimee Strasko (1994). "What's Behind the Twentysomething 'Movement?'" *Extra!* (March/April), pp. 6–7.

Sella, Marshall (1992). "Jock Citadel." *New York Times* (July 19), p. 3 of "Style" section.

Senate Subcommittee on Terrorism, Narcotics, and International Operations of the Committee on Foreign Relations (1988). 100th Congress, 2nd Session, "Report on Drugs, Law Enforcement and Foreign Policy," no. 1.

Shapiro, Eben (1992a). "In Light of Election Results, Companies Stress 'Change.'" *New York Times* (November 9), p. D7.

——— (1992b). "Getting a Running Shoe in the Door." *New York Times* (August 13), pp. D1, D12.

Sheinkman, Jack (1992). "We Demand an Answer." In *Paying to Lose Our Jobs,* edited by Charles Kernaghan. New York: National Labor Committee Education Fund in Support of Workers and Human Rights in Central America.

Shudson, Michael (1989). "Advertising as Capitalist Realism." In *Advertising in Society,* edited by Roxanne Hovland and Gary Wilcox. Lincolnwood Ill.: NTC Business Books. Pp. 73–98.

——— (1978). *Discovering the News: A Social History of American Newspapers.* New York: Basic Books.

Siegel, Joel (1993). "The Job Mob." *Daily News* (New York, April 25), pp. 5, 31.

Silverstone, Roger (1988). "Television Myth and Culture." In *Media, Myths, and Narratives: Television and the Press,* edited by James W. Carey. Newbury Park, Calif.: Sage. Pp. 20–47.

Sklar, Holly (1993). "Young and Guilty by Stereotype." *Z Magazine,* Vol. 6, No.7/8 (July/August), pp. 52–61.

Sloan, Pat, and Marcy Magiera (1993). "Mo' Better News: Spike Lee Wants to Be Ad Agency." *Advertising Age* (August 9), pp. 1, 29.

Smith, Roberta (1990). "Michael and Hope and Julian and Francesco." *New York Times* (April 1), pp. 2-35, 2-40.

Soley, Lawrence C. (1989). "The News Shapers: The Individuals Who Explain the News." Minneapolis: University of Minnesota Press.

Spethmann, Betsy (1992). "Focus Groups Key to Reaching Kids." *Advertising Age* (February 10), p. 51.

Steinem, Gloria (1990) "Sex, Lies & Advertising." *Ms.* (July/August), pp. 18–28.

Strong, Morgan (1992). "Portions of the Gulf War Were Brought to You by . . . the Folks at Hill and Knowlton." *TV Guide* (February 22), pp. 11–13.

Taylor, Steven T., and Morton Mintz (1991). "A Word from Your Friendly Drug Co." *The Nation* (October 21), pp. 480–484.

Tetzlaff, David (1992). "Popular Culture and Social Control in Late Capitalism." In *Culture and Power,* edited by Paddy Scannell, Philip Schlesinger, and Colin Sparks. London: Sage.

Times Mirror Media Monitor (1993). "TV Violence: More Objectionable in Entertainment Than in Newscasts." Times Mirror Center for The People & The Press (March 24).

Treaster, Joseph B. (1993). "2 Judges Decline Drug Cases, Protesting Sentencing Rules." *New York Times* (April 17), pp. A1, A27.

Tuchman, Gaye (1978). *Making News: A Study in the Construction of Reality.* New York: Free Press.

TV Guide (1992). *Violence on Television: A Symposium and Study Sponsored by the Editors of* TV Guide.

Uchitelle, Louis (1993). "Strong Companies Are Joining Trend to Eliminate Jobs." *New York Times* (July 26), pp. A1, D3.

Valley, S. (1992). "Potential Jurors in King Beating Trial Get Questionnaires." *Los Angeles Times* (February 6), p. B1.

Wasko, Janet (1993). "Hollywood in Europe: An Update." Paper delivered at the International Association of Mass Communication Research (IAMCR) conference held in Dublin, Ireland (June).

Weinberg, Bill (1993). "Cops—and Civil Liberties." *Columbia Journalism Review* (May/June), p. 6.

Weinstein, Judge Jack B. (1994). Decision issued in *Ayeni v. CBS Inc.,* United States District Court, Eastern District of New York, Brooklyn (March 17).

Wernick, Andrew (1991). *Promotional Culture: Advertising, Ideology and Symbolic Expression.* London: Sage.

Whitney, D. Charles, Marilyn Fritzer, Steven Jones, Sharon Mazzarella, and Lana Rakow (1989). "Geographic and Source Biases in Network Television News 1982–1984. *Journal of Broadcasting and Electronic Media,* No. 33, pp. 159–174.

Williams, Raymond (1980). *Problems in Materialism and Culture.* London: Verso/NLB.

Williams, Terry Moses (1989). *The Cocaine Kids: The Inside Story of a Teenage Drug Ring.* Reading, Mass: Addison-Wesley.

Williams, Wendy S. (1991). "Two New Surveys Show the Industry's Reach." *Washington Journalism Review* (November), pp. 24–25.

Williamson, Judith (1978). *Decoding Advertisements*. London: Marion Boyars.

Wines, Michael (1992). "Bush Tones Down Criticism of Clinton Visit to Moscow." *New York Times* (October 10), p. A9.

Wolff, Craig (1993). "Lawyer Says Ex-Officer Ready to Admit Charges." *New York Times* (June 10), p. B3.

About the Book and Author

To what extent does the advertising industry influence what we see on TV? What is the political and cultural environment that provides for the phenomenon of the corporate shaping of the mass media?

Robin Andersen addresses these questions, which ultimately intertwine with the very concept of democracy: How can citizens participate in political culture when the information they receive through their mass media is molded by corporate and commercial demands? She discusses and analyzes the impact of the consumer imperative on popular news and TV programs and talk shows, the psychology of consumer culture, the differing narratives of the 1992 presidential election, how representations of the Gulf War resembled advertisements, and the overall escalating commercial imperative of the mass media. Andersen has done a splendid job of accessibly presenting to mass audiences and students a subject of enormous gravity—the steady penetration of marketing and advertising strategies into the very fabric of both news and entertainment television.

Robin Andersen is associate professor of communication at Fordham University.

Index